For Doug, who knows the road
for the ideal, + will take
it all with a grain of salt,
with all best wishes from Rich

3/02

The Real and the Ideal

The Real and the Ideal

Essays on International Relations in Honor of Richard H. Ullman

Edited by
Anthony Lake and David Ochmanek

A Council on Foreign Relations Book

ROWMAN & LITTLEFIELD PUBLISHERS, INC.
Lanham • Boulder • New York • Oxford

ROWMAN & LITTLEFIELD PUBLISHERS, INC.

Published in the United States of America
by Rowman & Littlefield Publishers, Inc.
4720 Boston Way, Lanham, Maryland 20706

www.rowmanlittlefield.com
12 Hid's Copse Road
Cumnor Hill, Oxford OX2 9JJ, England

British Library Cataloguing in Publication Information Available

Library of Congress Cataloging-in-Publication Data
The real and the ideal : essays on international relations in honor of Richard H. Ullman / edited by W. Anthony Lake and David Ochmanek.
   p. cm.
  Includes bibliographical references and index.
  ISBN 0-7425-1555-9 (alk. paper)
   1. International relations 2. International relations—Philosophy. 3. United States—Foreign relations. I Lake, Anthony. II. Ochmanek, David A.
JZ1242 .R428 2001
327.1'01—dc21   2001019919
Printed in the United States of America

Contents

Preface and Acknowledgments

Neither of the editors of this volume particularly enjoys salesmanship. But, unlike normal efforts to create a volume of essays, getting people to contribute to a volume honoring Richard Ullman involved neither persuasion at the outset nor nagging at the conclusion. Quite the contrary: Everyone we contacted asking if they would be interested in participating in this effort— the authors, the Council on Foreign Relations, Rowman & Littlefield Publishers, the Harris and Eliza Kempner Fund, and the Center for International Studies at Princeton—all expressed their eagerness to participate, and, when it came time, all made good on their promises of support. If one measure of a life well lived is the respect and admiration of one's friends, then Dick has lived very well.

Credit for taking the initiative to create a celebratory volume of essays, or *Festschrift*, for Richard Ullman goes to Michael Doyle, Edward S. Sanford Professor of Politics and International Affairs, and director of the Center of International Studies at Princeton University. When Michael approached us in the summer of 1998 and asked if we would be willing to consider pulling together this effort we jumped at the chance. Throughout the process, Michael has been steadfast in his support for the project and has played important roles at critical junctures. He organized and hosted a conference of the volume's authors at Princeton in November 1999, giving each contributor a chance to share his ideas with other contributors and with Dick himself. Michael also reviewed several of the essays in the volume and offered ideas about its overall shape and themes.

Les Gelb, president of the Council on Foreign Relations, was an enthusiastic supporter of the project from its conception, seeing it both as an appropriate means of honoring Dick's many contributions to the field, as well as a way of bringing together the ideas of a select set of scholars and practitioners on issues relevant to post–Cold War international relations. The editors and authors are grateful to him for his support. We are also indebted to David Kellogg, publisher at the Council on Foreign Relations, whose substantive insights and expertise in the realm of publishing helped us to ensure that the volume was attractive to potential publishers. He worked assiduously to ensure a good match between the draft manuscript and its publisher. Once that match was forged, Patricia Dorff, director of publishing at the Council, was indefatigable in her efforts to push the project through to its completion.

This effort would not have succeeded without the generous support of the Harris and Eliza Kempner Fund of Galveston, Texas, and Princeton University's Center for International Studies (CIS). Dick has been associated informally with the Kempner Fund for many years, advising them on international projects, particularly focusing on U.S. organizations that seek to promote economic growth in developing countries. In recognition of Dick's efforts the fund contributed to the Council a grant sufficient to cover a substantial portion of the cost of publication. Professor Aaron Friedberg, deputy director of the CIS, agreed that the Center would contribute a like amount. We are deeply grateful to both institutions for their support.

Finally, we wish to acknowledge the many contributions made by the staff at Rowman & Littlefield Publishers, and in particular the careful attention shown by editors Jennifer Knerr and Christine Ambrose.

Foreword

Leslie H. Gelb

If there were a foreign policy school of commonsense liberalism, its father would be Richard Ullman. It would be a school that insisted upon decency, mutual respect for rights and interests, serious efforts to resolve disputes peaceably, international institution-building, and the belief in diplomacy by domestic and international example. Rights and dignity of people would sit always at the center of thought. But, and here is the twist Ullman watchers treasure, there would be no idealism for idealism's sake. Rights, liberties, and ideals would be tempered always by the vagaries of lawlessness and necessities of power.

The Ullman School can be captured intellectually. It possesses a historical consistency, a consistency of values and purposes, a kind of relentless questioning about whether or not the actions of great powers are accomplishing what they intend. These traits can be seen from Ullman's earliest writings about Britain and Russia at the end of World War I, through his wrestling with Vietnam, Nicaragua, and the Balkans, to his ceaseless examination of the influence of Wilsonianism in America's passions with the world.

The word "passion" might stop those who have known Dick Ullman casually. He seems so reserved, dignified, and professorial. But his writings are suffused with passion for his beliefs. He knows full well as a historian that common sense, let alone liberalism, requires constant battle. They are not the natural order of things. Indeed, in his classrooms or at the rostrums or around the dinner table, his words are cool and polite. It is rather in his writings that his will to do battle finds full release.

The reader will see all this in this marvelous tribute organized for Dick by Tony Lake and David Ochmanek and carried out by a small legion of admirers and former students, true friends of Dick, every one of them. The essays contained herein are admiring of their professor and colleague, as celebrations of a life and work usually are, yet they are quite clear-eyed as well.

I am honored and happy that Tony Lake and David Ochmanek asked the Council on Foreign Relations to copublish these celebratory essays and asked me to write this foreword. As with the other contributors to this volume, I began as Dick's student and evolved into a colleague and friend. And I now have the privilege of managing an organization that has been so near the heart of Dick's foreign policy writings. Dick Ullman served gracefully and with intellectual force as the Council's director of studies, as a senior fellow here, and as project director and participant in countless Council study groups and other gab fests. Princeton University has been Dick's home for almost forty years, and the Council has been a second home.

Forgive me for what might seem, but is not, a moment of excess. This world-class diplomatic historian, this founder of commonsense liberalism, this cherished professor and friend, and good man, has marked countless lives well. He holds us all to the highest standards of honesty and intellect that he has set and met for himself. You will see as much when you read the pages of his mind in this book.

1

Richard Ullman and His Work: An Appreciation

Anthony Lake, David Ochmanek, and Scott Vesel

> Let such teach others who themselves excel
> And censure freely who have written well.
>
> —Alexander Pope

To those who may wonder why Richard Ullman should deserve—even require—this collection of substantive essays, this *Festschrift* written by some of his former students, rather than a more traditional, strictly personal tribute to this extraordinary teacher, the answer is this: When any of us runs into him, on the streets of Princeton, Washington, or Cambridge, or at a conference, or, now, perhaps on a golf course, our faces light up for two reasons. We are his friends, like all his former students, as far as we can tell. And we know that we are about to discuss with him some interesting idea that he has been turning over in his searching mind. For Dick is not only a friend to us. He is a friend to ideas—and the difference that ideas can make in a world about which he cares with a genuine if gentle passion.

He is a great teacher because he cares not only about his own thoughts but also about those of his colleagues and students. One characteristic of conversations with Dick—even light-hearted ones—is an occasional delay in Dick's reaction—be it a smile or a counterpoint—to what you say to him. He delays, we believe, in order actually to think carefully about what was said. This, in part, is why we take him so seriously: because he takes others seriously—in some cases, perhaps, more seriously than we deserve.

It is wrong to have referred to ourselves as his former students, for we remain his students. Not because we sit at the feet of a didactic instructor, waiting for his revealed wisdom. Indeed, one of the hallmarks of Dick's seminars has always been vigorous debate—a tradition that continues with this volume. One or the other of us has disagreed with almost every one of the ideas that Dick has put forward over the past decades of his extraordinary scholarly and policy-related work. Rather, we remain his students because of the way he taught and teaches. From Dick we learned that the bite of the right question is more important than the apparent (and perhaps dangerous) certainty of a glib or dogmatic answer; that the effort to marry the demands of principle and the necessity of the practical is, and always will be, a work in progress; that this effort is both right and more interesting than finding refuge in pure idealism, pure pragmatism, or the purely theoretical.

From Dick his students have also learned, if sometimes poorly applied, the lesson of the importance of consistency and honesty in argument, taking the logic to its rightful conclusion. But also this: a careful skepticism about all human thought and endeavor, even one's own argument. And thus, a willingness, an invitation, to work through an issue in a communal search for the best answer, rather than the sterility of a competitive debate over who is right. Even when we have disagreed with Dick's conclusions, his thoughts have stimulated his students to search for their own ways to the principled ends Dick has outlined.

And from Dick we learned that the making of foreign policy, by a government or by a society, is an enterprise conducted by idiosyncratic human beings, subject to larger forces of history but not bound by them. Thus, the bad decisions of governments are produced more often by chaos than conspiracy. (We have seen little in our own careers that would contradict this view.) And thus, more important, the health of a democracy is dependent not only on its institutions but still more on the civic culture and sense of responsibility of its citizens.

This is not only what Dick has taught in his classes and writings. It is what Dick has been throughout his life and career—an engaged and responsible citizen, in the original sense of the word. And it is this, the light of his example, which has made him such a teacher. And such a friend.

Dick was born in Baltimore, Maryland, on December 12, 1933. He grew up in San Antonio, Texas. As an undergraduate at Harvard, he concentrated in chemistry and physics for three years before the competing pull of public policy—he was editorial page editor of the daily *Harvard Crimson*—caused him to transfer to the Department of Government, from which he graduated in 1955. The winner of a Rhodes Scholarship and intending on a career in journalism, he embarked at Oxford on a two-year B.Phil. in politics.

Dick had already accepted a reporter's job on the *Washington Post* when, in January of his second Oxford year, an article he published in the journal

World Politics, "The Davies Mission and United States-Soviet Relations, 1937–1941," caught the eye of George F. Kennan, who wrote that he would be in Oxford the following year as Eastman Visiting Professor and hoped to meet Dick. On the strength of Kennan's warm letter, Dick secured a third year from the Rhodes Trust and the *Post*'s consent to postpone arriving in Washington, and began work on a D.Phil. dissertation aiming to do with Anglo-Soviet relations what Kennan was then in the process of doing with the early years of U.S.-Soviet relations.

Once embarked on such a course, Dick determined to complete it. To do so he secured a dissertation grant from the Social Science Research Council, a research fellowship at St. Antony's College, Oxford, and another stay from the *Post*. The newspaper's patience went unrewarded, however. Completely out of the blue came a letter from the chairman of Harvard's Department of Government. Word had come that Dick was finishing an Oxford doctorate. If so, the department would like to invite him back as an instructor. The idea had its charms. Dick accepted, bade goodbye to the *Post*, and began teaching in February 1960. Five years later, with his first Anglo-Soviet volume published, came another offer—an associate professorship jointly in Princeton's Department of Politics and its Woodrow Wilson School of Public and International Affairs. The school was to be Dick's academic home for the remainder of his career. In 1988 he was appointed the first David K. E. Bruce Professor of International Affairs.

The Princeton years were to be punctuated with forays outward. Two such forays were for government service—in the Pentagon and at the National Security Council in 1967–1968 and in the Department of State in 1999–2001. Another was in the world of foreign policy think tanks: He served as director of studies at the Council on Foreign Relations from 1973 until 1977. And yet another was at *The New York Times*, where during 1977–1978 Dick was the newspaper's principal editorial voice on matters of foreign policy and defense. His stint at the *Times* was followed by two years as editor of the quarterly journal *Foreign Policy*.

Finally there was Oxford. Coming full circle from his student days, Dick served as the George Eastman Visiting Professor in 1991–1992. For Dick and his wife, Gail, it was the most enjoyable and stimulating year of their lives. It brought Dick's list of Oxford colleges to four: New College, Nuffield, St. Antony's, and now, with the Eastman chair, Balliol. In 2000, St. Antony's (the college closest to his heart) elected him to an Honorary Fellowship.

THE WORK

Even a cursory review of Richard Ullman's published work makes clear that he has been engaged intellectually in the most salient foreign policy and security issues of our time. His books, articles, and lectures have dealt with such problems as the management of relations between the Soviet Union and the West; how to reduce the risks of war and, in particular, the danger of nuclear weapons; how to promote peace and stability in such regions as Europe and the Middle East; and the nature of national security itself. The obvious relevance of these issues notwithstanding, Dick's work has also ranged well beyond the subjects preoccupying the writers of the day's op-ed pages. At least since the 1970s, Dick has been concerned with the tensions in U.S. foreign policy between the Wilsonian impulse to activism abroad and potential for overreaching and abuses inherent in such activism. Over this same period, he has also pondered the conditions under which the international community should intervene to protect the fundamental rights of people being victimized by their own governments. In these and other areas, by looking beyond the surface phenomena of international relations, Dick has blazed intellectual trails in areas of great relevance to scholars and policy makers today.[1]

The Soviet Union and the West—Coming to Terms

Dick's doctoral dissertation at Oxford was published in 1961 by the Princeton University Press as *Intervention and the War*.[2] It deals with British policy toward Russia in the twelve months between the Bolsheviks' seizure of power and the armistice with Germany in November 1918. In it, Dick explores how the interests—perceived and real—of the countries involved in the war against Germany shaped British policy toward the new Soviet state. Dick's analysis goes well beyond a conventional assessment of the interplay of national interests, however. He examines the bureaucratic dynamics underlying British policy, noting that policy making toward Russia at the time was dominated by the War Office and, hence, largely governed by the imperative of reopening the Eastern Front. In the immediate aftermath of the Russian Revolution, the British sought some form of accommodation with the Bolsheviks. As it became clear that this would be impossible, however, Her Majesty's Government hatched a grandiose and highly implausible plan in which it was hoped that "loyal" Russians would rally around intervening British, American, French, and Japanese troops to fight the Germans.

The improbability of this hoped-for scenario points to two themes that appear elsewhere in Dick's work; namely, the "fog" in which policy makers frequently operate due to imperfect information and the ways in which preconceived notions shape their interpretation of that information and resulting policies. In this work Dick also casts a skeptical eye on the notion (cherished by conspiracy theorists of all stripes) that "grand schemes" lie behind most state policies. More often, the truth lies in a more prosaic incrementalism: Policies result from isolated choices made on the fly by policy makers preoccupied with other matters and coping with the immediate problem at hand.

Dick's research at Oxford also led him to observe a tendency that must have resounded eerily later on when he served in the Johnson administration during the Vietnam War. In attempting to explain the British government's attachment to a policy of intervention that was, in retrospect, so obviously futile (indeed, counterproductive), Dick concluded that the policy "was born of a desperate feeling that something—anything—had to be done to relieve the pressure on the Allied forces in the west."[3] Feeling such pressure, government officials may grasp at straws or take initiatives that give the appearance of purposeful action but that, in actuality, are little more than empty gestures. Such initiatives are likely to be especially seductive if they are regarded as "cheap." As Dick wrote:

> Basically, [the intervention] was a policy aimed at getting something for nothing—recreating an Eastern Front without sacrificing any Allied resources which might have been brought against the enemy in the west. For that reason, it was a policy based on so many invalid assumptions; its seeming cheapness induced a blindness to its defects.[4]

How many times have policy makers in Washington and elsewhere been seduced into approving actions that seemed attractive because they appeared to offer some chance of achieving the desired goal while consuming few resources and presenting a low level of risk? One thinks of the Bay of Pigs invasion, the dispatch of U.S. Rangers to Mogadishu in 1993, and the initial steps in Washington's efforts to preserve the independence of South Vietnam. More often than not, the result has been similar to the British experience: failure to achieve the desired goal and a set of unforeseen and unintended consequences that left the nation worse off.

Following the publication of *Intervention and the War*, Princeton University Press asked Dick to produce a second volume examining the years immediately following the war. Dick agreed, and when the U.K. government then changed its policy on releasing government documents to a thirty-year rule, Dick gained access to so much additional material that he decided to split the planned second volume into two. The first of these, *Britain and the Russian Civil War: November 1919–February 1920*,[5] focuses on "the process by which a great Power extricated itself from a civil war in which it was the leading foreign participant, after it became clear that the war could not be won without the payment of a wholly unacceptable price."[6]

Again, Dick found that Britain's support for the Whites came about largely inadvertently, as the original decisions on intervention as a means of bringing about a reopening of the Eastern Front led, almost inexorably, to a commitment to seek the overthrow of the Bolsheviks. Dick observes that "Having fostered the growth of 'new anti-Bolshevik administrations' in order to use them against the Germans, the Allies could not simply let them fall before the Bolsheviks once the War had ended."[7] Once again, a series of seemingly minor decisions, many of which were made implicitly or by low-level officials, created a momentum for intervention that was not tempered by reflection about what resources would actually be needed to bring the operation to a successful conclusion. Ultimately, the manifest failure of the policy resulted in a consensus in London that the political and military resources available to the United Kingdom and the other participants in the intervention were not sufficient to bring success. The book was awarded the George Louis Beer prize of the American Historical Association.

The third volume of the trilogy, *The Anglo-Soviet Accord*,[8] examines the politics and the policy-making process that took place following Britain's disengagement from the Russian civil war and the signing of the Trade Agreement that represented Great Britain's de facto recognition of the Soviet government. By 1920, policy toward Russia was no longer dominated by the War Office; rather, it was shaped primarily by foreign policy and domestic concerns. Accordingly, the third volume focuses much more closely on internal politics in the United Kingdom than the preceding volumes, paying close attention to the perceptions, attitudes, and actions of key players such as Lloyd George, Winston Churchill, and Sir Henry Wilson, chief of the Imperial General Staff.

In this book, Dick also uncovers the roots of what would become the hallmark of British foreign policy in the interwar period: appeasement. He points out that, at its origin, Lloyd George's conception of appeasement was, at least in part, a noble one, based on a desire to reintegrate Germany and Russia into the community of nations—sort of the détente of its day. The worldview that underpinned this conception was that Britain had no permanent enemies and that her interests were best served by balancing off potential rivals against one another. Indeed, as Dick observes, many in Britain at the time viewed France and the United States as more serious potential rivals in some dimensions than Germany and Soviet Russia. The Trade Agreement between the United Kingdom and Russia was also sought after because trade and commerce were seen as means of "civilizing" the "barbaric" Soviet regime. In point of fact, trade between the United Kingdom and Russia never amounted to much, and Lenin and company proved to be far more recalcitrant than Lloyd George and others had hoped.

As in the United States, coming to terms with the Soviets was highly controversial in the United Kingdom Lloyd George's policies were vigorously opposed by a number of his political opponents, including Churchill and Wilson. In one of several historical "scoops" uncovered by Dick over his career, chapter VII of *The Anglo-Soviet Accord* brings to light the story of how Wilson came to suspect that Lloyd George might be a traitor and a "Bolshevist." On the strength of these suspicions, Wilson laid the groundwork for a conspiracy to bring down the government. In the end, no coup was attempted, but the circumstances surrounding the conspiracy and its undoing (Churchill played a pivotal role in scotching it) make for fascinating reading.

Reducing the Nuclear Danger

In 1972, as the third volume of his trilogy was being published, Dick published an essay in *Foreign Affairs* calling for a policy of no first use of nuclear weapons.[9] In this piece, Dick frankly recognized that a credible no first use policy could, at least on the margins, undermine deterrence of conventional attacks. But he concluded that, on balance, this cost would only be "overwhelmingly high" in instances "where there exist major tensions that might lead to conflict, and where there are significant disparities in non-nuclear military capabilities."[10] Dick judged, in 1972, that this combination was not present in Central Europe, Korea, or other areas where the United States had defense commitments. Besides raising the threshold of nuclear use, he felt that the adoption of a no first use pledge by the United States would have the added advantage of prompting America's European allies to spend more on conventional forces for their own defense, thus bolstering deterrence and alleviating existential doubts about the willingness of American leaders to risk their own cities for Europe's security.

The 1972 essay goes on to suggest and to evaluate three ways in which a U.S. no first use pledge might be effectuated: through bilateral or multilateral agreements (in conjunction with the resolution of other arms control issues), through a unilateral declaration, or through a congressional check on the ability of the executive to launch a first strike. Dick concluded that each of these approaches had differing merits and drawbacks, but that a congressional check might be the most feasible. At the time, Congress was considering the adoption of the War Powers Resolution and Dick suggested that the legislation include a restriction on the president's ability to cross the nuclear threshold. Dick argued that, whatever the outcome of the debate, the momentous issue of when and under what circumstances the United States might be prepared to initiate the use of nuclear weapons deserved more serious public discussion than it had had up to that point. He concluded:

An unequivocal 'no first use' position undoubtedly entails certain risks. But a careful and thoughtful examination might judge them lesser risks, and risks more easily hedged against, than those inherent in blurring the line between conventional and nuclear weapons, and thus jeopardizing the long-lasting nuclear truce.[11]

Dick returned to the issue of reducing the dangers associated with nuclear weapons in an article in *Ethics*, which appeared in April 1985.[12] The central point of the piece was that although the genie of nuclear knowledge can never be put back into the bottle, it may nevertheless be possible to remove nuclear weapons as a dominating factor in international relations; that is, to "denuclearize international politics." This denuclearization could come about "if it came to be generally perceived that nuclear weapons were retained in national arsenals solely to deter their use by other nations."[13] This, in turn, led Dick to argue again for the adoption by the United States of a no first use pledge (something Moscow had done in 1982). As before, no first use in the West had foundered on the rock of extended deterrence—NATO's reliance on nuclear weapons to offset its inferiority in conventional arms. Hence, Dick argued as well for heightened efforts to achieve a balance between conventional forces in Europe via reductions in Soviet forces.

In the *Ethics* article Dick expressed dissatisfaction with nuclear arms control negotiations as they had been practiced up to that time, observing that too often military-industrial bureaucracies faced with the prospect of cuts in weapons levels had been bought off with the expansion of programs not covered in the agreements. For this reason, Dick supported the idea of a nuclear freeze as a basis for subsequent arms reduction negotiations. Finally, Dick returned to a theme foreshadowed in his 1972 article—the need for some formal, institutional check on the executive branch's ability to employ nuclear weapons. He pointed out that nuclear weapons are fundamentally incompatible with democratic governance because

> They place the most awesome decision an organized society could ever face in the hands of a very small number of persons who at the moment of decision would almost certainly be totally isolated from, and thus unable to consult with, the publics in whose name they would presume to act.[14]

By diminishing the incentives and possibilities for nuclear war fighting, Dick argued that his proposals would help "diminish some of the most profoundly antidemocratic aspects of a national nuclear capability."[15]

Dick's study of nuclear weapons and their implications led him to what was perhaps the most remarkable "scoop" of his career. During the course of more than one hundred interviews on both sides of the Atlantic from 1987 to 1989, Dick uncovered a long-standing program of covert U.S. assistance to the French government's nuclear program. He broke the story in an article in the summer 1989 issue of *Foreign Policy*.[16]

From the earliest days of the U.S. nuclear program, Washington's policy had been to restrict tightly the dissemination of information about the design and fabrication of nuclear weapons. Only the government of the United Kingdom was permitted access to such information. The Kennedy and Johnson administrations both actively opposed nuclear collaboration with France on the grounds that, in a crisis, small, vulnerable "third country" forces could invite a preemptive Soviet attack. Dick, in fact, argued that U.S. opposition to France's nascent *force de frappe* as well as Washington's refusal to share with the allies the power of decision over its nuclear forces were among the key reasons why de Gaulle withdrew France from NATO's integrated military command in 1966.

Nixon and Kissinger, recognizing the value of France's nuclear forces to Western security, reversed this policy. They hoped that by sharing information about the design of nuclear warheads they could help the French find short cuts in the costly research and development process and that the money thus saved would be applied to the modernization of French conventional forces. In conversations with French Foreign Minister Michel Jobert, Kissinger initiated a procedure that permitted U.S. experts to provide to their French counterparts so-called negative guidance. Under this procedure, French engineers would describe to American interlocutors what they were planning to do and the Americans would, in the style of a game of "twenty questions," let the French know whether they were on the right track.

Although initiated under the Nixon administration, nuclear cooperation reached its peak between the two countries under the Carter administration. The concrete results of the effort have been difficult to gauge, as information about both countries' nuclear programs remains classified. However, it does not appear that the French redirected significant resources toward their conventional defenses in the 1970s. Nevertheless, in the judgment of those with whom Dick spoke in the course of his research, the cooperation contributed mightily to a productive and more trusting security relationship between Washington and Paris. More broadly, the nuclear cooperation was probably a significant factor in France's rapprochement with NATO during the 1970s and 1980s, and its de facto reintegration into NATO's command structure via participation in contingency planning and other activities.

While acknowledging that the Franco-American cooperation had yielded benefits for both sides, Dick criticized the fact that it was undertaken covertly. Covert programs, he wrote, "are almost always costly in one sense or another."[17] One cost of the tight compartmentalization of the information was undoubtedly that fewer experts in France would have access to it than would otherwise have been the case. Too, the program could have a "negative demonstration effect" on third countries that might follow the American example of providing covert nuclear assistance behind a facade of nonproliferation rhetoric. Finally, Dick asserted that covert cooperation was to be avoided because it could not "generate political will." In his view, the most important result of cooperation between democratic allies in the security arena was that it generated "public awareness both of the commitments that governments have made and of the instruments they have adopted to fulfill them."[18] In this way, formal undertakings between governments become commitments between societies and, as such, they are more likely to survive the test of crisis and war.

Bringing Peace to the Middle East

Dick has long been concerned with the knotty problems of the Arab-Israeli conflict and has sought ways to bring peace to the Middle East. In two provocative articles that appeared in 1975, he argued that a formal U.S. security guarantee for Israel might be the best way to promote a settlement that met the security needs of all parties to the dispute.[19] The articles came on the heels of the 1973 Yom Kippur War, the ensuing Arab oil embargo that sent world oil prices skyrocketing, and the 1974 summit of the Arab League in Rabat that resulted in the PLO's emergence as a pivotal factor in intra-Arab politics. Dick's analysis of intra-Arab politics pointed to the need for some initiative to break the cycle of violence in which Arab political leaders in the "confrontation states," Palestinian territories, and elsewhere saw overwhelming incentives to take radical, anti-Israeli positions. As Dick put it in the first of his two essays, "Revolutionary politics favors the extremist and the fundamentalist over the moderate and the compromiser."[20] In this context, Dick saw a U.S. guarantee of Israel's security as a means both of deterring future Arab attacks on Israel and of restraining Israel from provocative actions, including preemptive strikes. Only such an initiative was likely to solve the "overarching dilemma," namely,

> To give the Israelis sufficient assurance of future security from Arab attacks so they will give up the territory they now hold and at the same time satisfy the Palestinians to the extent that they stand firm against the extremists in their own midst.[21]

Assuming that the United States would, under the right circumstances, be prepared to shoulder this burden, the problem would be how to make the guarantee credible to Israelis. As Dick observed, this would require convincing them "that the identity of interests between Israel and the United States was perceived by Washington as being far-reaching indeed, and not one which might be easily disavowed by a future administration."[22] Dick's examination of U.S. interests vis-à-vis Israel convinced him that a large number of Americans, including many outside the Jewish community, perceive an intrinsic value in the preservation of the Israeli state. He saw these feelings as being based partly on the emotional reaction to the fate of the European Jews during World War II and partly on the "intrinsic value" most Americans place on "preserving and extending nonauthoritarian government."[23]

Undertaking a formal commitment to defend the state of Israel would not be without its drawbacks, and Dick examined them in his essays. Among these would be the irreducible uncertainties about the willingness of the United States to make good on its pledge should the Arabs test it. Here, Dick concluded that a U.S. commitment, once entered into, would not easily be broken and that it should be, from the Israelis' point of view, "at least as satisfactory a source of security as continuing to hold occupied territory."[24]

The United States and the World

In several articles written between 1975 and 1983, Dick explored questions about the role of the United States in the international system and U.S. national security strategy. On the eve of the bicentennial of American independence, Dick compared two competing approaches to advancing U.S. interests in a turbulent world, positing the two poles of the "Washingtonian" and "Wilsonian" approaches.[25] Both approaches emphasize American exceptionalism and a desire to protect American democracy. But the former, according to Dick, seeks to secure that objective through "detachment" from the foreign world, while the latter calls for an activist approach that seeks to promote the spread of democracy abroad.

Dick's choice of words—detachment as opposed to isolationism, the more common label placed on our first president's prescription—is significant. In his essay, Dick did not see much support, either in official circles or in the public at large, for crudely drawn approaches that would seek to isolate the United States from the rest of the world. He did, however, perceive a tendency in some sectors toward unilateralism, and in others a mistrust of government-sponsored foreign adventures undertaken in the name of national security. The Washingtonian view is animated, in part, by concerns that as foreign policy grows in scope and importance, it increases inexorably the power of the executive branch and thereby risks disrupting the balance essential to the preservation of American liberties. The Wilsonian view, by contrast (which predates Woodrow Wilson's presidency), springs from the conviction that supporting democracy abroad against the forces of reaction was the best way to promote peace and, at the same time, make the world "safe for democracy."

In Dick's view, the Wilsonian approach has generally predominated in U.S. foreign policy since 1945, though at times (including 1975, when he was writing), the Washingtonian view has come to the fore. At its outset, the strategy of containment was premised in part on the notion that the survival of democracy in America depended on its preservation elsewhere, though this idea quickly became distorted in the execution of the strategy. Too often, U.S. preoccupation with anticommunism led to policies that supported reactionary and repressive regimes so long as they were "with us in the struggle against communism."[26] One result of such policies was the erosion of American credibility and moral standing in the eyes of democrats at home and abroad.

In the period following World War II, the key turning point away from ambitious Wilsonianism was Vietnam. "Wilson's spirit was laid to rest once again," wrote Dick, "in the ashes of Vietnam (and Watts, Newark, and Detroit?)."[27] The revelation by the press of unconstitutional policies by the Nixon administration, including the "abridgment of the rights of American citizens, undertaken by agents of the executive from the president on down,

all in the name of an endless campaign on behalf of 'freedom,'"[28] highlighted
for many the need to restrain the executive from pursuing far-reaching and
ambitious foreign adventures. Senator George McGovern's words from his
landmark speech accepting his party's nomination for president in 1972 to,
"Come home, America" expressed this sentiment.

Yet, as is characteristic of his work, Dick saw other nuances in the situation.
He perceived that the embers of democratic idealism still glowed in the United
States, noting that the maintenance of public support for foreign policy depends on a concern for "ends beyond those of accommodation."[29] He noted
too that the crushing of dissent in one nation poses a threat to the well-being
of Americans not only because it sets a negative precedent, but also because it
diminishes the quality of critical discourse worldwide. Repression in one place,
therefore, can affect the quality and responsiveness of politics elsewhere.

This critique of a robust and militarily oriented posture of containment
evolved in Dick's thinking and in 1983 he published an influential article that
sparked debate on the nature of security itself.[30] In this work, he criticized
the tendency among American political leaders since the late 1940s to define
U.S. national security in narrow terms, centered on military threats and solutions. He wrote that, "Politicians have found it easier to focus the attention of
an inattentive public on military dangers, real or imagined, than on nonmilitary ones."[31] Not surprisingly, therefore, "political leaders have found it easier to build consensus on military solutions to foreign policy problems than
to get agreement on the use (and therefore, adequate funding) of other
means of influence."[32] Dick warned that this tendency is dangerous both because it causes states to overlook potentially more serious nonmilitary
threats and because it can contribute to a militarization of international relations, with detrimental effects on regional and global stability and security.

Dick formulated this critique of the U.S. approach to foreign policy during
the early 1980s, when the Reagan administration was sharply increasing U.S.
defense spending while cutting resources devoted to "other dimensions of
security." In order to challenge conventional thinking about the nature of national security, Dick proposed an original definition of what would constitute a threat to it. A threat, he wrote, should be conceived as:

> An action or sequence of events that (1) threatens drastically and over a rela-
> tively brief span of time to degrade the quality of life for the inhabitants of a
> state, or (2) threatens significantly to narrow the range of policy choices avail-
> able to the government of a state or to private nongovernmental entities (per-
> sons, groups, corporations) within the state.[33]

Stated this way, it becomes clear that the government is responsible not
only for protecting its citizens against "traditional threats," such as war, re-
bellion, or blockade, but that it also has a role in managing the effects of natural disasters, epidemics, droughts, and so on.

A drastic deterioration in environmental quality . . . [or] urban conflict at home [may be as consequential as] interruptions in the flow of critical resources, . . . terrorist attacks, or restrictions on the liberty of citizens in order to combat terrorism.[34]

Dick pointed out that there exists a huge disparity in the expenditures made to prevent or to cope with these various types of threats. For example, expenditures on research that might lead to programs to head off or ameliorate resource scarcities or environmental degradation are also only a small fraction of defense expenditures. Dick stated that nongovernmental entities have important roles to play in raising public awareness of these and other nonmilitary dangers, but he expressed little optimism that a change in consciousness or policy was in the offing any time soon.

In 1998, Dick revised and refined his redefinition of security in a chapter on relations between Russia and the West after the Cold War.[35] On the semantic level, he rejected his previous lumping together of military and nonmilitary threats under the rubric of national security, arguing that the "war problem" is conceptually distinct from the threats posed by natural disasters, environmental degradation, or urban violence. On the practical level, however, the public policy dilemma he had sketched out in "Redefining Security" remains. Most states, Dick points out, "find it extraordinarily difficult to make even a rough calculation of benefits and costs between resources devoted to military purposes and those devoted to other societal needs."[36] The case in point that inspired the article was the trade-off between military expenditures and foreign aid for Russia.

The situation, Dick writes, was described quite succinctly by President Bush: "Democrats in the Kremlin can assure our security in a way nuclear missiles never could."[37] Writing in the aftermath of the Russian financial crisis, Dick distills from Bush's statement a practical policy question: "What does more to enhance American security—a U.S. contribution of one or five or ten billion dollars toward a fund for stabilizing the ruble, or the same expenditure on military forces?"[38] Attempting to answer this question is further complicated by the fact that both military expenditures and foreign financial aid are examples of what Dick calls "threshold phenomena."[39] Expenditures below a certain threshold are useless, yet it is impossible to know precisely where the threshold is.

As so often in his writing, Dick's purpose here is not to score academic points or to make specific policy prescriptions but to raise the level of policy debate. In a section entitled "The Changing Problem of Security," Dick writes:

Not only do the United States and Russia no longer threaten one another: in the international order now evolving, the majority of states face literally no traditional military threats to their security. That is what makes it particularly urgent

that states acquire not only the habit but the techniques and political mechanisms for comparing the contributions to their well-being of military and of nonmilitary spending.[40]

His main policy recommendation is that the West needs to set an example
for Russia to follow of how to think through this policy problem and determine the right mix of guns and butter. For the United States an imbalance in
expenditures on military forces and other national priorities results in nothing worse than an inefficiency or "sub-optimal result." But for Russia, whose
resources are so scarce, it may present a dilemma whose incorrect resolution—getting the mix of guns and butter wrong—can make the difference
between a successful transition to a stable democracy and a delayed or even
unsuccessful one.

Another Ullman essay on U.S. strategy that has resonance today was a critique of "trilateralism"—an idea much in vogue in the mid-1970s that advocated ever-closer cooperation among the United States, Europe, and Japan
on matters relating to their common interests.[41] Trilateralism emerged in part
out of a reaction to a unilateralist thrust that came to dominate the foreign
economic policy of the Nixon administration. The OPEC oil embargo and
strident calls by leaders in the Third World for a "new international economic
order" also prompted some in the industrial democracies to seek greater
unity.

Writing in October 1976, Dick pointed out that the notion of a triangular relationship among the three major democratic-industrial power cen-
ters remained more aspirational than real. For one thing, the thick lines of
trade and security links that connected the United States to Europe and to
Japan were largely missing between the latter two vertices. And of the
three, only the United States had a truly global (as opposed to regional)
perspective or the military means to act extraregionally. These facts suggested that, trilateralist rhetoric notwithstanding, the United States was often going to find it difficult to gain European and Japanese support for
U.S. positions and initiatives that reached beyond their immediate, regional concerns. This has, in fact, been a central conundrum for U.S. foreign policy makers in the 1970s, 1980s, and on into the post–Cold War period. Dick concluded that "there is and will continue to be less to
trilateralism than meets the ear."[42] But he acknowledged the existence and
the relevance of shared values and interests among the three corners of
the triangle and suggested that the most effective way to protect those values was to strengthen formal and informal mechanisms that specifically
relate to them. Rather than trying to assert a commonality of interests
across the board, then, Dick recommended that U.S. leaders work on specific policy areas where that commonality exists, such as in the areas of
human rights or trade policy.

Intervention and Human Rights

Dick's views on intervention in the Third World are nuanced and informed by deeply held humanitarian instincts. Two articles published five years apart in *Foreign Affairs* illustrate this. In this first of these articles, "Human Rights and Economic Power: The United States versus Idi Amin," written in 1978, Dick called for U.S. leadership to bring down an evil regime through economic intervention.[43] In the second, "At War with Nicaragua," written in 1983, he called for an end to U.S. intervention.[44] In both cases, his primary concern was for the well-being of the people of these countries, while his focus was on U.S. interests, as defined by a distinctly long-term perspective.

Idi Amin ruled Uganda through terror and repression. In this, he was far from alone. But the scope of his regime's brutality was exceptional: By 1978 it was estimated that the Amin regime was responsible for the death of between 100,000 and 300,000 Ugandans. In the face of such brutality, Dick saw an imperative for action. Given the reluctance of regional actors to intervene (the Organization for African Unity had long refused to takes sides in the internal affairs of its members), it was up to the West to do something. Fortunately, the requisite leverage was at hand: Four fifths of Uganda's hard currency earnings were derived from the export of coffee to the West, and one third of this came to the United States. Moreover, those export earnings were controlled directly by Amin, who used them not to compensate the growers of the coffee but rather to pay off loans to Libya and other Arab countries, to buy weapons (mostly from the Soviet Union), and to supply his army, police, and civil service with luxury goods.

In light of this, a boycott of Ugandan coffee seemed the perfect way to put pressure on Amin. Surprisingly, the Carter administration had opposed such a boycott on the grounds that it would violate rules of the General Agreement on Trade and Tariffs (GATT) and, therefore, weaken the international trading regime. Dick challenged the administration's position as being rooted in a conviction that the economic and political spheres can be treated separately. He then dismissed this distinction as being more rhetorical than real and, in any case, trivial in comparison to the human stakes involved. A boycott of Ugandan coffee, Dick wrote, would indicate that the U.S. government "is prepared to say that there are boundaries of decency beyond which other governments must not pass in their treatment of their own citizens."[45] This position put Dick at odds not only with the Carter administration but also with more than 300 years of international law on the sovereignty of states. It was a position that would wear well more than two decades later, as the international community confronted atrocities carried out by governments against "their own" people in the former Yugoslavia, Rwanda, East Timor, and elsewhere.[46]

Dick's position against U.S. intervention in Nicaragua was founded on two judgments: First, he argued that the regime against which the Reagan

administration was working was, in many ways, an improvement over the
one it had replaced. "Nicaragua under the Sandinistas," Dick wrote, "is no
longer a state in which the bulk of the population is terrorized by its own
armed forces. In that respect it is nothing like as repressive as some of its
[non-communist] neighbors."[47]

Second, Dick felt that the means chosen by the administration for undermining the Sandinistas—supporting the Contra rebels—were, in fact, counterproductive to U.S. objectives. Having visited Nicaragua in August 1983
with other members of the board of directors of Oxfam America, Dick came
away with the clear sense that, far from being likely to liberalize or overthrow the communists, the Contras were strengthening the hands of hardliners in the Sandinista regime and solidifying their support among the peas-
ants. "In a dozen peasant communities I heard the same thing from scores of
people," Dick wrote, ". . . nothing had rallied them to the Sandinist cause as
much as the Contras had done."[48] In light of the injustice of U.S. policy and
its perverse consequences for U.S. interests, Dick concluded the article by
urging members of Congress to deny the administration funds for continuing
the Contra war.

Ending the Cold War

In fall 1988, on the eve of U.S. presidential elections, Mikhail Gorbachev
had been in power in Moscow for three years. Dick Ullman saw in Gorbachev the opportunity of a lifetime—literally to end the Cold War. Accordingly, he published in *Foreign Policy* an article by that title that argued for
some major changes in U.S. foreign and defense policies.[49] While some have
since argued that the Reagan defense buildup, particularly the Strategic Defense Initiative (SDI), accelerated the decline and fall of the Soviet Union,
Dick took the opposite tack. He took seriously Gorbachev's stated determination to reform and restructure the Soviet economy and society and reasoned as follows:

- Gorbachev's primary focus is in the domestic arena.
- International affairs—especially military expenditures—distract attention and resources away from Moscow's domestic priorities.
- Perceived foreign policy failures could bring down Gorbachev and lead
  to his replacement by a leader with a less benign agenda.
- Only international tranquillity—a sort of détente plus—can allow Gorbachev to remain focused on domestic imperatives (hence the Soviet
  leader's emphasis on arms reduction initiatives).
- The United States therefore should work to create an international environment supportive of Gorbachev's reform efforts.

Dick argued that, for the first time, the Soviet Union had the potential to become a "normal state," one that

> Derives few domestic benefits from propagating a view of the international system that emphasizes the presence of powerful enemies . . . and whose policies are not driven by . . . an imperative for expansion through the reproduction of its own political system and ideology.[50]

Obviously, the transformation of the Soviet Union into a normal state would represent a boon to the security of the rest of the world. While tensions between the United States and the USSR would remain, the two powers would increasingly see their security in terms other than the zero-sum game that had characterized their relations through the Cold War.

In order to maximize the probability of achieving this state of affairs, Dick urged that the West take steps to assuage points of conflict between the Soviet Union and the West and to facilitate economic reform. Specifically, he called for an abandonment of President Reagan's SDI program and for the United States to abide by the ABM Treaty. He also urged support for Moscow's application for observer status at the GATT and for some formal link with the International Monetary Fund (IMF). To those who argued that "a prosperous bear is a more dangerous bear," Dick responded that economic liberalization in the Soviet Union would almost certainly be accompanied by liberalization in the political sphere.

In retrospect, while Dick's analysis of Gorbachev's position led to sound policy prescriptions, it (like almost everyone else's at the time) was based on a flawed understanding of the resiliency of the Soviet regime. Dick asserted that Gorbachev's regime "may be the first [in Moscow] secure enough in its own domestic standing not to feel threatened by questions about the legitimacy of regimes in Eastern Europe."[51] Whether Gorbachev and those around him might, in fact, have felt secure in their domestic standing, it is now clear that the regime he inherited was remarkably fragile. Such was the cynicism of the Soviet people toward their political system that, once the winds of change were unloosed, it took little more than a stiff breeze to rip the entire structure from its foundation. Nevertheless, Dick's call in 1988 for decisive steps to hasten the end of the Cold War stands out as a clear vision of the possibilities inherent in the Gorbachev transition and that which followed.

Securing Europe

This vision kept pace with the accelerating pace of change that swept over the Soviet Union and its empire in the ensuing four years. In 1991, after the Soviet empire abroad had collapsed and just prior to the disintegration of the Soviet Union itself, Dick published *Securing Europe*, a prescient and insightful assessment of the qualitatively new security situation in and around Europe.[52] In this volume, Dick was among the first to recognize that international relations in Europe were entering a period in which historical models and analogies had become largely irrelevant. Dick identified several factors that lay behind this transformation. The first was the dual recognition by the Soviet regime that its most pressing priority was internal reform and that its future survival was no longer bound up with the preservation of communist regimes in Central and Eastern Europe or with the expansion of communism elsewhere. Because of this, Dick argued, the Soviet leadership understood that it faced no problems for which the external use of military force could provide a solution.

Other factors figured as well in the new, more stable Europe:

- The declining value of territory as a military or economic resource
- The fact that Europe's peace had become "divisible"; that is, that conflicts in the Balkans or elsewhere in Eastern Europe would be unlikely to ignite a larger war drawing in the great powers
- Germany's transformation (through decades of experience with the West in the Federal Republic and, finally, through unification) from a revisionist power to a status quo power

Together, these developments converged to create a situation in which Western leaders had "the opportunity to banish, perhaps forever, warfare among the major powers of Europe."[53] In this new situation, reductions in military forces, the adoption of more "nonoffensive defense" postures, and other measures aimed at reducing the risk of inadvertent war were called for. Dick foresaw that ultimately, if and when Russia evolved into a truly democratic state, NATO would be transformed into a "European Security Organization" open to all democratic polities in the Euro-Atlantic region. Dick also recognized that the focus of European and American defense planners would shift to "out of area" problems on Europe's periphery and the need to prevent conflicts in these areas from spilling over into the new "zone of peace" through terrorism, the use of weapons of mass destruction, or other means.

Of course, Dick was not the first to proclaim an end to the feasibility of war among the major powers in Europe.[54] But his analysis pointed to structural changes of such a profound nature that many of us became convinced that, this time, the optimists had it right. At the same time, there were other voices decrying the collapse of bipolarity in Europe as a prelude to renewed instability and conflict.[55] Prominent analysts of the so-called Realist school argued that the reemergence of a multipolar distribution of military power in Europe would lead inexorably to state behavior similar to that which led to catastrophe in the early decades of this century. We would, wrote one, "soon miss the Cold War."[56]

Dick was unsparing in his criticism of this "Realist" analysis. By focusing almost exclusively on military structure, he wrote, the Realists exclude from consideration the very factors most responsible for the transformation of the international system in Europe. He also took issue with the Realist view that small conflicts in Eastern Europe would inevitably draw in larger powers, especially Germany and the Soviet Union.

> The revolutionary events of 1989–1990 have left Germany and the Soviet Union with no vital interests in Eastern Europe except the negative one of seeking assurance that the region will not become a place where threats aimed at them can originate. Because neither has claims against the other, or interests that can be furthered only at the expense of the other, neither has any interest in enlisting the states of Eastern Europe in alliances aimed against any other state.[57]

Dick concluded by calling on the governments and the people of the West to make the most of the opportunities presented by the new situation and to work vigorously to extend stability and peace outward. This would depend in large measure on helping to "rebuild the shattered and demoralized societies of the Communist part of Europe and to realize the latent human potential in people who were regimented and suppressed for so long."[58]

Dick's understanding of the new dynamics of the security situation in Europe have proven to be remarkably accurate. He was thus well-equipped to assess the prospects for and the implications of conflicts in the Balkans during the 1990s. As editor of *The World and Yugoslavia's Wars*, and author of that book's introduction and one of its chapters, Dick stated that a central lesson of the modern Balkan wars is predicated on his earlier assessment that Europe's peace today has become divisible.[59] He wrote that, "there has, in fact, never been a high probability that any of these scenarios for a wider war would become actual."[60] Indeed, from the standpoint of Western policy makers the biggest problem created by the wars over Bosnia and Kosovo has been in getting the leading members of the international community to commit the resources needed to bring the situation under control. These policy makers are caught on the horns of a dilemma. On the one hand, they recognize that their states have no "vital interests" at stake in Yugoslavia. Yet, because of modern communications and a growing, if still inchoate, sense of responsibility for upholding universally held norms against unjust violence, they cannot escape pressure to act to stop the killing. As Dick wrote:

> There is a point . . . when interest and embarrassment merge. When television sets worldwide nightly show pictures of massacred civilians, governments that previously have not perceived an important interest at stake in a specific outcome of a conflict discover that they have a real interest in ceasing to appear— to their own publics and to the world—as not only callous but impotent.[61]

Embarrassment, of course, is not a strong basis for policy, and the international community stumbled badly during the first three years of the conflict in Bosnia. Writing after NATO's forcible intervention in Bosnia in 1995, but before Operational Allied Force in Kosovo in 1999, Dick was pessimistic about the prospects for rapid change: "States in trouble," he wrote, "would be advised to have other remedies at hand" than waiting for international intervention.[62] The international security institutions that have been set up to prevent such wars—the United Nations, the Organization for Security Cooperation in Europe (OSCE)—were not up to the task. Neither was the United States. The self-proclaimed "indispensable power" was, in Dick's words, "consistently inconsistent" in its policies toward the Bosnian crisis and when it did intervene forcefully, congressional support for U.S. involvement in the Implementation Force (IFOR) to implement the Dayton Accords was precarious.

In short, the "divisibility of peace in Europe" that Dick celebrated in 1988 has turned out to be a two-sided coin, with the lack of vital interest in the outcome of "out of area" conflicts helping to ensure peace among the major powers of Europe, but breeding at the same time a certain indifference to such horrors as "ethnic cleansing." Writing prior to NATO's intervention in Kosovo, Dick likened the United States and its allies to bystanders who sit idly by as street crimes are committed before their eyes. NATO's subsequent action in the Kosovo crisis has altered Dick's judgment somewhat. However, governments will remain generally reluctant to commit military forces to the resolution of conflicts caused by other governments' repression of "their own" populations.

THE MAN AND THE WORK

What shines through all of Dick's writing is the presence of a large and many-faceted mind at work. We see the mind of a policy maker, weighing the manifold and sometimes conflicting interests at stake in complex situations and keeping them in balance. We see as well in this policy maker's mind an appreciation for the constraints and pressures under which officials in the "real world" must operate and, in light of this, a rejection of superficially appealing or ideologically pure solutions that would ultimately be unworkable.

We see the mind of a scholar, who delights in unraveling complex problems of human relations and in understanding what makes them tick and identifying the main features of the landscape without either getting lost in the minutia or oversimplifying the picture. We see, in fact, the mind of the best sort of scholar—one that does not shrink from challenging the conventional wisdom if that is where his scholarship takes him.

We see the mind (and heart) of a humanitarian, which prompt a readiness to look beyond narrow, traditional definitions of national interest and to accept that the United States and its partner democracies have a real and growing responsibility to help prevent the worst abuses of human dignity in this imperfect world.

We see the mind of a journalist who relishes the chance to break a good story, not for its own sake but for the sake of advancing our knowledge and understanding of important events and relationships.

We see the mind of a critic who does not shrink from pointing out the failings of his own country when it falls short of carrying out its responsibilities. But we see too the mind of a patriot who loves what is best and most worthy of emulation in his country's democratic traditions.

And, fortunately for those of us who have had the privilege, we see the mind of a teacher who is willing and able to share his hard-won insights with others and to challenge his students to probe deeply beneath the surface phenomena of international relations.

As policy analyst, scholar, humanitarian, journalist, and critic, Dick's work stands on its own and speaks for itself. As a teacher, the other contributions in this volume represent a few examples of the nfluence Dick has had on the thinking and the careers of his students.

NOTES

1. This chapter draws on selected works by Richard Ullman. A complete bibliography is found in the appendix.

2. Richard Ullman, *Intervention and the War* (Princeton: Princeton University Press, 1961).

3. *Intervention*, p. 333.

4. *Intervention*, p. 333.

5. Richard Ullman, *Britain and the Russian Civil War: November 1918–February 1920* (Princeton: Princeton University Press, 1968).

6. *Britain*, p. viii.

7. *Britain*, p. 348

8. Richard Ullman, *The Anglo-Soviet Accord* (Princeton: Princeton University Press, 1972).

9. Richard Ullman, "No First Use of Nuclear Weapons," *Foreign Affairs*, July 1972.

10. "No First Use," p. 673.

11. "No First Use," p. 683.

12. Richard Ullman, "Denuclearizing International Politics," *Ethics*, April 1985.

13. "Denuclearizing," p. 567.

14. "Denuclearizing," p. 587.

15. "Denuclearizing," p. 587.

16. Richard Ullman, "The Covert French Connection," *Foreign Policy*, Summer 1989.

17. "Covert," p. 27.

18. "Covert," p. 33.

19. Richard Ullman, "After Rabat: Middle East Risks and American Roles," *Foreign Affairs*, January 1975; and Richard Ullman, "Alliance with Israel?" *Foreign Policy*, Summer 1975.

20. "Rabat," p. 276.

21. "Alliance," p. 19.

22. "Rabat," p. 291.

23. "Rabat," p. 294.

24. "Alliance," p. 27

25. Richard Ullman, "The 'Foreign World' and Ourselves: Washington, Wilson, and the Democrat's Dilemma," *Foreign Policy*, Winter 1975–1976.

26. "Washington, Wilson," p. 107.

27. "Washington, Wilson," p. 110.

28. "Washington, Wilson," p. 112.

29. "Washington, Wilson," p. 116.

30. Richard Ullman, "Redefining Security," *International Security*, Summer 1983.

31. "Redefining," p. 129.

32. "Redefining," p. 129.

33. "Redefining," p. 133

34. "Redefining," p. 134

35. Richard Ullman, "Russia, the West, and the Redefinition of Security," in *Russia and the West: The 21st Century Security Environment*, ed. Alexei Arbator, Karl Kaiser, and Robert Legrold (New York: M.E. Sharpe, 1999).

36. "Redefinition," p. 190.

37. Cited in "Redefinition," p. 192.

38. "Redefinition," p. 192.

39. "Redefinition," p. 193.

40. "Redefinition," p. 201.

41. Richard Ullman, "Trilateralism: Partnership for What?" *Foreign Affairs*, October 1976.

42. "Trilateralism," p. 16.

43. Richard Ullman, "Human Rights and Economic Power: The United States versus Idi Amin," *Foreign Affairs*, April 1978.

44. Richard Ullman, "At War with Nicaragua," *Foreign Affairs*, Fall 1983.

45. "Idi Amin," p. 540.

46. As Dick's article went to press, Congress was debating the adoption of a boycott on Ugandan coffee. The boycott legislation passed. As it happened, not long afterward the Ugandan armed forces collapsed in the face of a Tanzanian invasion.

47. "Nicaragua," p. 46.

48. "Nicaragua," p. 42.

49. Richard Ullman, "Ending the Cold War," *Foreign Policy*, Fall 1988.

50. "Cold War," p. 132.

51. "Cold War," p. 135.

52. Richard Ullman, *Securing Europe* (Princeton: Princeton University Press, 1991).

53. *Securing*, p. 153.

54. Famously, Norman Angell wrote that the use of military power to advance a nation's economic and political standing "belongs to a stage of development out of

which we have passed . . . that war, even when victorious, can no longer achieve those aims for which people strive." The year was 1911. Norman Angell, *The Great Illusion* (New York: G. P. Putnam's Sons, 1911), 381–382.

55. See John Mearsheimer, "Back to the Future: Instability in Europe After the Cold War," *International Security*, Summer 1990.

56. See John Mearsheimer, "Why We Will Soon Miss the Cold War," *Atlantic Monthly*, August 1990.

57. *Securing*, p. 153.

58. *Securing*, p. 153.

59. Richard Ullman, ed., *The World and Yugoslavia's Wars* (New York: Council on Foreign Relations, 1997).

60. Ibid., p. 3.

61. *Yugoslavia*, p. 5.

62. *Yugoslavia*, p. 25.

2

Legitimacy and World Politics

David C. Gompert

RICHARD AND MIKHAIL

I first heard Richard Ullman explain the strategic importance of the legitimacy of states not in a Princeton lecture bowl but in a Manhattan hotel suite late one evening in 1984. A group of American and European experts had gathered to ponder Mikhail Gorbachev's "new thinking" about the Soviet system. Convinced that change was imperative, Gorbachev had embarked on the political reform known as *glasnost* (openness) and its economic sibling, *perestroika* (restructuring).

Rising above the evening's cackle of (cognac-enhanced) interpretations of Moscow happenings, Ullman offered an elegant explanation: Gorbachev knew that Soviet communism must be made legitimate if it was to last. Both Gorbachev and Ullman understood that the Soviet regime's lack of domestic lawfulness was not merely hard on its citizens but also a one-way ticket to failure.

Making communism and the Soviet Union lawful would be a tall order—too tall, as it turned out. In his article "Ending the Cold War," Ullman wrote: "Legitimacy is a troubling issue for regimes that owe their present hegemony to a past seizure of power and that have not adopted mechanisms such as genuinely democratic elections to show they no longer hold power arbitrarily."[1] It would thus take more than a paint job to save the Soviet state from oblivion.

But Gorbachev's understanding of legitimacy was narrow and naive. A favored son of the Soviet system, he believed that there was virtue at the heart of both the ideology and the union. He had been trained to regard capitalism as unjust, free markets as corrupt, and democracy as inferior to conscientious

25

communism. Stalin had perverted and Brezhnev had nearly suffocated what to Gorbachev remained a noble idea and grand multinational state. He therefore thought making the system more open and clean—"draining away the poison"—would suffice. Going further than that never crossed his mind.

By improving Soviet internal and external behavior, Gorbachev hoped to earn international respectability, reduce tensions with the United States, escape from a costly and losing military competition, and obtain badly needed Western technology and capital. He made participation in the Soviet bloc voluntary—discarding the Brezhnev Doctrine in favor of the Sinatra Doctrine[2]—as if this would quell unrest in Eastern Europe and cool the fever of disaffected national minorities within the USSR.

Far from saving communism, Gorbachev's measures exposed its deepest flaws, which he had neither the vision nor the means to mend. Even shedding an illegitimate empire, from Tallinn to Tashkent, could not save an illegitimate core. He and his associates turned out to be "the victims of an enormous hoax—the premise in Marxism-Leninism that through the prism of intense coercion could be refracted the image of a truly just, humane, and even prosperous society."[3] The rest, to say the least, is history.

To most of us, the bonfire of Soviet communism illuminated something new: a cause-and-effect relationship between the lawlessness of a system of government and its weakness when put to a true test. To Ullman, it confirmed a long-held belief that legitimate government is both righteous and rugged; its opposite both fiendish and frail.

What is this "legitimacy" that can explain such momentous developments? How does it affect the stability, strength, and performance of states? How is the lawfulness of states related to domestic, international, and transnational security? Does sovereignty provide legitimacy, or is it the other way around? What will become of the system of sovereign nation-states if legitimacy becomes a criterion for sovereignty?

Answering these questions to the full satisfaction of the venerable professor would exceed both the allotted length of this chapter and the ability of this former student. But the very fact that they have become defining questions of international politics underscores the truth of Ullman's conviction that the doctrine of human freedom should and can apply at the global level.

DEFINING LEGITIMACY

Clearly, legitimacy is more than decency and openness, though these are common ingredients. To be legitimate, a government must at least "achieve office through constitutional processes and rely on constitutional processes, not repression, to remain in office."[4] It is not enough for a state to permit its people a margin of freedom in their social, intellectual, and economic lives. It must permit *them* to decide the extent of freedom they will have. Thus, benign regimes are not necessarily legitimate: if they determine their own tenure, they are benign out of choice not obligation. To make the grade, a regime must answer to the people, not merely care for them.

Yet achieving office constitutionally does not in itself make a regime legitimate, even if it enjoys continuing popularity, as Hitler's Reich did until it destroyed itself and Germany. A legitimate regime arrives, governs, and departs according not only to the people's wishes but also to the laws and institutions that embody and safeguard their rights and the rights of future generations.

The elected Zimbabwe government of Robert Mugabe respects only the laws that are consistent with its continuation in power and the desires of its constituents. Despite Mugabe's appalling management of the Zimbabwe economy, his orchestration of the wrongful seizure of white-owned farms helped produce the needed, narrow margin of victory in the last election. Few would dare argue that this regime is legitimate, since it is clear that neither it nor its slim majority feels bound by the rule of law.

In a law-based democracy, a government that behaves illegally can and will be excised, not rewarded, by the governed through constitutional methods. Conversely, one that is merely unpopular or ineffective will continue to enjoy the people's obedience until it is replaced. It takes "high crimes," not high incompetence, to impeach and remove a U.S. president.

Nixon was undone by his own wanton lawlessness; the lapsed legitimacy of his administration stood in sharp contrast to, and became a casualty of, the enduring legitimacy of American democracy. If a regime's existence is lawful, it must behave lawfully or else go out of existence. Facing this sanction for misrule, law-based democratic regimes are more likely than others to rule benignly. The likes of Hitler, Mugabe, and Milosevic are the exceptions that prove the rule: Democracy implies accountability to the people *and* to the law; the absence of either means true accountability to neither.

If so, can only democracies be legitimate? Or does such a claim merely reveal a Judeo-Christian blindness toward the virtues of other political cultures? What about benevolent monarchies, in which most of the people accept, even revere, the regime, and in which the regime abides by the constitution and is dedicated to the well-being of the people? How can we have witnessed the outpouring of Jordanian grief at the death of King Hussein and yet claim that the Hashemite Kingdom is illegitimate?

On this question, Ullman considers democracy desirable but not essential for legitimacy. "There are a few polities left whose rulers derive their authority by lineal descent and whose legitimacy derives from universal respect for the traditional meaning of those processes, but there are not many." He cites Saudi Arabia and the Gulf emirates.[5]

Maybe so. But it is hard to see how elections on a regular schedule could but help, even where there is no precedent. After all, winning a free and fair election is the surest test of whether the regime and its particular laws are truly accepted or merely endured. Moreover, denial of religious and female rights clearly undermines any claim of legitimacy, whether or not supported by tradition.

Elections and universal suffrage might not come naturally to some non-Western cultures; but their absence makes it difficult to determine whether a ruler in fact enjoys "universal respect." To say that a regime is tolerable to its citizens is not to say that they would rather have it than one of their own choosing. The Sandinistas were regarded as legitimate by themselves and their supporters, only to lose office at the first chance Nicaraguans had to vote.

Popular appeal does not equal legitimacy. King Abdullah, heir to Hussein, appears to be as kind and capable as his father. But if he were not, what options short of riot or regicide would the people of Jordan have? It is all too easy for a rich regime to co-opt the people or for a charismatic one to charm them. The wealth of Gulf emirs—attributable entirely to fossil luck—does not confer legitimacy on their rule any more than the talent to arouse virulent nationalism conferred it on the presidency of Slobodan Milosevic.[6]

Two current trends are making democracy a prerequisite of legitimacy, if it is not already. First, the spread of information technology, along with the ideas and truths it propagates, is whetting the appetite for authentic democracy even in relatively open authoritarian states. Their citizens are becoming more able to make informed decisions on matters affecting them, rather than deferring to a ruling family or elite. Thomas Jefferson got it right—two centuries before the information revolution!—when, in a letter to James Madison, he wrote: "And, say, finally whether peace is best preserved by giving energy to the government, or information to the people. This last is the most certain, and most legitimate engine of government."[7]

Second, among "emerging" countries, the processes of marketization and integration into the global economy are heightening demands of the rising middle class for political rights and freedom to go with their expanded economic possibilities.[8] While the privileged few can live without democracy, and illiterate masses are malleable, an informed and growing middle class will not long regard as legitimate any regime it has not had the choice to select. If only to protect their economic activities and gains, they insist on government that lives by the rule of law or can be removed if it does not.

Recent research at RAND confirms empirically that because of this middle-class phenomenon democracy generally will not be far behind economic liberalization.[9] As the aftermath of the 1998 Asian financial crisis shows, when "crony capitalism" distorts markets, retards reform, stalls economic growth, and damages confidence, traditional and transitional regimes may be compelled to open up or get out of the way. The East Asian model itself—a quasi-democratic, single-party (or single-family) system that buys legitimacy by "delivering the goods"—looks unconvincing now that the "tigers" are being thrust toward real democracy by the need to get on track economically.

For our purposes, then, we can equate legitimacy with the democratic rule of law.[10] And, with Ullman as guide, we can explore how such legitimacy affects world politics.

LEGITIMACY AS STRENGTH

It is now broadly understood that the most robust and secure states are the law-based democratic ones. But this was not always the prevailing view: Recall the West's awe of Soviet power. That state was commonly viewed as both mighty and durable. That the Kremlin had to answer neither to its people nor to its "allies" was even deemed to give it an edge over the law-abiding but unruly West.

Even Ullman, in 1984, cited the Soviet Union as an example of a repressive state that was nevertheless stable—an error he shared with almost every other analyst of world politics.[11] But he also had early inklings that domestic legitimacy was a strategic asset. Twenty years ago, when asked to explain the concept of trilateralism, he suggested that tolerance of dissenting views largely accounted for the economic and technological success of the United States, Western Europe, and Japan.[12] The timing of this observation is significant, for it was made before the information revolution revealed a definite that pluralistic democracy does indeed contribute to national strength by fostering initiative.

Some attribute this advantage to the growing importance of "soft" power—economic, technological, and ideational—which the Western democracies possess in abundance.[13] But it is increasingly apparent, and no coincidence, that the most legitimate states also have superior "hard" (i.e., military) power, especially with the expanding role of information technology in warfare.[14] The U.S. lead in information technology, including for military use, is attributable to exceptional openness and, more specifically, to state noninterference in this critical sector (having deregulated telecommunications and never regulated computers).

After the United States, the best armed forces in the world are those of its West European allies, whose societies are also free and open. In contrast, states that deny economic and political freedoms are severely handicapped in creating, absorbing, and using information technology, whether for civilian or military applications. The "revolution in military affairs" is an option not open to closed societies. Such rogue states as North Korea and Iraq have no hope of offsetting their military inferiority with information technology. This growing disparity, favoring the legitimate over the illegitimate, makes the latter vulnerable to intervention by the former.

Undemocratic states were not always technologically "challenged." By assembling, controlling, and if need be enslaving scientific talent, the Nazis (in rockets), Imperial Japan (in torpedoes), and the USSR (in space) were able to gain temporary leads. The centralization of nonaccountable power had certain industrial-age advantages, especially as part of war preparations. In sharp contrast, the creation and application of information technology blossoms outside, arguably in spite of, the state.

Even before the information age, openness was a potential source of enduring strength for legitimate states. Now, information technology taps that potential by expanding the ability of private and public institutions to network and thereby mobilize the human capital, ideas, and initiative that are distributed throughout a free society. As the old tokens of strength—steel, ships, tanks, explosives—become less important and information becomes more important, open societies and their democratic states are able to function more effectively, internally and externally, than closed, centralized ones.

STRONG STATES AND WEAK STATES

If illegitimate states monopolize domestic power yet are ineffective, should they be considered strong or weak? How can a state disperse its power and yet become stronger?

The most important quality of a strong state, according to Ullman, is "that its government enjoys legitimacy among the vast majority of the persons who reside within the geographic space over which it claims to be sovereign."[15] In other words, what makes a state effective is the respect and allegiance of its people, not its internal security forces. States that perform well what their citizens ask of them and otherwise show restraint are more likely to enjoy such respect and allegiance than are states that reach too far. Put differently, the concentration on "core functions" that is now the rage in the world of business is also applicable to the world of politics.

Take Costa Rica: With no army, it is among the strongest states in Latin America. Its government is indisputably legitimate; its per capita GDP is comparatively high; its citizens are content, its streets clean, and its forests unspoiled. (A recent up-tick in violent crime suggests that law enforcement is, if anything, *too* gentle.) Costa Rica controls its borders with ease; its sovereignty is respected, even by some very unsavory actors in the neighborhood.

Or consider South Korea, where the reduction of the state's role in the economy and the dismantling of state-sanctioned industrial-banking conglomerations are considered so crucial for economic recovery that markets recoil at any sign that they might be reversed. The opening up of South Korea's politics, exemplified by the election of former outsider Kim Dae Jung, has helped reinvigorate the economy, earned foreign confidence, and created a stronger state.

While there are other important examples from the developing world—Mexico and Nigeria are showing promise—the most powerful evidence of the correlation of legitimacy and strength is right under our noses. Generally speaking, the oldest continuously functioning states in the world are the Atlantic democracies, none of which is now seriously threatened from within or without. Of these, the strongest is the United States. True, this is in part because of its size, its natural blessings, and its emergence, unscathed, from World War II. But it has especially surged since the 1980s, thanks to the information revolution and related retreat of state power.

Most Americans see their government as more, not less, legitimate to the extent that its role in their markets and lives is limited. They want a state of circumscribed but predictable competence. As the political nine lives of William Jefferson Clinton show so poignantly (if jocularly), the American people expect little else from their chief executive as long as he does not botch his modest part in managing their economy.

Much of the rest of the world now wants a go at the American model. Even as they decry the excesses of American capitalism, most European societies, starting with Great Britain's Thatcher-to-Blair revolution, are trying to reduce the role of government. The West European "welfare state" is now viewed as infirm, as well as less legitimate than it once was. Similarly, the improved economies and cohesiveness of many countries of Latin America and East Asia can be credited to the supplanting of state dominance with democracy.

Ullman's comforting equation—state strength = legitimacy—contradicts the traditional image of state power. The paradox is more than semantic. A state can indeed monopolize power, especially the old industrial forms of it, and yet be feeble. While it can flex and use its muscles against its people or its neighbors, its weakness and ineffectiveness can become manifest, even fatal, when tested.

In modern history's most extreme cases, Nazism and communism depended vitally on concentrated state power. It made them what they were and sustained them temporarily. But their strength was like that of the pumped-up body-builder who must increase his dosage of steroids until they cause his system to fail. Consider, for instance, the former German Democratic Republic—a power-state that proved to be a weakling when put to the most elementary test of legitimacy: will its citizens stay when given a chance to leave? In the information age, such extreme concentrations of power are inherently self-defeating because the dominant technology both requires and fosters the distribution of power.

STATES AND NONSTATES

Some have suggested that *all* states, democratic and not, will be undermined
by the compound effects of the information revolution and globalization. Increasingly, nongovernmental organizations and other nonstate actors offer
alternative pathways for people to pursue collective interests—pathways
that often appear more promising than sclerotic political institutions, including states. Because they ignore borders, such transnational economic and
political associations are bound to weaken purely national ones.

Provided they do so lawfully and affirmatively, it is healthy for states to resist this erosion—thus, their own obsolescence. (Analogously, it is good for
political parties to try to regain their relevance, corporate boards the confidence of their stockholders, and labor unions the support of their members.)
For all the interest in nongovernmental organizations, internetworked communities, and other transnational actors, they are not constitutionally an-
swerable to all the people they affect, the way law-based democratic governments are. Better to make duly constituted political institutions more
effective than to let them be overrun by shadowy special interests, well-
meaning or not.

Democratic states can be more easily bypassed than other states precisely
because their citizens may make full use information technology and join
whatever groups they wish. But this does not mean that democracies will be
weaker, or badly weakened, because of information technology, globalization, and transnational movements. Pressures to be more responsive are the
headwaters of reform. Those states that sense and respond to such pressures—typically, law-based democracies, because they must—should become even more effective and strong.

Thus, the states that have never tried to monopolize or abuse political
power are the least likely to lose it. Their legitimacy makes them competitive
with nonstate actors. Democratic societies have least to fear from the erosion
of state power because they depend on it least.

In contrast, as undemocratic regimes are forced by the global market to retreat from dominant roles in their national economy, their lack of political legitimacy becomes ever more exposed. This brings us to the world's most
crucial case of legitimacy deficit: China.

LEGITIMACY, STABILITY, AND SECURITY

As China grows, its state shrinks; indeed, the shrinkage of the state facilitates
the growth of the country. This is most obvious in the economic sphere,
what with the shedding of insolvent state-owned enterprises, the decentral-
ization of decision making, the growing role of foreign direct investment,

and the acceptance of World Trade Organization constraints on government subsidies and protections.

Politically, the Chinese state remains entrenched. But signs of its retreat are everywhere: its ideology survives in name only, democracy is bubbling up from the local level, religious practice is on the rise, alternative political models (e.g., Hong Kong and, over the horizon, Taiwan) are in play, and accurate information about the country and the rest of the world is increasingly available.

Ironically, China's rapid economic expansion and the improvement in the lives of most Chinese, owing to nonstate forces, have purchased time for a regime that would flunk the Ullman legitimacy test. However, the tolerance of the swelling middle class for the state's lack of accountability will decline, especially if economic growth slows and soaring expectations go unmet. There are indications of this already.

On the defensive and under pressure for change, Chinese leaders are obsessed with order. Former Red Guards are now gray guardians of the political status quo. (Jiang's antidote to Western liberalism is just the opposite of Mao's.) That the regime chooses to suppress dissent in order to maintain stability betrays its core weakness and its erroneous, preinformation-age belief that stability can be commanded and policed in perpetuity. China's leaders seem to think that the way to achieve China's overarching goals of modernization and security is to give the Chinese people economic freedom and deny them political freedom. They are drawing the wrong lesson from Gorbachev's mistakes.

The argument that freedom must be sacrificed to achieve security is often made, self-servingly, by regimes with little to gain and much to lose from granting freedoms.[16] As Ullman has pointed out, legitimate states can maintain their own security without infringing on the security of those they govern.[17] The requirement that a government act through due process of law does not significantly hamper it from bringing its authority to bear against those who use violence against it or flout its laws.

In contrast, examples abound—North Korea, Iraq, Serbia, Cuba, Syria, Congo, Afghanistan, perhaps Pakistan—of illegitimate regimes producing insecurity, externally and internally. They have a propensity to create enemies, real and imagined, domestic and foreign. If they have a greater need to use force against internal enemies, it is precisely because their illegitimacy breeds determined opposition. The potential for internal instability is more often a consequence of authoritarianism than a fair justification for it. It is in the nature of such states to wield violence as an instrument of policy with little compunction, unless faced with superior power. (More later on "criminal states.")

At the global level, the correlation between democracy and security is striking. The descendants of two vicious aggressors, Nazi Germany and Imperial

Japan, have threatened no one since they embraced democracy. The twentieth century's most dangerous regions, Europe and East Asia, have become more stable and peaceful in the course of becoming democratic. In contrast, the most dangerous region at century's end, the Middle East, has few democracies. And an undemocratic Russia would surely be a more unstable and dangerous Russia.

Sub-Saharan Africa, never tranquil, has become a region of widespread, continuous, grisly violence. While European colonialism still deserves some blame, half a century later, for disregarding or exploiting tribal distinctions, it is more the unevenness and frailty of democracy that accounts for the spreading chaos. The promise of the legitimate South African state, for all its problems, contrasts with the bleak and bloody prospects of Congo (nee Zaire), which has been ravaged by lawless government and, lately, predatory neighbors. Lately, the United States and Europe have become active advocates of democracy throughout Africa—if only this had come much sooner!

Evidence that democracy engenders stability bears out the Wilsonian tenet that the United States can improve its security by exporting its political values. At the same time, it runs against the grain of pragmatism in American foreign policy. For the sake of forestalling turmoil, U.S. administrations of both parties have supported assorted illegitimate regimes—Cuba's Batista, the Shah of Iran, Nicaragua's Somosa, the Philippines' Marcos, Somalia's Siad Barre, Zaire's Mobutu, and Indonesia's Suharto, to name some of the worst. America's interests, Foggy Bottom pros would say, sometimes must take precedence over its ideals. Consequently, in some cases, the United States has not pressed for reform until it was too late.

But for the Carter administration, which was widely accused of softheadedness in foreign policy, the United States has been tolerant of authoritarianism and human rights violations on the part of numerous states on which it depended for some U.S. national security function. Sometimes it was military base rights; other times it was to prevent a "front line" state from falling victim to subversion by a power that was hostile to the United States.

While it lasted, the East-West struggle provided a generic justification for sheltering and excusing illegitimate regimes. After all, how much could the oppression of far-away peoples matter when our own way of life hung in the balance? To be fair, American policy makers during the Cold War thought that people under pro-Western dictatorship would be worse off under Marxist dictatorship. (Evidence that this was actually so has not been produced.) Moreover, our understanding of foreign societies is rarely good enough to be confident that pressing hard for democracy will produce the desired outcome. Still, the American-led "free world" of the Cold War contained many states whose people were far from free.

The Soviet Union has disappeared, but Washington's habit of supporting undemocratic friends has not. We still see, especially throughout the Middle

East, that U.S. foreign policy will tolerate a lack of legitimacy when the strategic or material stakes are perceived to be great. There is no stomach in Washington for pressing the likes of the Saudi royal family, steward of the status quo—and all that oil—to accelerate liberalization.

It is as if reform is a luxury the world's greatest power cannot always afford to support. One would think that the combination of U.S. successes (Philippines, South Korea) and failures (pre-Castro Cuba, Iran under the Shah) would have convinced its policy makers that dictators and monarchs do not produce stability and that democracy is not too risky to try. Odd that the country that defines the democratic advantage would not champion it everywhere, most of all where it has strategic interests. Odder still that the same foreign policy establishment that insists that democracy would benefit China fears that it might harm U.S. client states.

Ullman has never known a despotic U.S. "friend" he did not detest, not only out of concern for human rights but also because he has seen illegitimate states as trouble down the road for the United States. States that repress are ultimately unstable because they engender opposition yet give it no scope for democratic protest.[18] And "societies which are ultimately unstable are clearly weak foundations upon which to raise security structures."[19] Ergo, supporting repression does not enhance U.S. security.

Sure enough, one by one, unsavory U.S. clients have been swept aside, often by the very revolutions and chaos the State Department had hoped to avert by standing by them. The results—Castro, the mullahs, anarchy in central Africa—have hardly been rewarding. In contrast, where the United States worked actively, if belatedly, for change toward legitimate government—in South Korea, the Philippines, Thailand, South Africa, El Salvador, Indonesia, and elsewhere—the results have been good for U.S. security and good for the local peoples.

Ullman has never had difficulty reconciling the calculated pursuit of U.S. national interests with upholding U.S. values, at home and abroad. Where others see a chasm between doing good (promoting values) and doing well (promoting interests) in foreign policy, he sees a sturdy bridge.

CHANGE AND NEW DANGERS

Debates over interests and values often revolve around the pros and cons of change. To a classical geopolitical thinker, the United States, being the world's leading power, should favor stability and try to maintain the status quo. Yet how can anyone dispute that the tumultuous changes of the last ten years have been good for the United States? Stability is not necessarily good, and when sustained by illegitimate states it is fool's stability. Genuine stability is achieved through adaptability, which is a hallmark of states that answer to their citizens.

The importance of legitimacy in coping with change is a recent Ullman insight.[20] As the world economy integrates, the United States and others face a set of emerging nonstate threats to the safety and quality of their citizens' lives: drug trafficking, cyber-war, international crime, willful ecological damage, terrorism (potentially with weapons of mass destruction), untreated disease, mass or sudden migration. Legitimacy can aid in combating such threats.

While the United States is well-equipped to defend its interests and friends against the armies of hostile states, its military superiority is of little value against most of these sub- and transnational challenges. Nor can it create FBI field offices everywhere. Therefore, the United States wants strong states that can control what is happening on their territory and crossing their borders. The kind of control needed is not that of a police state but that which results from genuine respect for the rule of law by citizens and government alike.

This might sound like a rear-guard action to defend the nation-state against the new transnational forces that would erode it—in a way, it is. Ullman's call for strong states means that U.S. foreign policy ought actively to promote legitimate regimes, the most effective of which are liberal democracies. He recommends specifically gearing U.S. foreign assistance to the strengthening of legitimate states, which can in turn improve defenses against the new threats to our society.

Dictators, juntas, and other illegitimate regimes are often so preoccupied with internal power and security that they neglect external problems. (Their won-lost record in wars is quite pitiful!) They are better at creating trumped-up external threats as a diversion from their domestic messes than they are at confronting real ones. Military-dominated states can be particularly inept in the face of nonstate challenges. And a politically powerful military can be like a tumor within a state, displacing organs needed for health and performance.

Dangerous transnational actors, such as terrorists and drug traffickers, commonly seek safe haven or material support from illegitimate states. If they cannot always exploit the weaknesses, divisions, and cynicism that plague unlawful states, they can at least buy the political protection they need. Consequently, the sovereignty of illegitimate states can shield nonstate elements that harm the societies of legitimate states. Pressure will grow on the latter to do something about this, be it to encourage democracy or to infringe on the sovereignty of dictatorships.

CRIMINAL STATES

The ranks of illegitimate states are being thinned by the democratic-information revolution. But some of the worst survive by relying on concentrated state power, the denial and manipulation of information, self-isolation, and imposed stability. If they fail to eliminate internal opposition, they collapse—a hazard that removes any inhibition about using force domestically. They are the antitheses of Ullman's "strong states."

By substituting savagery for legitimacy—polar-opposite sources of state power—these regimes might be able to hang on for some time, indifferent to the eye-watering poverty of their people. The citizens of illegitimate states pay the price for their rulers' survival and misconduct. Moreover, because the tenure of despots is independent of their performance in office, government incompetence—except in the crafts of repression—is chronic. North Korea, Cuba, Serbia, Iraq, Sudan, and Belarus are among the world's sickest economies, owing to a combination of brutalized citizens, maladroit policies, anemic markets, and international embargoes imposed in response to their misdeeds.

The North Korean regime is a particularly frightening example of where this can lead. Its economy trashed by its own lawlessness, the regime has been backed into utter dependence on raw military power to survive. But even that source of power is running down, as the state's military industries buckle and the lack of information technology leaves its conventional forces inferior to those of its enemies. At the same time, the option of making peace with its enemies is fraught with danger for North Korea. So it grasps for types of military power that do not require a healthy national economic base: weapons of mass destruction. The North Korean case suggests that as illegitimate regimes become desperate, they can become extremely dangerous.

HUMANITARIAN INTERVENTION

Even if felonious states do not threaten either international peace or the interests of powerful states, there are limits to international patience with them. In this regard, the reaction to Serbia's assault on the Albanian population of Kosovo province could be a watershed.[21] Over Chinese and Russian objections, the Atlantic democracies took international law into their own hands by waging what they considered a just war against Serbia.[22] Though lacking a mandate from the United Nations, which had itself proved incapable of curbing the crimes of the Serbian regime, NATO decided that an illegitimate state that commits genocide behind its borders should not enjoy the prerogatives and protection commonly associated with sovereignty, including the sanctity of those borders.

Adding insult to injury—more accurately, indictment to intervention—an international tribunal has charged the Yugoslav president with war crimes. And a United Nations administrator, backed by NATO forces, now controls Kosovo, despite its being a long-recognized province of Serbia. Thus, in all but the most formal sense, Kosovo has been detached from Yugoslavia and made a ward of the Atlantic democracies. The Kosovars are protected not *by* their sovereign but *from* it. This barrage of blows to the sovereignty of the Belgrade state is entirely a consequence of its illegitimacy, lawlessness, and resulting weakness.

Critics of the Kosovo war argue that NATO attacked a sovereign state without legal grounds or authority. Chapter VII of the U.N. Charter provides for the possibility of armed intervention when, in the Security Council's view, domestic conflict threatens international peace.[23] Also, Articles 55 and 56 suggest an obligation on members "to take joint and separate action to promote universal respect for . . . human rights." But the charter does not sanction armed intervention for the latter purpose when international peace is not threatened.[24]

Supporters of NATO's action respond that sovereignty is not absolute and must not be allowed to shield barbarism. In this instance, the latter view prevailed, politically and militarily. The implication is that sovereignty, in the new era, may be only as strong as the legitimacy of the state that claims it. Although such an idea is on thin legal ice, international law (especially) "evolves from international notions of moral conscience that rise to the level of obligatory."[25] Supporters of humanitarian intervention can point out that just such an evolution is underway.

Because of their internal and external misconduct, the current North Korean and Iraqi states have also lost degrees of sovereignty. Imposed no-fly zones, security enclaves, intrusive inspection regimes, international control over the internal distribution of aid, and unabashed campaigns to effect regime change, not to mention the occasional air strike, are among the measures being taken with little compunction by democratic states against egregiously illegitimate ones. If genuine sovereignty means that others respect it, the current Iraqi regime has little or none left, since the democratic powers want that regime gone.

Criminal states are not completely at the mercy of the powerful democracies. Despite military and economic disaster, Saddam Hussein survives, for now. But as illegitimate states lose the ability to protect themselves physically and politically, they become not merely isolated but vulnerable to interference, coercion, intervention, and eventual extinction. In the end, even the ability to ward off external threats can be compromised by a regime's own illegitimacy, which leaves its economy in ruins, its generals corrupt, its armies demoralized, and its people hungry. Illegitimate states cough up their last bit of sovereignty when they commit acts, within or beyond their borders, which legitimate states decide cannot and will not be tolerated.

Thus, although international law and institutions have not kept pace, the world's democratic powers—the strongest of strong states—increasingly have both the might and, in their view, the right to brush aside claims of sovereignty by states that attack humanity behind such claims. While crossing this threshold does not necessarily obligate the democracies to intervene wherever human beings are oppressed—in Rwanda and Congo, they did not; in Kosovo, Haiti, and East Timor (with Indonesian acquiescence), they did—it does suggest that they presume to have the license to do so. They will obtain the authority of the Charter and the Security Council if they can, but proceed without it if they decide they must.

Yet any license to intervene in one instance is weakened by the choice not to do so in another. The evolving moral authority to act against unlawful states that act lawlessly implies a *responsibility* to do so when feasible, for otherwise it would be tantamount to a prerogative, or even a privilege, of power. And because of the military superiority of the United States and its democratic allies, their interventions cannot easily be blocked or defeated—though they may be deterred by the fear of casualties. So this responsibility must be borne with care and consistency.

In very real ways, inconsistency in humanitarian intervention can be dangerous. The license invites abuse: Hitler's pretext for invading Czechoslovakia was to protect the Sudeten Germans. Moreover, the expectation of intervention can incite an uprising by an oppressed group, which is then butchered when the intervention does not ensue. Conversely, the failure to intervene in one case may embolden other oppressors and thus increase the need to intervene, or the consequences of not intervening, in the next case.

The Bosnian Moslems had their hopes raised, then dashed, in the early years of the Clinton administration, and they paid a heavy price. The Serbs, in turn, may have concluded from NATO's hesitation toward Bosnia that they could cleanse Kosovo of Albanians without risk of intervention, so they tried and brought on a war.

The lower threshold for intervention by the Western powers in the Balkans than in Africa, where it might be easier, fans suspicions that the high-minded democracies place less value on African lives than on European ones. Using force to save humans in one place but not in another betrays a lack commitment to save humans. If the rights and lives of humans transcend sovereignty as a matter of principle, they must do so everywhere.

For these reasons, there is a need for a consistent and responsible basis for multilateral intervention by democratic states against those that represent a threat to humanity. The starting point should be the precept that sovereignty depends on lawfulness, not only in a state's behavior but also in the basis for its existence. This does not warrant armed intervention against states solely because of their illegitimacy, but rather against illegitimate states that turn on their own people. At a minimum, the commission of recognizable "crimes against humanity" would seem easily to justify intervention—provided it is proportionate and efficacious—in order to rescue that humanity.

In the new era, sovereignty is being eroded in so many ways, profound and mundane. Why should it be left standing as a wall behind which lawless regimes commit unspeakable acts? Surely not because one or two members of the Security Council believe it should.

THE FUTURE OF THE STATE SYSTEM

The nation-state system, formalized in the Treaty of Westphalia of 1648, which ended the Thirty Years' War, is based on the principle that rulers are sovereign, and must be treated as such, if they control their territory. The monarchs of the time erected state sovereignty as a bulwark against the seventeenth-century version of transnational conflict: the religious wars that had swept across Europe. Sovereign states could be attacked only when they threatened other sovereign states. Their character and conduct within their territory were nobody's business but their own. Intervention was strictly taboo.

For the sake of European order, human beings and their nonstate associations were subordinated to the state. Internally, of course, they were already subordinate to their rulers; but Westphalia codified this among states. Because there were no democracies at the time, legitimacy (if it could be called that) was a derivative of sovereignty—a simple fact of territorial control. There was no need to be lawful in the eyes of ones subjects, or act lawfully toward them, if one was lawful in the eyes of neighboring kings.

Again, this 350-year-old proscription against intervention is weakening. As President Clinton said after defeating Serbia, if human beings are under assault and we can do something about it, we will (the "we" being the United States and its allies). Even the West Europeans, typically skittish when it comes to using force, staked out similar positions. This sentiment is even reflected in the evolving military rationale of the Atlantic Alliance, which is predicated on the possibility of projecting collective power to protect its members' shared interests *and values.*

This means that *how* states exercise territorial control matters. Yugoslavia forfeited sovereignty over Kosovo precisely because of the way it tried to exercise it; by seeking to rid its territory of ethnic Albanians, it invited intervention and so lost control of that same territory. At the very least, then, sovereignty cannot be sustained by exterminating or depopulating one's territory of potential opponents. That single exception to the Westphalian principle means that sovereignty is contingent on internal human conditions, and thus on legitimacy.

Following this reasoning to its extreme, sovereignty can be sustained only by the willing support of the governed and acceptance of the rule of law; otherwise, the power of the state may be unchecked, in which case extermination and depopulation are available options. To be accepted as sovereign by other sovereigns, a regime must be lawful and act lawfully not only toward them but also toward its people. This is equivalent to saying that only law-based democracies can be sovereign, because others can, if they wish, rely on coercion, repression, or worse to maintain control.

This might have seemed a radical idea until recently. But the number of democracies is growing steadily, and most other states are in transition toward democracy. Furthermore, as Ullman points out, effective territorial control in the face of transnational threats increasingly requires legitimate (i.e., strong) states. In the information-globalization age, dictators might be able to maintain control, but their brutality should not and will not qualify them for sovereignty. Therefore, via another route, we come to the same conclusion: Sovereignty requires legitimacy.

Such notions do not please all strategic thinkers. As Henry Kissinger wrote in reference to NATO's intervention in Kosovo: "Those who sneer at history obviously do not recall the legal doctrine of national sovereignty . . . emerged at the end of the devastating Thirty Years War, to inhibit a repetition of the depredations of the seventeenth century, during which 40 percent of the population of Central Europe perished in the name of competing versions of universal truth. Once the doctrine of universal intervention spreads and competing truths contest, we risk entering a world in which, in C. K. Chesterton's phrase, 'virtue runs amuck.'"[26]

Yes, of course, we should recall history, and not sneer at it. But this view does not take into account that today's interveners are democratic, which is just any "competing version of universal truth" but the *only* version that reconciles state sovereignty with human freedom. Such reconciliation is not so far out of reach to be futile to pursue.

Does this mean that law-based democracies should hereafter refuse even to extend diplomatic recognition to illegitimate (e.g., undemocratic) states? No, for that would so upset international relations and the world economy as to be impractical and imprudent under current conditions. However, it is an outcome toward which the trend is pointing. This is surely a long way off. It does not spell the end of nation-state sovereignty, as long as states earn it by their lawful internal and external behavior. But it spells the end of a system wherein sovereignty confers lawfulness rather than the other way around—done in not by supranational authority, religion, or ideology, but by the ideals and muscles of democratic states.

It is possible, then, that as legitimate states become more numerous and strong, illegitimate states will become an endangered species. The security of the planet, the well-being of its inhabitants, and the interests of the United States would benefit from such progress. To be clear, Ullman has not gone this far in his writings. But it is a reasonable extrapolation from his lesson that legitimacy is the touchstone of world politics.

With such profound changes underway, we need the most insightful and expansive minds at work. We urge Richard Ullman to keep pondering and writing, so that we can keep learning from him.

NOTES

1. Richard Ullman, "Ending the Cold War," *Foreign Policy*, Fall 1988, 130–151.
2. An allusion to "I'll do it my way," a line from the 1980s Frank Sinatra hit, *My Way*.
3. Richard Ullman, "Enlarging the Zone of Peace," *Foreign Policy*, Fall 1990.
4. Richard Ullman, *Strong States, Strong Hopes* (Washington, D.C.:Aspen Institute, 1997).
5. *Strong States*, p. 9.
6. Although Milosevic has won a number of elections, this made him neither democratic nor legitimate. His control over broadcast media and ruthless manipulation of domestic politics rendered Serbian and Yugoslav elections a sham.
7. Lipscomb and Bergh, eds., *The Writings of Thomas Jefferson* (Washington, D.C.: The Thomas Jefferson Memorial Association, 1903–1904), Volume 6, 392.
8. Samantha Ravich, *Marketization and Prosperity: Pathways to East Asian Democracy* (Santa Monica, Calif.: RAND, 1996).
9. Ibid.
10. Alternatively, we could define genuine democracy to exclude states in which the disregard for inconvenient laws improves popularity and assures reelection. This would place Hitler and co. where they belong: outside democracy's walls.
11. Richard Ullman, "Human Rights and American Foreign Policy," *The Center Magazine*, Vol. XVII, No. 1 (March–April 1984): 21–29.
12. Richard Ullman, "Trilateralism: 'Partnership' for What?" *Foreign Affairs*, October 1976, 1–19.
13. See Joseph S. Nye, *Born to Lead: The Changing Nature of American Power* (New York: Basic Books, 1990).
14. David Gompert, *Right Makes Might* (Washington, D.C.: National Defense University Press, 1998).
15. *Strong States*, p. 4.
16. The parallel argument that democracy must be subordinated or postponed to allow economic development has also been exposed as bogus and largely self-serving.
17. Ullman, "Ending the Cold War," op. cit.
18. Ibid.
19. "Human Rights and American Foreign Policy," op. cit., p. 7.
20. *See Strong States*.
21. For our purposes, Serbia, Yugoslavia, and the "Former Republic of Yugoslavia" will be used interchangeably, given Serbia's dominant position and the strong desire of Yugoslavia's other remaining republic, Montenegro, to break loose.
22. Although the Security Council did not authorize military intervention, it did reject a Russian attempt to condemn it, by such a wide margin that a U.S., U.K., or French veto was not needed.

23. This was the legal justification given by NATO for its intervention, though its public, political justification was to stop ethnic cleansing. In any case, Chapter VII does not authorize intervention without Security Council approval, which was not forthcoming.

24. Charles B. Shotwell and Kimberly Thachuk, "Humanitarian Intervention: The Case for Legitimacy," National Defense University *Strategic Forum*, number 166, July 1999.

25. Ibid., p.4.

26. Henry Kissinger, "The End of NATO As We Know It?" *Washington Post*, LA Times Syndicate, August 19, 1999.

3

Ethics and International Relations: A Speculative Essay[1]

Michael W. Doyle

What should we make of statements such as the one by Vaclav Havel that the war in Kosovo was a (perhaps, he says, *the* first) humanitarian war, a war motivated by ethical concern? How do we square the judgment of that widely respected, contemporary statesman with the words of William Wordsworth, that great earlier poet of democratic revolution, with his ever-so-devastating comment on his times: "Earth is sick; And Heaven is weary, with the hollow words; Which states and kingdoms utter when they talk: Of truth and justice."[2]

To many in our field of international politics—asking just what is the role of ethics in foreign policy is like asking what did Chopin's sonatas contribute to the success of the New York Yankees or Manchester United. But to wiser heads different questions and different answers arise. Richard Ullman is one who has identified important markers for the role of ethical judgment in international relations. In "Human Rights vs. Economic Power: The US vs Idi Amin," he argued that ethically outrageous treatment by a state of its own citizens could breach national rights to nonintervention and give rise to justified international interference. Governments, especially governments with the commitment to human rights that should animate the U.S. government, should be "prepared to say that there are boundaries of decency beyond which other governments must not pass in their treatment of their own citizens."[3] In this case, ethical concerns warranted a foreign boycott of Ugandan coffee, on whose sales the regime was especially dependent, particularly when one could show that the impact of the embargo would be felt mostly by the target regime, and not by the already victimized ordinary Ugandans. Similar ethical concerns for the well-being and autonomy of people cut the

other, noninterventionist, way when regimes with a claim to furthering the
well-being of their population were being interfered with for reasons that
we could judge to be remote from an effort to promote the interests of the
affected population. The not so covert campaign against the Sandinistsas
in Nicaragua fit this latter instance as Richard Ullman showed in "At War
with Nicaragua."[4] Moreover, by fostering emergency conditions in
Nicaragua, the armed intervention probably strengthened and hardened
the Sandinista regime, harming the one potentially ethical goal that should
have been and could have been a legitimate aim of another more re-
spectful U.S. policy—a more democratic and less dominated Nicaraguan
society. So whether it was the Carter administration's failure to interfere or
the Reagan administration's intervention, ethical and pragmatic concerns
should have been at the core of U.S. policy (and were not)—and could
have readily worked together.

The persuasive power of Richard Ullman's two essays rests on the under appreciated conjunction of ethical concern and pragmatic, long-run,
national self-interest.[5] But the two do not always, of course, coincide and
Richard Ullman's extensive discussion of international intervention in the
Russian civil war explores many of the confusing trade-offs that often arise
in world politics among decent goals and absent means (as well as the
common but unfortunate coincidences of exploitative ends and readily
available means). In this vein, Richard Ullman has commented on the desperate search by British statesmen for "moderates"—"saner elements of
the left"—with which to ally in their effort to manage the Russian Revolution and consequent civil war. Dick then warned: "Civil wars are polariz-
ing experiences; leaders who can supply the discipline and efficiency necessary to win are not likely to be 'moderate' (although they may be by
most people's lights 'sane') whether they come from the Right or the
Left."[6]

Arnold Wolfers is another scholar who has highlighted the nature of the
trade-offs that Richard Ullman noted in Russia's civil war and the rarity of co-
incident ethics and interests. His famous essay, "Statesmanship and Moral
Choice" begins: "Nowhere does the contradiction between professed ethical
principles and actual behavior appear so patent and universal as in the conduct of foreign relations." But he then ends in the spirit invoked by Richard
Ullman: those "who have non-perfectionist and non-nationalistic moral con-
victions dare not evade moral judgment whether of their own political acts
or of the acts of others."[7] The two statements are in an obvious tension that
many argue is the core of international ethics: In international relations (IR)
ethics are more than difficult; in IR moral judgment should not and cannot
be evaded. In this chapter I discuss why ethical judgments should not and
cannot be evaded, and end with why they are so difficult and troubling in international politics. I explore three issues:

- Why international ethics should not and need not be evaded through three classic but dangerous simplifications, each of which serves as an excuse for dismissing ethical judgment.
- The roles that considerations of ends, means, and consequences can play in ethical judgments of international politics.
- Why ethical principles so often leave us so far from ethical outcomes in international politics.

THE NEED FOR ETHICS IN INTERNATIONAL POLITICS

First, why is it that international ethics should not and need not be evaded through three classic simplifications—simplifications that should be rejected as partial truths, so partial as to be dangerous?

- Ethics cannot, should not, be limited to private life, supposedly because public political life is necessarily a separate world of dirty hands. This is the Machiavellian Problem.
- Ethics should not be domesticated, seen as fit only for domestic politics and judged to be inherently absent from, and irrelevant to, international politics, which is the Hobbesian Problem.
- Ethics cannot be dismissed as being inherently a set of hypocritical or merely self-serving political slogans. We could call this Wordsworth's Problem.

The first and most prevalent reason why we are told that ethical judgment can be ignored is that it is inapplicable to political decisions. As Dean Acheson, former U.S. secretary of state, once said, "Moral Talk was fine preaching for the Final Day of Judgment, but it was not a view I would entertain as a public servant." This is often called the ethics of public responsibilities. Engaging in politics means, requires, "learning to be cruel to be kind" (as Shakespeare's Hamlet intoned).[8] In political theory, this is the Machiavellian Problem. "A wise prince," Machiavelli said, "knows how to do wrong when it is necessary." And it is often, very often, necessary to act, he adds "contrary to truth, contrary to charity, contrary to humanity, contrary to religion—if the Prince wishes to sustain his government."[9]

Ethics, it is said, are for stay-at-homes, those happy men and women who till their own gardens, secure in the knowledge that they are able to do so safely. But princes, it is added, have no choice but to be like the "ferocious beasts," for the moral life available to private men and women is neither safe nor sufficient for them. "Princes must be like a very savage lion and a very tricky fox." But why "must"? First, for themselves: for without beastlike force and fraud, they will be overthrown. And second and more tragically, for us:

for without the political order of government we would all have to be beasts, too, or perish under the attacks of thieves and murderers. Our making ethical judgments of specific political acts is therefore inappropriate and an act of bad faith, so many simple Realists have said.

But this is too simple. Machiavelli knew it was, and so should we. Princes can and should be making moral choices. Not every prince is the leader of a threatened coup, everywhere and with everyone at war. Old, traditional princes would do themselves harm if they acted like new princes, the successful coup masters. Rules and traditions are the bulwarks of traditional princes.

As important, we private men and women in our gardens can hardly claim the virtue the political amoralists grant us. Are we, in fact, free from moral conflict? Are we free from contrariness worth respect to truth, charity, humanity, and religion? Machiavelli, author of the *Mandragola*, knew we were not. In that racy, sexual comedy, the wily Callimacco, deeply in love, tricks old Nicias into allowing him to sleep with his beautiful young wife Lucrezia. With Lucrezia's connivance, Callimacco invents a curse that the first man to sleep with her will suffer a painful death. Gullible Nicias allows Callimacco to "suffer" for him. Private men and women—Callimaccos and Lucrezias—are as crafty and ruthless as any foxlike public prince.

Machiavelli thus says private life, too, is not without moral corruption and authentic moral conflict. So should we. Moreover, we do. We do not grant our politicians a moral hunting license. Indeed, we may hypocritically hold them to standards we rarely meet. In short, we share a moral universe with politicians. If we endorse their ability to punish or even kill in the name of the state, it is because we allow ourselves to use force in self-defense. They can be said to do it for us, because we are prepared to do it for ourselves. We hope they will do it more impartially—for public ends—and are often disappointed. But both public and private individuals can make moral choices and often face dreadful trade-offs. The world often requires some very hard trade-offs where rules of moral conduct confront the moral value of public survival, and these are choices both we and our leaders understand.

If all politicians are not inherently different, inherently absent from moral judgment, maybe say the second set of critics it is the international politicians who fall outside ethical standards. The minister of health and the town mayor are in the ethical world; Bismark and Kissinger, the foreign minister and the secretary of defense, are out.

Hobbesians argue that nation-states exist in a condition of international anarchy with no superior world state to provide law and order. There follows a general struggle for power—all against all—fueled by competing desires for scarce goods, by fear of what others might do, and by hunger for glory. Internationally, nations have no choice but to compete, because the competition is for survival. Domestically, ethics can be established once a state establishes law and order. Then promises will be enforced, social norms will be decreed, and those norms will be taught to the young. Lacking an international government of law and order, all is uncertain. Anything goes in the struggle for survival. This is the condition of complete struggle that Sherman had in mind when he told the citizens of Atlanta, after he burned their city, "War is cruelty and you cannot refine it."[10]

But again moral life is not so simple. International politics is not an absolute struggle of all against all. Contemporary relations between the United Kingdom and France, Germany and Belgium, and the United States and Canada bear no similarity to that Hobbesian model. Relations are safe from war and shaped by international law.[11] Even the genuine representation of citizens becomes mixed. Both the U.S. Midwest and Canada cause acid rain, but Ottawa's greater concern for the consequences may better represent a downwind New Englander than does Washington. Even in war, most states have come to accept the principle that the struggle is not "against all." Rules of war forbid struggle against noncombatants, against children, the ill in hospitals. And some modern Hobbesians fail to ask what is the meaning of survival—national or state survival. States are artificial beings not natural ones. They exist, as Wolfers has noted, for the purposes of their inhabitants, not their inhabitants for states.[12] Some citizens shuck off their sovereign Leviathans as the British did in 1688, the American colonists did in 1776, and the former Soviets did in 1991. Moreover, the moral meaning of survival is frequently contested—up for domestic political competition—as it was in France in the 1940s. Was France to survive physically and conservatively as it did under Marshall Petain's Vichy regime or be risked, grandly, as it would be under General de Gaulle's Free French Resistance?[13]

States represent, or can represent, not merely our fears (as Hobbes argues) but also our hopes and our ethical commitments. Goals and values therefore define what normal survival means, what is worth protecting in both domestic and international politics. U.S. civilian and military officials, for example, swear to preserve the Constitution, a set of principles. Our ends define what is worth sacrificing for and shape even the international behavior of states.

The third objection to international ethics accepts the view that politicians can be as ethical as we are (or no worse) whether they are engaging in foreign or domestic affairs. But, as the skeptics like Wordsworth have said, politicians, regularly, just about always choose not to be. Their international ethics is all ordinary cynical hype and nothing more. They can be ethical. They choose to be hypocritical, paying the small tribute vice pays to virtue. Preaching ethics to them is thus like preaching chastity in a bordello.

Speaking as a former member of the U.S. Air Force and noting that some of my best friends were in the Navy, let me tell you of a truly pathetic instance of convenient political morality. In 1949, the Navy decried the A-bomb, then the sole property of the Air Force, as immoral. By 1951, two years later, as the Navy started to assemble its own atomic arsenal and plans for a nuclear submarine force, atomic bombs suddenly became necessary to the survival of the free world. Of course, neither their criticism nor defense was thought convincing.

Again we should hesitate to generalize the hypocrisy. Ethical arguments need not be altruistic to be convincing and some seem even to masquerade as self-serving advantage. At the Teheran Conference in 1943, Stalin suggested to Churchill that after the defeat of Hitler, all 50,000 of the German Officer Corps should be summarily shot by the Allies. Churchill replied, "The British Parliament and public will never tolerate mass executions. They would turn violently against those responsible after the first butchery had taken place."[14] Churchill's fear of reprisals from the British public does not wash. Indeed, shouldn't we suspect hypocrisy in reverse? Appalled by the indiscriminate slaughter Stalin proposed, Churchill invents the self-serving logic of electoral advantage and political survival to appeal to the ruthless Stalin and, perhaps, soothe his own discomfort with "moral talk."

ENDS, MEANS, AND CONSEQUENCES

International ethics thus is not impossible because politicians unlike us must be beasts, nor because international politics is a universal jungle, nor because nothing but hypocrisy and partisan advantage can influence a politician. What then is international ethics? What can and should it be?

Like all ethics it is the inescapable judgment that precedes action. Not all judgment, however, is or needs be ethical. Prudential judgment prescribes productive strategies in the pursuit of given ends for a given person. Aesthetic judgment asks what is best, good, or beautiful. Ethical judgment combines prescription (like prudence), overridingness (what is best like aesthetics), and impartiality—what should be done not just by or for me, but by or for anyone in the same position. You should, as I should, fulfill an ethical duty because it is designed to apply to us all, like the "golden rule" of doing unto others as you would have them do to you.

Three concerns shape ethical judgment. In a fine book on *Nuclear Ethics*,[15] Joseph Nye calls them motives, means, and consequences. Let us call them ends, means, and consequences.[16]

An ethical end is necessary. Only ends justify, if any thing can, the means we employ. In simple terms, it is ends that make some wars just defensive wars when, that is, they seek to protect the borders, the territorial integrity, and political independence, that allow people to determine their own lives freely. Related ethical arguments can justify some humanitarian interventions across borders to rescue people from genocide and other grievous and systematic violations of their basic rights. People can't shape their lives collectively if they are being repressed and slaughtered.

Good ends, however, are not sufficient to justify our acts. The theologian Paul Ramsey has shown why not in a striking parable. If we really, truly, sincerely, deeply wanted to end, once and for all, the deaths and injury to tens of thousands each year in auto accidents—a worthy end surely—there is a simple and sure-fire means. All we have to do is tie, in as comfortable way as possible, babies to the front and rear of our automobiles. Can anyone doubt that, slowed to a fully moral crawl, our cars would successfully avoid thousands of traffic accidents?[17]

The problem here is in the means: the anguish to innocent infants, and perhaps even more the anguish to parents, none of whom is individually responsible for the collective tragedy of auto fatalities. Some ethicists have condemned nuclear deterrence for just these reasons: Deterrence terrorizes innocent civilians.

Third, even with good ends and acceptable means, we need to consider and anticipate consequences. Our sense of ethical ends (e.g., national self-defense, national self-determination) and ethical means (e.g., in war, respecting noncombatant immunity because noncombatants pose no direct threat) are powerful and inherited and learned intuitions. They are taught by parents, learned at our mothers' knee (or, as Acheson once said, some other low joint). They are part of now-traditional, evolved social conventions.

We need to govern these intuitions or rules by a consideration of consequences. It is wrong to lie in ordinary morality, but only a fool would tell a known murderer the location of his prospective victim. Similarly even if Kissinger is correct that the United States fought in Vietnam in order to prevent South Vietnam from falling prey to a totalitarian communism from the North,[18] and if the United States had fought the war justly, minimizing where possible civilian noncombatant casualties, the war could and would have been morally flawed if the United States failed to consider the suffering that would result from trying to win against a guerrilla movement supported by a large fraction of the population in a culture that the United States did not understand for a local government that had little support from too few of its own people.[19] A similar moral wasteland was emerging in Serbia in the spring of 1999 when NATO looked at the prospect of destroying by October or November of that year tens of thousands of noncombatant Serbs, through the disease and medical deprivation that in a modern society accompanies the destruction of electricity, transportation, and trade—all traditionally legitimate targets for bombing. The ends and means were justifiable: rescuing and returning thousands and thousands of noncombatant Albanian Kosovars "ethnically cleansed" from their homes and avoiding in the process as much as was feasible the bombing of noncombatant Serbs. It was the indirect consequences on the ability of the Serb population to provide essential services needed for health that were becoming morally unacceptable.[20] Goals and means become disproportionate when warriors find themselves destroying villages in order to save them or killing more noncombatants in order to save fewer noncombatants.

Unavoidably violent means need to be proportionate to legitimate ends. And to do this, we need to consider all the available alternatives and weigh the consequences of each.

THE PERSISTENT GAP BETWEEN
ETHICAL PRINCIPLES OUTCOMES

Last, if ethics is not impossible in international relations and if ordinary ethical judgment is identifiable and applicable, why, as Wolfers said, do we find such a gap between ethical principles and actual behavior in foreign relations?

The simplest and predominant reason is that the behavior may or may not in particular instances be motivated by ethical principles. More troubling is that even when it is (and we often have little reason to assume not) it does not have the same civilizing effects as ethical behavior in domestic politics. It is much more constrained because international politics is conflictual, confused, and uncontrolled.

There are at least four reasons for this unfortunate outcome:[21]

- Anarchy—no enforcement
- Moral diversity—conflicting values
- Uncertainty—as to adversary, intentions
- Uncertainty and lack of control over our responses

International anarchy does not make ethical behavior impossible. As noted, statesmen are moral and immoral beings like the rest of us, but it does make ethical behavior difficult and the international good problematic. The lack of a world government capable of enforcement means unethical behavior lacks adequate punishment, and evil is insufficiently deterred. The Vietnam War was widely criticized in the 1960s. And Idi Amin met with widespread moral condemnation in Africa in the 1970s for his human rights violations. But as long as Washington was a superpower and Amin controlled the Ugandan army, arresting, trying, and correcting wrongs meant war. Intervention against the United States was suicidal. Intervention against Uganda was unacceptable as long as invading Uganda was unacceptable to Ugandans and to Uganda's African neighbors. Until 1979, that is, when Amin finally provoked Tanzania—inciting in the process international enforcement by an African neighbor. Given international anarchy, furthermore, even ethically motivated states need to take measures of self-help to defend themselves. These measures restrict the resources that might be otherwise spent in aiding the poor economically, or helping to enforce just behavior among states.

Second, complicating international anarchy is moral diversity. There is not a practical international consensus on right and wrong. There are some nearly universally recognized values, including human dignity, various human rights specified in the Universal Declaration of Human Rights, and, in practice, avoiding nuclear war. But they are thin. States have diverse ideologies and values and these lead to conflicts.[22] A sincere communist has much to disagree with when he meets a sincere liberal. Marxists think they can identify progressive forces scientifically; liberals should be, but are often not, more skeptical. Fundamentalist Islam is said to be in a "clash of civilizations" with the Christian West.[23] Even if exaggerated in its impact, differences between Islam and the West over women's rights and freedom of the press clearly occasion strife.

Even with a wider consensus on principles, ethical conflicts over application can be extreme, when social and environmental circumstances differ and when power and authority become involved. When a group of desperately poor immigrant farmers seeks to settle in the seemingly less than fully used lands of a society of nomadic hunters, both do and, perhaps, justly can claim rights: the farmers to settle and hunters to resist the destruction of their hunting and way of life. As Locke once said, in these circumstances one "appeals to heaven" and thus wars ensue. In less extreme circumstances, and even when states share a broad consensus on basic human rights and the efficacy of market economies, the threat of foreign imposition—Washington dominance—leads to strife over national honor and independence.

Third, international politics, even more than domestic politics, is full of uncertainty. In one gruesome example, the casualties at Hiroshima and Nagasaki were five times more than expected partly because U.S. planners expected that the cities would take the protective measures other Japanese cities had taken when they were first bombed. But the lone atomic bombers failed to trigger the protections.[24] The United States undoubtedly still would have bombed in any case, but the arguments made at the time in favor of a warning explosion were probably weakened by the false lower estimates of Japanese casualties.

Sometimes we do not know whether to support or oppose or ignore not merely because other principles may be disputed, but also because the facts are unclear. Liberals can wonder whether Cuba or China or Eritrea are socialist democracies (as some of their apologists claim) suffering trying times and tolerating restrictions on freedom such as those that characterized U.S. politics between 1776 and 1781 and 1861–1865. Or, are they dictatorships of a single ideology consolidating autocratic rule? Or something else altogether?

It is hard enough to understand what is happening in Boston, New York, London, or Chicago; do we know what to approve or condemn in Eritrea? Was the Vietnam War a civil war in which foreigners had no legitimate role or Northern Vietnam's aggression on South Vietnam? Judgments such as these can make enormous ethical difference.

And fourth, we do not control our responses very well. When states wind up trying to punish the behavior of other states that elements of their own bureaucracies have provoked, ethical behavior loses its effectiveness, even its meaning. If the U.S. Congress supported aid to the Contras in Nicaragua because and only because the Contras could help deter the Nicaraguans from external attacks on Honduras (where the Contras were based), and if it did not know that a CIA operation funded the Contra's and directed the Contras in cross-border raids against Nicaragua, then the first action (supporting Honduras), justifiable as it may be on its own terms, is undermined ethically by the covert actions that accompanied and preceded it; for the Nicaraguans were engaged in just reprisals when they crossed the Honduran frontier.

In short, as citizens outside the university and scholars within it, there is no need to refrain from ethical judgment of those who claim as public officials to act for us. Ethics is not impossible. But not all ethical arguments are equally convincing—we need to hold our public officials as well as ourselves to careful considerations of ends, means, and consequences.

When we do so, we cannot be either optimistic or crusading. Ethical judgment and behavior are difficult. Statesmen too often pursue narrow self-advantage. Even when ethical concerns motivate political leaders, we should not expect international good automatically to follow because many international conflicts are fought over ethical differences. And we can't expect international good to follow because the circumstances of international anarchy, confusion, and lack of control often leave us desperate, driving in the dark, without lights, and with a loose steering wheel. All of which are grounds for cautious modesty in the practice of international ethics, but not for abandoning ethical judgment in international relations.

NOTES

1. An earlier version of this chapter was delivered as the Benjamin Meaker Professorial Lecture at the University of Bristol, United Kingdom, on June 6, 1999. I am grateful to the organizers and audience and to Richard Ullman, Amy Gardner, Richard Little, and Mark Wickham-Jones for comments and suggestions.

2. William Wordsworth, *The Excursion*, Book V *Collected Works* (London: Edward Moxon, 1814), lines 378–381.

3. Richard Ullman, "Human Rights and Economic Power," *Foreign Affairs*, 1978, 540.

4. Richard Ullman, "At War with Nicaragua," *Foreign Affairs*, Fall 1983, 39–58.

5. Richard Ullman discusses potential conjunctions of ethics and interest in "Both National Security and Human Rights Can Be Served Simultaneously," *Center Magazine* (March/April, 1984): 21–29.

6. Richard Ullman, *Britain and the Russian Civil War* (Princeton: Princeton University Press, 1968), 352.

7. Arnold Wolfers, "Statesmanship and Moral Choice," *Discord and Collaboration* (Baltimore: Johns Hopkins University Press, 1962), 47, 63.

8. This is also Max Weber's argument from "Politics as a Vocation." For this issue see Michael Walzer, "Political Action: The Problem of Dirty Hands," *P&PA* 1 (Winter 1972): 160–180.

9. Machiavelli, *The Prince*, tr. Harvey Mansfield Jr. (Chicago: University of Chicago, 1985), 14.

10. William T. Sherman, *Memoirs* (New York: D. Appleton and Co., 1875), 119–120; and see Michael Walzer, *Just and Unjust Wars* (New York: Basic, 1977), 32–33 for discussion.

11. Anne-Marie Slaughter, "Law among Liberal States: Liberal Internationalism and the Act of State Doctrine," *Columbia Law Review* 92, No. 8 (December): 1907–1996; and Richard Ullman, *Securing Europe* (Princeton, N.J.: Princeton University Press, 1991).

12. Arnold Wolfers, "Statesmanship and Moral Choice," op. cit.

13. Marc Bloch, *Strange Defeat* (Oxford: Oxford University Press, 1949).

14. As quoted by Hans Morgenthau, "Human Rights and Foreign Policy," in W. Thompson, ed., *Moral Dimensions of International Politics*.

15. Joseph Nye, *Nuclear Ethics* (New York: Free Press, 1986). Other valuable introductions to the topic include *Ethics and International Affairs* by J. E. Hare and Carey Joynt (New York: St. Martins, 1982).

16. Motives are not quite the same as ends. My dentist may be motivated only by money when he drills my teeth, but what distinguishes him from the torturer also motivated by a generous salary is the end of the act he is performing—fixing cavities rather than coercing confessions.

17. The example is Paul Ramsey's from *The Just War* (New York: Scribner's, 1968).

18. Henry Kissinger, *The White House Years* (Boston: Little Brown, 1979), 228.

19. This is part of Michael Walzer's criticism of U.S. intervention in Vietnam, from *Just and Unjust Wars* (New York: Basic Books, 1977), 188–196.

20. The Clinton administration was aware of this issue and the danger's replicating the moral morass that had emerged in Iraq after years of a debilitating sanctions regime. Special measures were taken to ensure that the destruction inflicted on power plants and electrical grids would be repairable before the onset of winter (including the use of chaff to short circuit the grids, rather than bombs to destroy them). (Private communication with U.S. NSC officials.) But recent United Nations High Commissioner for Refugees (UNHCR) reports from Belgrade suggested that NATO overestimated the sustainability of Belgrade's civilian infrastructure. Severe shortages of fuel complicated by the blocking of the Danube and the destruction of the Danube bridges and slow repairs to the water system hampered the provision of electricity.

21. I draw these distinctions from Locke and his discussion of the troubled "state of nature," for discussion see Michael Doyle, *Ways of War and Peace* (New York:

Norton, 1997), chapter 6. For a thoughtful analysis raising similar points see Stanley Hoffmann, "International Law and the Control of Force," in the *Relevance of International Law*, ed. Karl Deutsch and Stanley Hoffmann (Cambridge, Mass.: Schenkman, 1971) and his recent essay, "The Politics and Ethics of Military Intervention," in *World Disorders* (Lanham, Md.: Rowman & Littlefield, 1998), 152–176.

22. Michael Walzer discusses the implications of thin and thick moral conventions in *Thick and Thin: Moral Disagreements at Home and Abroad* (Notre Dame, Ind.: University of Notre Dame Press, 1996).

23. Samuel Huntington, *Clash of Civilizations and the Remaking of World Order* (New York: Touchstone, 1996).

24. Hare and Joynt, *Ethics and International Affairs*, p. 90.

4

The Realist Illusion
and a Patriarchal Reality

Robert Hunt Sprinkle

At the Conservative Party Conference at Blackpool, England, in October 1999, Baroness Margaret Thatcher, once a barrister and later illustrious as prime minister of Great Britain and commander-in-chief of British forces in the Falklands War, condemned the house-arrest and then-impending extradition of another former commander-in-chief, Augusto Pinochet. He had come to London for back surgery and been detained postoperatively for crimes against humanity, their multiplicity pared down to torture. She made her case standing before a huge projection of a grandfatherly Pinochet warmly cuddling beaming children.[1] Whatever he may have done, the implication seemed to be, he had done as a patriarch. He had been acting within and for his family, which, plausibly enough, was Chile. Awkwardly for Lady Thatcher's purpose, the slim slices of humanity against which some of Pinochet's deeds constituted arguably actionable crimes had included members of families less plausibly his own.

Pinochet was trying to evade extradition not to Chile, where he still expected to be secure, but to Spain and perhaps then to other states, each offended either by the murder of its nationals in Chile or the murder of Chilean nationals on its territory. In the end, after sixteen months, Pinochet got home not through a claim of innocence or extenuation or immunity, nor through a hole in national or international law. Rather, he got home through a claim of mental incapacity, a claim Britain's home secretary seemed determined to accept. Pinochet's spry walk and bright behavior at welcoming ceremonies in Santiago suggested that the true incapacity in this affair was not mental and not his.[2]

Lady Thatcher's visually patriarchist defense recapitulated in forensic cliché one side of a long and harsh debate distinguished by the brilliance of its major protagonists, the inadequacies of their proofs, and the mundane ubiquity of the behavior discussed. Indeed, as to this last point, most beneficiaries of patriarchal privilege have not been heads of state engaged in civil rivalry or foreign war; they have been heads of household. The penalty for abusing one's own slave, spouse, or child, even fatally, has immemorially been lighter than for likewise maltreating a freeborn neighbor or stranger. Even in advanced societies, innumerable victims, their rights to asylum waived fatalistically or revoked procedurally, have died following "repatriation" to brutal homes.

Great crimelike acts of state, of course, seem altogether distinct, for reasons jurisdictional, substantive, and stylistic, surely, but also because they are, demonstrably, *great*. They could not be accomplished without the durable allegiance of an audacious cohort and the forbearance of most everyone else. Their very accomplishment, consequently, is evidence of moral authority, and, however malevolently used, moral authority makes a difference. Realistically, and to realists, it can make prerogative.

The spirit conjured at Blackpool is easy to sense and hard to dispel. It routinely leads us to presume that power within a family—or within a community, corporation, or nation—signifies moral authority, that no family's business is the business of others, and that most any measure taken to smooth a family's functioning or to defend one family from another, perhaps simply to advance one beyond another, is taken justly. A contrary spirit, more welcome in temperate airs but quick to vanish when temperate turns torrid, objects that no one in any family deserves to be abused, that the suppression of abuse is the business of any and all, and that the moral licenses issued for governance and competition are limited. The first spirit calls anarchy to order. The second calls patriarchy to account. The tension between them is ageless, and their conflict has long complicated politics.

The apprehension, indictment, prosecution, and punishment of major political criminals has rarely been straightforward, even when facilitated by collapse of the conspiracies the criminals once led or served. Intervention to stop, suppress, or prevent major political crimes, ranging from cross-border aggression to within-border persecution, has rarely been easy to organize, notwithstanding evident capacity to act successfully at acceptable cost. Efforts to speed political development through the installation of liberal civil procedures ignoring or demeaning indigenous modes of legitimation have so often ended badly as to make "nation building," as a progressive policy, notorious. Political and economic relations with internally abusive states have regularly become confused, sometimes through the diplomatically ordinary conflation of government with governed, sometimes through the personalization of state-to-state contact.

Not only have such frustrations occurred in temporary circumstances promising logically to obviate them, but they also still occur frequently today despite an emboldening of liberal expectations worldwide. Explanations have typically centered on weaknesses in international legal regimes, disincentives to collective action, and perversities in political culture. Other explanations might prove usefully complementary. This chapter considers two, both evoked by arguments in seventeenth-century political philosophy. The first, a once-momentous topic long shunned as a scholarly embarrassment, is *patriarchal privilege*. The second is, as I have called it, *the realist illusion*,[3] which depends psychologically, just as it does rhetorically, on a presumption of moral anarchy among artificial persons. The two may merge, and merge fatefully, for in the realist illusion patriarchal features, and other features as well, are chronically, convincingly, and dangerously misperceived. The realist illusion is very old, patriarchal privilege far older.

A LOST ARGUMENT

Politics may have had its origins in a state of nature, but not one with humans in it. Politics, apparently, long antedated our own speciation. Structured observation of nonhuman animals, and most provocatively nonhuman primates, reveals behaviors readily analogous to the politics described within and between, if not among, human groups. Nonhuman primate political behaviors, including "domestic" and "foreign" aggressivity, even vary group-to-group, suggesting the influence of circumstance and, to apply a human term to nonhuman leaders and followers, personality.[4] If they follow the geographic pattern recently delineated for nonhuman primate "culture"—distinctions in tool use, social interactions, phonations, and the like[5]—then these political behaviors would also vary region-to-region. They unambiguously vary species-to-species; the chimpanzee, the now famously matriarchal and ambisexual bonobo, the gorilla, the macaque, and others, we must accept, are different political animals.[6] Yet these creatures all share a behavioral ancestry with each other, as we do with them, and much of that ancestry now may be inferred from objective reports. Taken together, these reports suggest much about the traits now mixed in us and the paleontogeny of basic expectations we hold for ourselves, our families, our fellows, and our institutions.

Of singular interest is what modern behavioral primatology suggests about the essence of moral authority. What we express by "moral authority," even by "legitimacy," clearly has an evolutionary meaning, one understood with species-specific variation throughout, and well beyond, the primate order. What we express by these terms is evidently *innate* to some substantial degree, its motivational pressure felt by individuals *as* individuals. Put differently, moral authority *in* a group may be recognizable from outside that group—or from outside any group. If so, then intragroup moral authority has

an extragroup reference and legitimacy a standard, one fundamental to cus-
tom and law and only in elaboration and peculiarity their artifact.

Among the English *virtuosi* of the seventeenth century's Scientific Revolution, natural philosophy and political philosophy were accepted as having a
common origin, yet the existence of innate ideas, including innate moral
ideas, was denied. A prominent physician, John Locke, whom England's rising lord high chancellor correctly credited with both the rejuvenation of his
health and the maturation of his thought, claimed that the human mind was
a "white Paper" at birth, that we were expelled from the womb ready to learn
but knowing nothing. Surely a knowledge of God would have been chief
among our innate ideas if we had any, yet revelation had been necessary and
instruction *about* revelation was necessary still. Furthermore, no idea was so
natural as not to be questionable, no rule so transparently right as not to be
breakable.

Like other animals, humans did, though, have "natural tendencies."[7] These
were argumentatively handy. Dismissing the innateness of ideas was credible as long as natural tendencies were kept nearby, set to cover gaps that
even the broadest sheets of "white Paper," however diligently inscribed by
experience and teaching, could never convincingly span. Locke's error—a
scientific one, really, more than a metaphysical—lay not in ignoring natural
tendencies but in disregarding their foundational role in the building of
ideas, especially moral ideas, and the behaviors grounded upon them.[8]

That said, and giving virtuosity its due, perhaps this "error" was strategic.
Locke's principal goal, after all, was not dismissal of the innateness doctrine
but dismissal of the *patriarchal* doctrine it made plausible.

In the 1630s, Sir Robert Filmer, a gentleman of Kent, had begun circulating
among his friends an argument no contractarian, no consent theorist, authoritarian or liberal, could like. Some of his work had entered publication over
succeeding decades but with little notice or effect. Then, in 1680, the author
long dead but the Stuart Restoration desperate for rhetorical defense, royalist
operatives arranged to publish Filmer's major work, *Patriarcha: The Naturall
Power of Kings Defended Against the Unnatural Liberty of the People.*[9]
Reception within the aristocracy—in Virginia no less than in England[10]—was
resounding.

Filmer, like all his contemporaries, knew no natural history whatsoever, nor
even that there was a primate order, let alone one in which he held membership. But he did still have a sense of political-behavioral inheritance, however
unlikely we might now judge his version of its origin and descent, and he was
offended by the increasingly clamorous argument that all people were somehow naturally free-born and were therefore free to chose, to form, and even
to invent and dismiss their own governments. "Consent" was the key.

Filmer objected that consent was a fable in politics and a fraud in political
theory. Politics, law, and legitimacy itself were first seen in families and re-

tained all their naturalistic features even as families became nations. Consent had nothing to do with this process, as was evident in human history, whose long premodern phase, fully recorded and open to inspection in the Old Testament, and more recent phase, profusely described in secular chronicles, demonstrated beyond questioning that patriarchy and, thus, monarchy were ineluctable. Occasional dalliances with democracy had proved this through the uniformity of their failure. The earliest transfer of power had been from Adam, the first and universal king, to his eldest son, and the legitimacy of all subsequent transfers within tribes, nations, and empires had been a function of the effort to honor this ideal form. Much the same could be said about power's artifact, property, to which no one enjoyed a right inconsistent with royal will and favor. In sum, no limitation of kingly power had ever made sense, even during corrupt reigns, divine judgment being both sure and sufficient. Yes, popular forms incrementally had entered the English constitution, and rightly so, but only with the agreement, and supposedly through the grace, of a king—or, bridging intervals in male lines, a queen. Fathers ruled families naturally by divine right, just as kings ruled nations, and families and nations alike prospered through submission to legitimate power. Indeed, if any law was "natural" it was the law of fathers and families, not the law disingenuously said, by Hugo Grotius and others, to have been established by fanciful first contractors. Consent was a secular creation myth, a rationalization disrespectful of scripture, contemptuous of history, alienated from experience, and ruinous in prospect.

Filmer's core argument was no novelty, nor were attacks on its more familiar features unknown. It was an ancient case, stated worldwide with more cultural variation than Filmer could have imagined. Confucianist political philosophy was, and remains, a major manifestation. Julius Nyerere's *ujamaa*, or "familyhood," policy was to be another.[11] By Filmer's day, as he correctly said, patriarchy had been rejected only rarely and even then transiently. It needed no introduction. Yet here, finally, was a manifesto, complete, sincere, and disarmingly unoriginal—necessarily unoriginal, as it claimed not to innovate but merely to substantiate. In the England of 1680, *Patriarcha* was a weapon, its publication a sly move, a signal event. For liberals it was a threat, for consent theorists and natural-law romantics a well-earned minor rhetorical embarrassment. For John Locke, both as celebrated physician and epistemologist and as anonymous political philosopher, it was a high-priority target.

Locke was well along with his *Essay concerning Human Understanding* when *Patriarcha* appeared. When the *Essay* itself finally appeared, in 1690, safely beyond the Glorious Revolution of 1688 and fully acknowledged by its author, Locke seemed to be leaving Filmer and absolutism unengaged. Not so; Filmer had written a book about the ease with which legitimacy was recognized in patriarchal structures and the difficulty, rarity, and impermanence with which it was recognized in consent-based structures. He regarded these latter not just as unbiblical and otherwise unhistorical but also—and here was the battle Locke assigned mainly to the *Essay*—unnatural. By demoting innate ideas to the level of natural tendencies, the *Essay* shifted the foundation upon which Filmer had built his thesis, straining *Patriarcha's* structural elements sufficiently to preclude comfortable intellectual habitation.

Written concurrently with the *Essay*, at least with its latter parts, and in 1689 published anonymously, Locke's *Letter on Toleration*[12] and *Two Treatises of Government*[13] gave whiggery the struts it would stand on for centuries to come. In these secret works, Locke reworded—"disguised" might better convey his purpose—the innateness-and-naturalness line he was soon to publish in a less political context under his own name in the *Essay*. But the line can still be followed.[14] In the *First Treatise*, written explicitly against *Patriarcha*, it was overtly instrumental and quite fruitful. The *First Treatise* was not a simple rebuttal of divine-right monarchism but a watershed in the history of political thought and, surprisingly to some these days, feminist thought as well.[15] Filmer's exposition had been awkwardly and unnecessarily scriptural, and Locke took full advantage, thrust after thrust spearing exegetic pretense and the royalist intellectualism standing behind it. The *Second Treatise*, with a consent-theory garden scene explicit enough to excite yet demure enough not to embarrass, further advanced the edge of liberalism, anticipating its famous declarations and roughing out its lasting institutions.

Oddly, then, Filmer's antiquated argument, "the most refuted theory of politics in the [English] language,"[16] seems in one key element—its observational premise—more modern than the consent-theory consensus that banished it. Indeed, if secularized, generalized, simplified, made descriptive rather than prescriptive, recast to be objective and falsifiable, and trucked off from philosophy to evolutionary psychology, it would today seem unexceptional, a piece of "normal science," a researchable hypothesis: patriarchy or matriarchy, one or the other, is the organizational and moral norm in the primate order. To this hypothesis we may add a corollary for ourselves alone, for *Homo sapiens*: however deeply submerged it may be in the flow of political progress, patriarchy remains in ebbing tides a hazard to moral navigation.

AN HONORED ERROR

One such ebbing tide had left Thomas Hobbes in Paris during the English Civil War. Born, like Filmer, in the year of the Great Armada, coming to adulthood in the first years of the Stuart dynasty in England, Hobbes in his maturity watched his country disintegrate. It became his life's work to prevent another such catastrophe, another grand fratricide, by elaborating a true science of politics through whose practice England and other Protestant

Christian states, many just emerging from the Thirty Years' War, could ensure domestic stability. In 1628, he had presented as his first published work a translation of Thucydides's *History of the Peloponnesian War*, a book about societal self-destruction. Then in 1651, out of a long exile, Hobbes published the third and lasting version of his own—and the first ever—political science, *Leviathan, or The Matter, Forme, & Power of a Common-wealth Ecclesiasticall and Civill*. It "was occasioned by the disorders of the present time,"[17] wrote its author, and fit its purpose well.

Modern presentations of realist theory are almost exclusively international in focus—not intranational, not transnational, not intracorporate, and just occasionally intercorporate. They all pivot on an assumption of anarchy.[18] Analysis of state behavior cannot be "reduced" to analyses of human behavior or internal state structure[19] since states exist in an anarchical "system" disciplined by no common and supreme ruler. Relative state power determines the pattern of international initiative and dictates the terms of dispute resolution, and rational-choice decision making guarantees an "ethic" of self-interest and self-help. It is the anarchy assumption that allows modern realist theory to turn smoothly away from global ethical obligation, and it was in *Leviathan's* oft-quoted chapter 13, its state-of-nature chapter, that the anarchy assumption first found clear expression.[20]

Leviathan is so well-known for this one chapter that many of its forty-six other chapters could disappear with little scholarly notice. Indeed, the second half of the book is excluded entirely from at least one modern edition. To today's audience, parts one and two, "Of Man" and "Of Common-wealth," seem vital members of a living body, while parts three and four, "Of a Christian Common-wealth" and "Of the Kingdome of Darknesse," the second of these viciously anti-Catholic, seem intellectually vestigial. This is too bad. Hobbes wrote carefully in a dangerous time. He expected his 1651 book to be read as a whole, as we can infer from its concluding comments and, more pointedly, from its sequential argumentation. Studied in parts and remembered in pieces, *Leviathan* has impressed students of international ethical theory in ways Hobbes may not have foreseen.

What Hobbes offered was a domestic theory with international inputs and implications, but it was not, as "scientific" orthodox modern realism would claim to be centuries later, a theory derived from the idealized actions of unitary rationally acting states existing within an international system. His international relations theory was not systemic at all but reductionist—a human-behavioral theory and, in his thinking, a state-behavioral theory.

Unlike Filmer, Hobbes set out to redefine legitimacy, to *rederive* it, and not scripturally but "scientifically," even mechanically—from "motion," no less.[21] His goal was civil stability, and that, he claimed, required political absolutism. Unanimous consent, which could be historical and could even be assumed, rather than elicited, brought political absolutism into line with an idealized parliamentary sovereignty, and majority rule could make of such a sovereignty a single being with a clear mind. Political absolutism, however realized, required national autonomy, which in turn required the discrediting of Roman Catholicism, Hobbes's obsession, and collaterally all secular catholicisms as well.

Thus was moral universalism condemned, but inconsistently. In more famous passages it was condemned as fiction, but in less-read reaches of the book as anything but fiction—indeed, as the main cause of domestic discord. Following his forty-seventh chapter, Hobbes appended "A REVIEW, and CONCLUSION," wherein he offered a candid gloss on his argument for the state's immunity to moral censure.[22] Here, as if to reward the relentlessness of the reader, Hobbes admitted that the reason he placed sovereign action outside the bounds of moral judgment was not that he truly believed in or had proved the ethical rightness of such an exemption. Not at all. He had simply decided that the no-moral-judgment rule was necessary to maintain domestic stability—a consequentialist escape from deontology.

Hobbes could have reached absolutism through an aggrandizement of patriarchy, however messily established, but he could not then gracefully have entertained the sovereignty of assemblies, such as England's then-triumphant parliament. Nor could he have kept absolutism autonomous, which is to say free of transnationalism, most immediately the patriarchal transnationalism of the bishop of Rome. Hobbes's solution to the simultaneous equation here implicit was, of course, unanimous, solemn, and irrevocable consent to absolute authority. Yet not only did this mode of consent, or some approximation of it, fail to solve his country's problem. It failed even to solve his book's problem.

We may excuse as well meant the absolution of post-consent tyranny. We may excuse as unintentional the faint implication that election must have legitimized even the pope's power. We may not, though, so easily excuse Hobbes's contradictions on political morality, especially regarding its locus in international life. Hobbes did not believe the space between nations was morally anarchic. To the contrary, he feared this space, for spirits mobilized there could cross a border, oblige a priest, sway a mob, divide an assembly, corrupt an army, kill a king. For Hobbes, international anarchy was not an axiom, as it is for modern realists; he *deduced* international anarchy from the nature of human beings, which he imagined to be mechanistic, and from the internal nature of the state. He did not argue *from* the international state of nature. He argued *toward* it and even *for* it, urging Protestant Christendom to recognize the danger that a lack of international anarchy posed to civil peace.

Patriarcha was no match for *Leviathan* philosophically or artistically, and neither one was a match for the *Two Treatises* politically—or for the flow of events. *Patriarcha's* most intriguing feature, its protoanthropological critique of consent theory, was swept aside in a general Western rush toward liberalism. With divine-right rule the deadest of secular letters but gender inequity at last a respected complaint, the patriarchist view now appears far less dangerous than long ago but in important ways decidedly more offensive. *Patriarcha's* absolutist legacy, of course, has been almost wholly obscured by *Leviathan's*, which itself has held honors only in the theory of international relations, where its author's interest was roundabout. But it *has* held them there.

A COMPLICATING SIMPLIFICATION

When at the close of the Second World War modern political realism scratched its way up through a rubble of failed hopes and false philosophies, international moral anarchy seemed, at once, everywhere and nowhere. The unregulated competition of nations had lately been flagrant, as was usual in war. Yet an alliance of nations, some of them democracies fighting for other democracies, had just overturned great evil at high cost. In Nuremberg, Tokyo, and Singapore, tribunals of that alliance were soon to judge the conduct of deposed leaders and surviving loyalists. And in San Francisco, New York, and Geneva, the alliance itself was about to become, supposedly, a global moral order.

As was soon enough apparent, though, morality was not about to be globalized. It was more nearly to be nationalized, or divided between alliances, holy and unholy, as if for a war of religion: liberal egalitarianism versus socialist authoritarianism. International life was looking as Hobbesian as ever, perhaps more so. Throughout the West analysts settled comfortably into the realist illusion, a perspective most often remembered from *Leviathan* but elaborated and greatly refined by later scholars, especially those of the Cold War.

Within the realist illusion moral judgment based on ordinary criteria seems unsuitable, since all protagonists are in every way imaginable extraordinary. They are not simple, but compound, yet still for any practical purpose unitary and personifiable. They are not short lived, but persistent, even immortal; not law abiding, but law giving unto themselves; not subject, but self-determined and self-helping. They are jealous of power, yet selfishly rational in its pursuit and application. They are leviathans rampant on a field of nations, and into them, into these artificial persons, these indispensable fictions,[23] guilt diffuses, like blood into the sea. Competing nearby on less privileged ground are more accountable giants: corporations, "lesser Common-wealths in the bowels of a greater, like wormes in the entrayles of a naturall man."[24] For them, as for the states they resemble, the amoral pursuit of self-interest not only is rational but also in the long run may be excused as having enhanced the general welfare through intensification of competition, through striving one against the other for profit and prominence—a liberal extension of realism much influenced by market theory. Into these "lesser Common-wealths," in contrast to states, the guilt that diffuses is almost always civil, while the guilt that attaches to individuals, to officers and employees, may well be criminal, the product of actions that corporations themselves may or may not have exposed but ultimately will disown.

Guilt has origins, simple or otherwise, and spreads a traceable scent. In global political life, various forms of retribution, from informal score settling and victor's justice to conscientiously conducted war-crimes trials and truth-commission proceedings, demonstrate the urge to individualize responsibility for past wrongs, at least recent ones. It is exactly this urge to individualize that the realist illusion ordinarily attenuates. The foremost exception over the last half century, an illusion lifter for even the strictest of realists, has been genocide, an audacious family killing hate crime whose *unindividualized* punishment, were it executed, would necessarily be collective, could fairly be condemned as retaliatory, and could easily come to resemble genocide itself.

Realism as theoretically informed practice has endured, even thrived, not just through extension but also, and more importantly, through restriction. Its most formidable antagonist, liberalism, has in leading countries conveniently blocked the forbidding old Hobbesian prospect of domestic authoritarianism, thus making realism safe for democracy—indeed, making realism potentially convincing as the *safeguard* of democracy at home. Liberalism has also helpfully superimposed upon the realist world-of-states view an international legal regime, often denigrated yet increasingly functional. The "modern liberal realist," to coin a term, may these days see all leviathans as foreign and may see the misbehaving ones less as threats to the sovereign independence of neighbor states than as threats to themselves, harming the "natural liberty of the people" denied illiberally by Filmer and, despite a presumption of consent, by Hobbes.

The realist illusion is an independent factor in a range of political behaviors, including many of the more troubling and less successful ones. As for more troubling, it simplifies the formation of policy but obscures the truth that genuine individuals are at every chosen policy's sharp end. As for less successful, it again simplifies but this time blurs the near-certainty that the policies of foreign governments will have been formed by individuals or factions themselves in competition with each other locally. Sometimes these effects interact, as when China's full inclusion in the world's commerce is opposed on human-rights grounds, the strategy being to force "China," the indispensable fiction, to stop abusing "China," the composite corporeal fact.

Whether clarifying or confounding, the realist illusion is not peculiar to the leaders of political, military, and economic competitions or to the scholars of these competitions. It can also be perceived convincingly by citizens, soldiers, and employees, whose commitment to communal efforts and acceptance of collective fates make large-scale leadership and, hence, competition possible.

"Commitment" and "acceptance"—how human these behaviors sound, how easily attributable to the making of a social contract, to the general and durable granting of consent. In fact, these behaviors *are* almost exclusively human, but not quite. In our very closest patriarchal relatives, chimpanzees and gorillas, just as in humans, dominated males tend to stay with, to stay committed to, to remain accepting of, their natal groups—their "nations," in the oldest sense of the word.[25]

A PROBLEM ABROAD

As political-psychological terms, rather than as anthropological or primatological classifications, "patriarch" and "patriarchy" have never well supported the definitional loads placed upon them. They sagged even under the weight applied by Filmer and must now accept additional meanings he would never have lifted his pen to defend. What he called a "patriarch" in truth may be young, as he knew, may be female, may be thoroughly secular, may be elected, may be *communal*, the legitimate bearer of moral authority rather than personally its source, or may simply be powerful, though perhaps only temporarily. What Filmer called a "patriarchy"—the word itself is a hindrance—is better said to be any complex order compelled principally by moral authority and structured by rank. Some institutions in the modern world are inherently and unapologetically patriarchal. Virtually all institutions, including egalitarian democracies, have patriarchal features, try as they might to expunge them.

Such an order—which need not be morally used to be recognizable as morally compelled—may be or may become roughly coterminous with a state. In this case, not an uncommon one, the term "nation-state," which is often too casually applied, may fit rather well. Observers within the realist illusion will respect this complex order as a whole, and they may respect its personification at face value. They may show less respect, sometimes none whatever, for the predicaments, aspirations, and complaints of individuals and groups disaffected, frustrated, or misused within. Yugoslavia's personification, Josip Broz Tito, living and dead, was widely respected in this way both abroad and in-country, while more enduring lower-level allegiances awaited fuller and disruptive expression.[26]

When a complex order compelled principally by moral authority is coterminous not with a state but only with *itself* the realist illusion is characteristically unreliable. A stateless nation, a race, tribe, clan, or "outlaw band," a linguistic or religious group, a trades union or "radical" political party, or most any other substantially sized and strongly self-identified community may confound statist expectations. It may later come conversely to fulfill these same expectations, with diplomatic recognition the result, on occasions when political friction has heated sovereignty into flux. Most regrettably, the realist illusion may single out for respect a complex order compelled principally or excessively by *force*, with compellence by force often signifying a workable degree of moral authority within a faction but, simultaneously, an irremediable moral bankruptcy beyond it.

Though its historical analysis may come to rest upon subtleties not as yet appreciated, the Pinochet case at the moment seems a classic of patriarchal indulgence aggrandized by realist illusion. It may already have become a prototype,[27] if an ambiguous one. As Pinochet was waiting to fly home, Chad's deposed President Hissene Habre was abruptly indicted for crimes said to have been committed while in power. He was charged not by Chad but by his host, the previously gracious Senegal.[28] Then, a week following Pinochet's repatriation, a little-noticed affair involving another reputed torturer recapitulated the new motif more faithfully, but this time *prestissimo*. An officer credibly accused of atrocities furthering President Alberto Fujimori's suppression of press freedoms in Peru was admitted into the United States and tracked. When about to exit the country, he was detained—but only for about a day.[29]

The Pinochet case is not all new, of course. It is a precedent with many antecedents, some exalted. The first French emperor, Napoleon Bonaparte, who was thought a monster of the worst sort by his conquering enemies, was initially *given* a court, on Elba, not arraigned in one. Kaiser Wilhelm II successfully "retired" to Holland after losing a world war he was believed to have plotted. Emperor Hirohito laid down his divinity and took up marine biology, while his wartime prime minister, Hideki Tojo, agreed to recant his loyal-subordinate defense and be hanged.

Many abusive leaders in recent decades have been pushed into exile or in some other way sequestered. Others have been shunned. Some have been jailed by their successors or killed in revolutions, but almost none has been punished in the criminal due-process sense, not even Pol Pot. Uganda's deposed president, Idi Amin, was kept safe, though he is unlikely ever to leave his asylum in Saudi Arabia. Radovan Karadzic and, with rare exceptions,[30] other reputed criminals of the recent Bosnian conflict have remained cautiously at liberty in a status that might be termed "enclave arrest."[31] Slobodan Milosevic, indicted for war crimes in Kosovo, likewise was long at liberty, and he was also fully in power, the democratically chosen president of what was incongruously still called Yugoslavia, until he too obviously cheated in the first postwar election. He remained until then "a man to be dealt with"— a phrase once used pointedly by Jordan's late King Hussein in reference to

Iraq's pertinacious President Saddam Hussein after the latter, a domestic repressor in the Stalinesque style, reached abroad to ravish his long-coveted neighbor, Kuwait. Saddam Hussein, of course, was subject to determined vilification before, during, and after the Persian Gulf War, whose justification in public discourse in the democracies allied against Iraq depended heavily upon his reputation as a political and genocidal murderer. Yet, during the war, efforts to kill him were always supposedly incidental to the purely professional selection of targets. One of the United Nations Security Council resolutions authorizing the whole enterprise provided for the arrest of war criminals; it was much cited in the support-building stages of the effort, but not at war's end, when it could have been invoked to warrant a transformative application of force, military or political or both. Indeed, no acknowledged effort was made to win Saddam Hussein's delivery, even for an interview, or to pursue and capture him. Deposing him, along with his Baathist comrades, was a goal the victors repudiated or, at any rate, a goal from which they shrank. Saddam Hussein was not even indicted, just left to his own reflections, while the heterogeneous and mutually hostile groups collectively called "his people" were immiserated further by internal reprisals and external sanctions, the latter directed at a leadership largely unaffected, if not perversely assisted, by them.

After-the-fact deference may have before-the-fact and during-the-fact counterparts, though their rationalizations tend to differ. The most controversial recent examples were the decisions of the North Atlantic powers, both separately and as an alliance, to refrain from intervening militarily in the closely watched and unmistakably genocidal wars of Yugoslavia's disintegration. These examples were made all the more controversial by the rapidity with which intervention, when it did occur, succeeded, first in Bosnia and then in Kosovo. These wins may have been comparatively easy because they were well-timed, but their ease could also suggest that they had been unnecessarily delayed.

Reluctance to intervene may be explained by many factors, including inattention, indifference, self-absorption, cynicism, timidity, incapacity, good judgment, and the courage to leave bad enough alone. Doctrinal adherence may also be involved; in American statecraft, Washingtonian principles of diplomatic detachment and executive restraint have traditionally been preferred to, though they have frequently been superseded by, Wilsonian principles of engagement and initiative.[32] In explaining a specific reluctance to intervene, respect for sovereignty may be cited first, but it may only be first— or even last—on a list whose very existence, not to mention its length and variety, implicitly disrespects sovereignty. Respect for sovereignty if reason at all should be reason enough. Supposedly it was when the Carter administration, which had placed human rights higher on its internationalist agenda than had any of its predecessors, opposed a boycott of Ugandan

coffee, the source of Idi Amin's personal fortune, lest the international system, especially along its trading dimension, be weakened.[33]

Failure to intervene may be explained also by fear of failure *when* intervening. The history of regrets here is long, with many errors more alike psychologically than the diversity of their details suggests. A common theme is the expectation that local modes of legitimation, if recognized at all, will be
subordinated to the statist modes recommended by the intervening power,
which may be a state itself, an intergovernmental organization, or a nongovernmental organization. Local modes may be inconveniently idiosyncratic,
may be overtly patriarchal in some troublesome way, or may be uncon-
scionably regressive, misogynistic, caste-ridden, religiously or racially intoler-
ant, or permissive of slavery—or in some other way overdue for improvement.
In the 1960s, the U.S. government misunderstood the Buddhist priesthood in
South Vietnam, in the 1990s, the clan structure of Somalia, and so forth.

Intervention can fail in yet other ways relating to the dysfunctional recognition of moral authority. One is particularly well-known. Fighters in groups
may become so closely bonded to each other and to their leaders that loyalty to a properly constituted external command structure is supplanted. On
the unit level, in theoretical terms, patriarchy grows to block all view of the
authorizing state, usurping its authority. Rogue action is the characteristic
sign, sometimes on a scale hard to ignore, as at My Lai. The preemption or
modulation of such bonding is easy to devise but may atomize otherwise
functional units.

Another class of moral-authority problem is less obvious but potentially no
less serious. Invaders, colonizers, interveners, and private soldiers, even aid
workers and businesspeople, may adopt what seems to be the lowest ambi-
ent behavioral standard in-country, doing unto others as others do unto each
other. The problem here is not blindness to local patterns but opportunism
based on their recognition. Abetting this opportunism, and compounding its
offensiveness, is an implicit arrogation of "family" privilege.

A contrasting variation, well-known from migrations and conquests and
freshly remembered from "ethnic cleansings," is the tendency for cruelty
abroad to be esteemed as charity at home. The most compelling example is
away-child killing by home-child benefactors, wherein the protection and
promotion of one's own family leads logically and coldly to the annihilation
of another's, nationalism mutating into nation-killing, into genocide. General
Philip Sheridan's frontier army, in an egregious example, campaigned ex-
pressly against Native American children as well as against their parents
when clearing lands on which future generations of immigrant Americans
could make for their own sons and daughters the prosperous homes they deserved. Many conquerors, ancient and modern, genocidal and otherwise, not
a few of them proud of their work, have exhibited similar behavior. So have
chimpanzees in the wild.[34]

SUMMARY JUDGMENT

The realist illusion undervalues individuals in politics and individualism in political ethics, while patriarchal privilege assigns to prominent individuals an exceptional value, through the leverage of which they may act audaciously with a highly robust personal impunity. The realist illusion and patriarchal privilege, which may operate separately or together, are genuine psychological phenomena with clear evolutionary antecedents and numerous nonhuman analogues, most explicitly among our primate cousins. They are also regressive in that they interfere with the advancement and protection of human rights at the fundamental—the individual—level.

The politics here is more behavioral than institutional or legal. Its mechanisms are emotional and deeply seated, rather than simplistically rational and self-interested. Sharp motivational insight would not be expected among the practitioners involved, not even one-by-one, let alone as policy teams, and clean case-by-case theoretical distinctions would unduly simplify what must usually be a swirl of perceptions and concerns, conscious and not.

This discussion might be mistaken for a commentary on the perseverance of primitive thought. It appeals to primatological and anthropological observation. It reviews arguments from an era when conscientious people in leading countries took more seriously the political rights of royal pretenders than the human rights of women. It describes conduct found alike in preindustrial societies, atavistic states, and modern liberal alliances. Yet the persevering thought being discussed is not primitive so much as permanent, the manifestation of what may jarringly be called, in seventeenth-century terms, an innate idea. Its avoidance is not feasible, nor is its ultimate mastery, but its management could surely improve. Awareness is the first step.

NOTES

1. Warren Hoge, "Once Again in Public Eye, Thatcher Acts as Conservative Lightning Rod," *New York Times*, October 7, 1999, p. A1.

2. Anthony Faiola, "Pinochet steps into uproar: Apparent vigor sets off debate about release," *Washington Post*, March 4, 2000, p. A1.

3. Robert Hunt Sprinkle, *Profession of Conscience: The Making and Meaning of Life-Sciences Liberalism* (Princeton: Princeton University Press, 1994), 116–120, 154–155.

4. P. Buirski, R. Plutchik and H. Kellerman, "Sex differences, dominance, and personality in the chimpanzee," *Animal Behavior* 1978 Feb, 26(1):123–129.

5. R. W. Wrangham, W. C. Mcgrew, F. B. M. de Waal, and P. G. Heltne, eds., *Chimpanzee Cultures* (Cambridge, Mass.: Harvard University Press, 1994). A. Whiten, J. Goodall, W. C. Mcgrew, T. Nishida, V. Reynoldsk, Y. Sugiyama, C. E. G. Tutin, R. W.

Wrangham, and C. Boesch, "Cultures in chimpanzees," *Nature*, vol. 399 (17 June 1999): 682–685.

6. Frans de Waal, *Chimpanzee Politics: Power and Sex Among Apes* (Baltimore: Johns Hopkins University Press, 1989). Frans de Waal, *Good Natured: The Origins of Right and Wrong in Humans and Other Animals* (Cambridge, Mass.: Harvard University Press, 1996). Richard Wrangham and Dale Peterson, *Demonic Males: Apes & the Origins of Human Violence* (Boston: Houghton Mifflin, 1997). Frans de Waal and Frans Lanting, *Bonobo: The Forgotten Ape* (Berkeley: University Of California Press, 1998).

7. John Locke, *An Essay concerning Humane Understanding* (London: Eliz. Holt for Thomas Basset, 1690), presented as John Locke, *An Essay concerning Human Understanding*, Peter H. Nidditch, ed. (Oxford: Clarendon Press, Oxford University Press, 1975), 67–95.

8. Sprinkle, *Profession of Conscience*, pp. 43–47.

9. Sir Robert Filmer, *Patriarcha and Other Writings*, Johann P. Sommerville, ed. (Cambridge University Press, 1991).

10. David Hackett Fischer, *Albion's Seed: Four British Folkways in America* (New York: Oxford University Press, 1989), 220–225, 252–256, 274–280, 321–326.

11. Julius Nyerere, *Ujamaa—Essays on Socialism* (Dar es Salaam: Oxford University Press, 1968).

12. John Locke, *Epistola de Tolerantia: A Letter on Toleration*, Raymond Klibansky, ed., and J. W. Gough, ed. and trans. (Oxford: Clarendon Press, 1968).

13. John Locke, *Two Treatises of Government: In the Former, the False Principles and Foundation of Sir Robert Filmer, and His Followers, Are Detected and Overthrown. The Latter is an Essay Concerning the True Original, Extent, and End of Civil-Government* (London: Awnsham And John Churchill, 1698), presented as John Locke, *Two Treatises of Government: A Critical Edition with an Introduction and Apparatus Criticus*, amended reprinting, Peter Laslett, ed. (New York: Mentor Books, by arrangement with Cambridge University Press, 1960 and 1963).

14. Locke, *Two Treatises*, pp. 215–216, 244.

15. Locke, *Two Treatises*, pp. 210–216.

16. Peter Laslett in *Patriarcha and Other Political Works of Robert Filmer*, Peter Laslett, ed. (Oxford: Basil Blackwell, 1949), 20.

17. Thomas Hobbes, *Leviathan, or the Matter, Forme, & Power of a Common-Wealth Ecclesiasticall and Civill.* (London: Andrew Crooke, 1651), presented as Thomas Hobbes, *Leviathan*, C. B. Macpherson, ed. (London: Penguin Books, Ltd., 1968), "A Review, and Conclusion," p. 728.

18. Kenneth N. Waltz, *Theory of International Politics* (New York: Random House, 1979), 102–128.

19. Waltz, *Theory of International Politics*, pp. 60–78.

20. Hobbes, part I, chapter 13, pp. 185–187.

21. Hobbes, part I, chapter 3, p. 94.

22. Hobbes, "A REVIEW, and CONCLUSION," pp. 721–722.

23. Edward Hallett Carr, *The Twenty Years' Crisis, 1919–1939: An Introduction to the Study of International Relations*, 2nd ed. (New York: Harper Torchbooks, Harper & Row, Publishers, 1964), 148–149.

24. Hobbes, part II, chapter 29, p. 375.

25. A. H. Harcourt, "Strategies of emigration and transfer by primates, with particular reference to gorillas," *Z Tierpsychol* 1978 Dec; 48(4): 401–420.

26. Richard H. Ullman, "The Wars in Yugoslavia and the International System after the Cold War," in *The World and Yugoslavia's Wars*, Richard H. Ullman, ed. (New York: Council on Foreign Relations Press, 1996), pp. 9–41, at pp. 9–11 and p. 37, Note 4.

27. Anthony Faiola, "'Pinochet Effect' Spreading," *Washington Post*, August 5, 2000.

28. Norimitsu Onishi, "An African dictator faces trial in his place of refuge," *New York Times*, March 1, 2000.

29. Karen Deyoung And Lorraine Adams, "U.S. frees accused torturer," *Washington Post*, March 11, 2000.

30. Marlise Simons, "Nato Troops Seize a Top Serb Facing War Crime Charge," *New York Times*, April 4, 2000.

31. Carlotta Gall, "Karadzic Still Plays Hide-And-Seek With U.N. in Bosnia," *New York Times*, August 7, 2000.

32. Richard H. Ullman, "The 'Foreign World' and Ourselves: Washington, Wilson, and the Democrat's Dilemma," *Foreign Policy*, Winter 1975–1976.

33. Richard H. Ullman, "Human Rights and Economic Power: The United States versus Idi Amin," *Foreign Affairs*, April 1978.

34. J. Goodall, "Infant killing and cannibalism in free-living chimpanzees," *Folia Primatol* 1977; 28(4):259–89.

5

The Reasonable Public
and the Polarized Policy Process

I. M. (Mac) Destler

We live in curious times. We seem to have a rational public and an ideological ruling class. Average Americans are basically centrist, prone to balance, compromise, fair shares, reasonable resolutions. Their Congress is polarized, hyperpartisan, responsive to "cause" activists of left and right. Washington regularly misreads the former and bemoans the latter.

Exhibit A was the impeachment of President William Jefferson Clinton. Showing astoundingly bad judgment and an excruciating lack of self-control, he indulged himself in an affair with a White House intern, then lied about it—in legal proceedings, and to the American public. He had also, by some combination of skill and luck, presided over a national prosperity—soaring income and productivity growth and low inflation complete with fiscal surplus—that virtually no one thought possible on January 20, 1993. And his empathy with Americans' goals and needs was uncanny. The public's conclusion? Bad man, good president. Censure him and move on. The congressional resolution? Haul out the heavy guns. A year of bitter wrangling, driven by activists on the Clinton-hating right, ending in a partisan House vote for his ouster and acquittal by the Senate (also along mainly partisan lines) and no censure resolution at all. Meanwhile, Washington vacillated between certainty that the latest juicy revelation would finally destroy Clinton's public support and wishing that statesmen would emerge to lead us out of the mess.

We were taught in school that our founding fathers sought a republic, not a democracy, to provide buffers for extremes in public sentiment. But today's America has turned James Madison on his head. It is the people that seem sensible and stable. The passions are in the men and women who purport to represent them, and in the activist minorities to whom these "representatives" respond. It is not just "a growing gap between the interests of political elites and the preferences of average Americans,"[1] important though that be. It is that the politicians seem to be pulling apart even as the people, by and large, stay together. And there was no fundamental break from this pattern in the initial months of the George W. Bush administration.

* * *

The above seems a strange start to an essay on the politics of American opinion and American foreign policy. Unmentioned are the dilemmas that follow Cold War victory, the choices the nation faces in a twenty-first-century world. But there is an eerie connection—reflected, for example, in the Senate's bitter partisan wrangle over, and rejection of, the comprehensive nuclear test ban treaty in October 1999. In matters international as well as domestic, our leaders are blessed with a "rational public"[2] that supports reasonable action, sensible governmental engagement, reflecting values as well as interests. Leaders are often blind to this blessing—in important part because their polarized, day-to-day Washington political environment reflects so little of it. But a steady, humane, constructive American foreign policy may depend on their discovering it, building on it, exploiting it.

WHAT AMERICANS THINK— AND WHAT WASHINGTON THINKS THEY THINK

Through most of the 1990s, it was conventional wisdom in Washington that Americans wished to pull back from global engagement. In semistructured interviews conducted with eighty-three policy practitioners in early 1996, part of a comprehensive research project carried out by the author and Steven Kull in 1995–1998, three-fourths of them expressed this view. Half of these same practitioners thought citizens to be negative toward the United Nations (just one-fourth believed them favorable). Two-thirds saw the public as opposed to foreign aid in principle. By contrast, over half believed the public wanted either to maintain or increase the level of spending for national defense. Belief in public neoisolationism was particularly strong on Capitol Hill, and among members of the media.[3]

The actual views of Americans were and are quite different—if public opinion surveys are to be believed. Sixty-plus percent consistently want the United States to "play an active part in the world," unchanged since the Cold War.[4] Overwhelming majorities support the United Nations, and majorities or pluralities consistently favor participation in U.N. peacekeeping and full U.S. payment of back dues. There is a strong preference for multilateral, as opposed to unilateral, U.S. international engagement. Americans do want to cut foreign aid, but this is apparently because they estimate U.S. spending at 15 to 30 times its actual amount; they support it overwhelmingly in principle, however, and favor at least current spending levels when informed what they are.[5] They also back, overwhelmingly, a robust defense, but when they learn how enormous U.S. defense spending remains compared to that of other nations, they tilt toward serious reductions.

When these results—drawing on all extant opinion surveys—were presented to sophisticated Washington practitioners, they expressed skepticism, and suggested that such public support is soft: a mile wide perhaps, but surely an inch deep. Asked to make their challenges concrete, they suggested multiple ways that Americans' responses to survey questions might be misleading. Asked to propose alternative questions that would uncover the isolationism they felt is present, they responded intelligently and creatively. But citizen responses to *their* questions did not change the fundamental picture.

- One challenge reflected the view that *issues play differently in the heat of election campaigns*; in that context, it was said, voters opt for candidates who favor cutbacks, whatever they might state generally. We tested this view several different ways: the most vivid was in the form of "attack ads" denouncing a fictional incumbent for supporting foreign aid or payment of U.N. dues. Ads and incumbent "responses" were checked with campaign professionals for their plausibility, then read to poll respondents. But on foreign aid those polled backed the incumbent by 53 to 37 percent; on U.N. dues, the margin was 56 to 37 percent.

- A second line of skepticism saw *support for international engagement as soft*: critics held their views more intensely, it was argued, and were more likely to hold to them when challenged. But surveys showed that those who felt "strongly" were as likely to be positive as those who did not. To test for *resilience*, we presented three strong contrary arguments to supporters and opponents of foreign aid, and did the same for supporters and opponents of participation in U.N. peacekeeping. It turned out that the views of critics were a bit *less* resilient than those of supporters.

- A third plausible suggestion was that supporters were less attentive to the issues and less active politically. We tested this by comparing respondents according to their answers to questions about how closely they followed international issues, whether their votes were influenced by candidates' foreign policy stands, and whether they had contributed to a campaign or contacted Congress on an international issue. The attentive and active proved significantly *more* proengagement, though those who had contacted Congress were somewhat less positive toward the United Nations.

- It was argued further that the public would cut international programs if faced with the sort of trade-offs Congress must address. So we gave respondents the opportunity to reallocate the money that the average taxpayer provides for the discretionary federal budget. They made substantial changes. Spending for human capital (education, job training, medical research) fared best, but international spending (State Department, United Nations, foreign aid) came in second, up no less than 77 percent. Defense was the big loser.

- Finally, it was argued that, since members of Congress should know their constituencies, we could assume that representatives with very strong antiengagement records represented voters who felt likewise. So we conducted separate polls in the districts of four members who had voted consistently against aid and the United Nations. But views in these districts were, for the most part, indistinguishable from those in the national sample.

Thus the challenges from practitioners were generally refuted: public support remained. So we shifted the focus of our analysis from the public to the Washington community. Our study found a number of plausible explanations why they might be misreading the public, all supported by evidence from interviews.

- Policy practitioners may misinterpret dissatisfaction with the United States playing a hegemonic (world policeman) role, and a consequent desire for more international burdensharing, as a public wish to disengage. (The public does tend to think the United States is doing too much, and doing it alone.)
- They may misread the vocal public—constituents who express discontent at district meetings—as the majority and fail to seek more comprehensive information about public opinion.
- They may assume that congressional action is a faithful reflection of citizens' preferences. (The press is particularly prone to do so, and Capitol Hill in turn often sees the public through media eyes, creating the possibility of a "closed loop.")

We also developed a systematic political analysis of why this particular misreading of the public (the belief that it wants to pull back internationally) could arise and persist.[6]

- *Why did it get established in the first place?* From a Washington perspective, the belief that the American public wanted to disengage was *plausible*, consistent with major, visible recent developments abroad and at home. There was the sudden end to the Cold War, the ongoing driver of U.S. internationalism since 1947. This was followed by the unraveling of President George Bush's reelection campaign in 1992, as challenger Bill Clinton drew blood with the charge that he had spent too much time on foreign affairs. A more complicated contributor was the rise in American politics, over the past quarter-century, of forces labeled "conservative." The most visible conservative platform of the nineties, the "Contract with America," included attacks on U.S. involvement in U.N. peacekeeping. And voters gave its proponents a smashing electoral victory in 1994.

- *Once established, why did it persist?* Because the political market doesn't provide a corrective. The American public doesn't give priority to international issues when it goes to the polls. The executive branch doesn't give priority to public opinion when it makes foreign policy. The legislative branch cares a great deal about public opinion, but not opinion on international matters and especially not as it is reflected in polls. Members of Congress have no overriding stake in getting that opinion right because they are unlikely to lose elections for getting it wrong. And executive and legislative branch officials don't challenge the conventional belief in public neoisolationism because they fear they'll be labeled unrealistic, even naive, undercutting their influence. For all these intertwined reasons, the belief that the public wants to withdraw has proved persistent, even *self-reinforcing*, once it is established.

Finally, once established, the belief that the public wants to disengage has been *convenient* for those whose priorities have been elsewhere. Clinton was elected on a primarily domestic agenda ("the economy, stupid!") in 1992. Republicans stressed home issues two years later. With leaders in both White House and Congress inwardly focused, not wanting to give energy to campaigning for international engagement, the view of a negative public offered a nice rationalization, highlighted in the view repeatedly expressed to us by members of Congress: "We'd do more but the American people won't let us."

THE POLARIZATION OF PARTY POLITICS

An important additional part of the story, however, is that American political leaders have been spending less and less of their time seeking viable consensus in the center, and more of their time fighting for partisan and ideological advantage. They have not been listening to the majority public because their minds and hearts have been elsewhere. In this context, their assertions about public opinion have tended to be opportunistic, weapons in a bipolar battle. Nowhere has this been more evident than in our political parties, our Congress, and the cause-based interest groups with which they interact.

Our political parties have become more ideological. Two decades ago, amidst bitter domestic conflict over U.S.-Soviet relations and arms control, Thomas L. Hughes pointed to the evisceration of the center and its destructive

impact on U.S. foreign relations.[7] Things have gotten worse since. Drawing on
the voluminous data compiled by the American National Election Studies at
the University of Michigan, David C. King demonstrates how polarization has
grown, especially since 1980. Americans have become somewhat more conservative and significantly more Republican, but they remain clustered near
the political center.[8] But "the parties are becoming more extreme . . . increasingly distant in their policies from what the average voter would like. . . .
Strong Republicans have become more conservative, and . . . party activists
are drawn almost entirely from their ranks. Likewise, strong Democrats have
become more liberal, though the ideological shift has not been as steep."[9]

Congress has reflected, indeed magnified, this trend. The percentage of
centrists in Congress "declined from about 25 percent of all members in 1980
to 10 percent in 1996."[10] By 1999, this trend had reached its logical culmination, as reflected in the annual *National Journal* voting survey. "In the Senate, for the first time since *National Journal* began compiling vote ratings in
1981, every Democrat had an average score that was to the left of the most
liberal Republican." In the junior chamber, *NJ* found that "only two Republicans . . . were in that chamber's more-liberal half on each of the three issue
areas. . . . And only two Democrats . . . ranked in the more-conservative
half." (One of them left the Democratic Party in January 2000.) "The findings
help explain why so little got done in Congress last year. . . . Votes were cast
to highlight partisan political differences."[11] And this conclusion from data-
based journalism finds support in data-based political science: in a thor-
oughgoing analysis of the causes of policy gridlock in Washington, Sarah A.
Binder writes:

> The effect of party polarization is perhaps the most striking. Despite the faith of
> responsible party advocates in *cohesive* political parties, the results here suggest
> that policy change is *less* likely as the parties become more polarized and the
> percentage of moderate legislators shrinks.
>   Such results confirm the sentiments of the many members of Congress and
> observers who claim that partisan polarization limits the legislative capacity of
> Congress. The "incredibly shrinking middle"—as Senator John Breaux called
> it—seems to hamper substantially the ability of Congress and the president to
> reach agreement on the issues before them.[12]

Over the same period, *the public has become increasingly alienated from
government and the political process.* In the 1964 University of Michigan survey 76 percent of Americans said they had confidence that the government
would "do the right thing" always or most of the time. Thirty years later this
number had dropped to 19 percent (Yankelovich Partners).[13] And as sum-
marized in a recent survey by Steven Kull's Center on Policy Attitudes
(COPA), "Confidence that the government serves the nation as a whole has
plummeted over this same time period."

In 1964, a strong 64% majority said that the government "is run for the benefit of all the people," while only 29% said that "the government is pretty much run by a few big interests looking out for themselves." In 1972, a majority (53%) said for the first time that "the government is pretty much run by a few big interests." From 1990 through 1999 those saying "the government is pretty much run by a few big interests" were always 69% or more, while the percentage saying that the government is run for the benefit of all never went above 27%. National Election Studies (NES) found 31% in November 1998; COPA's 19% result in January 1999 was back in line with most results through the 1990s.[14]

This decline of confidence in government has been accompanied by a growing sense of separation from that government. To quote COPA again:

In response to the statement, "Public officials don't care much what people like me think," in 1960 only 25% agreed. Agreement started an upward movement [thereafter], reaching a majority for the first time in 1976 and 63% in 1990 (58% in the current [1999] poll).

In response to the unequivocal statement, "People like me don't have any say about what the government does," only 27% agreed in 1960. The numbers rose thereafter, but not until 1990 did the number of those in agreement surpass the number of those disagreeing. The number agreeing in the current poll (56%) matches the previous high of 1994.[15]

The decline in public trust is clearly correlated with the rise of polarization, and the public perceives a connection: in the November 1998 survey by National Election Studies (NES), 73 percent said that the phrase "too involved in partisan politics" described Congress well. But is there in fact a direct link? King's research suggests that there is. For he finds that the most alienated citizens are those farthest from the two extremes. "The more distant the parties are from [individual] respondents, the more likely [these] respondents are to say that they mistrust government."[16] Hence, "The growing gap between elites and the rest of us is being filled with cynicism, mistrust, and frustration that our leaders do not care about 'our' problems."[17] And to the degree that people in the center "drop out" by failing to vote, the extremes are reinforced.

Congressional movement toward the extremes has been encouraged and reinforced by the rise of activist, "cause" groups on the left and right. In the words of Richard Neustadt (paraphrasing Hugh Heclo), a growing political role has been played by "movements . . . imitative of the civil rights movement . . . environmentalists and feminists—then, in reaction, right-to-lifers."[18] The end result is "warfare among elites, waged since the 1960s in the name of causes, not compromises, fueled by technology, manned by consultants, rousing supporters by damning opponents, while serving the separate interests of particular candidates and groups at given times."[19] This pattern has been evident in such domestic issues as abortion, gun control, social security, and health care. And it has led, in the main, to policy stalemate.

POLARIZATION AND FOREIGN POLICY

In the past, foreign policy issues have been somewhat insulated from this pattern. To be sure, there has been polarization within the foreign policy elite—on arms control policy in particular. During the Carter administration, for example, left and right waged ideological warfare with the public in the middle: wanting a strong defense, being skeptical of the Russians, *and* supporting arms control if verification and compliance could be achieved. And partisan and cause-group conflict were prominent in controversies from the Panama Canal Treaties of 1977–1978 to selling AWACS to Saudi Arabia in 1981 to NAFTA in 1993 and the Chemical Weapons Convention in 1997. But as these also attest, presidents have generally prevailed on the most prominent issues through persuasion and bargaining with a swing group of senators or representatives. (And on some issues, like NATO expansion in 1998, division on partisan lines was largely avoided.)

But in Clinton's second term, several key issues suggested the emergence of a new pattern, where partisan conflict not only complicated but often overrode the quest for foreign policy consensus, even on first-order issues. The most prominent example was the Senate rejection of the Comprehensive Test Ban Treaty (CTBT) in 1999. Also victims of the new polarization were legislation to authorize new trade negotiations and funding for U.S. dues to the United Nations and broader nondefense international operations.

Test Ban Fiasco

The CTBT was the international issue where partisan conflict surfaced in rawest form. Substantively, the treaty was a centerpiece in the administration's policy against proliferation of nuclear weapons, and the president personally signed it in 1996, making the United States the first country to do so. More than 150 other countries followed (though only about one-third had ratified it by fall 1999). It was sent to the Senate Foreign Relations Committee in 1997, where Chairman Jesse Helms bottled it up, refusing to hold hearings until the administration submitted and the full Senate voted on (and presumably rejected) amendments to the ABM Treaty negotiated in 1997 and the Kyoto Protocol on climate change. The CTBT was also viewed with skepticism, however, by former officials in Republican administrations not associated with the far right—Brent Scowcroft and Henry Kissinger, for example.

The United States had not conducted nuclear tests since 1992, and in mid-1999 the administration was pressing India to sign and preparing for a special international conference on the treaty in early October. To the White House and the State Department, ratification was overwhelmingly in the U.S. interest. But Republicans controlled the Senate 55–45; to have any chance at all of winning the 67 votes required, Clinton would need the support of Republican centrists like Armed Services Committee Chairman John Warner, senior Foreign Relations member Richard Lugar, and rising internationalist Chuck Hagel—and the cooperation, at the very least, of Majority Leader Trent Lott. Rather than undertake the hard, slogging work of building a bipartisan majority, however, the president worked with Senate Democrats in a public campaign to embarrass and put heat on the Senate Republicans, to make the issue a political winner if not a legislative winner. On July 20, Clinton called for Foreign Relations Commitee hearings in a Rose Garden statement, while Senator Byron Dorgan (D-ND) released a letter on the same day urging such hearings signed by all forty-five Senate Democrats. Dorgan also released a poll, conducted jointly by a Democratic and a Republican polling firm, which found 82 percent of Americans (84 percent of Democrats, 80 percent of Republicans) believing that the United States should ratify the CTBT.[20]

Senator Dorgan upped the ante on September 8, telling his colleagues that until Lott allowed consideration of the CTBT, "I intend to plant myself on the floor like a potted plant" and block any routine business. Other Democrats joined in, including ranking Foreign Relations Democrat Joseph Biden, and explained their strategy two weeks later to presidential national security adviser Samuel Berger. Unknown to them, however, hard-line Senate treaty opponent John Kyl had been working quietly with Helms for months to solidify Republican votes against the CTBT, and had commitments from well over the necessary thirty-four. Lott then called the Democrats' bluff. He reversed himself on September 30 and offered to take up the treaty, with a vote in two weeks. Democrats, thinking they had a shot at persuading enough Republicans, quickly agreed.[21] They learned within a week that they had no chance of winning, and suddenly became alarmed about the global impact of a Senate rejection. (The Senate had not voted down an important treaty since the Treaty of Versailles in 1920.)

By early October the White House and Minority Leader Tom Daschle had taken an 180-degree turn and were negotiating with Lott to *avoid* having a vote. Sixty-two senators, including twenty-four Republicans, signed a letter initiated by Warner and Democrat Pat Moynihan urging that the matter be put off until 2001, and the president formally requested to Lott that he "postpone consideration." But this now required either unanimous consent in the Senate or an extraordinary procedural vote. Hard-line Republicans, wanting to sink the treaty once and for all, blocked the first way out. Lott was unwilling to call for, or acquiesce in, the second. So on October 13, the Senate voted 48–51 against ratifying the treaty, with only 4 Republicans in favor.[22]

"Never before," declared the president, "has a serious treaty involving nuclear weapons been handled in such a reckless and ultimately partisan way." He did not state that his own party bore its full share of the blame.[23] Nor did his national security adviser help matters when he gave an impassioned speech eight days later attacking "the isolationist right in the Congress" for the treaty's defeat.[24]

Trade Stalemate

More complicated was the conflict over trade legislation, where the division was not precisely along partisan lines. Since the completion of the Uruguay Round negotiations in 1994, Clinton had lacked the "fast track" authority granted all of his predecessors since Richard Nixon.[25] In principle, the president and Republican congressional leaders both supported such legislation. Arrayed against them were the majority of Democrats (reflecting virulent labor opposition) and a sizable minority of Republicans (reflecting Buchanan-style populism). But Clinton wanted to broaden trade negotiations to include labor and environmental standards; Republicans were overwhelmingly opposed to this. And it was this ideological/political division that would prove decisive.

Unwilling to reopen the political wounds with labor sustained in the NAFTA battle, Clinton and his highly political trade negotiator, Mickey Kantor, rebuffed Republican attempts to renew fast track in 1995. Then, with reelection safely behind him, the president took until September 1997 to present a specific proposal. This gave labor and environmental critics ample time to mobilize, while business held back until it knew the precise content of Clinton's bill. By September, most Democrats were locked into opposition, and in quest of a heavily Republican House majority Clinton followed their wishes and largely excluded labor and environmental measures. In the end, vote-counts found a maximum of 21 percent of Democrats in favor (65 percent had backed the Uruguay Round/WTO bill three years earlier), and Speaker Newt Gingrich could not make up the difference.

Clinton first had the vote delayed, then asked that the bill be pulled in order to avoid what seemed certain defeat. Gingrich complied. But he then resurrected the bill over Clinton's objections in September 1998, in a primarily partisan move designed to squeeze Democrats caught between labor and business constituencies. The vote was 243–180 against, with just 29 of 200 Democrats recorded in favor. Prominent among those working in opposition was Public Citizen, the "consumer" lobby, and it built on the momentum gained by these victories to disrupt the Seattle WTO Ministerial Conference in December 1999.

This again was an issue where the public was in the middle: favoring trade expansion and reciprocal reduction of trade barriers, but also supporting, by strong margins, the broadening of the agenda to include labor and the environment.[26] But on this issue, as on some others, the political extremes were less internationalist than the center, so their reinforcement posed a particularly severe challenge. In substance, compromise was clearly conceivable, one that would both reflect public concerns and "advance the cause of global labor and environmental standards while authorizing the negotiation of new agreements to reduce barriers to trade."[27] But polarization was too deep, and trust was largely absent.

Uncle Sam as Deadbeat

A third prominent victim of partisan polarization has been funding for U.S. international involvement, particularly the payment of U.S. back dues to the United Nations. Here the public has been consistently supportive, despite persistent myths to the contrary.[28] And presidents of both parties have pressed for funding, Bush at least as much as Clinton. But with resistance from Foreign Relations Chairman Helms in the Senate and right-to-life Republicans in the House, the going has been extraordinarily hard.

By U.N. calculation, U.S. arrears for regular dues and peacekeeping assessments rose from $287 million at the end of 1992 to $1.4 billion four years later. (The administration estimated the debt at $1 billion.) This generated serious financial problems for the organization, and growing international criticism of the United States. In June 1997, the administration came to a complex agreement with Helms and ranking Foreign Relations Democrat Biden. This provided for payment of $819 million over three years—$200 million less than the administration had requested and another $400 billion below the U.N.'s estimate—and only if administrative reforms were undertaken and the U.S. share of the total U.N. budget lowered from 25 to 20 percent.

But House Republicans were pressing another agenda. They attached to the legislation a rider that denied U.S. funding to U.N. population programs, because some organizations that were instruments of these programs were involved in the provision of abortions. (U.S. policy has long barred use of U.S. aid funds for this purpose.) President Clinton, under pressure from pro-choice groups and because he thought it bad policy, refused to accept this proviso in 1997, and again in 1998. Finally, in the fall of 1999 compromise abortion language was negotiated and the funds were appropriated. In the meantime, the United States twice narrowly avoided losing its vote in the General Assembly because of its arrearages. (Helms did make a peace offering of sorts, visiting the U.N. headquarters himself and inviting officials down for a hearing in early 2000.) The record was no better on the broader funding of U.S. international engagement.[29]

On all three issues (CTBT the most, trade the least), the public supported constructive U.S. international action and favored compromise that balanced competing values. On all three, Congresses of prior decades would surely have found a way forward, or at minimum, a way to avoid the United States humiliating itself internationally on a matter of high national security concern. But Washington political actors—particularly members of

Congress—saw the issues through partisan and ideological lenses and failed to display the readiness, or maintain the communication, that was necessary for compromise to come about.

THE SPLINTERING OF LIBERAL INTERNATIONALISM

But there remains one final question. Why, on issues where the public is clearly with them, don't the liberal internationalists do better on Capitol Hill? Why didn't the consistent majority favoring payment of U.S. dues carry more weight politically? Why does Congress consistently cut spending for "Function 150" (the budget category for State, USAID, the United Nations, and multilateral programs) and provide unsought money to the Pentagon?

The answer does not lie in the general structure of public—or leadership—opinion.[30] In his comprehensive analysis of the results of the quadrennial Chicago Council on Foreign Relations survey, Eugene R. Wittkopf found nonisolationist opinion in the United States divided three ways in the post-Vietnam era. *Hardliners* favored military toughness but were skeptical about cooperative measures—aid, arms control negotiations, and so forth; *accommodationists* took the opposite stand; *internationalists* back both the "hard" and the "soft" instruments of global engagement. But the balance was not tilted toward the hardliners: they were generally fewer in number than accommodationists among both the mass public and the leaders, and they never reached 25 percent of the population.[31]

Nor, aside from the issue of abortion, do we find activist groups of the right exercising disproportionate sway. U.S. legislative processes on the United Nations, or U.N. peacekeeping, or foreign aid do *not* feature prominent, let alone dominant, lobbying groups pressing Washington to cut or eliminate public funding.

But neither do they feature strong organized groups in support. The United Nations Association, for example, may have 180 chapters and 30,000 members, but it lacks the cutting-edge energy that it (and predecessor movements) possessed half a century ago. Today the forces of cooperative internationalism are fragmented—the main energy goes not into supporting a broad liberal international agenda for the United States, but into specific causes: the environment and human rights in particular. These cause groups target other internationalist forces, business in particular. They also target government. In their campaigns to increase membership, raise funds, and mobilize support, they are prone to trash, even demonize, the policies and structures that others have built to enhance global welfare. The Public Citizen campaign against "GATTzilla" and its WTO successor is a particularly egregious example. But more generally, such groups play upon, and enhance, the skeptical, can't-trust-government mood that is so pervasive in today's America.

WHAT MIGHT BE DONE?

For supporters of U.S. international engagement who believe in cooperative, multilateral approaches to world problems, the good news is that the American people are with them. The public is willing to support reasonable efforts and proportionate expenditures. It is ready to be led if leaders evoke widely shared values: doing our fair share, helping people in need, pursuing programs that work. And this readiness to go along extends to putting American troops in harm's way, if the ends are just and the means seem workable. Washington was surprised when (in an atmosphere of bitter partisan discord over the issue) public opinion surveys showed majority support for the NATO campaign to save Kosovo.[32] Those who had studied previous polls on Somalia, or Haiti, or Bosnia, or U.N. peacekeeping, or humanitarian intervention in general, were not surprised. People favor U.S. participation in multilateral action to right grievous wrongs if it offers reasonable prospects for success.

The bad news is that general public support isn't enough. On international engagement, Americans are permissive, not demanding. And their politicians are as far away from them than they have been in this author's lifetime, driven by ideological views and pressures and partisan animosities that the public, by and large, does not share.

Thus, while building a political base for U.S. international engagement can and should begin with responsiveness to *real* public attitudes and concerns, it cannot end there. It must also seek ways to both bridge and mute the partisan divide. The president must make this a high priority—for reasons extending beyond the international realm.

One strategy George W. Bush might pursue is to cite, repeatedly and explicitly, poll evidence in support of U.S. international engagement.[33] In seeking decent funding for the Function 150 account (as Clinton never seriously did), President Bush should stress that strong majorities of Americans are in favor. In arguing for troop deployments in future Kosovos, the president should stress that Americans *want* to do their share in international peacekeeping, particularly in cases of egregious ethnic cleansing. He should not allow Jesse Helms to dominate the media with assertions that Americans view the United Nations "with disdain,"[34] when every survey shows majority support for the organization and most Americans want the United Nations to be stronger.

Reference to public opinion needs to be artful. If the president sounds like he is taking actions *only* because of the polling numbers, he will bring down an avalanche of criticism on his head. References to public opinion need to be blended with, and often subordinated to, arguments that a line of policy is right in substantive terms. But with this caveat, it can only strengthen the case for a policy if it can be shown to be consistent with what Americans want to have happen in the world.

In this spirit, the president and his senior aides should place particular stress on the *values* that Americans hold. In pressing for trade compromise, for example, they should note that the public backs open competition *and* help for trade-displaced workers *and* the enhancement of labor and environmental standards worldwide.[35] On issues like global warming, they should stress that citizens are strong supporters of measures to protect the earth, but do not share the antigrowth perspective of some in the environmental community.[36] Such arguments will not, by themselves, win policy battles. But they will help to frame the debate, invite competing interests to join and bargain, and encourage individual members of Congress to move toward the center on specific issues—as some would indeed like to do.

Of course, this sort of public presentation strategy will have, at best, only modest impact on the ideological divide itself. Its roots run deeper, and are not to be found primarily in the foreign policy sphere. So constructive U.S. government action on international issues will require heavy doses of old-fashioned politics: compromise, logrolling, deal making, giving something to both sides, all of the above. And it will require old-fashioned comity—a word and a condition not very visible in today's Washington. The president must/should reach out to leaders of the other party, as Bush has done to some degree. Recognizing that they will not be with him on most issues, he needs to build a basis for ongoing communication so they can help him, and he them, on some crucial issues. And by meeting regularly with Senate and House majority and minority leaders together, he might help them improve their bilateral relationships, particularly in the venomous lower chamber.

For a range of reasons, restoration of personal trust has become impossible for Bill Clinton. But his successor, George W. Bush, entered office with a "new shave," as *Washington Post* cartoonist Herblock gave even Richard Nixon in 1969. Hopefully, he will make the most of it.

I am grateful to Josh Pollack for research assistance on the Test Ban Fiasco section.

NOTES

1. David C. King, "The Polarization of American Parties and Distrust of Government," in Joseph S. Nye Jr., Philip D. Zelikow, and David C. King, eds., *Why People Don't Trust Government* (Cambridge, Mass.: Harvard University Press, 1997), 178.

2. Benjamin I. Page and Robert Y. Shapiro, *The Rational Public: Fifty Years of Trends in Americans' Policy Preferences* (Chicago: University of Chicago Press, 1992).

3. The data from this study is presented in full detail in Steven Kull, I. M. Destler, and Clay Ramsey, *The Foreign Policy Gap: How Policymakers Misread the Public* (College Park, Md.: Center for International and Security Studies, University of Maryland,

October 1997); and more concisely in Kull and Destler, *Misreading the Public: The Myth of a New Isolationism* (Washington, D.C.: Brookings Institution Press, 1999).

4. John E. Reilly, ed., *American Public Opinion and U.S. Foreign Policy 1999* (Chicago: Chicago Council on Foreign Relations, 1999), 12.

5. *Misreading the Public*, chapter 5. The survey by the Chicago Council on Foreign Relations (Ibid.) is less positive, finding Americans "split [47–45%] on the overall idea of giving economic aid to other nations." (*American Public Opinion 1999*, p. 21.) But Pew, *The Washington Post*, and PIPA find 76–87 percent wanting to provide at least some foreign aid. (*Misreading*, pp. 117–118.)

6. For the full-blown analysis, see *Misreading the Public*, chapter 11, from which this summary language is drawn.

7. Thomas L. Hughes, "The Crack-Up," *Foreign Policy*, no. 40 (fall 1980, pp. 33–60. See also I. M. Destler, Leslie H. Gelb, and Anthony Lake, "From Establishment to Professional Elite," in *Our Own Worst Enemy: The Unmaking of American Foreign Policy* (New York: Simon and Schuster, 1984).

8. When asked to identify themselves on the political spectrum, an average of 77 percent of voters in the 1972–1976 period labeled themselves middle of the road, slightly liberal, or slightly conservative, or said they didn't know or hadn't thought about it. In 1990–1994, the average was 75 percent. Comparing the same two periods, the margin of Democrats over Republicans fell from 20 percentage points to 11. (Calculated from tables in King, "The Polarization of American Parties," pp. 158 and 163.)

9. Ibid., pp. 165, 172.

10. Calculated by Sarah Binder, reported ibid., pp. 166, 168.

11. Richard E. Cohen, "Going to Extremes: Our Annual Vote Ratings," A Special Supplement to *National Journal*, February 26, 2000, p. 4.

12. "The Dynamics of Legislative Gridlock, 1947–96," *American Political Science Review*, Vol. 93, No. 3 (September 1999): 527–528. The causes of this polarization are beyond the scope of this chapter. One is surely the decennial congressional redistricting process, dominated by the drive for safe seats for incumbents and ethnic groups. To the degree this is successful—and it has been very successful—it makes *intra*party politics the primary influence on who is elected, reinforcing the impact of party activists with polar views. Other plausible forces include the rise of television, which may reward confrontational approaches, and the impact of activist "cause" groups, treated later in this analysis.

13. There have been fluctuations within the period. As measured by a "Trust in Government Index" calculated from responses to the question posed biennially by the University of Michigan's National Election Studies—"How much of the time do you think you can trust the government in Washington to do what is right?"—confidence plummeted from a high of 61% in 1966 to 29% in 1974 and 27% in 1980, rose to 47% in 1986, and then plunged to a record low of 26% in 1994. It has rebounded slightly since. A convenient source of data and analysis is Joseph S. Nye Jr. et al., eds., *Why People Don't Trust Government* (Cambridge, Mass.: Harvard University Press, 1997). The numbers here are from Table 4–3 on page 129. Because it gives different weights to strong and moderate responses ("all of the time" vs. "most of the time," for example) the numbers differ from those in our text, but the trend is the same.

14. Center on Policy Attitudes, *Expecting More Say: The American Public on its Role in Government Decisionmaking* (Washington, D.C.: Center on Policy Analysis, May 1999), section 1.

15. Ibid.

16. King, "The Polarization of American Parties," p. 176.

17. Ibid., p. 178.

18. Richard Neustadt, "The Politics of Mistrust," in Nye et al., *Why People Don't Trust Government*, p. 185.

19. Ibid., p. 187.

20. Craig Cerniello, "White House, Key Senators Intensify Push for CTBT," *Arms Control Today*, July–August 1999.

21. John M. Broder, "The Tactics: Quietly, Dextrously, Senate Republicans Set a Trap," *New York Times*, October 14, 1999.

22. Eric Schmitt, "Senate Kills Test Ban Treaty in Crushing Loss for Clinton," *New York Times*, October 14, 1999.

23. Dave Boyer, "Senate Rejects Treaty on Nuke Testing," *The Washington Times*, October 14, 1999.

24. Samuel R. Berger, "American Power: Hegemony, Isolationism, or Engagement," Address to Council on Foreign Relations, October 21, 1999 (available on White House website). The assistant also attacked the "new isolationists" for "devastating cuts to our foreign affairs budget."

25. I. M. Destler, *Renewing Fast-Track Legislation*, Institute for International Economics, Policy Analysis No. 50, September 1997, esp. part I.

26. Steven Kull, *Americans on Globalization: A Study of U.S. Public Attitudes*, Program on International Policy Attitudes, Center for International and Security Studies at the University of Maryland, Washington, D.C., March 28, 2000.

27. I. M. Destler and Peter J. Balint, *The New Politics of American Trade: Trade, Labor, and the Environment*, Institute for International Economics, Policy Analysis No. 58, p. 65.

28. Kull and Destler, *Misreading the Public*, chapters 3–5, 7–8.

29. See Robert C. Kaiser, "Foreign Disservice," *Washington Post*, April 16, 2000, p. B1.

30. The CCFR results suggest that American leaders generally are not polarized to anywhere near the extent that political party leaders and activists are.

31. Eugene R. Wittkopf, *Faces of Internationalism: Public Opinion and American Foreign Policy* (Durham, N.C.: Duke University Press, 1990), pp. 26, 116. His analysis draws on the CCFR surveys of 1984 through 1996.

32. Steven Kull, *Americans on Kosovo: A Study of U.S. Policy Attitudes*, Program on International Policy Attitudes, Center for International and Security Studies at the University of Maryland, Washington, D.C., June 1999.

33. This should not be done simply to score political points, as the release of new CTBT poll numbers in August 1999 most have seemed to Republicans, but in parallel with serious administration efforts to work the issue with opponents and fence-sitters to win a constructive resolution.

34. *Washington Post*, October 8, 1997.

35. Kull, *Americans on Globalization*, pp. 5–25.

36. Richard J. Ellis and Fred Thompson, "Culture and the Environment in the Pacific Northwest," *American Political Science Review*, Vol. 91 (December 1997): 885–897.

6

Politics, Humanitarian Values, and American National Interests

Thomas G. Weiss

Humanitarian ideas have become central to defining American interests and making foreign policy in the post-Cold War period. Although often disparaged by humanitarians as obstacles to realizing their objectives, calculations by decision makers explain why intervention occurs, or does not.

Modern humanitarianism is usually dated from the Biafran War of 1967, but the importance of humanitarian values has been growing gradually, albeit fitfully, since the founding of the International Committee of the Red Cross (ICRC) in the middle of the nineteenth century. Their prominence since the end of the Cold War is another illustration of Richard Ullman's prescience in his 1983 article that expanded the notion of national security.[1] Perhaps more than any other arena, humanitarian action demonstrates the pertinence of an expansive definition.

Ideals and *Realpolitik* often mix in the murky waters surrounding Washington's foreign and defense policies. Michael Doyle's chapter in this volume explains why Machiavelli, John Hobbes, and William Wordsworth would take issue with attempts to infuse values into State Department, Pentagon, and White House calculations. For those seeking to enhance the role of values, the work of Reinhold Niebuhr is more relevant. He rejected idealism as well as the depravity of man (and woman). He avoided lapsing into either utopianism or cynicism.

Niebuhr's approach is relevant for this volume and chapter. He appreciated the limits of values in the making of foreign and defense policies but nonetheless left room for their intrusion. "If conscience and reason can be insinuated into the resulting struggle," he wrote, "they can only qualify but not abolish it."[2] Greater moral attention from policy and decision makers will not bring peace on earth but can be conducive to protecting and even improving the fragile character of what we should unashamedly call "civilized life." This is no small achievement.

The past decade has witnessed the dramatic growth in the weight of humanitarian values to justify American diplomatic and military action. "In the 1990s," summarizes Adam Roberts, "humanitarian issues have played a historically unprecedented role in international politics."[3] In the dramatic example of the military campaign in Kosovo, Michael Ignatieff notes that "its legitimacy [depends] on what fifty years of human rights has done to our moral instincts, weakening the presumption in favor of state sovereignty, strengthening the presumption in favor of intervention when massacre and deportation become state policy."[4]

This chapter concentrates on the veritable revolution in ends that is driving foreign policy. Limitations of space prevent dealing with the means and consequences of humanitarian intervention that Doyle includes in his ethical template. Moreover, I have written extensively elsewhere about these issues,[5] and both Michael O'Hanlon and David Callahan analyze in some detail means and consequences of military force in Kosovo in this book.

Yet, a brief aside is in order because there can be no doubt that this decade's experiments with the application of American military might on behalf of humanitarian efforts have been decidedly mixed. There are not humanitarian solutions to fundamentally political problems. Humanitarianism is ambiguous. On the one hand, it can reduce suffering and save lives. On the other hand, it can be counterproductive by freeing up local resources and fueling armed conflict. Or humanitarianism can make the lives of many victims worse than without it. Or worse yet, it can be an alibi that impedes more vigorous responses. The appearance of "doing something" in the face of a tragedy permits cheap moralizing but can prevent riskier sorts of commitments that are necessary to resolve a crisis. The well-fed dead in Bosnia prior to Dayton aptly illustrate that a humanitarian veneer can help make collective spinelessness a more palatable policy option than collective defense or security.[6] The July 1995 tragedy in the "safe area" of Srebrenica, in the words of the United Nation's own hard-hitting inquiry, "will haunt our history forever."[7]

Notwithstanding this caveat, the role of humanitarian values in U.S. military intervention in northern Iraq, Bosnia, Haiti, Somalia, Rwanda, and Kosovo is noteworthy and encouraging. As President Clinton told NATO's May 1999 fiftieth anniversary summit in Washington, the war in Kosovo was declared to halt "the slaughter of innocents," a theme that he embroidered in his September 1999 address to the U.N.'s General Assembly when he argued that the intervention "helped to vindicate the principles and purposes of the U.N. Charter."[8] The disappearance of Westphalian barriers to humanitarian intervention should not be mourned, although conservative pundits like Charles Krauthammer are skeptical about "humanitarian war" and concerned about the use of military force for such purposes.[9]

American vital interests were not involved in Somalia and Rwanda, and many analysts would say something similar about the former Yugoslavia and Haiti, although European stability and Caribbean refugees are normally seen as more central than suffering in Africa. Only in Iraq were geopolitics controlling. And even there the humanitarian intervention in April 1991 should be distinguished from the Gulf War because the efforts, still ongoing, on behalf of the Kurds are more striking as a formidable intrusion into the prerogatives of a sovereign state than as a *Realpolitik* calculation.

This chapter briefly discusses tragedies in the 1990s as background for the changing role of humanitarian ideas, in the United Nations and in Washington. It concludes with an analysis of the evolving nature of international society at the dawn of the twenty-first century.

BAD NEWS: SUFFERING IN THE 1990s

Since the fall of the Berlin Wall and the implosion of the Soviet Union, the parameters of international security have changed.[10] The ebbing in bipolar confrontation initially facilitated both the resolution of lingering regional conflicts and a renaissance of the United Nations[11] However, the initial binge accompanied by the celebratory rhetoric of President George Bush's "new world order" quickly changed to a post-Cold War hangover. For every local war that ended, at least one new one erupted. The population of refugees and other war victims exploded. At the end of the decade, the number of refugees had shrunk to about 13.5 million from earlier totals almost twice that high, but the number of internally displaced persons (IDPs) had grown considerably larger (at least 17–18 million). When IDPs were first counted in 1982, there were only a million, at which time there were about 10.5 million refugees.[12]

Whatever the exact numbers and categories of victims, they are horrific and undoubtedly will remain high. The punch line for pundits and the opening line in many a scholarly article is that *international* security remains an awkward and challenging subject when virtually all armed conflicts are internal[13] and the conduct of belligerents, in William Durch's dramatic understatement, is so "uncivil."[14]

Nationalistic, ethnic, and communal tensions are the predominant factor in contemporary war and involuntary displacement. Until recently, the most essential humanitarian principles (neutrality, impartiality, and consent) had been relatively uncontroversial along with the key operating procedure of seeking consent from belligerents. These principles too have become casualties in the 1990s. A host of factors have challenged the classical posture: the complete disregard for international humanitarian law by war criminals and even by child soldiers; the direct targeting of civilians and relief personnel;

the use of foreign aid to fuel conflicts and war economies; and the protracted nature of many so-called emergencies.[15] War has returned to Europe. In spite of the indictment of a sitting head of state (Slobodan Milosevic) and his eventual incarceration, genocide is alive and well. In many ways, international humanitarian law seems to have been formulated to deal with a different world—one populated by governments and regular armies whose interests were often served by respecting the laws of war.[16] In writing of old-fashioned humanitarianism, David Rieff has gone so far as to suggest "the death of a good idea."[17]

The United Nations and regional institutions of all stripes have deployed peace operations. Hardly the collective security of the U.N. Charter variety,[18] they nonetheless have helped to resolve, manage, or render the outcomes of wars somewhat less painful than they might otherwise have been. We have not yet arrived at what the editor of *Foreign Affairs* prematurely identified in 1994 as "the springtime of intervention."[19] But outside military efforts to pick up the pieces from armed conflicts have become a prominent, some would say fashionable, feature of contemporary international relations and part of a policy and scholarly growth industry.[20]

Amid these depressing developments has also arisen a willingness by states on occasion to act on the humanitarian imperative. What has led to what Edward Luttwak has dubbed "Kofi's Rule . . . whereby human rights outrank sovereignty"?[21]

News: The Secretary General and Intervention[22]

One of the secretary general's ceremonial tasks is to open the U.N. General Assembly, but Kofi Annan's September 1999 speech was anything but routine. The 54th session's dual focus was on globalization and humanitarian intervention. But his stance on the latter touched a raw nerve: "States bent on criminal behavior [should] know that frontiers are not the absolute defence . . . that massive and systematic violations of human rights—wherever they may take place—should not be allowed to stand."[23]

These were powerful words from the bully pulpit. They continued at the September 2000 Millennium Summit after they had appeared earlier at Ditchley Park.[24] Annan consciously sought to contradict the stereotype of a secretary general, especially a national from a former colony, who did not "preach a sermon against intervention." Instead of the usual handful of responses during the general debate, there were almost fifty along with four plenary sessions between October 6 and 11; the Security Council had a two-day session in late November to discuss implications;[25] and developing countries have sought to establish an open-ended working group to dispute Annan's approach.

No one is upset with the "most pacific" part of his intervention "continuum," the standard bill-of-fare of international relations. But Annan's statements on the "most coercive" ones, military force, amount to arguing that "sovereignty is no longer sacrosanct."[26]

The lowered threshold for coercion to enforce minimal human rights is approaching conventional wisdom. It is one thing for the Organization for Security and Cooperation in Europe (OSCE) to approve a new charter that proclaims local conflicts to be the legitimate concern of all European states, or for President Clinton in his General Assembly address to plead "to stop outbreaks of mass killing and displacement."[27] It is quite another to hear directly from the secretary general how few sovereign clothes remain on emperors who are war criminals. The host of military interventions in the 1990s add up to a set of powerful precedents. Nonintervention, the organizing principle of international relations since Westphalia, is not what it once was.

GOOD NEWS: SHAPING AMERICAN
INTERESTS WITH HUMANITARIAN VALUES

Although many generalizations are contested, the post-Cold War era has certainly been characterized by considerable flux in the search for consensus about fundamental threats and interests. Judith Goldstein and Robert Keohane have demonstrated the importance of ideas to the foreign policy process, particularly as at the present moment when "periods in which power relations are fluid and interests and strategies are unclear or lack consensus."[28] To argue that humanitarian values are important in and of themselves does not mean that they are divorced from power and interests. Quite the contrary. Because humanitarian ideas explain what is driving much of Western foreign and defense policy, it is useful to apply four insights from the literature about the impact of ideas in foreign policy[29] to intervention and state sovereignty: Ideas inform the definition of what constitutes interests; ideas are important in setting priorities; ideas are crucial in forming new political and bureaucratic coalitions; and ideas become embedded in institutions. Looking through the prism of humanitarian coercion over the past decade shows how ends have changed and how ideas operate causally and operationally.

First, humanitarian values have influenced the composition of national interests. Kosovo jumps to mind, but numerous operations in the 1990s substantiate that military force may be employed for human rights and humanitarian purposes. Rather than examining more successful cases, one way to appreciate the role of ideas in framing vital interests is by posing a stark counterfactual to the Somalia debacle—what would have happened with Harry Truman instead of Bill Clinton?[30] What constituted U.S. interests was not predetermined and fixed but could have been shaped creatively by a leader. With the residue of Vietnam still very much in the corridors, the orthodox view about troop withdrawal from Somalia is that vital interests were not at stake.[31] In the wake of the dramatic images of American soldiers dying in a distant place with no connection to core interests, the argument goes, the president had no alternative besides retreat.

Yet he could have responded to both conservatives and liberals. He could have stressed that Washington's credibility was on the line and that teenage grenade-launchers from a fourth-rate African military power could not get away, literally, with the murder of eighteen Rangers and hold U.S. foreign policy hostage. He also could have emphasized respect for universal standards and international commitments, in this case the Security Council's authorization to protect humanitarian space.

Domestic criticism could have been muted and Presidential Decision Directive 25 (PDD-25) could have looked different from the document that has, since its signing in the midst of the Rwandan genocide, restricted Washington's participation in peace operations and its approval of others' operations. There is no need to prop up a straw man of a consistent intervention policy. Neither the United States nor the larger community of responsible states can respect a universal humanitarian impulse. Selective indignation and selective intervention are inevitable. Decision makers are required to ask routinely whether, how, and why. However, if we fast forward to March 1999, it would have been unnecessary for Clinton to promise to avoid the use of ground troops in Kosovo. Rather, he could have framed American interests as sufficiently threatened by a tidal wave of Kosovar refugees and the legitimization of ethnic cleansing to risk lives on the ground rather than initially make matters worse in remaining at 15,000 feet to soften up the Serbs.

The American population is not as casualty-averse or as mindlessly prone to unilateralism as is commonly assumed, as I. M. Destler's contribution to this volume suggests. The Persian Gulf War is one illustration as is the 1989 invasion of Panama. If interests are at stake and an effective case is made, the population will support a military effort and endure casualties. A different sales pitch along with a different framing of U.S. interests could have given different results in Somalia as well. In fact, many observers interpret Clinton's September 1999 address to the General Assembly as an indication of a waning "Vietmalia syndrome."

Second, ideas are crucial in helping states to set priorities among conflicting norms and provide a road map when strategists need to choose. Specifically, humanitarian ideas are key in addressing the conflict between sovereignty and human rights. Respect for the former has traditionally been viewed as the bedrock of international order, whereas the latter requires the expectation that outside military coercion may halt massive abuses of rights.

Should human rights violations justifying external intervention prevail over the doctrine of sovereignty? On occasion, the answer clearly is "yes." The definitions of sovereignty and of national interests have been dramatically expanded to include humanitarian values. Bryan Hehir has noted that "The contemporary interest in military intervention (much to the dismay of realists) is driven by normative concerns."[32] The policy relevance of voices advocating justified humanitarian intervention has increased.[33]

The rapid, in historical terms, evolution of measures on behalf of IDPs and the embrace of their plight by intergovernmental (IGOs) and nongovernmental organizations (NGOs) demonstrate the increasing weight of humanitarian values in state decision making.[34] In a number of publications, the Secretary General's Special Representative on IDPs Frances Deng assumes the continuing centrality of the Westphalian system and seeks pragmatically to reconcile intervention with the traditional prerogatives of the state through "sovereignty as responsibility."[35] To the three characteristics usually considered to be attributes of a sovereign (territory, a people, and authority), Deng adds a fourth (respect for a minimal standard of human rights). The secretary general himself has not gone as far as French activists Bernard Kouchner (former minister and head of the U.N. operation in Kosovo) and Mario Bettati would like because he espouses no duty or obligation to override sovereignty.[36] But Annan is approaching Deng's notion, which joins political philosopher Charles Beitz's earlier argument that nonintervention is a derivative of more basic principles of justice.[37]

The power of this approach resides in underscoring a state's responsibilities and accountabilities to domestic *and* international constituencies. Accordingly, a state is unable to claim the prerogatives of sovereignty unless it meets internationally agreed responsibilities, which include respecting human rights and providing life-sustenance to its citizens. Failure to meet such obligations legitimizes intrusion and even military intervention by the society of responsible states. "In the real world, principles often collide," Clinton told the General Assembly, "and tough choices must be made." The language of U.N. resolutions and of such public policy discourse as Annan's and Clinton's speeches is not fluff but the veritable stuff of priority-setting when norms clash.

Third, humanitarian intervention has made possible new coalitions—the media and the public can demand that something be done, the military can respond, and relief agencies can ask for help because on occasion they require both the war-fighting and logistic capacities of the armed forces. Commitments by major powers rest largely on their leaders' calculations of domestic costs, benefits, and risks. The arithmetic in part reflects the success of domestic and transnational constituencies in mobilizing support for humanitarian action and in altering conceptions of interests and rewards.

One example is Washington's change of tack on Haiti in 1994 after effective lobbying by the supporters of Jean-Bertrand Aristide, especially

TransAfrica and the Congressional Black Caucus.[38] American leadership in Haiti beginning in September 1994 and in Bosnia after the Dayton Accord in November 1995 (a year and two years, respectively, after the October 1993 fiasco in Somalia) suggest that when interests are perceived to be sufficiently involved and foreign policy framed accordingly, minds can be concentrated and changed. In Kosovo, humanitarian arguments managed to carry the day even when aerial bombing entailed deterioration in Washington's relations with Moscow and Beijing. As was the case in northern Iraq, and despite the Vietnam and Somalia syndromes, American interests were framed in Haiti, Bosnia, and ultimately Kosovo to merit military intervention with significant humanitarian motivations and certainly significant humanitarian consequences.

A pertinent, more recent example is the "Ottawa process" on antipersonnel land mines. This case is worth examining because of what its dynamics portend for the future even if the mind-set in Washington remains for the moment more respective of the U.S. military's preferences than of the humanitarian values that have penetrated more deeply the foreign policies of other countries. A transnational coalition successfully imbued the domestic politics of a sufficient number of states with enough humanitarian concern to redefine state interests in a way that led to the treaty.[39] Unlike most cases of transnationalism, this one touches directly on the high politics of security.

This example suggests the importance of substate and transnational actors in influencing, framing, and ultimately redefining state interests. The initial impetus in the anti-land mines campaign was provided by a formidable coalition of civil society organizations. The International Campaign To Ban Land Mines, founded in 1993, grew out of private advocacy organizations whose main orientation was domestic and public (that is, oriented toward change in *state* behavior). Its success depended on co-opting *states* (and notably Canada, the Scandinavian countries, and South Africa), in "determin[ing] what states want."[40] Their support depended not only on the moral appeal of the cause but also on the consideration of domestic and international political interests and risks.

State involvement was necessary to translate social pressure into international law. The key to the outcome was to move states and alter definitions of perceived interests by persuading politicians. A basic aspect of the process was to remove land mines from the apolitical (that is, essentially nonpartisan) realm of military strategy and to place the issue firmly in the political realm of domestic constituencies.

Humanitarian values are in the forefront of concerns motivating the societal forces that determine leaders' perceptions of interest. In commenting on the intervention in Kosovo, Max Frankel concluded that "It's those pictures of almost unfathomable atrocity that once again drive our politics."[41] This is not the place to discuss the so-called CNN effect, which influences both the perception of tragedy and the pace of decision making.[42] However, the increasing reach and efficiency of international communications along with the related growing influence of transnational and nongovernmental actors point toward a changing domestic environment and decision-making context. Armed with graphic images of suffering, these nonstate actors help shape definitions of state interest. We are not witnessing a phenomenon of ceding state authority, but rather of its being influenced from outside by coalitions of actors with humanitarian values. Their agendas to some extent and in some circumstances become those of their governments.

Fourth, and this discussion can be brief because of its obviousness, humanitarian ideas have become embedded within institutions and thus takes on a life of their own. New institutional structures in virtually all Western governments and their militaries as well as in IGOs and NGOs attest to the organizational manifestations of humanitarian priorities.[43] Careers, military and civilian, are being made and promotions given as a result of humanitarian business over the last decade. This is a fact of the budget processes in Washington and Brussels, and in U.N. and NGO headquarters. Another indication is a major theme in publications from the United Nations, the Organisation for Economic Co-operation and Development (OECD), and such alternative critical sources as *The Reality of Aid*—namely that emergency funding is replacing development assistance.[44]

INTERNATIONAL SOCIETY, NOT INTERNATIONAL COMMUNITY

International society, a constellation of states seeking to regulate their relations while maintaining autonomy, rests on the mutual acceptance of the principle of equal sovereignty. To reiterate, humanitarian values are intruding into American perceptions of national interest, but there has been no change in the commitment to sovereignty by the United States or other states. Indeed, this is a central reality in Edward Luck's explanation of America's fundamental ambivalence toward the United Nations.[45]

Governmental rhetoric continues in large part to be framed in Westphalian terms. The norm of nonintervention is intact but seriously dented. The meaning of sovereignty is evolving as a result of normative developments as well as international action. The most promising development, at least for those who espouse humanitarian values, is the unequivocal challenge to the notion that official recognition implies an absolute obligation of nonintervention in domestic affairs. It emanates from those who argue that the right to status as a sovereign is associated with respecting generally agreed standards about the treatment of citizens. It builds on the Universal Declaration of Human Rights and helps to finesse the contradictions in the U.N. Charter between the rights of individuals and of states. It also is an extension of actions in the 1960s, 1970s, and 1980s to apply economic coercion against white-majority rule within the borders of Rhodesia and South Africa—which opened the flood-gates in terms of domestic policies being framed as threats to international peace and security.

As discussed in contributions to this book by David Denoon and Thomas Banchoff, the erosion or evolution in state sovereignty is fostered in part by globalization and technological advances that permit activities across national boundaries that are essentially outside state control.[46] But the normative dimensions are at least as striking. Arguably, Western liberal values over the last century and a half have been moving toward moral obligations that go beyond family, beyond tribe, and beyond nation. The impalpable moral ideal is concern about the fate of other people, no matter how far away. Henry Dunant's efforts to establish the ICRC[47] can be contrasted with the more geographically circumscribed approach of his Swiss compatriot, Jean-Jacques Rousseau, who had emphasized the importance of kin, kith, and ken: "It appears that the feeling of humanity evaporates and grows feeble in embracing all mankind, and that we cannot be affected by the calamities of Tartary or Japan, in the same manner as we are by those of European nations."[48]

In terms of international relations theory, the space occupied by humanitarian values in Hedley Bull's paradoxical "anarchical society" is expanding. Order within this society is based on common interests, rules, and institutions. The essential common interest of states lies in their shared acceptance of the elementary goals of social life (survival, truth, and property) and derives from fear "of unrestricted violence, of the instability of agreements or of the insecurity of their independence or sovereignty."[49] Individual members of the society of states share an interest in the preservation not only of their own sovereignty but also of this principle as it applies to other states.

The contents and interpretation of this principle are, however, not cast in concrete but rather, in the term preferred by ideational theorists, "constructed."[50] We have seen how ideas and values about humanitarian intervention have been important in defining interests and identities, setting priorities, constituting coalitions, and adapting institutions. The weight of humanitarian values has increased in calculations about foreign and defense policies throughout the Western world in the 1990s. Indeed, very little else seems to be motivating governmental action. The rejectionism of many developing countries coincides with the fervent negativism from such conservative critics as Charles Krauthammer, Michael Mandelbaum, and Richard Haass.[51] They are worried that the wide-ranging demand for intervention will waste resources and distract Washington from truly important issues of national security. Officials from many developing countries have not set aside their postcolonial memories; they are fearful that U.S. resources will be expended in exactly the ways that conservative American pundits fear.

Depending on perspectives, 1999 was the *annus mirabilis* or *horibilis* for intervention. Kosovo constituted a "humanitarian war."[52] In the West, and

Washington particularly, intervention for humanitarian purposes was crucial enough to risk worsened relations with both Russia and China. And in some ways, the international reaction to East Timor is even more remarkable because only area specialists and stamp collectors could have located it on a map a few years ago.[53] But in spite of official and initially strong objections from the world's fourth most populous country, enough international pressure was exerted that Djakarta "requested" the deployment of the Australian-led coalition in Timor, which was followed by U.N. trusteeship. Comparable actions are out of the question in Chechnya, Tibet, or Kashmir; but efforts against Indonesia suggest that humanitarian intervention is an option against more than powerless or failed states, even without formally overriding sovereignty.[54]

The continual expansion of concerns about IDPs and their treatment suggest that the tensions between state sovereignty and human rights at the heart of this issue are being resolved in favor of the latter. In many ways, Deng's notion of sovereignty as responsibility—controversial but less radical than David Gompert's far-reaching treatment of legitimacy in this volume—suggests how central humanitarian values have become to foreign and defense policies over the last decade. If the abuses of human rights are grave enough, a country's sovereignty temporarily disappears; and the prospects for outside interference, including the deployment of military forces, increases.

Nonintervention is affirmed in Article 2(7) of the U.N. Charter. "[E]ssentially within the domestic jurisdiction of any state"[55] formerly was interpreted to cover state-society relations and general welfare, including human rights. This narrow interpretation is increasingly contested, even if its staying power is evident from the language of Security Council resolutions and the hostility of China, Russia, and a host of developing countries.

This orthodoxy is, however, in profound tension with contemporary state practice. Admittedly, there is inconsistency in the application of international coercion to deal with complex emergencies involving the territorial integrity of important U.N. member states or their allies. At the same time, visceral anti-interventionist biases have been overturned enough times that a norm about contingent sovereignty is emerging. Chapter VII action to enforce humanitarian decisions can no longer be seen as exceptional, and certainly not "unique," after international intervention in northern Iraq, Somalia, Bosnia, Rwanda, Haiti, Albania, Kosovo, and Timor. There are numerous differences among these cases, but one thing links them. The U.N. Charter's contradiction between sovereignty and justice has been resolved in favor of the latter, and responsibility is becoming an additional attribute of statehood.

In short, the definition of national interests is evolving, and this can facilitate intervention. "It is important to realize that respect for sovereignty has not been an important inhibitor of reaction to the various crises," Richard Falk writes. "[C]rucial members will not support such activities in a sustained and sufficient manner if the initiative is mainly undertaken as, and is perceived to be, an altruistic reaction to human distress."[56]

Hence, national interests are not an "obstacle to effective action," as Annan argues, but the explanation for whatever action occurs or does not. "Common interests" are not superceding national interests, as he implies at one juncture in his General Assembly speech, but rather *raisons d'État* are being redefined to include human rights. The secretary general is on much safer ground when speaking of a "more widely conceived definition of national interests" so that, for instance, states acknowledge that eliminating ethnic cleansing as a policy option *is* in their vital interests. As Kathryn Sikkink has demonstrated, "The adoption of human rights policies represented not the neglect of national interests but a fundamental shift in the perception of long-term national interests."[57]

Public policy discourse usually juxtaposes the role of *Realpolitik* and idealism in the making of foreign and defense policy, but there is considerable space between them. The advantage of the so-called English School, "international society," as Barry Buzan has noted, is that it bridges structural realism (a mild version of anarchy) and regime theory (a mild version of idealism).[58] In thinking about humanitarian intervention, the role of power is normally seen in opposition to justice, and the standard operating procedure of nonintervention is contrasted with what in France has been championed as the purported right or even duty to intervene.

In the making of U.S. foreign and defense policy in the 1990s, humanitarian values have become weightier. Mort Halperin, then director of the Policy Planning Staff, and James Michel, a USAID counselor, chaired an interagency review of U.S. government civilian humanitarian and transition programs at the end of the Clinton administration. The report was careful "not to imply that humanitarian considerations will, or should, dictate foreign policy outcomes." At the same time, the report argued that American "global humanitarian interests have become more complex and vital to our foreign policy" and that the "line separating the USG humanitarian stake from our other key foreign policy goals has been erased."[59]

Solidarity with victims and international society's interest in legitimacy have on occasion in the post–Cold War period meant that American decisions to act have been based on the notion that for sovereignty to be legitimate, it has to be responsibly exercised. Otherwise, outside military intervention can be justified in spite of objections from sovereign authorities.

We undoubtedly never will have an "international community" of 189, and counting, U.N. member states sharing values and aspirations. However, an international society has emerged to respond to several humanitarian tragedies in the post–Cold War era. It is not strong enough, nor does it respond quickly enough, to prevent genocides in the former Yugoslavia and

Rwanda or the catastrophe in Timor. However, American foreign and defense policies no longer reflect what were the more *Realpolitik* and less humanitarian security calculations of the Cold War era.

CONCLUSION

The old Westphalian structure is being modified, but a new one has yet to emerge. Traditional interpretations of unlimited sovereignty are under siege. There is a growing consensus that states must be held accountable for massive abuses of human rights. There remains, however, considerable uncertainty and inconsistency as well as much debate about legitimacy, trigger mechanisms, and compliance. Annan's call for standards that are "fairly and consistently applied, irrespective of region or nation" is a clarion call. This laudable even if unrealistic proposition is the predictable part of a secretary general's sermon. As he knows better than social scientists, states will pick and choose which principles they will apply and which they will flaunt.

Proposals to establish definitive criteria to govern humanitarian intervention fly in the face of political reality. Even if we could somehow determine the "can" or "should" of intervention, we still could not determine when states "will" or "must" intervene. Governments ultimately will determine what costs and benefits are worth sustaining. Using a poker analogy, it seems that we are often willing to be "in for a dime but not for a dollar." Could we raise the ante to a quarter?

To reiterate, humanitarian values have not superceded traditional conceptions of vital interests but rather have become increasingly a part of their definition. There is a persistent tendency in the discourse of international relations to juxtapose ideals and *Realpolitik*. Humanitarians with hearts on their sleeves lament the pernicious influence of politics. But politics explains action or inaction. There is little that is immutable about perceived interests, particularly when survival is not at stake. Both realism and neoliberalism view state interests as exogenous instead of examining the forces behind them. Despite the dramatic growth in numbers and significance of transnational actors, states remain the most important actors within the international system in general and humanitarian affairs in particular. Getting state authorities to take seriously their obligations to citizens is more sensible than searching for mythical common interests or a "space of victimhood."[60]

This chapter does not question that states act on the basis of power and interests. As President Clinton told the U.N. General Assembly in September 1999, "the way the international community responds will depend upon the capacity of countries to act, and on their perception of their national interests."[61] Leaders ultimately determine the shape of humanitarian action after calculating benefits, risks, and costs. Political interest is continually being redefined as a result of calculations within fluid domestic and international contexts.

As the millennium dawns, neither Reinhold Niebuhr nor Richard Ullman would be displeased with the increasing importance of humanitarian values in American foreign and defense policies. They both have argued, as does Doyle in this volume, that there is no escape from moral reasoning in international politics. What was described at the outset as a "revolution in ends" means that conscience and reason have been insinuated with considerable prominence into decision-making struggles in the 1990s. At the same time, "[o]ur moral ambitions," writes David Rieff, "have been revealed as being larger than our political, military, or even cognitive means."[62]

Greater attention to humanitarian values from policy makers has not brought utopia but made the world a somewhat more livable place than it would have been otherwise. It is inconceivable, for instance, that a responsible Western leader could have made the same argument about Kosovo as Neville Chamberlain did about Czechoslovakia. Although vigorous action was too slow in East Timor, at least the outcry over Indonesia's military and militia atrocities was immediate; an Australia-led force was deployed and followed by a full-fledged experiment with U.N. trusteeship.

Friends or foes of humanitarian intervention should not get too excited or exercised. In April 1991 after action in northern Iraq, many humanitarians argued ebulliently that anything was possible; three years later after Rwanda's genocide, they concluded pessimistically that doing nothing was the dominant mode. Care should be taken about extrapolating from 1990s headlines about humanitarian interventions.

There may not be many but there will be some Kosovos and Timors. This likelihood has particular resonance in light of NATO's efforts in the Balkans after earlier dithering by NATO countries in the U.N.'s efforts in Bosnia.[63] Adam Roberts argues that "Operation Applied Force will contribute to a trend toward seeing certain humanitarian and legal norms inescapably bound up with conceptions of national interest."[64] Joseph Nye writes that Kosovo is the latest indication that, despite their shortcomings, humanitarian crises "raise moral concerns that the American people consistently include in their list of foreign policy interests. Policy experts may deplore such sympathies, but they are a democratic reality."[65]

Humanitarian values have become central to defining vital interests by interveners as well as to plotting by dictators and war criminals. Notwithstanding this decade's mixed record of humanitarian intervention, the eternal policy challenge in an eternally imperfect world is to reduce the discrepancy between rhetoric and reality. The humanitarian glass is nine-tenths empty, but it is getting fuller.

NOTES

1. Richard H. Ullman, "Redefining Security," *International Security* 8, No. 3 (Summer 1983), reprinted in Sean M. Lynn-Jones and Steven E. Miller, eds., *Global Dangers: Changing Dimensions of International Security* (Cambridge, Mass.: MIT Press, 1995), 15–39. Although he subsequently called for distinguishing "war" from other threats to "well-being," the expansion of the term and of vital interests to include other than military threats remains valid. See Richard H. Ullman, "Russia, the West, and the Redefinition of Security," in Alexei G. Arbatov, Karl Kaiser, and Robert Legvold, eds., *Russia and the West* (Armonk, N.Y.: M. E. Sharpe, 1999), 189–209.

2. Reinhold Niebuhr, *Moral Man and Immoral Society* (New York: Scribner's, 1960), xiii. For discussions, see Robert G. Kaufman, "E. H. Carr, Winston Churchill, Reinhold Niebuhr, and Us: The Case for Principled, Prudential, Democratic Realism," *Security Studies* 5, No. 2 (Winter 1995/96): 314–353; and Patricia Stein Wrightson, "Morality, Realism, and Foreign Affairs: A Normative Realist Approach," *Security Studies* 5, No. 2 (Winter 1995/96): 354–386.

3. Adam Roberts, "The Role of Humanitarian Issues in International Politics in the 1990s," *International Review of the Red Cross* 81, No. 833 (March 1999): 19.

4. Michael Ignatieff, "Human Rights: The Midlife Crisis," *The New York Review of Books* XLVI, No. 9 (20 May 1999): 58.

5. For a discussion of the costs and benefits of U.S. military intervention, see Thomas G. Weiss, *Military-Civilian Interactions: Intervening in Humanitarian Crises* (Lanham, Md.: Rowman & Littlefield, 1999).

6. Thomas G. Weiss, "Collective Spinelessness: U.N. Actions in the Former Yugoslavia," in Richard H. Ullman, ed., *The World and Yugoslavia's Wars* (New York: Council on Foreign Relations, 1996), 59–96.

7. *Report of the Secretary-General Pursuant to General Assembly Resolution 53/35* (1998) (New York: United Nations, 1999), paragraph 503.

8. William Jefferson Clinton, "Remarks to the 54th Session of the United Nations General Assembly," September 21, 1999.

9. Charles Krauthammer, "The Short, Unhappy Life of Humanitarian War," *The National Interest*, No. 57 (Fall 1999): 5–8.

10. For an overview of the changing perceptions of security analysts, see Craig Murphy and Thomas G. Weiss, "International Peace and Security at a Multilateral Moment: What We Seem To Know, What We Don't, and Why," *Contemporary Security Policy* 20, 3 (1999): 116–141.

11. See Thomas G. Weiss, David P. Forsythe, and Roger A. Coate, *The United Nations and Changing World Politics*, 3rd ed. (Boulder, Colo.: Westview, 2001).

12. On the low side of the estimates, see U.S. Committee for Refugees, *World Refugee Survey 1998* (Washington, D.C.: U.S. Committee for Refugees, 1998): 2–6; and U.N. High Commissioner for Refugees, *The State of the World's Refugees, 1997–98: A Humanitarian Agenda* (Oxford: Oxford University Press, 1998): 2–3 and 286–289. On the high estimate side, see Jamie Hampton, *Internally Displaced People: A Global Survey* (London: Earthscan, 1998).

13. See Peter Wallensteen and Margareta Sollenberg, "Armed Conflict, 1989–98," *Journal of Peace Research* 36, No. 5 (1999): 593–606.

14. William J. Durch, ed., *U.N. Peacekeeping, American Policy, and the Uncivil Wars of the 1990s* (New York: St. Martin's, 1996).

15. For more extensive discussions of this landscape, see Michael Maren, *The Road to Hell: The Ravaging Effects of Foreign Aid and International Charity* (New York: The Free Press, 1997), and Alex de Waal, *Famine Crimes: Politics & the Disaster Relief Industry in Africa* (Oxford: James Currey, 1997). This debate was initiated by Alex de Waal and Rakiya Omaar, *Humanitarianism Unbound? Current Dilemmas Facing Multi-Mandate Relief Operations in Political Emergencies* (London: African Rights, 1994), Discussion Paper No. 5. For a discussion on the disarray among humanitarians, see, for example, John Borton, "The State of the International Humanitarian System" *Overseas Development Institute Briefing Paper* 1998 (1), March 1998; Myron Wiener, "The Clash of Norms: Dilemmas in Refugee Policies," *Journal of Refugee Studies* 11, No. 4 (1998): 1–21; and Mark Duffield, "NGO Relief in War Zones: Toward an Analysis of the New Aid Paradigm," in Thomas G. Weiss, ed., *Beyond U.N. Subcontracting: Task-Sharing with Regional Security Arrangements and Service-Providing NGOs* (London: Macmillan, 1998), 139–159. For a look at the political economy of conflict, see, for example, Mark Duffield, "The Political Economy of Internal War: Asset Transfer and the Internationalisation of Public Welfare in the Horn of Africa," in Joanna Macrae and Anthony Zwi, eds., *War and Hunger: Rethinking International Responses to Complex Emergencies* (London: Zed Books, 1994), 50–69; David Keen, *The Economic Functions of Violence in Civil Wars* (Oxford: Oxford University Press, 1998), Adelphi Paper 320; and François Jean and Christophe Rufin, eds., *Economies des Guerres Civiles* (Paris: Hachette, 1996).

16. See Adam Roberts, "Implementation of the Laws of War in Late twentieth Century Conflicts," Part I and Part II, *Security Dialogue* 29, Nos. 2 and 3 (June and September 1998): 137–150 and 265–280; Thomas G. Weiss, "Politics, Principles, and Humanitarian Action," *Ethics & International Affairs* XIII (1999): 1–22, as well as "Responses" by Cornelio Sommaruga, Joelle Tanguy and Fiona Terry, and David Rieff on pp. 23–42; and a special issue on "Humanitarian Debate: Law, Policy, Action," *International Review of the Red Cross* 81, No. 833 (March 1999).

17. David Rieff, "The Death of a Good Idea," *Newsweek*, May 10, 1999, p. 65

18. For discussions, see Joseph Lepgold and Thomas G. Weiss, eds., *Collective Conflict Management and Changing World Politics* (Albany: State University of New York Press, 1998); George W. Downs, ed., *Collective Security Beyond the Cold War* (Ann Arbor: University of Michigan Press, 1994); and Thomas G. Weiss, ed., *Collective Security in a Changing World* (Boulder, Colo.: Lynne Rienner, 1993).

19. James F. Hoge Jr., "Editor's Note," *Foreign Affairs* 73, No. 6 (November/ December 1994): v.

20. For an analysis of 2,200 titles in English, see Cindy Collins and Thomas G. Weiss, *An Overview and Assessment of 1989–1996 Peace Operations Publications* (Providence, R.I.: Watson Institute, 1997), Occasional Paper #28. About one-fourth of the titles concern humanitarian and military interactions.

21. Edward Luttwak, "Kofi's Rule: Humanitarian Intervention and Neocolonialism," *The National Interest*, No. 58 (Winter 1999/2000): 57–62, quote at p. 60.

22. The argument here first appeared in Thomas G. Weiss, "The Politics of Humanitarian Ideas," *Security Dialogue* 30, No. 1 (Winter 2000): 11–23.

23. Kofi Annan, "Secretary General's Speech to the 54th Session of the General Assembly," September 20, 1999. Intervention was also a major theme in the annual *Report of the Secretary-General on the Work of the Organization*, document A/54/1.

24. Kofi A. Annan, *"We the Peoples": The Role of The United Nations in the 21st Century* (New York: United Nations, 2000), especially pp. 47–48. The theme of the possible need for intervention with especial reference to Kosovo was introduced in his speech on "Intervention," June 26, 1998, document SG/SM/6613/Rev.1.

25. See "Statement by the President of the Security Council," November 30, 1999, document S/PRST/1999/34.

26. Jarat Chopra and Thomas G. Weiss, "Sovereignty Is No Longer Sacrosanct: Codifying Humanitarian Intervention," *Ethics & International Affairs* 6 (1992): 95–118. Every issue of this journal since 1992 has contained articles on humanitarian intervention. See also, for example, Tim Dunne and Nicholas J. Wheeler, eds., *Human Rights in Global Politics* (Cambridge: Cambridge University Press, 1999); and Nigel Rodley, ed., *To Loose the Bands of Wickedness: International Intervention in Defence of Human Rights* (London: Brassey's, 1992).

27. Clinton, "Remarks to the 54th Session of the United Nations General Assembly."

28. Judith Goldstein and Robert O. Keohane, "Ideas and Foreign Policy: An Analytical Framework," in Judith Goldstein and Robert O. Keohane, eds., *Ideas and Foreign Policy: Beliefs, Institutions, and Political Change* (Ithaca, N.Y.: Cornell University Press, 1993), 26.

29. In addition to ibid., see also Martha Finnemore, *National Interests in International Society* (Ithaca, N.Y.: Cornell University Press, 1996); and M. E. Keck and Kathryn Sikkink, *Activists Beyond Borders: Advocacy Networks in International Politics* (Ithaca, N.Y.: Cornell University Press, 1998).

30. See S. Neil MacFarlane and Thomas G. Weiss, "Political Interest and Humanitarian Action," *Security Studies* 10, No. 1 (Autumn 2000): 166–198.

31. Richard A. Melanson, *Reconstructing Consensus: American Foreign Policy since the Vietnam War* (New York: St. Martin's, 1991); Tom J. Farer, "Intervention in Unnatural Humanitarian Emergencies: Lessons of the First Phase," *Human Rights Quarterly* 18, No. 1 (1996): 1–22; and Thomas G. Weiss, "Overcoming the Somalia Syndrome," *Global Governance* 1, No. 2 (May/August 1995): 171–187.

32. J. Bryan Hehir, "Military Intervention and National Sovereignty: Recasting the Relationship," in Jonathan Moore, ed., *Hard Choices: Moral Dilemmas in Humanitarian Intervention* (Lanham, Md.: Rowman & Littlefield, 1998), 30.

33. See, for example, Laura W. Reed and Carl Kaysen, eds., *Emerging Norms of Justified Intervention* (Cambridge: American Academy of Arts and Sciences, 1993); Stanley Hoffmann, *The Ethics and Politics of Humanitarian Intervention* (Notre Dame, Ind.: University of Notre Dame Press, 1996); John Harriss, ed., *The Politics of Humanitarian Intervention* (London: Pinter, 1995); Oliver Ramsbotham and Tom Woodhouse, *Humanitarian Intervention in Contemporary Conflict: A Reconceptualization* (Cambridge: Polity, 1996); Anthony McDermott, ed., *Humanitarian Force* (Oslo: International Peace Research Institute, 1997), PRIO Report 4/97; James Mayall, ed., *The New Interventionism, 1991–1994: United Nations Experience in Cambodia, former Yugoslavia, and Somalia* (Cambridge: Cambridge University Press, 1996); and Jan Nederveen Pieterse, ed., *World Orders in the Making: Humanitarian Intervention and Beyond* (London: Macmillan, 1998).

34. See Thomas G. Weiss, "Whither International Efforts for Internally Displaced Persons," *Journal of Peace Research* 36, No. 3 (May 1999): 363–373.

35. Francis M. Deng, *Protecting the Dispossessed: A Challenge for the International Community* (Washington, D.C.: Brookings, 1993); Francis M. Deng et al., *Sovereignty as Responsibility* (Washington, D.C.: Brookings, 1995); and Francis M. Deng, "Frontiers of Sovereignty," *Leiden Journal of International Law* 8, No. 2 (1995): 249–286. For more recent analyses and case studies, see Roberta Cohen and Frances M. Deng, *Masses in Flight: The Global Crisis in Displacement* (Washington, D.C.: Brookings, 1998), and Roberta Cohen and Frances M. Deng, eds., *The Forsaken People: Case Studies of the Internally Displaced* (Washington, D.C.: Brookings, 1998).

36. Bernard Kouchner and Mario Bettati, *Le devoir d'ingérence* (Paris: Denoël, 1987); and Mario Bettati, *Le droit d'ingérence: Mutation de l'ordre international* (Paris: Odile Jacob, 1996).

37. Charles R. Beitz, *Political Theory and International Relations* (Princeton, N.J.: Princeton University Press, 1979).

38. David Malone, *Decision-Taking in the U.N. Security Council: The Case of Haiti, 1990–97* (Oxford: Oxford University Press, 1998).

39. See Stephen Biddle, et al., *The Military Utility of Landmines Implications for Arms Control* (Alexandria, Va.: Institute for Defense Analyses, 1994).

40. Richard Price, "Reversing the Gun Sights: Transnational Civil Society Targets Land Mines," *International Organization* LII, No. 3 (Summer 1998): 617.

41. Max Frankel, "Our Humanity Vs. Their Sovereignty," *New York Times Magazine*, May 2, 1999, p. 36.

42. See Nik Gowing, *Media Coverage: Help or Hindrance in Conflict Prevention* (New York: Carnegie Commission on Preventing Deadly Conflict, 1997); Warren P. Stroble, *Late-Breaking Foreign Policy: The News Media's Influence on Peace Operations* (Washington, D.C.: U.S. Institute of Peace Press, 1997); Edward R. Girardet, ed., *Somalia, Rwanda, and Beyond: The Role of the International Media in Wars and Humanitarian Crises* (Dublin: Crosslines Publications, 1995); Johanna Neuman, *Lights, Camera, War: Is Media Technology Driving International Politics?* (New York: St. Martin's Press, 1996); Colin Scott, Larry Minear, and Thomas G. Weiss, *The News Media, Humanitarian Action, and Civil War* (Boulder, Colo.: Lynne Rienner, 1996); and Robert I. Rotberg and Thomas G. Weiss, eds., *From Massacres To Genocide: The Media, Public Policy, and Humanitarian Crises* (Washington, D.C.: Brookings Institution, 1996).

43. For overviews of the panoply of actors, actions, and arenas, see Thomas G. Weiss and Cindy Collins, *Humanitarian Challenges and Intervention: World Politics and the Dilemmas of Help*, 2d ed. (Boulder, Colo.: Westview, 2000).

44. Judith Randel and Tony German, eds., *The Reality of Aid 1997/8* (London: Earthscan, 1997).

45. Edward C. Luck, *Mixed Messages: American Politics and International Organization 1919–1999* (Washington, D.C.: Brookings Institution, 1999).

46. Ronald Diebert, *Parchment, Printing, and Hyperspace* (New York: Columbia University Press, 1997), 162–163.

47. See Michael Ignatieff, *The Warrior's Honor: Ethnic War and the Modern Conscience* (New York: Henry Holt, 1997); John F. Hutchinson, *Champions of Charity: War and the Rise of the Red Cross* (Boulder, Colo.: Westview, 1996); Nicholas O.

Berry, *War and the Red Cross: The Unspoken Mission* (New York: St. Martin's Press, 1997); Caroline Moorhead, *Dunant's Dream—War, Switzerland, and the History of the Red Cross* (London: Harper Collins, 1998); and David P. Forsythe, *Humanitarian Politics: The International Committee of the Red Cross* (Baltimore: Johns Hopkins University Press, 1977).

48. Jean-Jacques Rousseau, "A Discourse on Political Economy," in *The Social Contract and Discourses* (New York: Dutton, 1950), 301.

49. Hedley Bull, *The Anarchical Society: A Study of Order in World Politics* (New York: Columbia University Press, 1977), 69.

50. See Thomas J. Biersteker and Cynthia Weber, eds., *State Sovereignty as Social Construct* (Cambridge: Cambridge University Press, 1996). See Peter J. Katzenstein, ed., *The Culture of National Security: Norms and Identity in World Politics* (New York: Columbia University Press, 1996); and Alexander Wendt, *Social Theory of International Politics* (Cambridge: Cambridge University Press, 1999).

51. Krauthammer, "The Short, Unhappy Life of Humanitarian War"; Michael Mandelbaum, "A Perfect Failure," *Foreign Affairs* 78, No. 5 (September/October 1999): 2–8; and Richard N. Haass, "What to Do with American Primacy," *Foreign Affairs* 78, No. 5 (September/October 1999): 37–49.

52. See "The Meaning of Kosovo," including an Introduction by Alberto Coll and Essays by Tony Smith, Richard Caplan, Carl Cavanagh Hodge, and Martin L. Cook, in *Ethics & International Affairs* 14 (2000): 3–65.

53. See Brien Hallett and Ralph Summy, eds., *East Timor*, a special issue of *Pacifica Review* 12, No. 1 (February 2000); and Jarat Chopra, "The U.N.'s Kingdom of East Timor," *Survival* 42, No. 3 (Autumn 2000): 27–40.

54. Donald K. Emmerson, "Moralpolitik: The Timor Test," *The National Interest*, No. 58 (Winter 1999/2000): 57–62.

55. This article is only one of many codifications of the principle of nonintervention in both multilateral and bilateral international legal instruments. Bruno Simma provides a useful account of the evolution of the interpretation of this article as it concerns human rights in *The Charter of the United Nations: A Commentary* (Oxford: Oxford University Press, 1995), 141–154.

56. Richard Falk, "Sovereignty and Human Dignity: The Search for Reconciliation," in Francis M. Deng and Terrence Lyons, eds., *African Reckoning: A Quest for Good Governance* (Washington, D.C.: Brookings Institution, 1999), 25.

57. Kathryn Sikkink, "The Power of Principled Ideas: Human Rights Policies in the United States and Western Europe," in Goldstein and Keohane, eds., *Ideas and Foreign Policy*, p. 140. See also Thomas Risse, Stephen C. Rapp, and Kathryn Sikkink, eds., *The Power of Human Rights: International Norms and Domestic Change* (New York: Cambridge University Press, 1999).

58. Barry Buzan, "From International System to International Society: Structural Realism and Regime Theory Meet the English School," *International Organization* 47, No. 3 (1993): 327–352. This same point is made in relationship to regionalism by Mohammed Ayoob, "From Regional System to Regional Society: Exploring Key Variables in the Construction of Regional Order," *Australian Journal of International Affairs* 53, No. 3 (November 1999): 247–260.

59. *Interagency Review of U.S. Government Civilian Humanitarian & Transition Programs* (Washington, D.C.: U.S. Government Printing Office, 2000), 3 and 8.

60. François Debrix, "Deterritorialised Territories, Borderless Borders: The New Geography of International Medical Assistance," *Third World Quarterly* 19, No. 5 (1998): 827–846.

61. Clinton, "Remarks to the 54th Session of the United Nations General Assembly."

62. David Rieff, "A New Age of Liberal Imperialism?" *World Policy Journal* XVI, No. 2 (Summer 1999): 3.

63. See John Williams, "The Ethical Basis of Humanitarian Intervention, the Security Council and Yugoslavia," *International Peacekeeping* 6, No. 2 (Summer 1999): 1–23.

64. Adam Roberts, "NATO's 'Humanitarian War' over Kosovo," *Survival* 41, No. 3 (Autumn 1999): 120.

65. Joseph P. Nye Jr., "Redefining the National Interest," *Foreign Affairs* 78, No. 4 (July/August 1999): 22 and 30. For an indication of the kinds of issues increasingly before the public, see Roy Gutman and David Rieff, eds., *Crimes of War: What the Public Should Know* (New York: Norton, 1999).

7

Saving Lives with Force

Michael O'Hanlon

Was the NATO air campaign against Serbia just a one-time thing, or should we expect the United States and other like-minded countries to make a serious, sustained effort to stop genocidal wars around the world? Even though the war in the Balkans is over, and even though Australia led the mission to East Timor in late 1999, Americans may not be granted much of a reprieve before having to face this question again. In recent years the world has witnessed the 1994 Rwanda genocide, the 1992–1995 Bosnian civil war, and the 1992–1993 war-induced famine in Somalia. Even today, wars that have taken many more lives than the conflict over Kosovo remain unresolved in places such as Angola and the Sudan. As Yahya Sadowski has argued, such wars are not becoming more frequent or violent in the manner that global chaos theorists would have us believe. But neither are they fast declining.[1]

This chapter considers three key questions in intervention policy. First, leaving aside military and political constraints for the moment, in what situations should the world community intervene to save lives? Second, based partly on the answer to the first question, how should other countries, as well as the United Nations, improve their capacities for humanitarian intervention—and what can Washington do to help them in this effort? Finally, what should the U.S. armed forces do themselves by way of restructuring for these missions?

My own analyses of these problems are informed by several important guidelines that Richard Ullman conveyed to me and many of his other students during his teaching career. Characteristically, they were neither simplistic nor facile, and often left us struggling with competing concerns and arguments rather than emerging from the classroom confident that we had easy answers to the world's problems.

111

Dick taught on the one hand that principles and values matter greatly in international relations, both on their own merits and for their influence in shaping the character of the global community. He also taught, however, that military force is a very blunt, demanding, and dangerous instrument of policy, and should not be invoked lightly. He further argued, in his seminal book *Securing Europe*, that Europe's peace, and that of other important parts of the world presumably, is "divisible." We have the luxury in many cases of choosing to ignore conflict without any great risk to our own societies and peoples. That may be a reassuring thought to some. But it is also a sobering thought. As terrible as genocides and other massive war-related humanitarian disasters are, stopping them is simply not a fundamental national security interest, even in the interconnected world of the twenty-first century. That means it will generally be difficult to rally the country to use U.S. military force to save lives abroad. It also means we will have to be selective and hard-headed about conducting humanitarian interventions, since our resources are only adequate for doing so occasionally, and since political support for such efforts is bound to remain fragile. If we are unwise or injudicious about intervening, many millions of people may die who would not have otherwise. That leads to the questions that this chapter will consider.

WHEN TO INTERVENE?

We certainly cannot resolve every conflict in the world. But the international community can generally do something about the worst wars—if not in every case, then at least in most. Doing so requires a strong national stomach, however; despite NATO's intervention against Serbia, in which only two U.S. troops died (in a helicopter training accident in neighboring Albania), it will usually be necessary to risk dozens or even hundreds of Western combat deaths to stop a serious civil war.

How can we decide when and where to intervene, apart from just relying on the "CNN effect" and swings in public opinion? Under the 1948 U.N. Convention Against Genocide, the international community is in theory obliged to take major steps—up to and including the use of force—to stop genocide. But in reality, that is not such a clear guide to intervention. Even the term genocide is vague. The U.N. Convention defines it as an effort to destroy, "in whole or in part," a national, ethnic, racial, or religious group. But does that mean that a few, or even a few dozen, ethnically motivated murders should be considered genocide? Presumably not, since by that standard there are genocides going on all over the world all the time. Then at what point does the definition kick in?

Some cases are clear, such as the 1994 genocide in Rwanda—even though the Clinton administration, to its shame, refused to acknowledge that a genocide was underway there since it did not want to be pressured to intervene so soon after eighteen Americans died in Mogadishu in October 1993. But many cases are tougher. For example, was Serbia's war against the Kosovar Albanians a genocide? It is hard to say. On the one hand, in 1998 and early 1999, about 2,000 Kosovar Albanians were killed by Slobodan Milosevic's forces—a very modest number of combat-related deaths by comparison with many other wars around the world. On the other hand, Serbia's ethnic cleansing operations in the fall of 1998 and again in the spring of 1999 drove hundreds of thousands of Kosovar Albanians from their homes and left them at risk of death by starvation and exposure. That could have made the ethnic cleansing operations practically and morally tantamount to genocide.

Partly because of this ambiguity, former Congressman Stephen Solarz and I devised another way to focus attention on major atrocities in the world. We proposed that the international community seriously consider military intervention whenever the rate of killing in a country or region exceeds the U.S. murder rate several times over, whether or not that killing is genocidal (that is, focused on a particular, identifiable group).[2]

The moral premise of this framework for humanitarian intervention is that all human lives have equal value. One may make a distinction between civilian deaths and military deaths, but not between countries or regions.

To be sure, it would be a mistake, and an impossibility, to make the security policy of the United States and other major powers blind to geography. Some regions are more important than others for strategic or economic reasons, and most major uses of force will be driven by such interests even in the post-Cold War era, as Dick Ullman underscored as early as 1990. Also, even interventions driven by political vision and idealism will properly be focused more on some countries and regions than others, as policy makers seek to uphold young democracies and consolidate and broaden what Ullman called "zones of peace."[3]

But the guiding principle for interventions justified principally on humanitarian grounds should be geographically nondiscriminatory. It should be founded on universal U.S. human rights principles as enshrined in the Declaration of Independence and other important touchstones of U.S. democracy such as the Gettysburg Address. Scholars who deride such goals as international "social work" or as manifestations of Western cultural imperialism seem at times morally callous. In addition, they overstate the degree to which humanitarianism could ever be the central focus of U.S. security policy; even the Clinton administration, which bore the brunt of most such critiques, organized its military forces first and foremost around areas of core national security interest in the Middle East, East Asia, and Europe. The argument here is that, when shaping an international order and searching for principles on which to base and justify it, protection of human lives is not only nice to do, but essential if we are to convey what Western democracy is about and maintain a clear moral basis for our global leadership.[4]

Thus, to the extent they conduct humanitarian interventions, the United States and other countries should generally try to do so in ways that save the greatest number of individuals. That means they should intervene to stop major genocides or other war-related atrocities—as the Bush and Clinton administrations did, with more success than is often recognized, in starvation-ravaged Somalia, but as the Bush administration failed to do in Bosnia and the Clinton administration failed to do in Rwanda. It also means, however, that countries must be careful not to overtax themselves intervening in relatively minor civil wars. The opportunity costs of doing so are simply too high.

There is another, practical reason for restraint: The United States cannot be politically or morally expected to try to make other countries safer than its own domestic society. The annual U.S. murder rate is roughly 1,000 people for every 10 million in the total population. By the proposal Solarz and I advanced, the United States and other countries should strongly consider intervention in situations when the intensity of killing or war-related starvation crosses a threshold several times as great—say five to ten times that number. They should be skeptical about using force to save lives when levels of violence are, and seem likely to remain, much lower.

One should not be too precise in using this guideline. For one thing, exact data about death rates in wars is rarely available. Thankfully, there is data from a wide range of sources—ranging from journalistic accounts to the work of Amnesty International and Human Rights Watch to studies such as the *SIPRI Yearbook* to official government intelligence—that allows one to estimate casualty figures in most conflicts.

The world generally should not wait a whole year to determine an annual rate. In most severe cases, a military response should be attempted within weeks, and in extreme cases even within days, to save the greatest number of lives possible. When genocides or similar mass killings are underway, force should not be a last resort but an early resort.

As suggested above, there will sometimes be cases where fewer deaths justify an intervention that is at least partly humanitarian in purpose. For example, in Haiti in 1994 and in Kosovo in 1999, the fact that countries suffering civil violence were near to the United States and Western Europe provided added rationale for action; the same is true of the U.S. intervention in Panama in 1989. (In fact, the locations of these countries probably provided the principal justification for action in the minds of policy makers.) In practical terms, concerns about refugee flows, drug flows, and/or fears of a possible spillover of violence to neighboring countries reinforced the humanitarian impetus to intervene. In political terms, we have a special interest in making the Americas and Europe what Dick Ullman calls "zones of peace" that might gradually grow to encompass more countries and regions over time. But in general, this numerical guidepost based on comparisons with the U.S. murder rate can help us begin to answer the frequent question: how can we interevene anywhere unless we are going to intervene everywhere?

The criteria for intervention that Solarz and I devised narrows the list of conflicts in which we might intervene from dozens to a modest few. As we argued, there were about eight extremely lethal conflicts between 1992 and 1997. Specifically, death rates from war and war-related famine were most severe in six countries in Africa—Sudan, Somalia, Rwanda, Burundi, Liberia, and Angola—as well as in Bosnia and Chechnya.

Since Solarz and I first wrote on the topic, Congo, with its civil war and dis-integrated society, and North Korea, with its economic collapse and wide-spread starvation, may have joined the list of extremely deadly cases, mak-ing for a total of ten during the Clinton presidency. The North Korean case is different in that the widespread starvation apparently underway was a re-sult of tyranny, corruption, and rampant misgovernment rather than armed conflict. There was concern, in light of U.S. government reports that up to 200,000 Kosovar Albanian men were missing during the war there in 1999 and feared dead, that Kosovo had joined this group as well. Thankfully those fears turned out to be exaggerated, though that could not be definitively known at the time.

These ten cases have together accounted for more than 75 percent of all war-related deaths in the world since 1992. Wars in Algeria, Sri Lanka, Afghanistan, Iraq, the Ethiopian/Eritrean border, and a few other places have been severe in the 1990s, but in the end not nearly as lethal as the above group of ten. Insurgencies and counterinsurgencies in places like Turkey, Kashmir, and Burma, while themselves tragic and deeply regrettable, have been yet another order of magnitude less violent.

In which of these worst-hit countries would intervention have been, or perhaps still be, appropriate? This question must be answered carefully and convincingly. It is not enough to want to "do something" and therefore just to intervene. U.S. military resources are too few, the lives of our military per-sonnel too precious, and the potential for actually making a problem worse by using force—as happened initially in Kosovo during Operation Allied Force—too great for good intentions alone to guide policy. For a humanitar-ian intervention to be wise and ethical, it must only be attempted if the odds are excellent that it will make a bad situation better and not worse.

In devising strategies for intervention, well-intentioned proposals for "sep-arating combatants" and "disarming militias" should generally be discarded. Such antiseptic terms make humanitarian intervention sound bloodless and apolitical. In reality, intervening to save lives is a mission that will often be opposed by at least one local party to a conflict—meaning that the interven-tion will only make sense if we are prepared to employ lethal force against such a government or faction.[5] That does not mean that intervening forces should always be spoiling for a fight. In some situations, they will be able to mitigate most of the worst effects of a humanitarian crisis by establishing a safe haven or safe corridors for humanitarian relief, and do so at less risk to themselves as well as the political sustainability of the operation in their home countries.[6]

These observations lead immediately to several other conclusions. First, well-trained combat units are needed to conduct humanitarian interventions to stop genocide and comparably severe atrocities. Second, they need to be able to move fast. Third, they need to be ready to fight and win on the battlefield. Fourth, they must be deployed in sufficient numbers to protect not only indigenous populations at risk but also themselves. All of these issues are discussed further in subsequent sections of this chapter.[7]

In a small country like Rwanda possessing a rather weak military, it might have sufficed to send 10,000 to 15,000 disciplined and properly equipped troops. In a large one like Angola, with fighting spread throughout much of the country and no obvious place to enforce a partition line, or in a dangerous place like Kosovo in which an enemy has many tens of thousands of troops under arms and a good deal of heavy military equipment, an intervening force could easily require tens of thousands of forces itself.

The mechanics of conducting these types of interventions are generally rather straightforward—though they are also not for the faint-hearted. Discussions of a possible ground war against Serbia in Kosovo have underscored the logistical complications of deploying 100,000 or more fairly heavily armed forces to a remote part of the world with challenging terrain and underdeveloped infrastructure. Some have suggested these factors mean that any NATO ground invasion would have taken three or more months to prepare, though I believe that half that amount of time would have sufficed for an intervention that emphasized Army air assault and Marine Corps forces. Most interventions to stop genocide would be in countries where terrain and lack of infrastructure could be just as challenging as in Albania and Kosovo, but where the presumed enemy would not be as strong as Serbia.

In such situations, airborne and other light infantry forces, backed up by modest amounts of heavy weaponry, would generally be able to get the job done. The good news is that such units can be transported fast—10,000 to 20,000 can be moved virtually anywhere in the world within a couple of weeks, even to inland locations like Rwanda. The United States has a long-range aircraft, the C-17, that can use most short runways. If necessary, intervening forces can also deploy in long-range aircraft to a regional staging base and then transfer to smaller C-130 aircraft and helicopters for a final lift.

After NATO's partial success in Kosovo, we must be especially careful to avoid drawing the conclusion that air power alone can stop civil wars. Most civil wars involve few heavy weapons of the type that can be spotted and attacked from long range. Nor does it generally make sense to attack economic targets in the less-developed countries where such wars usually occur. Not only are the targets usually few and far between, but attacking them may exacerbate a humanitarian crisis without gaining great leverage over the militias and factions that generally wage such wars.[8] Air power may have important specific roles even in conflicts in poor countries between lightly armed militias. For example, it might jam or destroy hatemongering radio transmitters, replacing them with more benign reporting—as many now wish the international community had done in Rwanda. But such steps, though worthwhile on occasion, will only rarely be silver bullets capable of putting an end to conflict. In short, at least one key dimension of the Powell Doctrine—the notion that force, to be effective, must generally be applied decisively, whether it be in major theater war or more limited interventions—survived the war over Kosovo and should guide future uses of force as well.[9]

Since air power alone will not generally get the job done, we cannot usually expect humanitarian interventions to be as low-casualty operations as the recent war against Serbia. Ground combat missions are inherently dangerous. U.S. losses from interventions in Grenada, Panama, and Somalia— roughly twenty to forty Americans killed in each—were more indicative of how such operations are likely to unfold in the future. They can go considerably worse than that, as the Beirut barracks bombing tragedy of 1983 (which killed nearly 250 Americans) reminds us. For starters, airplanes have catastrophic accidents, especially in difficult terrain and airspace they do not know well—as the crash of Commerce Secretary Ron Brown's plane in Bosnia underscores. A lucky shot by a man-portable surface-to-air missile or even a rocket-propelled grenade could bring down an airplane or helicopter; that is how Rwanda's president died in 1994 in the opening stages of that country's genocide and how the Mogadishu debacle began for U.S. forces in 1993. Even poorly armed militias can successfully ambush Western forces in urban or forest settings.

That is the bad news. The good news is that two of the above-mentioned interventions were widely considered as successes within the U.S. policy and political debate. The overall message would seem to be that Americans will tolerate some losses in humanitarian missions as long as they are confident that the missions are well-run, likely to succeed, and justified. Those who caution about the casualty aversion of the American people frequently overstate their case.[10] On the other hand, one should not be dismissive of Americans' casualty aversion either. The Grenada and Panama operations were seen as having broader national security implications as well as humanitarian ones. This survey of recent cases leaves us unsure of how the American public would respond if twenty to forty U.S. troops died in an otherwise successful but strictly humanitarian intervention. (Polling data on this type of subject, some of which suggests a much higher casualty tolerance on the part of the public, cannot be trusted given that such polls cannot truly capture the emotions people experience when U.S. troops start dying in faraway places.[11])

If we do intervene, we will generally have three main types of options: (1) take sides, either overthrowing a reigning regime or helping one side in a civil war to defeat another; (2) impose and then enforce a partition line between two main geographic zones (not simply between different militias within a given city or region); or (3) simply set up and defend safe havens or humanitarian relief zones to protect a threatened population from murder and starvation without trying to resolve a country's underlying political crisis.[12]

Even if the United States and like-minded countries choose the right time and place to intervene, they could easily go about it the wrong way. For example, in Somalia, aggressively seeking to eliminate one particular militia from the country's political scene cost eighteen American lives unnecessarily, given that the Clinton administration and the country proved unwilling to sustain the operation after those eighteen deaths. Tactical mistakes by U.S. commanders, and planning mistakes by Pentagon officials such as Defense Secretary Aspin and Joint Chiefs Chairman Powell, may have contributed to the casualties, but this was inherently a dangerous operation. Policy makers should have either accepted the commensurate risks, or declined to have U.S. forces undertake attacks against Aideed partisans in the first place (sticking to food relief, despite the inherent limitations of that mission).[13] In Bosnia, setting up safe havens failed to make towns like Srebrenica anything close to safe. The U.N. mission also provided Serbs with hostages, complicating the ability of NATO forces to undertake air strikes.[14] The wrong intervention may well be worse, or little better, than no intervention at all—not just for our own country, but even for those we are trying to help.

Consider several of the cases mentioned above where using force to stop genocide or other mass killing was not appropriate. Intervening to stop Russia from killing tens of thousands of innocent Chechens would have risked major-power war between nuclear weapons states with the potential to kill far more people than the intervention could have saved. Invading North Korea to bring food to its starving people would probably precipitate all-out war on the peninsula, quite possibly killing as many civilians in Seoul (to say nothing of soldiers on both sides of the war) as the food aid would save in North Korea. Entering into the Angolan civil war would be a Hobson's choice: Would we support our long-standing anticommunist associate, Jonas Savimbi, a maniacal killer who has already violated two major peace accords, or the corrupt dos Santos government? There are other complicating factors that would drive up American force requirements and casualties in any intervention. Angola is very large, covered by vast tracts of jungle, and laced with land mines after decades of civil war. Also, both Savimbi and dos Santos enjoy ethnically based support in certain regions of the country. That means if we intervened, their troops could disappear within friendly civilian population bases—reverting to classic guerrilla tactics that would make it a prolonged, bloody process to defeat them.

In Rwanda, by contrast, the sheer scale of the killing—nearly a million dead in several months' time in 1994—meant that almost any intervention would have been better than standing by the side. The bloodshed in this war was so severe as to call for drastic and urgent steps. The international community should have quickly sent at least 10,000 forces to defeat militarily the genocidal Hutu militias that targeted Tutsi and moderate Hutu. Whether the world community then stayed on for years to help the country rebuild, or took the radical step of helping populations relocate so that Hutu and Tutsi would each have their own homelands within Rwanda's borders, would in this urgent case have been a secondary concern.

In Sudan, the world community should also have intervened in the early 1990s. In fact, the case for doing so may become compelling again, depending on the future of the war and most specifically on the future of war-related famine. The most natural solution to end the fighting and associated famine would be a partition of the country into two parts, a predominantly Muslim north and predominantly Christian south. That would not tend to please Western liberals who insist on promoting multiethnic democracies all over the world. But we must be careful not to make the perfect the enemy of the good. To save hundreds of thousands of lives quickly, and at modest blood cost to the United States, a partition would probably be the soundest approach.[15]

In Liberia, the total number of war victims in that country's civil war during the first half of the 1990s was much less than in Rwanda or Sudan. Nonetheless, the world should have intervened to stop the killing and help establish a coalition government and a professional military (in other words, nation building—or more precisely, state building). Ethnic hatreds were generally less severe, and the violence more arbitrary and wanton, than in many other wars. Under those conditions, chances are good that the bloodshed could have been quickly stopped. Liberia's modest geographic size is an additional factor that would have lent viability to a possible intervention.

Stopping the world's worst wars is not always practical. And in some cases, stopping the fighting may prove a temporary measure that costs Western lives and military resources in the short term with little to show for the intervention in the longer term.

But the international community should have intervened in Rwanda, Sudan, and probably Liberia as well this decade. In one or two cases, it would have been realistic to expect major U.S. allies—notably Great Britain, France, or perhaps Australia—to lead the intervention; in the others, that responsibility would have had to fall on the United States, if the operations were to be conducted at all. In addition, the international community was right to get involved in Somalia, Bosnia, and Kosovo. In at least the first two cases, hundreds of thousands of lives were ultimately saved—even if hundreds of thousands had already been lost by the time the interventions finally occurred. Conducting these six interventions in a forcible and timely way could have prevented perhaps half of the world's war-related deaths since 1992 and, depending on where one applies the term, its two or three worst genocides of the decade. Doing so would have required the United States to spend a couple percent more on defense than it did. More to the point, it might have cost dozens or even hundreds of American lives. But it could have saved literally millions of innocent souls in the process.

WHAT CAN OTHER COUNTRIES AND THE UNITED NATIONS DO?

Does the United States really have to do the lion's share of the work in forcible humanitarian interventions? That seems unreasonable—not to mention politically unsustainable. Saving lives should hardly be a uniquely American interest. In addition, the United States is alone among the major Western powers in maintaining a high degree of military vigilance in the Persian Gulf and the Korean peninsula.

Unfortunately, there is no way around this situation at present. In some cases, the United States could simply provide strategic transport and logistics support, letting other countries' troops do most of the patrolling and other infantry tasks. But strategic transport and logistics are critical, and major, military activities in and of themselves. That is particularly true in emergency situations where rapid response is required, and in less-developed countries where advanced infrastructure is often lacking.

Our European allies, and several other countries such as Canada and even Japan, should get better at being able to deploy modest numbers of troops to distant combat zones. But it would take them several years to develop the necessary capabilities—though the European Union's recent effort to organize itself more effectively for power projection suggests that many European countries may be getting serious about doing so. As for the neighbors of a country where genocide or highly deadly warfare might be occurring, most would not be militarily capable of conducting major military operations beyond their own borders.

In addition, proximity and familiarity can breed contempt. The neighbors of a given country may be seen as too interested in helping a given faction, or too implicated in the country's history, to play the role of a fair-minded outsider. Even if many countries in the world had the independent capacity for humanitarian intervention, it would not make sense to conduct all such missions using exclusively local and regional security institutions. So the American, and more generally the international, role in humanitarian intervention and peace operations will remain important; regional bodies can help, but they cannot supplant the role of a broader community.

The magnitude of the problem should not be overstated. Countries besides the United States already do a great deal in international peace operations. European countries are providing 80 percent of the NATO-led forces in Bosnia and Kosovo. Australia is leading the U.N. mission in East Timor. Almost none of the world's U.N. peacekeepers, typically numbering in the tens of thousands at any point in the last decade, are American. In Sierra Leone, Nigeria has borne the brunt of the responsibility for attempting to keep a lid on that country's tragic civil war. In all, these non-U.S. deployments typically have involved around 100,000 troops at a time in the 1990s. That falls short of the roughly quarter million American forces typically deployed overseas at any moment, but is hardly inconsequential.

But the present level of effort by most other countries devoted to keeping the global peace is not enough, for two main reasons. First, simply looking at the broad numbers of population, GNP, and military troop strength, the rest of the world combined should be capable of deploying at least twice the number of troops overseas as the United States, rather than being constrained to send no more than half as many as it is today. Second, with the exception of Britain and partial exceptions of a couple other major U.S. allies, no other countries are capable of large-scale forcible interventions in distant places. They can do peacekeeping, but not forcible humanitarian intervention. Many are also severely limited in how well they could respond to systematic violations of a ceasefire in a peacekeeping mission that went awry. That means such missions often cannot be conducted without a central military role for the United States; it also means that if they are conducted, the United States will generally bear disproportionate fiscal and casualty costs. In the 1990s, it was largely the major European allies and other participants in the Bosnia UNPROFOR mission that suffered significant casualties in peace operations, but in Desert Storm, Panama, and Somalia it was largely the United States (though Malaysian and Pakistani troops, among others, did suffer large numbers of casualties in Somalia as well).

What are realistic ways for other countries, and multilateral groupings of countries, to improve their military capabilities in the years ahead? Much of the debate over such matters focuses on institutional mechanisms for the use of force—to wit, whether the United Nations, NATO, Western European Union, Organization of African Unity, or other organizations should bear the major responsibility for conducting these types of operations. Such debates are important, but insufficient. In the end, I am generally agnostic about institutional mechanisms. It clearly is highly desirable that most operations be conducted with U.N. Security Council approval, both for the legitimating effect and for

the opportunity that it provides the United States to offer its advice and blessing for most operations. The fact that NATO had to undertake the 1999 war
against Serbia without such approval was regrettable, even if NATO did act
in a manner consistent with the U.N. Security Council resolutions of the preceding fall.[16] But more discussion should focus on developing military capability rather than institutional machinery. The following emphasizes the former.

Among the major Western European countries, the model for improving
peace operations and forcible intervention capabilities is clear. In a word, it
is Britain. Its military is actually smaller and less expensive than France's or
Germany's, but much more useful beyond its own borders. It is capable of
deploying perhaps 50,000 combat troops, with air support, well beyond its
territory within three to four months, and sustaining them indefinitely in that
theater. Based on the Blair government's recent strategic review, it should increase that number modestly within a few years. Many of these troops are organized in brigade-sized units that are well-suited to peace operations because they are capable of deploying overseas in modest-sized packages.
Britain is also planning to acquire more sealift and airlift to move these forces
fairly rapidly.

The smaller European countries cannot all be expected to use Britain as an
exact model, of course, but they can scale their efforts to some extent pro-
portionately. In certain cases—such as the low countries or Scandinavian
countries—they may wish to band together to purchase strategic lift capabilities as groups. In others, such as Italy or the Netherlands or Canada, it may
be preferable for individual countries to buy enough lift and a broad enough
array of forces to be capable of deploying themselves overseas even if most
of their alliance partners choose not to participate in a given mission.

Skeptics will point out, appropriately enough, that most European countries have no interest in increasing their defense budgets to fund the airplanes, roll-on/roll-off ships, trucks, and other logistics assets needed to develop a power projection capability for any purpose outside the
continent—be it for war fighting or for humanitarian intervention and peace
operations. An additional obstacle is that many European countries still depend on conscription to fill out their force structures. Often, there are legal
or political obstacles to sending conscripts away to distant lands on less-
than-vital military missions. In addition, conscripts, many of whom serve for
only a year or year and a half before returning to civilian life, are often not
skilled enough to conduct complex military operations effectively.

There are two elements to the solution for such countries, which include
France, Germany, Spain, and Italy among others. First, they should end conscription, as France is already in the process of doing. Modern military operations are too complicated to be conducted by quasi-amateurs, and troops
deployed after only several months of training must be viewed as just that.

Second, holding defense budgets roughly constant, most European countries and Canada should reorder their defense priorities. Large force structures are not needed. Today's non-U.S. NATO members have 2.5 million troops under arms—a million more, in aggregate, than the United States— yet cannot deploy and sustain many more than 100,000 overseas at a time. For the U.S. armed forces, the corresponding number is nearly one million. This imbalance should be rectified. European nations could collectively develop perhaps half the power projection capabilities of the United States with a total investment of some $50 billion—about 7 percent of their total defense burden if spread out over a five-year period. Even less ambitious and costly initiatives could make a major difference.[17]

European powers need not develop the full gamut of military capabilities themselves. For example, many have been interested in acquiring reconnaissance satellites, as has Japan. The United States should not object to seeing its allies develop such capabilities in theory. In practice, however, such acquisitions would probably compete directly with the lower-technology sealift, airlift, and logistics assets needed for power projection.

Were Germany and Japan to follow the above prescriptions, their neighbors might be highly agitated, worrying about their capacity for autonomous power projection. Such worries should not always be deferred to, but they do constitute a political reality in the case of Japan in particular. The simplest way to defuse—or at least contain—such concerns is to begin with modest ambitions. Germany and Japan could each develop only enough force to send two or three brigades of ground troops overseas, for example. That number would be utterly insufficient to pose any threat to even their smaller neighbors. Once they had reassured their neighbors that they would only participate in multilateral operations with nonimperial intent, they could eventually expand their capabilities further.

What about other countries? Most have far smaller defense budgets than countries such as Japan, Germany, or even Italy and Spain, so they would need lower aspirations at first. Expensive hardware, such as airlift capabilities, helicopters, and fighter aircraft, will generally be beyond their means in large numbers. It is more realistic in these cases to ask the countries at issue to develop well-trained and capable soldiers, proficient in basic combat and basic peacekeeping skills, and equipped with serviceable small arms, body armor, vehicles for transport, and logistics and communications support for sustained operations abroad. Even if such countries cannot be reasonably expected to lead forcible interventions, they can still play a very important role by providing credible combat forces into peacekeeping missions that would be capable of upholding ceasefires and peace accords that may wind up being challenged. As the world witnessed in Angola in the early 1990s, some of the worst and most deadly conflicts occur in countries where peace accords are reached, but later disintegrate.[18]

This approach is not applicable to every country in the world, of course. The international community might not wish to encourage, or aid, improvements in the militaries of countries run by strong-armed autocrats. It would also have to be careful not to upset delicate domestic balances of power by strengthening the military—or certain parts of it—at the relative expense of other national institutions.

But the presumption should be that, even for poorer countries, improved capacity for peace operations makes sense. After all, it is just such countries that often have the greatest interest in helping stop conflicts, since the wars often occur in their neighborhoods. For that reason, programs like the African Crisis Response Initiative (ACRI), created by the Clinton administration, should not only be continued, but also expanded. At present the ACRI funds only occasional training rotations for regional troops. It should do more, expanding its reach beyond the 5,000 to 10,000 foreign troops now participating annually, helping to provide them better equipment and helping them financially when they deploy to places like Sierra Leone, the Congo, and Angola.[19]

What about a U.N. capability in which individuals from various countries take a pledge to do the will of the U.N. Security Council, forming units and training as an international force? This idea may have some merit. There is even some basis in recent experience in nonstate military forces making a meaningful difference in civil wars.[20] Bßut the hurdles to making this approach more systematic and more internationally legitimate are high. First, to be useful, such a force would have to be capable of more than routine peacekeeping, since there are ample soldiers in the world for carrying out that mission. At a minimum, it would need to be able to undertake difficult peacekeeping missions at some risk of failing. Second, and relatedly, it would need to be reasonably large. That is because difficult missions can require well upward of 10,000 troops in moderately sized countries, because more than one mission could easily be required at a time, and because troops would need time to spend at their home bases to train and recover from deployments. It is hard to see how a force much smaller than 30,000 to 50,000 troops in all could be ample. If provided with good equipment, such a force could easily require $1 billion a year in equipment costs—and much more in the early going. Another $2 billion or so would be required in salaries, assuming that soldiers would be paid in effect at Western rates (since the U.N. system usually pays employees based on salary levels in the wealthier countries). On top of those costs would be the marginal expenses of actually deploying to overseas missions. So would any purchases of dedicated airlift or sealift that were made to permit the U.N. force full autonomy, which could easily add $3 billion to $5 billion more to start-up costs.

Leaving aside the political and legal complexities of creating the world's third or fourth largest power projection force and placing it under U.N. command, it is dubious that spending at least $5 billion a year on a U.N.

force would be the best way to enhance international capacity for peace operations today. Perhaps the situation will be different in a decade.

HOW SHOULD THE U.S. MILITARY BE RESTRUCTURED?

In the short term, responding to humanitarian emergencies will remain largely a U.S. job. The unfortunate reality is that other countries do not in general have the forcible entry capabilities or sustainable logistics to intervene in distant lands to save lives. That is, they do not have the long-range airlift and sealift, the mobile hospitals and equipment repair facilities, and the hordes of trucks and engineering equipment to operate at great distance from modern infrastructure for extended periods. Over time, this fact of international life can and should change. But to date it has not. Nor, in the next five years or so, will it likely change drastically. As much as the United States should encourage, and in some cases even aid, the evolution of other countries' power projection capabilities, as discussed above, it also needs to assume that in some cases it will continue to carry out such missions with only limited help from other countries.

Even if the international community does not conduct more interventions in the future than it has in the past, simply maintaining the same level of effort will require adjustments in the U.S. military. The post-Cold War era so far has been hard on a force built first and foremost for major war that, in practice, was also asked to feed Kurds in Iraq, help make and then keep the peace in Bosnia and Kosovo, relieve starvation in a hostile environment in Somalia, take care of refugees from Rwanda in Zaire, and push corrupt governments out of power in Haiti and Panama.

Some have suggested creating new types of formations dedicated to handling these missions. The logic for this proposal is either that humanitarian interventions and peace operations are so different from combat as to require a different basic type of expertise, or that combat units conducting such secondary missions lose their warrior spirit and combat edge. How strong are these arguments?

In fact, both arguments are weak. This is quite good news for proponents of humanitarian intervention, since it would drive defense budget costs up substantially to create dedicated units that would perform only one type of mission or the other. In today's military, a single type of unit can and does undertake both combat and peace operations, as circumstances require. Since the U.S. combat forces are sized conservatively, based on a so-called two-war strategy, there are generally combat forces available to conduct a secondary mission—provided that such missions are not conducted so frequently as to "break the force" by excessively taxing people and equipment. (In the 1990s, the U.S. armed forces probably approached their maximum

strain levels, though that was partly due to the way in which they were organized—as well as to missions in Iraq and Northeast Asia—and not entirely
to the humanitarian workload.)[21]

The suggestion that U.S. combat forces are incapable of conducting peace
operations well is belied by their admirable track record. Incidents of soldiers
overreacting to provocations from unruly mobs or otherwise using too firm a
hand in situations better handled quietly have been few and far between. Missions in places like Somalia, Haiti, and Bosnia that succeeded in some ways but
failed in others never failed due to the poor performance of troops on the
ground. In Somalia, political and military leadership made mistakes, but U.S.
soldiers still prevailed tactically in the infamous October 3, 1993, firefight. In
Haiti, it has proven very difficult to reform national institutions and create a
more constructive political environment—but these are not tasks that U.S.
troops would have been expected to carry out in any case. In Bosnia, the fact
that the three ethnic entities have not reintegrated themselves is explained by
the realities of the local politics, not by the weakness of NATO's patrols or other
deficiencies in its soldiers' performance. Perhaps the international community
needed to do a better job in these places. But NATO and U.S. troops were perfectly capable of establishing and maintaining security as requested, and of doing so without inflaming tensions through ill-considered uses of force.

Not only do soldiers seem capable of being peacekeepers, but sometimes
their soldiering skills come in handy as well. Many countries around the
world—several South Asian and Southeast Asian states, many smaller European countries, and others—are capable of providing competent soldiers
skilled in basic discipline and patrolling and small-arms use for traditional
peacekeeping missions where the threat of renewed violence is low. These
are not missions in which U.S. combat forces need generally participate, unless there is a pressing political need that they do so (as in the Sinai). American forces are needed precisely where combat is possible—such as in Somalia, or Haiti, or Bosnia. In cases where they do not wind up fighting, their
reputations as formidable warriors undoubtedly help to account for that.
This intimidation factor is desirable, and not one that should be sacrificed
lightly. Even in cases where local militias are not inclined to challenge outside forces, many of the operations involved in establishing control of a
country—taking airfields, protecting relief convoys, protecting against possible ambushes, flying helicopters around a potential combat zone—require
the prudence and tactics of soldiers.

As for the second allegation, that warriors should not be charged with
peace operations because it weakens their fighting spirit and detracts from
their training regimens, the concern is real, but the evidence supporting it is
generally weak. First of all, soldiers tend to like the work of peace operations, as evidenced by the relatively high reenlistment rates of soldiers who
have deployed to the Balkans. Second, they can train at the small-unit level
even while deployed. Third, restoring their large-unit maneuver and combat

skills admittedly takes a while—from three to six months, depending on which estimate one accepts. But if only 5 to 10 percent of the combat force structure is involved in carrying out a peace operation or recovering from one at a time, that burden is entirely manageable. Indeed, there is not enough strategic lift in the U.S. military to carry all forces to a combat theater in less than four to six months in any case. So, in the event of a major conflict (or two), units that have recently been engaged in peace operations can train while others deploy first.[22]

There are, to be sure, challenges involved in conducting such operations. For example, the Army overused the 10th Mountain Division in the early 1990s in Somalia and Haiti, putting most burdens for intervention on its shoulders in a way that probably hurt that division for a considerable spell and strained morale. The Army has also routinely kept units under strength in the 1990s, meaning that it would have to bring a deploying unit up to full manpower by raiding other units. That practice, attributable to the two-war construct that mandated keeping ten large active Army divisions, created a ripple effect through the force that caused far greater strain than modest-sized deployments should have.

So the main elements of the U.S. Army, and other services as well, do not require radical overhaul if peace operations and humanitarian interventions are to be an important part of their future workload. But some changes are still needed at the margin.

Certain types of units should be augmented in number. These include special forces with particular language and political skills, military police, and support units that provide water and food and medical care, not only to troops but also to indigenous civilian populations in many humanitarian missions. Some of these forces, a good number of which are found primarily in the reserve force structure since they do not require constant training and drilling to do their jobs in war, are being overused. It would be wise to place some of them in the active-duty force structure so that they can be deployed without causing excessive disruption to the lives of reservists who did not expect such duty short of a major national crisis. I do not have the detailed data to make careful arguments about which types of units require what type of buttressing. But the Pentagon's 1997 Quadrennial Defense Review, which focused some such attention on units like the Air Force's AWACS aircraft, suggests that the same approach if applied more widely across the force would not involve much more than 10,000 troops. Total associated annual costs might approach $1 billion—hardly insignificant. But the costs are hardly astronomical either.

The other major change that is required is to stop undermanning major combat units. By keeping many units at only 80 to 90 percent strength, the Army in particular sets itself up for the cascading problem noted above. It likes to deploy units overseas at full strength or even 105 percent strength, meaning that it must routinely rob from Peter's unit to fill Paul's. This practice is insidious, because it winds up involving at least a few people from many units even in small deployments. Instead, the Army should scale back its number of divisions and other major combat formations, keeping roughly the same amount of manpower but packing it into fewer units to keep them at fuller strength. Or it should reduce the canonical size of units such as Army divisions, accepting a somewhat lower theoretical combat capability from each in order to reduce the strain on the force that results when individual units deploy. The price to be paid in combat capability would be acceptable. The current force-sizing construct used by the Pentagon—two chronologically overlapping conflicts, each on a scale approaching that of Desert Storm—is quite cautious, particularly in light of the decline of the Iraqi and North Korean threats this decade. Given this, some alternative and less demanding form of a two-war strategy would appear to suffice.[23]

CONCLUSION

Using force to save lives cannot be the chief priority of the U.S. military, but neither should it be the last. In fact, whatever one's strategic and philosophical views on the desirability of using national military forces for humanitarian purposes, the post-Cold War track record of the United States under two different presidents of two parties (and two different congressional majorities) suggests strongly that these types of missions will be a fact of life. The real questions are how well will the United States and like-minded countries perform them, how well will they prepare for them, and how well will they decide when and where to intervene?

A radical agenda for reshaping the militaries and the foreign policies of the United States and other countries to conduct humanitarian interventions more effectively will not work. Political support for military missions to save lives is relatively shallow, national security imperatives to use force for such purposes are generally weak, and competing demands on nations' military and diplomatic resources preclude excessive attention to what is at best a difficult and politically rather unrewarding endeavor. But there is a great deal that can be done—without radical overhauls—to improve the U.S. and international capacity for doing such missions and doing them well. The effort is likely to be successful if guided by Richard Ullman's characteristic blend of pragmatic liberalism with hardheaded realism.

NOTES

1. Yahya Sadowski, *The Myth of Global Chaos* (Washington, D.C.: Brookings Institution, 1998), 121–144.

2. See Stephen J. Solarz and Michael E. O'Hanlon, "Humanitarian Intervention: When Is Force Justified?" *Washington Quarterly*, Vol. 20, No. 4 (Autumn 1997): 3–14;

Solarz and O'Hanlon, "Deciding When to Go," *Washington Post Outlook Section,* February 7, 1999, p. B1; see also my July 12, 1999 article in *The New Republic.*

3. Richard H. Ullman, "Enlarging the Zone of Peace," *Foreign Policy,* No. 80 (Fall 1990): 117; see also Robert S. Chase, Emily B. Hill, and Paul Kennedy, "Pivotal States and U.S. Strategy," *Foreign Affairs,* Vol. 75, No. 1 (January/February 1996): 33–51.

4. On the debate over the role of ethics and humanitarianism in U.S. security policy, see Michael Mandelbaum, "Foreign Policy as Social Work," *Foreign Affairs,* Vol. 75, No. 1 (January/February 1996): 16–32; Stanley Hoffman, "In Defense of Mother Teresa," *Foreign Affairs,* Vol. 75, No. 2 (March/April 1996): 172–175; and (on the "Asian values" notion), Kim Dae Jung, "Is Culture Destiny?" *Foreign Affairs,* Vol. 73, No. 6 (November/December 1994): 189–194.

5. See Stephen John Stedman, "Alchemy for a New World Order," *Foreign Affairs,* Vol. 74, No. 3 (May/June 1995): 14–20.

6. Richard N. Haass, *Intervention: The Use of American Military Force in the Post-Cold War World* (Washington, D.C.: Carnegie Endowment, 1994), 49–65.

7. See Michael O'Hanlon, *Saving Lives with Force* (Washington, D.C.: Brookings Institution, 1997).

8. See Ivo Daalder and Michael O'Hanlon, "Unlearning the Lessons of Kosovo," *Foreign Policy,* No. 116 (Fall 1999): 128–140.

9. The Powell Doctrine does not argue against humanitarian intervention, as some who confuse it with the so-called Weinberger Doctrine sometimes argue. See Colin L. Powell, "U.S. Forces: Challenges Ahead," *Foreign Affairs,* Vol. 72, No. 5 (Winter 1992/93): 32–45.

10. For one who overstated in this way recently, see Charles Krauthammer, "The Short, Unhappy Life of Humanitarian War," *The National Interest,* No. 57 (Fall 1999): 5–8; for a thorough, if also sometimes overstated rebuttal, see Steven Kull and I. M. Destler, *Misreading the Public: The Myth of a New Isolationism* (Washington, D.C.: Brookings, 1999): 35–112.

11. For some of this polling data, see ibid., pp. 106–110.

12. On the need for a dose of realist logic in humanitarian interventions, see Richard K. Betts, "Delusions of Impartiality," *Foreign Affairs,* Vol. 73, No. 6 (November/December 1994): 20–33; Barry R. Posen, "The Security Dilemma and Ethnic Conflict," in Michael E. Brown, ed., *Ethnic Conflict and International Security* (Princeton, N.J.: Princeton University Press, 1993), 103–124; and Chaim Kaufmann, "Possible and Impossible Solutions to Ethnic Civil Wars," *International Security,* Vol. 20, No. 4 (Spring 1996): 136–175.

13. For a very good account of how the U.S. soldiers fought and died in the October 1993 Mogadishu firefight, see Mark Bowden, *Black Hawk Down* (New York: Atlantic Monthly Press, 1999).

14. See Ivo H. Daalder, *Getting to Dayton* (Washington, D.C.: Brookings, 2000), 32, 41–42.

15. For a similar view, see Francis M. Deng, "Ethnicity: An African Predicament," *Brookings Review,* Vol. 15, No. 3 (Summer 1997): 28–31.

16. For more on this, see Ivo H. Daalder and Michael E. O'Hanlon, *Winning Ugly: NATO's War to Save Kosovo* (Washington, D.C.: Brookings, 2000).

17. Michael O'Hanlon, "Transforming NATO: The Role of European Forces," *Survival,* Vol. 39, No. 3 (Autumn 1997): 5–15; see also David Gompert and Richard Kugler, "Free-Rider Redux," *Foreign Affairs,* Vol. 74, No. 1 (January/February 1995):

7–12; and John E. Peters and Howard Deshong, *Out of Area or Out of Reach?: European Military Support for Operations in Southwest Asia* (Santa Monica, Calif.: RAND Corporation, 1995), 97–117.

18. See Stephen John Stedman, "Spoiler Problems in Peace Processes," *International Security*, Vol. 22, No. 2 (Fall 1997): 5–53; Barbara F. Walter, "Designing Transitions from Civil War: Demobilization, Democratization, and Commitments to Peace," *International Security*, Vol. 24, No. 1 (Summer 1999): 127–155.

19. See Adekeye Adebajo and Michael O'Hanlon, "Toward a Rapid Reaction Force," *SAIS Review*, Vol. 17, No. 2 (Summer–Fall 1997): 153–164.

20. David Shearer, *Private Armies and Military Intervention*, Adelphi Paper 316 (Oxford, England: Oxford University, 1998).

21. For an overview of the state of U.S. military readiness in 1998, see Michael O'Hanlon, *How to Be a Cheap Hawk* (Washington, D.C.: Brookings, 1998), 137–159.

22. See Statement of Army General George Joulwan before the House National Security Committee, March 19, 1997, pp. 12–14; Statement of Mark E. Gebicke, General Accounting Office, before the House National Security Committee's Subcommittee on Readiness, March 11, 1997, pp. 3–4; and Thomas F. Lippiatt et al., *Postmobilization Training Resource Requirements: Army National Guard Heavy Enhanced Brigades* (Santa Monica, Calif.: RAND Corporation, 1996), pp. xv–xviii, 1–21; Rachel Schmidt, *Moving U.S. Forces: Options for Strategic Mobility* (Washington, D.C.: Congressional Budget Office, 1997) , 79; and Frances Lussier, *Structuring the Active and Reserve Army for the Twenty-first Century* (Washington, D.C.: Congressional Budget Office, 1997), 7–11.

23. O'Hanlon, *How to Be a Cheap Hawk*, pp. 48–172.

8

The Irony of Kosovo: The System Worked Better Than It Usually Does

David Callahan

In a 1996 essay reflecting on the wars that tore asunder the former Yugoslavia during the early 1990s, Richard Ullman expressed muted faith that the Western democracies would do better in the face of future such conflicts. He observed that the wars of Yugoslavia had been a "searing" experience for the nations of the West and they will "undoubtedly give higher priority to preventive diplomacy" in the years to come. At the same time, he doubted that new acts of aggression comparable to the shelling of Vukovar or the massacres in Srebrenica would trigger a Western military response.[1]

This prediction was eminently sensible, given not just the West's inaction in Yugoslavia but also its passivity in the face of far worse carnage in Rwanda. The prediction reflected the view, prevalent among jaded liberal internationalists of the mid-1990s, that humanitarian interventionism would not soon become a centerpiece of Western foreign policies for many reasons: because of a lack of vital interests in many bloody conflicts, because of the ongoing failure to build strong collective security mechanisms that could galvanize action, and because of institutional or political constraints within various Western countries, most notably the United States, where the aftermath of the Somalia debacle in 1993 had led to a new skepticism of intervention sometimes called the "Vietmalia Syndrome." For Richard Ullman, a veteran witness to many lost opportunities to create a more humane and cooperative international order, the West's post–Cold War inability to rise to the challenges posed by internal conflicts surely came as no great surprise.

NATO's intervention in Kosovo in early 1999 shows how quickly circumstances can change in foreign affairs. The United States and its allies acted with greater determination and took more risks in Kosovo than it did in any of the earlier wars in the former Yugoslavia—or any of the other major internal conflicts of the post–Cold War era. President Clinton, in particular, took an enormous gamble in Kosovo: the kind of foreign policy gamble he'd spent his whole presidency avoiding. The most plausible explanation of this abrupt turnaround in U.S. and Western policy is actually rather simple: The West learned from history and changed its behavior. Such things do happen, after all.

From its earliest days, the decade-long crisis in Kosovo was seen by U.S. and Western officials as a place where they could get things right and practice effective preventive diplomacy. This sense was accentuated by the abysmal failure of U.S. policy in Bosnia. After 1992, many in the West were determined not to fail in Kosovo as they had in Bosnia. For this reason, Kosovo always occupied a prominent place in the Western diplomatic mind through the 1990s. By 1998, the lessons of Bosnia, and also those of Rwanda, had sunk in deeply, shaping a psyche of Western guilt. While there was much disagreement on those lessons in all of their specifics, there seemed to be a general view that the West could no longer allow mass killings to take place in plain view if there were viable options for stopping such slaughter. Thus, as the crisis in Kosovo escalated through 1998, it was seen as far more than just another war in the Balkans: It was a supreme test of Western will, a challenge that called into question whether the West had learned anything at all from years of ethnic conflicts and, more pointedly, from the deaths of over a million people in Bosnia and Rwanda.

The NATO intervention in Kosovo last March, while not successful in a number of ways, showed that the United States and its allies had indeed learned from the past. Kosovo stands as one of the few cases ever where the United States and its allies did almost everything right in the face of a major crisis driven by ethnic conflict. The West predicted the crisis, helped prevent its escalation for many years, and then intervened in a limited manner, fulfilling its threats to take action and accomplishing its military objectives. The U.S.-led international security system worked at almost every step of the way, with a few notable wrong turns.

What's disturbing, of course, is that the system failed egregiously at the same time that it worked. A major Serb-Albanian war was not prevented in Kosovo, and when Western intervention occurred, it backfired in a number of disastrous ways. Unavoidably, Kosovo must be seen as the graphic illustration of a stark reality: The international security system, however hard it tries, has limited power to prevent ethnic conflicts, or easily stop them once they escalate. This will come as no surprise to the disciples of realist paradigms of international affairs, some of whom believe the West should just let many bloody internal wars "burn themselves out." Instead, the Kosovo experience is far more sobering to those in the idealist camp, who have long entertained high hopes for the potential of preventive diplomacy and collective security.

This chapter begins by setting the challenge posed by ethnic conflict within the broader challenge of maintaining an internationalist foreign policy in the post-Cold War era. It then examines the various stages of the Kosovo crisis, focusing mainly on U.S. policy decisions. It looks at the three stages of policy responses: prediction, prevention, and intervention. It argues that in each stage the United States usually followed the best course of action, discussing why the system can be seen as "working." In closing, I discuss why the system failed even as it worked.

ETHNIC CONFLICT AND U.S. INTERNATIONALISM AFTER THE COLD WAR

The upsurge of ethnic conflict in the post-Cold War era has generated much confusion in the policy world. In the United States, policy analysts both in and outside of government have been slow to think through what this new violence means and what the United States might do about it. During the 1990s, Washington has had a few successes in handling ethnic conflicts; more often U.S. policies have been inconsistent at best and incompetent at worst. This maladroitness must be viewed in the broader context of an American internationalism that has not been successfully reconfigured for the post-Cold War era.

Through the twentieth century, American internationalism often centered on ambitious responses to clear-cut challenges. World War I and World War II were clear cases of what might be called "emergency internationalism." Likewise, the Cold War internationalism that followed World War II was based on great exigency. It aimed to thwart communism and avoid a repeat of German or Japanese aggression by creating a community of liberal states bound together by shared political ideals, economic interdependence, and American power. In the post-Cold War era, however, American internationalism has lacked its previous clarity and vigorous sense of purpose. In short, no emergency exists any longer.

Among both policy elites and the public, a rough consensus exists on the need to perpetuate American leadership of the central institutions of the Western community, such as NATO and the web of bilateral alliances in East Asia, and also on the need for a U.S. leadership role in containing rogue states like Iraq and North Korea. In addition, promotion of American economic interests gained new salience within the internationalist agenda during the Clinton years.

But none of these missions has the urgency of a global military emergency or the sweep of the vision laid by the architects of containment. Instead, the central objectives of post-Cold War internationalism have been the product of incrementalism and adaptation—or institutional inertia, as some have argued. Meanwhile, there has been little agreement on how to cope with a variety of more ambiguous challenges and secondary threats to international security. The confusion here has been about ends as well as means. Not only has there been disagreement in identifying national interests outside the traditional core areas of American concern, but there has been no clear understanding of what kinds of public support and financial resources can be tapped successfully to deal with challenges in these areas. For forty years, American foreign policy on the periphery was formulated by policy makers and explained to the public in the context of the Cold War struggle. During the 1990s, with the disappearance of the Cold War measuring cup to assess threats and justify sacrifices, American foreign policy on the periphery often wandered in a vacuum, and the United States' response toward ethnic conflicts was a series of ad hoc adventures.

In the former Yugoslavia, the United States committed a series of missteps in the early 1990s that reflected its lack of clear goals. When the country was first fragmenting, U.S. diplomats first called for continual unity yet also came to acknowledge the merits of the self-determination bids by the Yugoslav republics. Thus, Washington may have both encouraged the independence efforts of Slovenia, Croatia, and Bosnia, while seeming to sanction Serbian violence aimed at squelching those efforts—the worst of both worlds. Later, when the war in Bosnia was under way, the United States seemed to vacillate between backing a complete victory by the Bosnian government and a compromise solution that would accept Serbian gains won by aggression. It wavered between seeking to bring Serbian leaders to trial as war criminals and bringing them to the negotiating table as statesmen. In 1995, the United States negotiated a highly fragile peace to end the war. That peace, of course, did nothing to address the simmering Kosovo crisis.

In the Caucasus, the United States failed to lay out a well-defined policy for dealing with a swath of ethnic conflicts that were in full swing by the early 1990s. It resisted American intervention in this region while fluctuating between backing an active Russian policing role and issuing criticisms of Russian meddling. Beyond denying that the United States has recognized a Russian sphere of interest in the Caucasus, American officials have been vague about American interests and intentions in this part of the world. Washington's passive policies toward Russia on this score may have been one reason why Moscow felt free to use such excessive force in Chechnya. Many of the ethnic wars in the Caucasus have now wound down, but the Chechen conflict has flared again, with little coherent U.S. response. More generally, American policy makers have left unaddressed long-range questions about what kind of regional order can be built to prevent future instability in the Caucasus. There is likewise little creative U.S. thinking in regard to the plight of the Kurds, who are one of the largest stateless groups in the world and are likely to continue rebelling sporadically through the foreseeable future.

American foreign policy has not been wholly bereft of strategic thinking in regard to ethnic conflicts, even if that thinking has only been applied selectively. In the post-Cold War era, American officials have placed new emphasis on the preventive component of foreign policy, and this insight has generated some policies of prescience in ethnic hotspots. The Clinton administration saw clearly the potential for disaster in the Baltic states and pressed leaders there for better treatment of ethnic Russians. Both the Bush and Clinton administrations recognized the danger inherent in Albanian calls for a greater Albania and used a burgeoning American relationship with the Albanian government to temper such ambitions. (More about that later.) Under both Bush and Clinton, the United States has at least tried to play a mediating role in the dispute in Kashmir, even as such offers have been consistently rebuffed. Burundi has been the focus of substantial American concern since the massacres in Rwanda. Before the Rwanda crisis, moreover, the United States was engaged in an effort to defuse the mounting political crisis in that country.

In addition to seeking to prevent selected crises, the American government has also put some effort into improving responses to ethnic conflict. The politics and logistics of peacekeeping and humanitarian missions have received much attention inside the government. This work has been designed to improve American policy toward all internal conflicts, but its application to ethnic conflicts is obvious and far-reaching. American policy makers have sought to formulate guidelines about when, why, and how to intervene; who to intervene with under what command arrangements; how to conduct operations while intervening; and how and when to extricate American forces from an intervention. Long before the intervention in Kosovo, U.S. military operations in Somalia, Haiti, Rwanda, northern Iraq, and Bosnia had yielded an enormous number of lessons.

American political and military thinking about ethnic conflict has unquestionably come a long way since the end of the Cold War, but it still has far to go. American policy in this area remains impoverished at both the conceptual and tactical level. Signs abound of half-learned lessons and forgotten insights. Policy makers often stumble through situations without evidence that they possess either a strategic compass or a policy road map. Overall, the project of developing guidelines for American policy toward ethnic conflict remains incomplete.

Responding to ethnic conflict must be part of a broader strategy for reinvigorating American internationalism in the post-Cold War era. Since the days of Woodrow Wilson, the case for an internationalist foreign policy has always rested in part on a simple idea: that sustained American engagement to nurture peace and stability would lower the chances of war—that it was better to pay less now than to pay more later. This preventive logic has remained at the center of U.S. post-Cold War foreign policy toward the industrial areas of the world. In calling for a continued primacy in the West, American leaders have repeatedly invoked the lessons of past isolationist neglect. While recent internationalist policies for preserving the Western community have often been unimaginative and incrementalist, they have nonetheless won bipartisan support in Washington and among the public.

What has been missing in recent years is a vigorous application of this logic to foreign policy problems outside traditional core areas of American concern. Preventive efforts in peripheral regions have been lacking on three levels: First, American policies to address long-term causes of instability like poverty, overpopulation, and environmental degradation have remained poorly developed and funded, despite growing awareness of how these problems are linked to armed conflict. Second, American support for stronger collective security mechanisms that can promote stability in peripheral regions has been inconsistent. In addition to opposing many credible proposals to strengthen U.N. capabilities, the United States has often failed to play an activist role in trying to reduce conventional arms transfers, ensure human rights accountability, and institute new regional collective security measures. Third, the American record of short-term preventive diplomacy in crisis situations has been decidedly mixed; many dangerous situations have failed to make it on to Washington's radar screen and have slipped through the cracks, producing missed opportunities for constructive American engagement. Again and again, the United States has been surprised by ethnic conflicts or other wars on the periphery not because it lacks the capacity to predict these wars, but because it either hasn't devoted the resources to that goal or top policy makers haven't paid attention to the information that these efforts produced.

The case for an internationalism that stresses greater attentiveness to developments on the periphery, including far better efforts at predicting and preventing new conflicts, rests on two main arguments.

First, there is the simple matter of cost-effectiveness. Over the past thirty years, most of the massive humanitarian crises brought on by ethnic conflicts have elicited a major U.S. aid response. In the cases of Biafra, East Pakistan, Lebanon, the Kurdish exodus in 1991, and the refugee crisis created by the Rwanda genocide, the United States played a major role in dealing with the human suffering caused by ethnic conflicts. In some cases, the expenses incurred by this role have been enormous. The U.S. operations in Zaire/Rwanda in 1994 and Turkey in 1991 ran well over $1 billion. Moreover, these humanitarian operations, run by the U.S. military, have also put U.S. service personnel at risk. Clearly, if it is possible for the United States to predict and prevent crises that trigger expensive humanitarian interventions, every effort should be made to do so.

Second, attentiveness to the nascent conflicts on the periphery can be justified by a modified version of the cumulative threat argument of the Cold War. Just as too many setbacks on the periphery during the Cold War could weaken the Western position in core areas of concerns, so too can the proliferation of conflicts on the periphery damage core interests today. If zones of conflict and instability expand or multiply on the periphery, the well-being of the international system as a whole will suffer. Regions of the world that turn into battlefields often become dependent on aid from the developed world and cannot contribute to the growth of global prosperity. They become exporters of refugees, drugs, and terrorism. They require constant emergency attention from international organizations that should be working on long-term solutions to problems like economic inequity and environmental degradation. More dangerously, a United States that fails to track and accurately predict the trajectory of nascent ethnic conflicts in places like the Caucasus, Central Asia, and the Asian subcontinent may suddenly find itself facing crises that can escalate to threaten vital interests.

American policy toward ethnic conflict involves a dizzying array of calculations and an artful blending of realist and idealist foreign policy impulses. Difficult judgments must be made about the claims and merits of nationalist movements, their chances of creating viable states, the likelihood that a small insurgency will escalate into a large internal conflict, and the potential for outside powers to have any influence over the protagonists involved. Policy makers must also step back and look at the international system as a whole, assessing how ethnic struggles might impact on regional or global stability. And, most difficult of all, the United States must determine what national interests are at stake in conflicts and find policy instruments to employ that are commensurate with those interests.

None of these tasks is made easier by the wide variation among ethnic conflicts and the seeming uniqueness of each situation. Drawing lessons from one conflict to apply to others might appear a daunting, if not altogether misguided, exercise. That said, a close study of over a dozen ethnic conflicts that have attracted U.S. involvement during the past thirty years suggests that there are enough similarities in such situations to justify policy generalizations. In each conflict, the United States has used a standard array of policy tools in seeking to predict, prevent, and resolve the conflict.

In the case of Kosovo, all of these policy tools were vigorously employed at different phases of the crisis between 1989 and 1999. The American (and Western) experience in trying to influence the course of events in Kosovo yields new insights about each of these tools and has important ramifications for future U.S. policy toward other ethnic conflicts. In some cases, these insights provide encouragement; in others, they are a cause for acute pessimism.

PREDICTION AND PREVENTION

Ruined by war and sprinkled with mass graves, Kosovo stands today as a case study in the failure of preventive diplomacy. However, several years ago, Kosovo stood as a case study—unfinished to be sure—of successful preventive diplomacy. Even as war engulfed Croatia and then Bosnia, Kosovo remained at peace during the early and mid-1990s. This was a particularly notable feat given that Milosevic's nationalist crusade had been first trumpeted in Kosovo and most Western observers expected that a blow-up would occur in Kosovo sooner rather than later. That the blow-up came later is testament in large part to an enormous effort made by the United States and other Western powers. This effort made use of just about every tool of modern preventive diplomacy, including early warning measures for predicting violence. In the final analysis, however, Kosovo must be seen as evidence of how limited such tools are in the face of powerful nationalist passions.

In general terms, the explosion of violence in Kosovo in 1998 came as no great surprise. Western policy makers had been worrying about exactly such a contingency for nearly a decade. However, it appears that both the exact timing of the Kosovo Liberation Army's (KLA's) sudden rise in 1997 and 1998, along with Belgrade's specific choice of responses, was less clearly foreseen. This prediction failure, if it can be called that, illustrates the immense difficulties of mapping the likely trajectory of ethnic conflicts.

Predicting ethnic conflicts is no easy task. It involves hard judgment calls, often based on contradictory information. Secessionist movements and ethnic insurgents tend to be less predictable than state governments. They are often led by committed ideologues and are less likely to feel bound by treaties or conventions. The passions that fuel their efforts can be difficult for outsiders to comprehend and are different from the calculations of national interest that usually underpin state actions. Reliable information about non-state ethnic actors can be scarce. Often nationalist groups emerge suddenly and little is known about the personalities of their leaders or the nature of their governing organizations. There is no past track record by which to predict future performance. Basic details about internal debates in such groups can be difficult for intelligence agencies to obtain. Insurgent movements in particular often have very secretive governing processes that have been designed to thwart penetration by agents of the central state.

In addition, ethnic movements are often centered far away from national capitals in remote and even inhospitable regions. It is harder for embassy officials and intelligence agents to gather information in these places. Information from open sources is less plentiful because journalists have little incentive to visit remote regions until wars are already under way. Nonstate actors also have fewer means to communicate their motives and plans to foreign governments. American officials tend to be deeply hesitant about meeting with leaders of self-determination movements, for fear of seeming to lend them encouragement and angering national governments. Also, most nonstate actors do not have much of an apparatus to represent themselves abroad. The lack of contacts, both official and unofficial, between the United

States and self-determination movements denies policy makers an important source of intelligence.

All of these observations applied to the Kosovo Liberation Army. While the West became quite familiar during the 1990s with Ibrahim Rugova and the mainstream Kosovo independence movement, information about the KLA remained spotty and scarce during this same period. Formed in 1993, the KLA was an extremely secretive and shadowy group up until 1999.

Despite the obstacles posed by secretive secessionist groups and inscrutable nationalist passions, American officials have not always failed to predict ethnic conflicts. The Johnson administration had advance warning of the Biafra secession and American policy makers rightly believed that East Pakistan would make a bid for independence. Well before war exploded in Yugoslavia in 1991, the violent breakup of that country had been predicted within the U.S. government. Accurate predictions were also made of the violence in Rwanda, and the casualties it would yield. In addition, the United States did a very good job of monitoring instability in the Baltic states, where serious problems surrounded Russian minority populations during the early 1990s, and the situation in Romania, where instability was linked to a large Hungarian population.

Kosovo was highly unstable from the late 1980s onward because of systematic repression of ethnic Albanians by the Serb government in Belgrade. Following the revocation of Kosovo's semiautonomous status in 1989, Kosovars lost their right to political representation, lost control of the education system in Kosovo, experienced various kinds of cultural oppression, and were otherwise relegated to second-class citizenship within the Yugolsav republic. In addition, there was an upsurge in police abuses of ethnic Albanians in Kosovo, including the use of torture and extralegal executions. Milosevic's campaign of repression in Kosovo not only infuriated the Kosovar Albanians, but also inflamed the passion of their ethnic brethren across the border in Albania proper.

American policy officials were well aware of this situation and monitored it closely, fearing greater violence. When Warren Zimmerman became ambassador to Yugoslavia in 1989, he raised Kosovo in his first meeting with Milosevic, pressing for improvements in the human rights situation there. Milosevic's response was to not meet with Zimmerman for an entire year. Throughout the 1990s, Serb repression in Kosovo would continue, growing more severe at times. In late 1992, the United States received information that the notorious war criminal Arkan was moving to Kosovo to carry out ethnic cleansing. This information helped push the United States to threaten military action against Serbia, as will be discussed later.

Another factor behind the instability in Kosovo was support from outside the province for independence. Ethnic pockets are most destabilizing when the leaders of a neighboring state show a desire to rescue their stranded ethnic brethren. One of the most destabilizing periods of the Kosovo crisis came in 1992–1994, when the leadership of Albania spoke openly about a "greater Albania," implying a potential willingness to come to the aid of repressed Albanians in Kosovo and also incorporate the Albanian minority in Macedonia. This inflammatory rhetoric was accompanied by a number of violent incidents on the border between Kosovo and Albania. To their credit, American policy makers during the early 1990s closely monitored Albania's encouragement of ethnic secessionism in Kosovo, paying attention the rhetoric coming out of Tirana, analyzing the domestic factors fueling this nationalism, and creating levers of influence to use with the Albanian government to force a change in language, as well as behavior.

While American and Western involvement with Kosovo in the 1990s showed the effectiveness of efforts to predict instability and the gains that can come from being attentive to a nascent conflict, it also illustrated the limits of policies of prevention.

Even when American attention is fully engaged, which is rare, there is often little that can be done to alter the trajectory of an escalating ethnic conflict abroad. In most situations American leverage ranges from limited to nonexistent. Because ethnic conflicts tend to erupt outside of America's traditional sphere of interest, there are often few existing levers for influencing the actors involved. Typically, there are no large aid packages that can be suspended or major trading arrangements that can be reconsidered. And those levers of influence that do exist are often inadequate given the intensity of the passions involved. Ethnic groups in conflict tend to fear for their very survival. Foreign threats to withhold aid or trade may matter little in the face of stakes such as these. Outside coercion, moreover, works best with state leaders; it is less likely to affect the calculations of substate extremists like the KLA.

In the case of Kosovo, the United States had some leverage over Milosevic, who clearly was anxious to get economic sanctions lifted by the mid-1990s and not have them reimposed. The threat of airstrikes against Serbia, an industrial state with many economic and military assets, also conferred some leverage, although the limits of this leverage were made clear by the fact that Milosevic chose to endure NATO bombing rather than give up Kosovo without a fight. Meanwhile, the United States would turn out to have even less leverage with the KLA, a fact that became clear as peace talks foundered at various times in 1998 and 1999 due to the KLA's insistence on full independence for Kosovo. Overall, the crisis in Kosovo presented a classic example of the limited influence of outside powers in an ethnic conflict. In a number of other recent ethnic conflicts, of course, outside powers had even less influence.

To acknowledge the limits of policies to affect the course of ethnic conflicts is not to deny their virtues. The modest instruments available to the United States for preventing ethnic conflict have shown some worth in the past and there is much room for a more systematic approach to deploying these instruments in the future. In some cases, such as the Baltics, the United States has played a highly constructive role in helping to prevent ethnic conflict. In other cases, such as Chechnya, the United States squandered opportunities to possibly head off large-scale ethnic violence. Frequently, American policy toward nascent ethnic conflicts has been plagued by half-heartedness. American efforts have often come too late because of neglect and poor prediction, have not been backed by sufficient political and financial resources, have been inconsistent or abandoned while still inchoate, or have been poorly coordinated with allies, international organizations, and the NGO community. Occasionally, the United States has sanctioned the use of violence—either implicitly or explicitly—by a state intent on resolving an ethnic dispute only to see the situation escalate out of control.

By examining the historical record of American efforts to prevent ethnic conflict, now quite extensive, it is possible to develop a better understanding than currently exists of how, when, and where different types of preventive actions are likely to yield results. There is not room in this chapter to recount the full range of preventive U.S. efforts in regard to various ethnic conflicts over the past thirty years. However, the Kosovo crisis by itself provides an extremely rich case study of preventive diplomacy.

U.S. Preventive Diplomacy in Kosovo, 1989–1999

Given its importance and symbolic significance, Kosovo received far more attention from U.S. policy makers than many other hotspots of the 1990s. American efforts to prevent an explosion of violence in Kosovo covered a wide gamut of approaches over the course of nearly ten years: from official condemnation of Serbian repression and quiet diplomacy in Belgrade to the deployment of American forces in neighboring Macedonia, to a direct mediating role in negotiations, to open threats that the United States would use force to stop Serbian repression in Kosovo. Policy makers in both the Bush and Clinton administrations were moved to act by a sense of compelling national interests and by the belief that American actions could make a decisive difference. The national interests were varied and arguably nonvital, including the desire to prevent a wider war in the Balkans, a concern about human rights abuses, and the desire to signal U.S. and NATO resolve in the face of grave acts of internal repression. The opportunity was presented by the simple fact that Kosovo had, by 1992 and 1993, still not yet been sucked into the maelstrom that raged in much of the rest of former Yugoslavia. It was the one piece of the Yugoslav crisis that the United States had a chance to handle right.

The fate of ethnic Albanians in Kosovo was an issue that concerned the United States as early as the mid-1980s. Escalating repression in Kosovo caught the attention of Congress, which held hearings on the issue and passed resolutions calling for Yugoslavia to change its policies.[2] In early 1989

Kosovo became the subject of American concern when Milosevic used it to showcase his agenda of Serb nationalism. Proclaiming Kosovo to be a sacred Serbian homeland, Milosevic sought to take complete control of the republic's governing bodies and to deny the 90 percent Albanian majority any kind of autonomy from Belgrade. As mentioned earlier, when Warren Zimmerman arrived in Belgrade in March 1989, he carried a message from the Bush administration that the United States was deeply concerned about Kosovo and that good relations with Washington depended on an improvement of the human rights situation there.[3]

The crisis over Kosovo deteriorated rapidly through 1990. Serb authorities arrested thousands of political opponents and dismissed tens of thousands of Albanians from their jobs. As Serb intimidation and repression escalated, Kosovo's Albanians increased their demands, insisting on the right to form a republic separate from Serbia or to affiliate with Albania. In August, the United States took the lead in invoking the human rights mechanism of the CSCE process. In December 1990, Kosovo Albanians boycotted the national elections, despite advice from American diplomats that they should participate and seek to use a parliamentary minority to improve their situation. American diplomats in Belgrade also sought to alleviate the growing crisis by seeking to set up a meeting between Milosevic and the Kosovo Albanian leader Ibrahim Rugova. Rugova agreed, but Milosevic refused.[4]

Through 1991, as the Kosovo crisis escalated, the United States continued to press the Serb leaders to moderate their behavior. A comprehensive statement of American policy released in May 1991 strongly condemned Serb actions in Kosovo and announced that the United States would step up its efforts to address human rights abuses in Yugoslavia through CSCE mechanisms.[5] When Secretary of State Baker met with Milosevic in June 1991, Kosovo was high on his agenda and he confronted the Serbian leader about human rights problems there.

The outbreak of fighting in Croatia and Bosnia confirmed the worst about Milosevic's intentions and increased American fears about Kosovo. In August 1992, the United States conferred with other Western democracies at the London Conference on Yugoslavia and advocated, among other measures, deploying CSCE human rights monitors to Kosovo. Deputy Secretary Eagleburger said after the conference: "By moving the monitors in, we are at least beginning a process, I hope, of assuring that, in fact, outside forces will not be able to intervene in the Kosovo." The United States and its allies, said Eagleburger, had delivered clear warnings "to the government in Belgrade that they must be very cautious in regard to the Kosovo."[6]

The United States's failure to do anything to stop Serb aggression in 1992 —it wouldn't even enforce a no-fly zone over Bosnia—and the damage to American credibility that resulted made it all the more important to take a stand in Kosovo. The province would become the second line in the sand that George Bush drew during his presidency. In the fall of 1992, intelligence reports indicated that the Serbs might unleash a reign of terror in Kosovo in late 1992 or early in 1993. The notorious Serb war criminal and paramilitary leader Zeljko Raznjatovic, known as Arkan, had established a presence in Kosovo and tensions were rising.[7] The Bush administration's response was to threaten military action if new Serb aggression occurred. In a letter delivered in late December to Milosevic and the chief of the Yugoslav army, General Zivota Panic, President Bush stated that "in the event of conflict in Kosovo caused by Serbian action, the United States will be prepared to employ military force against the Serbs in Kosovo and in Serbia proper."[8]

According to former Bush administration officials, the American plan was to employ airstrikes against targets in Serbia. Pentagon plans for such attacks had now been in existence for some time, and despite past bluffing and American inaction in the former Yugoslavia, this threat was apparently real. "If in fact anything had happened we were prepared to do what we had said—that I promise you," Lawrence Eagleburger would later remark.[9]

The Clinton administration came into office determined to continue the tough policy on Kosovo. President-elect Clinton had been informed of Bush's December 1992 threat at the time and supported it. The new administration reiterated this threat and made it clear to Belgrade that American policy on Kosovo was unchanged. During their first year in office, Clinton and his aides would add two elements to that policy: the deployment of American troops to Macedonia and the pressuring of the Albanian government to tone down rhetoric that served to inflame the situation in Kosovo.

The decision to send a small number of American troops to Macedonia in mid-1993 came on the heels of the Clinton administration's failure to win European support for a new initiative to stop the war in Bosnia. Like the Bush administration, the Clinton team focused attention on Kosovo because there existed an opportunity to do something effective and to advance American national interests while not getting sucked into a shooting war. Containing the Balkans war was the next best thing to ending it, and appearing to do something big about a horrendous tragedy was the next best thing to actually doing something big. Announcing on May 12 that the United States might send troops to Macedonia, Clinton said: "We want to try to confine that conflict so it doesn't spread into other places, like Albania and Greece and Turkey, which could have the impact of undermining the peace in Europe and the growth and stability of democracy there."[10]

The deployment of 325 American troops to Macedonia in July 1993 as part of a small U.N. force was a symbolic move. Nobody expected a Serb attack on Macedonia and the troops were not prepared to intervene in Kosovo. The mission of the troops was to underscore in general terms American concern about Kosovo and Washington's willingness to project military force into the region if Serbia stepped up its provocations. The hope was to shore up

American credibility, which had fallen to an all-time low by summer 1993. The troop deployment was preceded by new warnings from Secretary of State Warren Christopher that the United States would not tolerate increased Serb repression in Kosovo.[11] These warnings were reiterated a few months after the deployment by Assistant Secretary of State Stephen Oxman, traveling to Albania in October. "We have said before we would regard as a very serious matter any conflict in Kosovo inspired by Serb actions and that we would respond," Oxman said. "The stationing of U.S. troops in Macedonia, sent as part of the U.N. mission, was also to send an important message that the United States would view with great seriousness any spillover of the conflict and we are determined to do what we can to prevent that."[12] Beyond signaling Belgrade, the deployment also was intended to show the European powers, that had forces in Bosnia under U.N. command, that the United States was now ready to commit more of its own power to the Balkans.

Having amplified its message to Serbia, the Clinton administration began devising a message to Albania and a strategy for delivering it. During the early 1990s, the Albanian government helped to stoke the flames of the Kosovo crisis by loudly supporting the claims of the secessionists there. It also contributed to instability in Macedonia, whose population is 30 percent Albanian, by backing nationalist politicians. Macedonian government officials accused Albania of going even further, and providing arms to Albanian extremists.[13] By late 1993, CIA intelligence reports were predicting that there was an unstoppable momentum in the region toward a "greater Albania."[14] The death of Albanian citizens in minor armed incidents on the Albanian-Yugolsav border in January 1994 led to acrimonious diplomatic exchanges between Serbia and Albania and served to increase tensions.

The Clinton administration's goal in this volatile environment was to get Albania to temper its nationalist rhetoric and become a proponent of moderate behavior among the ethnic Albanians in Kosovo and Macedonia. This was no easy task. While Albanian nationalism did not rival Serbian nationalism in its ferocity, the dream of creating a single state that included all six million Albanians in the Balkan region was a powerful force in Albanian domestic politics. In 1993 and 1994, there were strong incentives for Albanian President Sali Berisha to support Albanian militants in Kosovo and Macedonia.

The United States sought to counter these incentives by offering Berisha foreign aid and closer ties with Washington in exchange for moderating his behavior. In early 1994, the United States established a military presence in Albania, using a base in the country to fly spy missions over Serbia. Top American military officials visited the country regularly, and the American ambassador to Albania, William Reyerson, became an influential figure in government circles.

By summer 1994, President Berisha had significantly altered his position in regard to Albanians in Kosovo and Macedonia. Dropping his strong support for Kosovo's secession, Berisha began calling for talks between local Albanian leaders and the Serb government in Belgrade. He and Kosovo leader Rugova issued a joint statement on May 27 announcing this new concession. Berisha also met with Macedonian President Kiro Gligorov and promised to support the moderate, integrationist wing of the main Albanian party in Macedonia. Previously he had backed a militant faction.[15]

In July 1994, Defense Secretary William Perry arrived in Tirana to discuss American military assistance to Albania and closer security cooperation with the West. While dangling these carrots, he reiterated the message that Washington opposed support for Albanian nationalists in Kosovo and Macedonia.[16] Through the remainder of 1994 and into 1995, American officials continued to stress this point as they built closer ties to Albania. Tensions remained high in Macedonia and Kosovo, but the Albanian government was no longer actively fueling them as it once had.

In retrospect, some critics argue that Washington's policy toward Albania backfired disastrously by undermining Berisha's political popularity and leading to the breakdown of Albania's government in 1997—a development that resulted in a cascade of illegal arms flowing into Kosovo. This may be the case. However, the United States was clearly engaged in the correct policy when it took extensive measures to dampen calls for a greater Albania. It is sometimes said, as well, that the United States erred disastrously by not resolving the Kosovo situation during the Dayton peace talks that ended the Bosnia war in 1995. This is a spurious argument. If Kosovo had been included on the agenda of those peace talks, no agreement may ever have been reached on Bosnia.

The breakdown of the Albanian government in 1997 and the rise of the KLA, armed largely with black market weapons from Albania, dramatically changed the situation in Kosovo. Whereas the United States had previously been able to exert influence over three functioning states in trying to resolve the Kosovo crisis—Albania, Macedonia, and Serbia—it now faced the far more difficult challenge of trying to influence the behavior of a shadowy insurgent army and a Serbian government intent on crushing it. Not surprisingly, this effort would fail.

After the failure of the Rambouillet talks and the initiation of NATO airstrikes, there was extensive analysis of where the United States and its allies had gone wrong in their preventive diplomacy during 1998 and early 1999. To be sure, this period was fraught with miscalculations. Foremost among these was underestimating Milosevic's resolve in the face of threats of NATO military action. The argument has also been made that NATO was making excessive demands on Serbia and insisted on terms at Rambouillet that would have meant unacceptable infringements on Serbia's sovereignty. Conceivably, a different negotiating approach—perhaps one that involved mediation by the Russians and less intrusive demands—could have produced results.

INTERVENTION

The NATO intervention in Kosovo was a historic development in Western policy toward ethnic conflicts. Never before had outside powers intervened in a decisive military manner to stop a state from trying to repress a secessionist effort within its internationally recognized borders. Again and again, the West had stood passively by in the face of such crackdowns. In such notable cases as Biafra in the late 1960s, East Pakistan in 1971, Kurdistan in 1988, and Chechnya in 1995, the West took no military action in the face of bloody efforts to repress secessionist movements.

That said, the United States has employed its military forces in ethnic war zones on four other occasions besides Kosovo: in Lebanon in 1982–1983, in Kurdistan in 1991 and sporadically through the 1990s, in Bosnia from 1992 until the present, and in Rwanda in 1994. Except for Kosovo, only twice—in Lebanon and Bosnia—have American forces engaged in combat aimed at affecting the outcome of an ethnic conflict.

American policy makers have been reluctant to intervene in many ethnic conflicts out of respect for the norm of international sovereignty. However, quite apart from these political calculations, intervention in ethnic conflicts is an intrinsically difficult proposition for the United States. Since the United States rarely will have vital interests at stake in an ethnic conflict, it will almost always be inclined to use military force on a limited scale, if at all. It will seek to keep casualties low and minimize the national prestige that it lays on the line—goals that are notoriously hard to achieve. At the same time, the United States and other outside powers face a basic disadvantage in ethnic conflicts: Because ethnic extremists often see themselves as fighting for survival, many will be willing to pay almost any price and struggle for any length of time to prevail.[17] In a game of nerves with American leaders worried about domestic support, nationalist leaders will invariably have the upper hand.

In most cases, as well, American military power will be restrained in its potential effectiveness. Ethnic conflicts typically involve a great deal of guerrilla warfare or other types of low-intensity conflict. Insurgent or secessionist armies are likely to have decentralized and low-tech command and control arrangements that are not easily disrupted. Arms depots and supply lines will be dispersed and redundant. Military forces will be intentionally stationed among civilian populations. The terrain in conflict zones may often be inhospitable. Since combatants in ethnic conflicts are often substate actors, the United States will often not be able to target the high-value assets of a state as part of a strategy of coercion.

None of this means that American military force cannot have a decisive impact in some ethnic conflicts. But it does suggest that the odds will never be good and that the United States must approach the use of force with extreme circumspection. Any military action must be tied to a clear-cut and near-term diplomatic strategy for ending the war. There must, in other words, be a goal that American leaders think they can achieve through force and some way to measure when that goal has been met. Within the context of limited interests and thus limited engagement, the United States must be prepared to use force in a sustained and decisive manner once it has opted for a military option. Pinprick airstrikes or other symbolic actions are not likely to work. Finally, the United States should never undertake military actions that it does not believe will achieve its objectives, but nor should it paralyze itself by insisting on a quick or certain success, since this criterion will be impossible to meet in most conflicts.

In Kosovo, the United States made a remarkable effort to walk the fine line between doing nothing and not being sucked into a military quagmire. The effort was largely successful—the United States and NATO secured the withdrawal of Serb forces without the loss of life or the use of ground troops. However, once the bombs began falling, the war followed a very unpredictable course and several Western goals were undermined, including the desire to stop ethnic cleansing and prevent a broader destabilization of the region. Still, on balance, the Kosovo intervention can be viewed as bolstering the case for using limited military force to achieve limited political goals in regard to ethnic conflicts.

In authorizing military action in Kosovo, President Clinton disregarded a more cautious approach to intervention abroad, preached most fervently by former JCS Chairman Colin Powell. In the view of Powell and many like-minded national security specialists, the United States should only use military power abroad when there is a near-certainty of victory, a clear exit strategy, and strong support by the Congress and American public. Some also argue that vital interests must be at stake as well, although Powell himself was equivocal on that point.

Kosovo met none of the criteria of the Powell Doctrine. This was a limited war in defense of limited interests with no guarantee of success. While NATO's failure to mount a very heavy bombing campaign from the beginning and to keep open the option of ground forces were clear mistakes and confirmed the Powell Doctrine's emphasis on decisive force, more broadly, NATO's success in Kosovo has dealt a blow to the Powell Doctrine.

Powell was right to oppose the large-scale use of ground forces in difficult conflicts of dubious interest to the United States. But he was never persuasive in arguing against the use of limited military force in defense of limited interests. Well before Kosovo, NATO's successful intervention in Bosnia in 1995 made this clear. Even Somalia, arguably, showed the merits of a limited interests/limited response model: Only twenty-six Americans died in an operation that saved over a million people from starvation.

The excessive rigidity of the Powell Doctrine was predicated on a deep skepticism about air power. Some of this skepticism is warranted. For example, bombing could have done little to stop the genocide in Rwanda in 1994. Likewise, in Kosovo, the bombing campaign alone could not have won the war. Economic sanctions, persistent diplomacy, and military pressure by KLA forces contributed to driving Serbian forces from Kosovo.

Still, Kosovo can be seen as giving a major boost to air power advocates. Even while taking extreme precautions against casualties—both allied military and civilians—and even in the face of terrible weather and a slow start because of a shortage of aircraft, NATO forces slowly and methodically weakened Serb forces in Kosovo and the Serb military more generally. Through the use of pilotless drones, satellite reconnaissance, infrared imaging, and radar tracking systems, NATO was able to locate and destroy such elusive targets as mobile Serb artillery, camouflaged armored vehicles, and combat units on the move. Once NATO's aerial strike force became fully operational during the war's second month, Milosevic's capitulation became only a matter of time. Had NATO been willing to train and equip KLA fighters to direct air attacks, or sent in special forces for this purpose, the air campaign would have been even more effective.

True, air power alone did not win the war. But it did so without the use of NATO ground forces, which is the real test of whether air power was an effective tool of limited intervention. One can imagine other situations where Western air power could have been decisive in limiting the carnage wrought by an ethnic conflict. For example, if NATO had intervened in Bosnia in 1992 or 1993 with a massive bombing campaign, the Bosnian army would have been given an enormous advantage in the war and probably achieved stalemate with Serb forces much sooner, bringing the war to an earlier end and saving many lives.

But if the Kosovo case stands as compelling evidence that limited military force can indeed achieve decisive results on the battlefield, it also illustrates the extreme unpredictability of military intervention more generally. Here, again, the system can be seen as working, but not entirely well. NATO executed a successful air campaign that drove Serb forces from Kosovo without any loss of Western lives or a ground campaign. But the air campaign also greatly accelerated ethnic cleansing and mass killing in Kosovo and produced major negative fallout with both Russia and China. In this sense it was hardly a total success.

CONCLUSION

Even as Kosovar Albanians rebuild Kosovo, free at last from Serbian domination, the history of the Kosovo crisis offers an extremely sobering perspective on the West's capacity to resolve ethnic conflicts. At most points during the ten-year crisis, the United States and its allies took the proper course of action. They paid attention to growing instability in Kosovo and responded aggressively to that instability with the full range of preventive measures available. In retrospect, it is hard to argue that there were many preventive steps that the West should have taken but didn't. Likewise, in regard to NATO's military intervention, one can identify some mistakes, but by and large NATO took the right approach. Yet still there was enormous unforeseen fallout. In its totality, the West's handling of the Kosovo crisis produced a contradictory record of success and failure at the same time.

The Kosovo experience confirms inescapable realities about the nature of ethnic conflicts and about U.S. foreign policy in the current era. The stark truth about ethnic conflicts is that outsiders have little or no leverage over many such wars. For all the complexities of the Kosovo situation over the past ten years, the conflict arguably boiled down to a simple fact: Many Kosovar Albanians were determined to win autonomy from Serbian rule and the nationalist leaders in Belgrade were equally determined not to give it to them. A major war was probably inevitable, whatever the West did. The international community should always try to do something in the face of brewing ethnic conflicts, and in quite a few cases it will succeed in preventing widespread carnage. But it should not fool itself into believing that even the best designed system of preventive diplomacy will always produce success. A good analogy can be drawn here with medicine: often patients will die, no matter how first-rate the medical care.

The reality of mixed success in preventive diplomacy underscores a broader truth about U.S. foreign policy: constant frustration and a lack of clear-cut successes are simply permanent features of post-Cold War internationalism. That failures and frustrations are far more common in regard to U.S. policy toward the periphery is a leading reason why these policies are such easy targets for attack. Preventive diplomacy in places like the Balkans and central Africa is not the same kind of internationalism the public supported during the Cold War or easily supports today. There is no noble crusade here, no inexorable march toward victory—only a constant stream of nasty dilemmas that the public usually can't understand and that policy makers would prefer to avoid.

While skepticism of engagement on the periphery has been most vocally expressed by isolationists, there are also doubts among some internationalists, and understandably so. The limitless supply of problems on the periphery and the secondary nature of American interests there are possible reasons for focusing scarce resources on the core. Moreover, the internationalist project as a whole may be put at risk if its agenda is too expansive, too global, and if it includes goals so ambitious that disappointment is guaranteed. Because the liberal international order created in the mid-1940s is now at risk of decaying, it has been argued that the dominant task of U.S. foreign policy officials must be to shore up what has been called "internationalism on stilts."[18] Other primary foreign policy tasks, such as aiding Russia's transition to democracy, also require enormous attention. Adventures on the periphery are seen as a distraction from these central missions. Such arguments were often on display during the Kosovo crisis, with many critics saying that the intervention wasn't worth it because it undermined more important foreign policy goals, namely good ties with Russia and China.

In principle, this perspective has compelling elements. Sustaining and revitalizing the international order built over the past fifty years should be the chief goal of American foreign policy. Failures on the periphery can have an overflow effect, souring the public on international engagement generally. Busy policy makers do have to establish priorities as to where to expend their resources, and problems on the core should be at the top of their list.

In practice, the argument has two weaknesses. First, the core areas of traditional American concern do not exist in a bubble, but rather have myriad interconnections with less-developed parts of the world. The liberal international order will prosper best within a global system that is gradually becoming more stable and peaceful. This goal, in turn, requires containing zones of instability. A second pitfall of overfocusing on the core is that it is hard to see how humanitarian catastrophes can simply be ignored. In some cases, of course, this does occur. The brutal war in Angola, the continuing anguish of Sudan, and the descent into chaos of Afghanistan are all examples of nightmares that have been kept off the list of American foreign policy priorities in recent years. But the historical record going back to Biafra is equally replete with episodes that have galvanized American attention for month after month and have been impossible for policy makers to ignore. Just as presidents always discover that things like nomination fights and petty scandals regularly distract them from their big policy goals, so too do national security managers inevitably find that crises in peripheral regions demand their attention. Whatever the musings of grand strategists and the edicts crafted by interagency planners, policy makers often have little choice but to focus on less important priorities.

The key to minimizing the time and resources spent on ethnic conflicts on the periphery is not to ignore or downplay these problems. It is to give them enough salience in American foreign policy planning that they are worked constantly, at their earliest stages, so that they are not neglected and left to grow to the point that a full-scale effort is needed to handle them. Unfortunately, as the Kosovo case demonstrates, even such sustained efforts can sometimes fail in the end.

NOTES

1. Richard H. Ullman, "The Wars in Yugoslavia and the International System After the Cold War," in Richard H. Ullman, ed., *The World and Yugoslavia's Wars* (New York: Council on Foreign Relations Press, 1996), 36–37.

2. U.S. Congress, 99–2, House Foreign Affairs Committee. Hearings: *Persecution of the Albanian Minority in Yugoslavia* (Washington, D.C.: U.S. Government Printing Office, 1987); U.S. Congress, 100–2, House Foreign Affairs Committee. Hearings: *Developments in Europe*, 1988 (Washington, D.C.: U.S. Government Printing Office, 1988).

3. Warren Zimmerman, "The Last Ambassador: A Memoir of the Collapse of Yugoslavia," *Foreign Affairs*, Vol. 74, No. 2 (March/April 1995): 3.

4. Ibid., p. 8.

5. "U.S. Policy Toward Yugoslavia," *U.S. Department of State Dispatch*, June 3, 1991, p. 396.

6. Acting Secretary Eagleburger, "London Conference to Galvanize International Action," *U.S. Department of State Dispatch Supplement*, Vol. 3, No. 7 (September 1992): 9.

7. Paul Iredale, "Kosovo Seen as Possible Balkan Flashpoint," *The Reuters Library Report*, January 11, 1993.

8. Don Oberdorfer, "A Bloody Failure in the Balkans," *The Washington Post*, February 8, 1993, p. A1.

9. Ibid., p. A1.

10. Cragg Hines, "U.S. Plan Would Draw a Line in the Balkans," *The Houston Chronicle*, May 12, 1993, p. 1.

11. "300 U.S. Troops in Macedonia to Try to Contain Balkan War," *The New York Times*, July 13, 1993, p. 10.

12. "U.S. Warns Yugoslavia Against Spillover of Conflict," *Reuters*, October 22, 1993.

13. Llazar Semini, "Macedonia Using Shameful Old Serbian Plot, Albania Says," *The Reuters Library Report*, November 12, 1993.

14. David Binder, "CIA Doubtful on Serbian Sanctions," *The New York Times*, December 22, 1993, p. 3.

15. Yigal Chazan, "Albania Urged to Rein in Radicals Amid Fears of Greater Balkan Bloodbath," *The Guardian*, May 30, 1994, p. 8; Yigal Chazan, "Tempering the Dream of a 'Greater Albania,'" *The Christian Science Monitor*, July 20, 1994, p. 7.

16. Suzanne M. Schafer, "Perry Opens Talks on Military Assistance to Albania," *AP Worldstream*, July 20, 1994.

17. Robert Cooper and Mats Berdal, "Outside Intervention in Ethnic Conflicts," in Brown, *Ethnic Conflict and International Security*, p. 201.

18. John Ikenberry and Dan Deudney are the authors of this term.

9

Charles Evans Hughes Reconsidered, or: Liberal Isolationism in the New Millennium

Edward Rhodes

Since the 1940s, it has been unfashionable, particularly in elite and academic circles, to speak favorably of the liberal isolationist foreign policies pursued by the United States in the 1920s. Indeed, it has been unfashionable even to think seriously about these policies. Parodied, demonized, or dismissed out of hand as an error of catastrophic proportion, the liberal isolationist vision of international security that shaped the behavior of the Republican administrations of the 1920s has received little serious, balanced scholarly attention. A recent outbreak of realist neoisolationism on the far right of the American political spectrum—myopic in vision, reactionary in agenda, nationalist in rhetoric, populist in appeal, and mildly xenophobic in psychology—has only reinforced deeply held elite presumptions regarding the intellectual vacuity of isolationism.

Ironically, however, the liberal isolationism of the 1920s was in critical respects the mirror opposite of today's conservative neoisolationism. For liberal isolationist policy makers of the 1920s, the world was not an inherently violent place or a lawless, Hobbesian jungle to be avoided, nor was it demonized as a source of dangerous contagions. To be sure, then as now there were some in America who saw the world in such terms, but American foreign policy makers in the 1920s did not envision building American security by erecting a bulwark of economic, social, and political barriers against the world outside. Like their internationalist Wilsonian colleagues, successive Republican administrations in the 1920s believed in the possibility and necessity of constructing a peaceful world order, one that rested on shared values and the rule of law rather than on a balance of power or skillful *Realpolitik*. American policy in the 1920s was isolationist only in the sense that it presumed that peace could not be created through American political or military intervention in world politics, however well-intentioned, but would have to depend on the organic evolution of national societies around the globe. Peace, in this view, had to be constructed by changes in how peoples understood themselves and their interests. Neither peace nor this altered understanding could be imposed from above or from outside—though both would be aided by transnational economic and cultural contact and by skillful diplomacy aimed at resolving disputes before they inflamed national passions. A mature, liberal understanding of self-interest would lead to international bonds of amity, and these in turn would yield collective security. In the absence of an amity growing naturally from this liberal construction of identity, though, it was irresponsible or even dangerous to believe that collective security could be guaranteed by formal institutions. Since mature, liberal political systems could not be imposed from above or from outside, neither international institutions nor intervention offered the key to peace—however desirable the one, or sometimes necessary the other, might be.

The habit of cavalierly dismissing the American foreign policy of the 1920s as naive or wrong-headed is unfortunate, for it obscures or mischaracterizes a history in which Americans could reasonably take pride and from which considerable positive guidance could be derived. The liberal isolationist policies crafted by Charles Evans Hughes, secretary of state from 1921 to 1925, represented a diplomatic achievement of historic proportions and a high-water mark of American statesmanship. Pursuing a course remarkable for its conceptual clear-headedness and political skillfulness, Hughes adroitly silenced the voices of competitive nationalism and maneuvered through successive crises, consistently advancing the cause of world peace.

More to the point, unthinking condemnation of the liberal isolationist policies of the 1920s is unfortunate because these policies and the vision of world politics that lay behind them are relevant today. In the wake of the Cold War, America again faces a world in which no great powers challenge the status quo but in which great power rivalries loom ominously on the horizon and in which liberal democracy struggles to take root in new soil. Conventional wisdom in elite circles, based in no small measure on the lessons of the interwar experience and the tragedies of the 1930s and 1940s, is that in these circumstances there is no acceptable alternative to global American politico-military engagement and an American embrace of global collective security. A more realistic examination of the 1920s, however, argues the contrary: Not only does a liberal isolationist alternative exist, but it is also far more promising than a reprise of Wilsonian interventionism, with its focus on international institutions rather than on the organic processes of domestic political evolution and identity construction.

For a mainstream scholar, such an assertion is apostasy. Since the 1940s, American international relations scholars and political leaders have been raised in the belief that the 1920s "pathway of peace"[1] was a tragic wrong turn, both on America's road to mature responsibility and on the world's road to stable order. This interpretation of the 1920s has become an article of faith, an item in America's foreign policy creed, a part of the educational catechism. For two generations, intellectual and political "correctness" have demanded automatic, complete, and unquestioning abjuration of the sin of liberal isolationism. But however valuable this absolute and unquestioning devotion to the true religion of internationalism may have been during the Cold War, intellectual honesty and political survival now demand heresy.

In the spirit of Dick Ullman's work—which has always combined iconoclasm with a deep, yet nuanced commitment to liberal values—this chapter deliberately commits that heresy. To that end, I begin by exploring the assumptions and logic underlying liberal isolationism. I continue by explaining why it was psychologically and politically necessary to discredit the liberal isolationist policies of the 1920s. I then proceed to argue that these policies were, in fact, highly successful. I conclude by making the case that liberal isolationism is relevant to today's world and by sketching out the basic implications of it for foreign policy in the new millennium.

The starting point for such an exercise is with the recognition that the canonical interpretation of the 1920s, portraying it as a period of foreign policy stagnation, xenophobic nationalism, and naive idealism, is simply wrong and cannot withstand scrutiny. It ignores the liberal isolationist policy demarches that, *inter alia*, halted a destabilizing great-power arms race, reversed the rapid deterioration of Anglo-American relations, created Japanese-American accord, restored German-American amity and provided the basis for a reduction in Franco-German tensions, committed the imperial great powers to supporting a sovereign China, stabilized the great-power rivalry in the Pacific, threw American weight behind a number of important transnational technical and humanitarian efforts, encouraged the development of domestic democratic institutions around the world, and opened a new era in U.S.-Mexican and U.S.-Latin American relations.

Coming between the political cataclysm of World War I and the social and ideological maelstrom of the Depression and World War II, it is easy to overlook the 1920s. Good times rarely merit examination or explanation. And, at least relatively speaking, the 1920s were a good time. They were a period of peace and prosperity. They were a time of healing after a tragedy of unimaginable proportions. And they were a decade of constructive experimentation with liberal democratic institutions aimed at meeting the challenges posed by political modernity and economic development.

These happy realities were in no way foreordained, however. An intelligent student of world affairs observing from the vantage point of 1920 would have to be forgiven for pessimism: With the old social and political order in ruins, economies devastated, major territorial and diplomatic issues unresolved, nationalist sentiment enraged, and revolution in the air, the global picture looked bleak indeed. It is only in retrospect that we assign an in-evitability to the 1920s and conclude that peace was in the natural order of things. But in this case 20-20 hindsight is more misleading than the cloudy con-temporaneous picture. The happy order of the 1920s was created, not given. And its creation was in no small measure due to American foreign policy.

To be sure, American foreign policy in the 1920s was far from perfect. Er-rors—terrible errors—were made. Without question, the most serious of these came in trade policy. It would be difficult today to find an apologist for the protectionism of the 1920s. But it should be evident that America's pro-tectionist policies were not only logically distinct from the liberal diplomatic and military course steered by the State Department, they were logically *in-compatible* with it. Perhaps Hughes's greatest failure as secretary of state was his inability to recognize this inconsistency—his inability to understand that so long as the American tariff wall remained high, repayment of war debts by allies and payment of reparations by Germany would in the end prove im-possible, and that unless Japan were fully integrated economically into the liberal order its political integration would be fragile.[2] A consistent liberal iso-lationist policy would have embraced free trade, despite the parochial objec-tions of traditional Republican domestic constituencies. Other errors can also be identified. Congressional limitation of Japanese immigration (over Hughes's fierce opposition) was a racist blunder of serious proportions. And Hughes's refusal to recognize the Soviet Union, though not a significant blow to American or international security, was arguably short-sighted and unwise.

To levy these criticisms, though, is simply to fault the Republican admin-istrations of the 1920s for being insufficiently liberal and for being too sensi-tive to pressures from the business community and xenophobic nationalists. It is not to deny the basic political premises on which the liberal isolationist policy was built—which is what post-1941 critics have consistently done. Perhaps the best starting place, then, for an analysis of the successes and fail-ures of 1920s liberal isolationism and of its possible relevance today is an ex-amination of the logical and philosophical underpinnings of it.

WHAT IS "LIBERAL ISOLATIONISM," ANYWAY?

One of the problems encountered in analyzing and evaluating liberal isola-tionism, of course, is that not only has the term *isolationism* always been a pejorative, but it has been a pejorative applied to a wide range of policies.[3] The range of meanings given to isolationism has made it an easy target for caricature. The notion, for example, that America should cease to have eco-nomic or social contact with the rest of the world, becoming some sort of hermit kingdom, is patently silly and no serious voices, either in the 1920s or now, have advocated it. Similarly silly is a concept of isolationism that envisions the American state refusing to participate in any international regimes or institutions. In neither of these senses has America ever been isolationist. America in the 1920s, however, did pursue an approach to foreign policy and an approach to creating a secure and stable international order that was fundamentally different from that of the early republic, from that pursued during the Progressive period, and from that advocated by Woodrow Wilson, and, pejorative or not, it is reasonable to describe this approach as liberal isolationist. The approach reflected the melding of several important intellectual traditions in American thought, the continued effort to build a cohesive industrial society able to overcome the fissiparous class and ethnic pressures associated with industrialization and urbanization, a compromise between competing regional economic and political interest groups, and the struggle to give meaning to the Great War.[4] It would be an oversimplification, therefore, to credit or blame any single individual or small group of individuals with America's liberal isolationist policies of the 1920s. Certainly in practice and even to some significant degree in design, these policies were a pastiche rather than the embodiment of some unified conception. Nonetheless, in important ways Charles Evans Hughes was both the principal architect of America's liberal isolationist foreign policy and its clearest explicator. In the interest of defining "liberal isolationism" for discussion, therefore, and at the risk of appearing wrongly to single him out, it is convenient to focus closely on Hughes.

Charles Evans Hughes and the Logic of Liberal Isolationism

Now largely forgotten, Hughes was one of the great political figures of his age, both in America and on the world stage, and was very much the intellectual rival of his opponent in the narrowly lost presidential election of 1916, Woodrow Wilson.[5] Hughes's public career was distinguished and wide-ranging. A progressive Republican New York City lawyer catapulted overnight into the public eye by his service on public commissions investigating corruption in the utility and insurance industries, Hughes served as governor of New York from 1907 to 1910, stepping down to accept President William Howard Taft's appointment as associate justice of the U.S. Supreme Court. Despite pressure from supporters in the Republican Party, Hughes refused to leave the court to run for president in 1912; in 1916, he declined to seek his party's nomination (or, indeed, even to indicate a willingness to accept it) but having received it, stepped down from the court to take up the race against Wilson. Suspicious of party professionals, Hughes ran a badly managed and unimpressive campaign. Despite this, he nearly won (as in 1948, election night reports wrongly predicted a Republican victory).[6]

The campaign was waged primarily on domestic issues. For the most part, the foreign policy differences between Hughes and Wilson were not clearly articulated. In the campaign, Hughes criticized Wilson for insufficient military preparation, held that Wilson had not been firm or clear enough in warning Germany about the unacceptability of unrestricted submarine warfare, and faulted Wilson's Mexican policy on two grounds: first, that Wilson had intervened in Mexican domestic politics through his thinly veiled efforts to unseat Huerta and, second, that he had failed to intervene effectively to protect American lives from Villa's bandits.[7] At first blush, then, it might appear that Hughes was inconsistently blasting Wilson both for too much and for too little intervention. This, however, would be an error. Rather, Hughes was offering an argument he would make most famously in 1928 in Havana at the Sixth International Conference of American States. In 1916, as throughout his career in foreign policy, Hughes argued against any intervention in the affairs of another sovereign state directed at altering the government or policies of that state, regardless of whether or not such intervention was designed to advance liberal democracy. Simultaneously, however, he asserted what in 1928 he would term the right of "interposition," arguing that sovereign states had not only a right but also a duty to protect the lives and property of their nationals when anarchy or lawlessness threatened them. Though neither Hughes nor Wilson developed the point, this different understanding of what justified military entanglement in other states' affairs also explained their differences in policy toward Germany.

Following America's entry into the European war, Hughes threw himself into public service, personally chairing the New York City District Draft Appeals Board, and, at Wilson's request, heading a federal investigation of corruption in aircraft procurement. Hughes's high-profile legal career during this period included, most notably, his pro bono defense of Socialist Party legislators denied their seats in the New York State Assembly.

In 1920, president-elect Warren G. Harding asked Hughes to join his cabinet as secretary of state; following Harding's death Hughes continued in this position in the Coolidge administration. Resigning from the cabinet in 1925 to make provisions for his family's financial security, Hughes returned to public life in 1928 as a judge on the Permanent Court of International Justice in the Hague. Ever the advocate of international arbitration and American membership on the World Court, Hughes turned down repeated requests from president-elect Herbert Hoover to leave the court to return to Washington to again head the State Department, as well as Hoover's offer of the ambassadorship to the Court of Saint James's. In 1930, however, he yielded to entreaties from Hoover and the dying Taft to return to the U.S. Supreme Court as Taft's successor as chief justice. Hughes retired in 1941, having shaped the Court's tempered response to the New Deal's expansion of federal powers along the Progressive jurisprudential lines laid down during his first tenure on the Court and having led the fight against Franklin Roosevelt's court-packing proposal.[8] Although Hughes's service as secretary of state lasted only four years, Hughes's successors—Frank Kellogg and Henry Stimson—pursued the policies Hughes established, though (particularly in Kellogg's case) arguably with less adeptness and (in Stimson's case) in circumstances increasingly unlike those for which they had been charted.[9]

Although Harding and Coolidge gave him a free hand over foreign policy, Hughes was constrained and constantly harassed by an activist Senate, most importantly on the central question of the League of Nations. In many ways, the issue of the League represented the critical political battleground for liberal isolationism, and the issue that most clearly encapsulated the philosophical differences between the liberal internationalists, the liberal isolationists, and the realist isolationists.[10]

Beginning in 1916, Hughes consistently and publicly advocated the creation of some sort of international organization to promote and facilitate peace,[11] but from Wilson's first announcement of the proposed League, Hughes was a "Reservationist": he favored the League, minus its controversial Article X that created a collective obligation to respond to aggression. Hughes's biographer has Hughes averring to his wife as he first read the draft of Article X, "the American people will never stand for that."[12] Within weeks, however, Hughes explained his philosophical objections to Article X, and in general avoided attacking it on the grounds of political impossibility, preferring to focus on why the article was undesirable rather than infeasible. In his March 26, 1919, Union League speech, Hughes dubbed the collective security provision "a trouble-breeder and not a peace-maker,"[13] and articulated two objections.

In the first place, he argued Article X was short-sighted and likely to prove dangerously iniquitous. Always a Progressive in outlook, Hughes believed in the organic growth and evolution of polities and political relationships; any effort to freeze conditions would inevitably became a reactionary defense of the rights of the privileged against what might, in some cases, be the reasonable and legitimate demands of the dispossessed and the interests of the community as a whole. The League covenant, in his view, mistakenly conflated preservation of the status quo with justice, and Article X bound the United States and the other signatories to the support of this status quo. "The guaranty," he warned, "makes no allowance for changes which may be advisable. It ascribes a prescience and soundness of judgment to the present Peace Conference in erecting States and defining boundaries which no body in the history of the world has ever possessed. Even as to the new States, it attempts to make permanent existing conditions, or conditions as arranged at this Conference, in a world of dynamic forces to which no one can set bounds. It gives no fair opportunity for adjustments."[14] Were the other League members uninterested liberal national republics, there might have been grounds for optimism about the potential for peaceful adjustment to correct injustices and respond to changing realities. The recent history of hard, self-interested bargaining at Versailles, however, effectively dispelled any such naive hopes. Article X would offer the imperial powers a blank check. As a consequence, Hughes concluded that "the guaranty would be unwise even if it could accomplish its apparent purpose."[15]

In the second place, he reasoned that an American pledge to collective security was logically unnecessary, a bluff, or, worst, incompatible with democratic institutions. If the bonds of amity were such that America would come to the defense of the threatened parties, then the commitment was unnecessary. If such bonds of amity did not exist, and if Congress and the people refused to become involved, then the pledge would prove a sham and would tend to undermine international law and society. If the United States fulfilled its obligation despite the will of the American people, then the American state's democratic foundations would be shaken. Of these three possibilities, however, Hughes considered the second by far the most likely:

> Certainly, each Power will be the judge of what in good faith it should do. In the case of the United States, the guaranty will not be made good except by the action of Congress, and it will be for Congress to decide whether we are bound and what we should undertake. The course of recent debates has sufficiently indicated what the attitude of Congress is likely to be, if the resort to war pursuant to Article X is opposed to the opinion of the country. Congress not improbably will consider that it has not been put under any proper obligation to assume the unwelcome task. In such a case, the guaranty would merely serve the purpose of permitting the charge that we had defaulted in our obligation.[16]

The sensible path to collective security, Hughes reasoned, was not through creating an obligation but through creating a sentiment and will: The task was to educate Americans and others on shared interests, not to dictate that they act against their understanding. "I am not unmindful," Hughes observed,

> of the importance of making response to the importunate demand of stricken and suffering peoples that an organized endeavor should be made to prevent the recurrence of strife. I deeply sympathize with the purpose to provide international arrangements for conference, for the judicial settlement of disputes, for conciliation, and for cooperation to the fullest extent practicable and consistent with a proper regard for our national safety. But. . . . I think that it is a fallacy to suppose that helpful cooperation in the future will be assured by the attempted compulsion of an inflexible rule. Rather will such cooperation depend upon the fostering of firm friendships springing from an appreciation of community of ideals, interests, and purposes, and such friendships are more likely to be promoted by freedom of conference than by the effort to create hard and fast engagements.[17]

Even as he strenuously disputed the wisdom of Article X, however, Hughes continued to endorse an international organization of more modest ambition and to work with the "Mild Reservationists" in the Senate to try to bridge the unbridgeable gap between Wilson, who refused to budge on Article X, and the "Irreconcilables," who refused to accept any need for the League. To Senator Eugene Hale he wrote: "There is plain need for a league of nations, in order to provide for the adequate development of international law, for creating and maintaining organs of international justice and the machinery of conciliation and conference, and for giving effect to measures of international cooperation which from time to time may be agreed upon."[18]

In the campaign of 1920, Hughes was one of thirty-one prominent Republicans ("The Committee of 31") publicly pledged to bringing America into the League subject to a reservation regarding Article X commitments.[19] Hughes accepted Harding's invitation to serve as secretary of state believing the administration's policy would be to pursue membership in a modified League. Within days of the inauguration, however, it became clear that the administration would be blocked by diehard Senate "Irreconcilables," whose numbers and resolve had been bolstered by the anti-Wilson landslide in the election. Rather than resign immediately, Hughes chose to stay on, generally maneuvering adroitly around obstacles created by the Senate to pursue his vision of international order.

"Liberal Isolationism" in the 1920s

But what exactly was this liberal isolationist vision? Given the high-tariff trade policy being pursued, in what sense was the Republican foreign policy charted by Hughes "liberal"? And given both the intense public and private activity of America in global politics and Hughes's willingness to embrace international institutions other than those premised on commitments to collective security, in what sense was it "isolationist"?

Hughes's vision was liberal in the sense that it explicitly denied the dog-eat-dog premises of realism and embraced the notion of a natural, peaceful order. The world, Hughes argued, was not one necessarily ruled by power. It was not one in which might necessarily made right or in which conflict was inevitable. It was not simply the protection offered by the sovereign leviathan that prevented life from being nasty, brutish, and short. In a well-ordered, mature society, Hughes observed, there existed natural harmony of interests, and in such a society, whether domestic or international, peace and order rested on consent and adjudication rather than on coercion and intimidation. Order, in the context of international anarchy, could thus rest on foundations other than a balance of power, just as order in the context of a hierarchic domestic system need not imply a police state.

This faith in the possibility of achieving a harmonious, natural order rested on a particular Enlightenment view of human nature. Human beings might indeed at times be ruled by their passions, by emotions, by fears, by anger, and by lust for power, but these same human beings were also endowed with the capacity for reason, and reason might enable them to see their own best interests and permit them to cooperate in the achievement of those interests. As education could improve individuals, helping them rule themselves by reason rather than yielding to their baser passions, so progress might help national societies develop domestic institutions that subjugated emotion to reason and that therefore allowed them to discover the natural amity possible in international relations.

Hughes's view of democracy is significant. He never wavered in his commitment to democracy and his belief in democratic institutions, but it was the capacity for self-control that he saw as essential to good government, nationally and globally. Though desirable, democracy was neither a panacea nor an unmixed blessing. Democracy had to be coupled both with a cultural maturity that subordinated passions to reason and with a set of domestic institutions that permitted statesmanship and reduced the danger of demagoguery. "We have to take account of both the advantages and disadvantages of democratization," Hughes observed.

> It is generally thought that democracies are disposed to peace, but this is yet to be demonstrated where there is deep feeling and a national sense of injury. Great wars, involving vast populations, cannot be fought without public support, but the most serious causes of war are precisely those which carry popular appeal. The peoples of the warring nations were never so united as during the last war, and this was equally true of both sides. A sense of injury is easily created and confused with a sense of justice. A despot may be as indisposed to war as any people, and democracies never lack leaders to inflame popular passion. While we should expect peoples to be slow to war in minor exigencies, the test comes when national sentiment is deeply aggrieved.[20]

Hughes's constant battles with the Senate also made clear to him the particular challenges of statecraft in a democracy:

> it is necessary to reckon with the special difficulties inherent in democratic organization of government with respect to the endeavor to maintain peace by concluding international agreements. . . . Aside from honest criticism, modern negotiations between democracies furnish rare opportunities for the ready tongues of demagogues. There are today serious questions between peoples which ought to be taken up and settled in order to heal festering sores. But those in charge of foreign affairs do not dare to undertake to negotiate agreements because they know that in the presence of attack inspired by political or partisan motives the necessary adjustment could not receive the approval of the legislative branch and would evoke such an acrimonious controversy on both sides that matters would be made worse instead of better. The discussion of international agreements naturally and properly engages the attention of the public press, but that also not only gives opportunity for reasonable criticism, but for the pseudopatriots to seize a vantage point against the government they de-

sire to attack. . . . Democracies may be loath to go to war, but they are extremely difficult agencies of international compromises in the interest of peace.[21]

Ultimately, peace and a just order depended on *virtu*, understood in terms of the capacity for rational self-control. Though Hughes never resorted to the language of Machiavelli, much less Rousseau, his understanding of the functioning of a community, whether of national or international scope, can be seen as hinging on his image of republican *virtu*, an image rooted in the Scottish rationalist school.[22] It was the subjugation of passion to reason in human life and in national life that permitted the functioning of social and political institutions—not the reverse. For Hughes, the essence of a democratic republic was not its forms, its constitution, or its institutions, but the *virtu* of its members and leaders. "We must have a constant application of reason," Hughes concluded. "That is what free government means. We have come down the course of history winning the victories of democracy, and summed up in a word, they are the victories of public judgment over force."[23] As harmony in a national republic necessarily rested on this triumph of judgment and reason (not on the perfection of any forms, constitution, or institutions), so too would harmony in an international *res publica*—that is, in a global community composed of sovereign states.

Hughes was neither naive nor millenarian in his hope for a liberal peace between nations, but neither did he yield to despair. He always recognized that maintaining a peaceful order was an iffy process, an aspiration rather than an expectation. At times, in his frank acknowledgment of the failure of civilization to rein in the emotions that led to violence, Hughes sounded more like a realist than a liberal. War, he observed, had been a common and natural occurrence in the lives of nations, and he was not optimistic it could be eliminated. "We may gain something in our quest for peace," Hughes argued,

if we recognize at once that war is not an abnormality. In the truest sense, it is not the mere play of brute force. It is the expression of the insistent human will, inflexible in its purpose.

When we consider that the inability to maintain a just peace attests the failure of civilization itself, we may be less confident of the success of any artificial contrivances to prevent war. We must recognize that we are dealing with the very woof and warp of human nature. The war to end war has left its curse of hate, its lasting injuries, its breeding grounds of strife, and to secure an abiding peace appears to be more difficult than ever. There is no advantage in shutting our eyes to the facts; nor should we turn in disgust of panaceas to the counsel of despair. The pathway of peace is the longest and most beset with obstacles the human race has to tread; the goal may be distant, but we must press on.[24]

Recognition that war was not an abnormality and that the tendency to violent emotions was part of the basic fabric of human nature meant that pacifism held no appeal for Hughes and that, despite his abiding commitment to law, adjudication, and the pursuit of peace, he saw a continuing need for the nation to remain prepared for armed conflict. The United States might well be confronted by states whose passions or myopia led them to attack the liberal order in ways that threatened American lives, property, or vital national interests. In dealing with such unreasonable states, Hughes did not advocate turning the other cheek. No less than Wilson or Theodore Roosevelt, he concluded the necessity of American involvement in the European war, and when America entered that war threw himself energetically into its prosecution.

From a post-Cold War perspective, how should we make sense of the refusal of the liberal isolationists to yield to pessimism despite their acknowledgment of the normality of war? Two points are key. On the one hand, their dual view of human nature—that mankind was capable not only of egoism, passion, and inflexible will but also of reason, farsighted and empathetic appraisals of self-interest, and love of justice—sets them apart from thinkers we might describe as classical realists. On the other hand, their belief in an achievable harmony of interests sets them apart from both radicals and structural realists, whose understanding of interest or of anarchy implies the inevitability of conflict.

This belief in a natural international harmony and in the capacity of nations to develop institutions that would permit them to identify their shared interests and to rise above judgment-clouding passions did not, however, lead Hughes into the error of expecting, or even hoping for, some sort of liberal "end of history." Societies and their political institutions were never fixed, but constantly growing and changing. They could not be frozen at some healthy point. There was nothing inevitable about the preservation of liberal, democratic values and institutions once achieved. Subjugating passion to reason and nourishing liberal democracy were continuing daily challenges for every society—not simply in Europe and Asia, but for America herself. Significantly, he titled perhaps his theoretically most significant speech "Pathway *of* Peace," not "Pathway *to* Peace": peaceful relations between nations were something to be lived, not an end state.[25]

For Hughes, the greatest threat to America and the greatest challenge for Americans seeking to advance world peace was always *internal*, not external. The danger was not some insidious conspiracy or subversive ideology (despite his unconcealed distaste for communism and his abhorrence of its excesses, Hughes had no patience for those concerned with a domestic "Red Menace"), but complacency and inattention; the perversion of public policy to serve private gain rather than common good; and (especially) demagogic and emotional appeals to an immature or divided public. In his 1910 Yale lectures, delivered before he joined the Supreme Court for the first time, Hughes argued that

> No greater mistake can be made than to think that our institutions are fixed or may not be changed for the worse. . . . Increasing prosperity tends to breed indifference and to corrupt moral soundness. Glaring inequalities in condition create discontent and strain the democratic relation. The vicious are the willing, and the ignorant are the unconscious instruments of political artifice. Selfishness and demagoguery take advantage of liberty. The selfish hand constantly seeks to control government, and every increase of governmental power, even to meet just needs, furnishes opportunity for abuse and stimulates the effort to bend it to improper uses. . . . The peril of this Nation is not in any foreign foe! We, the people, are its power, its peril, and its hope![26]

Twenty-seven years later, speaking as chief justice and addressing both the rise of totalitarianism in Europe and Franklin Roosevelt's court-packing scheme, Hughes returned to the same themes.

> We still proclaim the old ideals of liberty but we cannot voice them without anxiety in our hearts. The question is no longer one of establishing democratic institutions but of preserving them. . . . The arch enemies of society are those who know better but by indirection, misstatement, understatement, and slander, seek to accomplish their concealed purposes or to gain profit of some sort by misleading the public. The antidote for those poisons must be found in the sincere and courageous efforts of those who would preserve their cherished freedom by a wise and responsible use of it. Freedom of expression gives the essential democratic opportunity, but self-restraint is the essential civic discipline.[27]

The Liberals Battle: Hughesian Isolationists versus Wilsonian Internationalists

Perhaps the key to understanding the "isolationist" quality to Hughes's vision, and to understanding why he and the liberal isolationists divided from Wilson and the liberal internationalists, is to note Hughes's argument regarding the superficiality of international institutions and the fallacy of relying upon them. International institutions were superstructure in his account. This did not mean that international institutions were not useful—indeed, very useful and well worth creating and supporting, as Hughes repeatedly argued in establishing international commissions, arbitration agreements, and courts. When the parties engaged were ruled by reason and understood their self-interest in cooperation, international institutions could facilitate this cooperation, in essence reducing transaction costs. The existence of a World Court and preexisting arbitration procedures, for example, made adjudication of justiciable disputes easier. Similarly, institutions to coordinate efforts against international crime and disease, and to create international standards and arrangements on technical matters, were highly desirable. Such institutions would tend to reduce the occurrence of conflicts between states or permit states to resolve such conflicts in a nonpolitical fashion, before national passions were engaged.

But in the absence of reason and the amity that reason bred, institutions for providing collective security would not work precisely when they were most needed. If the strong were not mature and wise, and if they had not used this maturity and wisdom to resolve the issues of discord between them, then no agreement, organization, or expectation would bind nations together, and international peace would prove impossible:

> in the field of conflicting national policies, and what are deemed to be essential national interests, when the smoldering fires of old grievances have been fanned into a flame by a passionate sense of immediate injury, or the imagination of peoples is dominated by apprehension of present danger to national safety, or by what is believed to be an assault upon national honor, what force is to control the outbreak? Great powers agreeing among themselves may indeed hold small powers in check. But who will hold great powers in check when great powers disagree?[28]

If passions were unchecked and grievances burned hot, then the world would slip back into the disorder that realists imagined, force not justice would rule affairs, and safety would lie in a favorable balance of power—not in institutions.

Hughes thus anticipated the failure of the League to restrain Germany, Italy, and Japan in the 1930s. Consulted by Cordell Hull in April 1944 regarding the design of the League's successor, Hughes similarly anticipated the weaknesses and limitations that the United Nations would face, cautioning that the effectiveness of the organization in promoting peace depended on a continued amity between the United States, Great Britain, and the Soviet Union; that in the absence of American-British-Soviet amity, U.N. institutions would be powerless; and that the great powers would be loath to yield to U.N. authority on questions of vital national interest.[29] "Structure of any sort, and any defined method," Hughes warned in 1946, "will bring nothing but disillusion unless they are infused by good will and permeated by a spirit of reasonableness which alone makes possible the effective use of any form of organization that may be devised."[30]

In Hughes's view, ultimately peace rested on the existence of states that desired peace—that is, it rested on the existence of states that recognized the benefits of peace and possessed the institutions that permitted them to pursue this maturely understood self-interest. It was bootless to hope that peace could rest on international institutions able to coerce states into acting against their desires. In the end, sovereign states would act on their perceived self-interest, whether this meant committing aggression to redress unresolved grievances or refusing to support the international institutions to which they had pledged themselves. The answer to the danger of violent self-help that was inherent in a sovereign state system lay not, as Wilson saw it, in the construction of collective security institutions for "enforcing the peace"—nor, for that matter, in the disengagement from world affairs advocated by the American founders or in the construction of countervailing alliances to balance aggressive powers, as the Cold War realists would undertake—but in building amity among peace-minded nations. Unless nations came to conceive of themselves in ways that revealed to them their shared interests, in moments of crisis they would renege on commitments to collective security, however earnestly such pledges might have been made. Hughes's focus on the need for amity implied a vastly different agenda than the one pursued by Wilson.

First and foremost, in Hughes's view, building amity was a domestic matter: it meant reigning in excesses of nationalism that would lead a people to ignore the legitimate concerns of others and it meant nurturing domestic institutions that restrained popular passions. Second, it meant working creatively to find just solutions to the disputes that naturally arose between peoples. "There is no path to peace," Hughes argued,

> except as the will of peoples may open it. The way to peace is through agreement, not through force. The question then is not of any ambitious scheme to prevent war, but simply of the constant effort, which is the highest task of statesmanship in relation to every possible cause of strife, to diminish among peoples the disposition to resort to force and to find a just and reasonable basis for accord. If the energy, ability, and sagacity equal to that now devoted to preparation for war could be concentrated upon such efforts aided by the urgent demands of intelligent public opinion, addressed not to impossibilities but to the removal or adjustment of actual differences, we should make sure approach to our goal.
>
> [T]he only real progress to abiding peace is found in the friendly disposition of peoples and . . . facilities for maintaining peace are useful only to the extent that this friendly disposition exists and finds expression. . . . War is not only possible, but probable, where mistrust and hatred and desire for revenge are the dominant motives. Our first duty is at home with our own opinion, by education and unceasing effort to bring to naught the mischievous exhortation of chauvinists; our next is to aid in every practicable way in promoting a better feeling among peoples, the healing of wounds, and the just settlement of differences.[31]

In modern political science parlance, for Hughes the heart of the problem of international order lay at the state and individual levels of analysis, not at the system level. Like Wilson whose liberalism he shared, Hughes saw the importance of building a world of peace-loving states. But where Wilson (and, even more so, the later designers of the United Nations and of the Cold War security system) saw the possibility of creating such a world from the top down, by imposing or enforcing it through international institutions and regimes, Hughes believed liberal democratic values and mature national institutions could only develop organically, from the bottom up. Peace depended on the separate, positive evolution and growth of human understanding and national societies around the world, fertilized by their peaceful contact and commerce with each other but nonetheless separate and each according to its own principles and nature.

This led Hughes to the conclusion that, in general if not in every instance, both intervention and the pursuit of institutional commitments to collective security were likely to be counterproductive as well as misguided. The argument against intervention was driven home by lengthening American experiences in the Caribbean: democracy and stable domestic institutions did not seem to flourish at the point of American guns. Reason and *virtu* could not be imposed, and without them the forms of democracy were empty and meaningless. Despite recognizing the poorness of intervention as a tool for building liberal democracy, Hughes did not foreswear intervention entirely. It might be necessary for either of two reasons. First, intervention might sometimes be a necessary means for protecting American lives and property: quite apart from its interest in world order, the American state had a duty to safeguard its citizens when they were threatened by the failure of other sovereigns to maintain order within their borders. Second, intervention might in some situations be a moral obligation, when chaos abroad threatened human rights and it was within American power to prevent humanitarian tragedies. Thus while Hughes sought to disentangle America from its role in maintaining domestic order in the Caribbean, he accepted that this disentanglement would be slow and that American troops might at times have to return.

As for collective security, Hughes made his arguments clear in 1919 and was never swayed from them. In the first place, Hughes worried that a commitment to collective security might result in a commitment to the status quo, even when the status quo was unjust or incompatible with the development of a stable domestic or international order. At the same time, he worried that the making of binding commitments either involved a bluff, which in the long run would be detrimental to international order, or undermined democracy: in a democracy, a decision as grave as one to go to war necessarily belonged in the hands of the people or their constitutionally selected representatives, and a decision to go to war to fulfill some international commitment despite the opposition of the people (however wrong-headed their opposition might be) would, to Hughes, be abhorrent. As always, in Hughes's view, the solution was not the proliferation of formal commitments but the creation of good relations that would result in a will on the part of the American people to assist a beleaguered friend.

Hughes's isolationism did not equate to passivity. Hughes saw an active, constructive role for both America and the American state in creating a stable, peaceful international order. American trade, investment, loans, and cultural contact could be enormously valuable in creating the soil in which stable, mature, liberal, democratic national institutions might grow. While the role of the U.S. government in these areas would, in general, be indirect, it could nonetheless be significant, as illustrated by Hughes's brainchild, the Dawes Plan and its corollary capital investment in Germany.[32] And American foreign policy could be directed at removing the irritants and suspicions that contaminated foreign relations, creating the potential for amity, making more obvious the natural harmony of interests, and establishing procedures for resolving future disagreements. Most notable in this regard, of course were the Washington Naval Treaties of 1922, which not only nipped in the bud an emerging Anglo-American-Japanese arms race and solved a classical security dilemma of global magnitude but resolved the principal issues troubling great power relations in the Pacific.[33]

Thus the notion that the liberal isolationist policies pursued by Hughes involved American disengagement from world politics or a retreat to some sort of Fortress America is distinctly odd, and certainly historically ungrounded. To be sure, there were important voices in Congress and in the American public that cried for reduced American involvement in world politics and spoke fondly of an imagined past in which the world pressed less closely on America. But this was hardly the stuff of American foreign policy, or what Harding meant by "a return to normalcy."

What the liberal isolationists rejected was not involvement in the world but the notion of that collective security could precede, or exist in the absence of, politically mature, self-disciplined societies. They rejected making prior commitments to allies whose narrow and short-sighted conception of self-interest led them to very different images of world order. It was a vision of international security built on the foundation of an Article X commitment to collective security that the liberal isolationists rejected. A comparison of Hughes's agenda for advancing world peace with Wilson's makes this point clearly. Even in 1916, before America's entry into the Great War, Wilson was arguing that "the time has come when it is the duty of the United States to join with the other nations of the world in any feasible association that will effectively serve these principles [of securing settled peace and justice], to maintain inviolate the complete security of the highway of the seas for the common and unhindered use of all nations, and to prevent any war begun either contrary to treaty covenants or without warning and frank admission of the provocation and causes to the opinion of mankind."[34] The liberal isolationists, by contrast, doubted both the wisdom and the effectiveness of such association.

One last point about the isolationism of the 1920s is perhaps worth making. Given the temptation to see the liberal isolationism of the 1920s as cut from the same cloth as the isolationism of the early American republic, it is useful to recognize the difference. This lies not simply in the fact that the United States had become a great power. Rather, the isolationism of the early republic was premised on the assumption that international politics was inherently conflictual, and that American foreign policy should be aimed at distancing America from these conflicts. Safety (in general) lay in nonentanglement. Hughes and his 1920s colleagues, by contrast, believed that international politics was not inherently conflictual and that America had an important and constructive role to play in the world. For the liberal isolationists of the 1920s, eschewing political-military commitments was desirable not because it best guaranteed American safety but because it offered the best route to creating a peaceful international order. No less than the Wilsonians (but far more than the leaders of the early republic) the liberal isolationists of the 1920s sought a transformed world: they simply envisioned a different path to it than the Wilsonians.

THE RECASTING OF LIBERAL ISOLATIONISM AS A SIN

The principal purpose of this chapter is to explore what liberal isolationism looked like in practice in the 1920s and at what, by analogy, a liberal isolationist foreign policy might look like today. But given the calumny to which the liberal isolationist policies of the 1920s have been subjected and given the ingrained, automatic reaction against even the mention of isolationism that still exists today, perhaps it is useful to digress and to investigate why these policies came to be so consistently and ritualistically denounced. How did the liberal isolationism of the 1920s end up outside the pale of legitimate discourse?

The heart of the image problem for liberal isolationism is that the 1920s came before the 1930s and 1940s: It is difficult to wax enthusiastic about any policy that led, even if only temporally and not causally, to those disastrous decades. This said, it is important, first, to recognize that the connection is indeed only temporal and not causal and, second, to understand why the assumption of a causal connection has become so deeply ingrained in American thinking. The argument that America's liberal isolationist diplomatic policies of the 1920s—as distinct from its antiliberal protectionist trade policies—contributed significantly to the breakdown of international order in the 1930s is, on examination, difficult to defend. But there are important reasons why we have closed our eyes and chosen to believe it, and if we are going to be honest about the 1920s it is useful to understand the influences that have discouraged such honesty in the past.

Perhaps least odd about the assumption that American liberal isolationist policies in the 1920s were somehow responsible for what occurred in the

1930s and 1940s is the retrospective hubris involved—the notion that whatever happened must have been caused or been strongly influenced by our action or inaction, rather than been the product of economic, political, and cultural forces deeply rooted in other societies over which we exercised only limited power. More odd, however, is the assumption that American liberal isolationism *in the 1920s* must be blamed for what happened a decade later. Even if one agrees, as most reasonable observers would, that with hindsight it is clear the Western powers in the 1930s mishandled their responses to the Great Depression, underestimated the danger from fascism and militarism, and responded too slowly to them, this in no way logically implies that American policies in the prior decade—apart from an unwise protectionist tariff—were misguided. Complaints that America failed to exert leadership during the 1920s misread the historical record: While the United States chose neither to lead in the direction of *Realpolitik* military balancing and alliances nor to lead in the direction of Wilson's League, it did in fact lead—both in Asia and Europe—as the Washington Naval Conference and the Dawes Plan make clear. Since in the 1920s there was no fascist threat to contend with and no aggression to deter, the case against the Republican administrations of the 1920s rests principally on their refusal to enter the League and secondarily on their embrace of arms control and failure to build up American military strength.

Failure to Join the League Caused World War II?

It is hard, though, to believe that American membership in the League would have made much of a difference when it came time for the West to respond to fascist aggression. The problem in the 1930s was not a lack of institutions to facilitate cooperation between the Western powers. The problem was a lack of insight and a lack of will. If the need to oppose fascism had been clear and if domestic support for the use of force had existed, the League would have been unnecessary. Absent these conditions, the existence of the League, even with American membership, would have been insufficient.

Consider the record. At no juncture prior to the invasion of Poland were any of the Western great powers willing to go to war to stop fascist expansion, despite effective consultations among them. In 1931, in response to Japanese aggression in Manchuria, the United States and the League worked along roughly parallel and surprisingly coordinated tracks; however, as neither was willing to risk the breakdown in relations with Japan that would have been caused by economic sanctions, much less by stronger action, it is difficult to see what difference it would have made had the U.S. representative in Geneva been authorized to speak, as well as to listen to the League's debates. In fact, by early 1932, bilateral Anglo-American consultations were intense, and it was the British, despite their League obligations to collective security, that acted as a restraining force on the supposedly isolationist Americans—not that Secretary of State Henry Stimson had much realistic hope of committing the United States to a forceful line against Japan, given the combined opposition of the president, Congress, and public. In sum, the problem was that at moments of decision in 1931 and 1932, relations with Japan were valued above Nine-Power Treaty commitments on both sides of the Atlantic, and avoiding war was regarded as a higher priority than preventing aggression.[35]

This was precisely the problem Hughes had predicted in the 1920s and that had led him to reject Wilsonian approaches to collective security. As he observed in 1923:

All contrivances for maintaining peace by economic pressure, as well as by military force, depend upon the sentiment which will apply the pressure and direct the force when the test comes. Such arrangements are likely to fail when they are most needed, because national interests are diverse and unanimity of action under stress of crises involving conflicts of opinion is well-nigh impossible.[36]

Similarly, in 1935 none of the great powers showed any great eagerness to use force to stop Mussolini, nor in 1937 was there a willingness to pay the price to halt Japanese aggression in China. In both cases, the policies of the Western powers were principally motivated by a hope of rebuilding amicable relations and bringing Italy and Japan back into the liberal fold. However faulty the judgments that underlay these policies, they would not have been altered by American partnership in the League.

But what about the West's response to Germany? Surely had America been a member of the League, the West would have responded in a more timely fashion to Hitler. However self-serving, Hughes's response to these arguments, offered in a memoir drafted between 1941 and 1945, is perhaps as clear, succinct, and convincing a rebuttal of this notion as could be sought.

The immediate precursor of the Second World War was Hitler's action in rearming Germany and his subsequent aggressive measures. But Hitler rearmed in violation of treaty and in the presence of Europe. There was no real secret about it. His development of Germany's air power was his boast and was well-known. The European powers could easily have stopped him but they did not. Even when he sent troops into the Rhineland, they did not oppose him. Why? I suppose that the controlling thought in Great Britain was that Germany had been harshly treated and that if she were permitted to regain her prestige and take her place again as a Great Power, she could be dealt with satisfactorily by diplomatic methods and war would be prevented. Neither Great Britain nor France wished war.

Can any well-informed person, who looks at the matter realistically, believe that we should have taken a different view and as a member of the League would have thrown our weight against the policy of Great Britain and France, insisting on military action? They were immediately concerned and they, not we, had the military power to hold Hitler in check before it was too late. But they did not desire to use that power. . . . It is vain to suppose that these tragic events would have been prevented if our government had been a member of the League!

This is not to say that our entry into the League with reasonable reservations would not have aided our collaboration in various enterprises of international importance. And, when the present war [World War II] ends, I trust that there will be a favorable climate of opinion for international cooperation and that we shall be ready to participate in an international organization designed to facilitate united action in dealing with the grave matters which inevitably will require international adjustment, in establishing a supreme tribunal to determine international controversies which admit of judicial settlement, in providing the machinery of conciliation, and generally in taking every practicable measure to prevent or stop aggression and to assure international peace.

But the experience of the League of Nations teaches that, despite international organization, when it comes to the use of force, the Great Powers who have the force and upon whose willingness to use it reliance must be placed will act or fail to act according to the policy which they believe to be dictated by their respective essential interests at the time. Formal international organization will provide a useful mechanism to facilitate united action in the interest of peace but will not insure that action.[37]

Hughes's argument, based on his reading of the 1930s, is that Wilsonian liberals' emphasis on and faith in *institutions*—an emphasis and faith shared by much of the liberal scholarship of the 1980s and 1990s—is misguided. Ultimately, when matters of national survival are at stake, Hughes suggests that liberals must pin their hopes not on institutional mechanisms (however helpful these may be in facilitating cooperation) but on a liberal *construction of identity and interest.* In the end, peace depends on societies being mature enough to understand that their long-term self-interest lies in peaceful cooperation rather than in a resort to force however attractive this might appear in the passionate heat of the moment. Confronted by aggression, cooperative action by peace-loving states to deter or respond in a timely fashion requires a mature appreciation of the bonds of amity linking these states together—that is, on a construction of identity that takes into account a harmonious sharing of interests—not an unenforceable prior institutional commitment. To be sure, the existence of institutions may influence the construction of identity: Interaction within an institution may generate awareness of common interests and alter habits of thinking. Nonetheless, the importance of institutions in this view is secondary, and when institutions and identities (and the conception of self-interest they imply) diverge, it is the latter that prevail. Reviewing the record, one is thus inclined to join with Hughes's conclusion: "There has been a disposition, on the part of some

who are more zealous for their cause than careful in historical analysis, to attribute the impotency of the League, in the face of the crises which have culminated in the Second World War, to our failure to become a member. I think
that this opinion is wholly unjustified."[38]

But surely even if American membership in the League would not have
prevented the war, it would have resulted in more timely and effective American involvement! When, with the invasion of Poland, the League powers finally bestirred themselves to act, American weight would have been decisive
in defeating the fascist powers quickly, would it not? Here, again, the real
counterfactual is difficult to discern. Regardless of membership in the League
and the legal or moral commitments to collective security that this would
have entailed, it is difficult to imagine a president being able to marshal
whole-hearted public support for war in 1939. Even if a declaration of war
could have been wrung from Congress, popular support for mass mobilization would have been weak. What the actual involvement of America in a
European or a world war would have looked like is unclear at best. Absent
a consensus in America that German, Italian, and Japanese actions represented a threat to the American republic sufficient to demand the sacrifice of
significant numbers of American lives and the disruptive wartime mobilization of the American community, legal obligations to Britain, France, China,
or the League itself might not have prompted effective state action.

The League as a Sword and Shield of Liberal Democracy?

There are, however, reasons for thinking that the 1920 decision to eschew
League membership was not only not an error but was actually wise. The notion, underlying much of the *post hoc* nostalgia for the League of Nations,
that the League somehow embodied liberal democratic values is a distinctly
dubious one. Certainly this was Wilson's vision in creating the League but, as
events at Versailles demonstrated, his ability to impose his vision on the
other great powers was limited. All historical parallels are dangerous, but
perhaps an apt one might be to the Concert of Europe, which whatever its
merits was hardly an instrument of democratic advancement or national self-
determination. As likely to be the instrument of British imperialism, French
revanchism, or Japanese expansionism as the handmaiden of Wilsonian liberalism, the League must be recognized as a victor's condominium aimed at
the preservation of the gains acquired at Versailles, whether or not this com-
ported with a just or stable peace.

Certainly this was the case in the 1920s. The League powers—Britain,
France, Italy, Japan—showed more interest in gaining control of former German colonies, expanding into areas of former German influence, and ob-
taining reparations than in building a liberal world, leading thoughtful liberals such as John Dewey to dismiss the League as "an unregenerate coalition

of governments whose selfishness had caused the war."[39] Far from an ally in building a new, liberal world order, the League was (to a significant degree until Hughes "disarmed" it at the Washington Conference, but to a lesser degree for the rest of the decade) the principal opponent. As a symbol and a battleground in this struggle, the island of Yap assumed almost comical proportions: The League's decision to hand this formerly German telegraph-station-cum-islet in the Pacific over to Japan as a mandate served as a test case of League members' efforts to use the League as a vehicle for divvying up the spoils of war. While the question of Yap was ultimately resolved in 1922 in the goodwill and general resolution of outstanding issues associated with the Washington Naval Treaties, the more significant issue of British efforts to shut America out of Mesopotamia remained in dispute until 1930.[40]

That America and Britain—and even more clearly America, France, Italy, and Japan—had very different visions of the world to be created was evident. Whether it would have been more effective to apply pressure from within the League rather than to apply pressure from outside is, of course, an unanswerable question. It is, however, revealing that the Wilson administration anticipated the need for a dramatic post-World War I *increase* in American naval strength as a means of putting continued pressure on its League allies, while Hughes, unencumbered by the League, was able to achieve a favorable resolution of world-order issues and still slash American naval power.[41] Far from an institution of principled adjudication embodying liberal values, the League was shaping up to be an arena for classical *Realpolitik* logrolling, a setting where might, not right, was the coin of the realm.

If the bare-knuckle nature of Anglo-American negotiations do not provide sufficient grounds for concluding that the League would have been a forum for contention rather than an instrument of consensus, the history of 1922 and 1923 offers considerable evidence that nonmembership offered America a better position for advancing its liberal agenda. During the Franco-German reparations controversy, neither Britain from within the League nor America from outside the League was able to bend France from the course that led to the Ruhr invasion of January 1923. From its vantage point outside the League, however, the United States was able to play an independent role, searching out a fair basis for resolving the dispute. In December 1922, in his American Historical Association speech, Hughes broached the ideas that would become the Dawes Plan, which broke the Franco-German logjam.[42] Membership in an "Article X" League would not have permitted the United States to impose its political will on France (or at least not at a cost that would have been acceptable); it would, however, have certainly complicated American efforts at conciliatory statesmanship and it might have heightened French stubbornness.

Obviously, American membership in the League would have facilitated a wide variety of American diplomatic initiatives and undertakings—which is precisely why Hughes and the other liberal isolationists had wished to join, subject to Article X reservations. Not being at the table in Geneva complicated a number of Hughes's efforts to resolve technical and justiciable matters. But a military guarantee to France, Japan, and Britain at a time when those powers were expanding and consolidating their empires in the Middle East and East Asia and pursuing short-sighted policies in Europe hardly seems likely to have been conducive to world order. Ideally, America would have participated in the League in the 1920s, while refusing to accept Article X commitments. This possibility, however, was ruled out by Wilson's implacable opposition and by the election results of 1920, which returned to the Senate a blocking coalition of "Irreconcilables." Under the circumstances, eschewing the League may well have represented the best real option.

Liberal Isolationism as a Scapegoat

If "unreserved" membership in the League would not have prevented World War II and would have complicated American efforts to build peace in the 1920s, why has liberal isolationism come to have such bad press? In the policy struggles of the 1940s, delegitimizing isolationism assumed enormous importance. Both for reasons of cognitive consistency and as a deliberate political strategy, the architects of postwar internationalism sought to discredit liberal isolationism and the Republican foreign policy of the 1920s. For the architects of postwar internationalism, the danger posed by liberal isolationism was simultaneously ideological and personal. The Roosevelt and Truman administrations needed to establish both the necessity for a world order based on the collective security institutions they sought—the United Nations and the Atlantic Alliance—and their own right to govern despite the collapse of international order that had occurred on their watch. To do so they would need to argue that liberal isolationism was wrong not only in the present and (since the institutions they advocated would have an indefinite life) the future, but also had been wrong in the past—that is, they would need to argue that liberal isolationism was *never* a good or wise policy for a mature, powerful America.

Obviously, given the cultural centrality of Washington, Adams, and Jefferson in American political life, and given the fact that their pronouncements regarding the wisdom of American noninvolvement in European wars could not easily be reinterpreted, the post-World War II architects of internationalism could not argue the isolationism was *always* wrong. Thus the necessary caveat: For a weak, immature power, isolationism was the counsel of the wise. The advice of the Founding Fathers was right for the time, but was based on the circumstances of the day rather than on anything fundamental about a liberal republic or world politics. For a great power, which America had become by the 1880s or 1890s, a more active role in creating a global military order was a practical if not a moral imperative. Oddly, this revisionist interpretation placed the liberal internationalists of Franklin Roosevelt's administration on the same page with Theodore Roosevelt and the realist internationalists of earlier times—strange intellectual bedfellows indeed, given the elder Roosevelt's vituperous dislike for Wilson and opposition to the League.

A key part of the problem for the architects of postwar internationalism came in assigning meaning to World War II and to the sacrifices America had made in it. If the cause of World War II were simply German and Italian fascism and Japanese militarism, then the roots of the tragedy lay in the flawed internal character or political development of those nations, not in the structure of the international system. For pessimists, this interpretation of the war logically implied that the Founding Fathers were right, and that the Old World was inherently violent and should be kept at arms reach. For optimists, it suggested that Hughes was correct in stressing the fundamental importance of the organic growth of democracy in societies around the world and the need to develop American policies that allowed healthy national institutions to grow, free from external coercion. For introspective observers, this understanding of World War II focused attention on the delicacy of America's own democratic institutions and on the need to solve America's internal problems. For pessimists, optimists, and introspective observers alike, this interpretation logically raised doubts about an American foreign policy based on collective security institutions. Equally bad from a psychological point of view, it offered no reassurance that the sacrifice America had made in the war reduced the risk of future war. World War I had eliminated the great autocracies but it had not kept Germany, Italy, and Japan on a democratic course; was there any reason to believe that World War II would be more successful in making the world safe for democracy, however complete the destruction of the fascist regimes?

Perhaps worst of all, though, this explanation of World War II suggested that the very leaders now proposing to build a new global order were (to whatever extent the United States had to share the blame) the very people responsible for the magnitude of that conflagration. It was the Roosevelt administration and Democratic majorities in Congress that sat back and failed to act as fascism and militarism took root and grew. Obviously, then, for both psychological and political reasons, some deeper explanation for the war needed to be found.

Blaming fascism, militarism, and the war on the Depression—however historically plausible—worked only slightly better. True, Roosevelt and the Democratic Congress could not be held responsible for the Depression as they could for American failure to act after 1933. But the policies of economic nationalism that spread, deepened, and prolonged the Depression were part and parcel of the New Deal. Further, if the war could have been prevented by liberal trade policies, then the implicit lesson was not the need for collective security institutions but for a free trade regime—a goal even isolationists (or at least those from export-dependent parts of the country) could support. And to blame the capitalist business cycle for the war made a mockery of America's sacrifice and played to the hands of the radicals. To leaders committed to collective security, interested in absolving themselves in responsibility for the war, and concerned about a domestic Red threat, an economic interpretation of the war was unappealing.

The solution, of course, was to blame the war on the failure of America to join the League of Nations. It was not the internal flaws and contradictions of German, Italian, and Japanese society nor the unbearable domestic pressures caused by the Depression that made war inevitable, but America's failure to embrace international institutions of collective security. Had America joined the League, the argument ran, the Japanese would not have invaded Manchuria, Mussolini would not have moved on Ethiopia, and Hitler would not have remilitarized the Rhineland—or had they done so, they would have been defeated before their power waxed. This neatly shifted responsibility for the war from Roosevelt and the Democrats, who despite their economically nationalist and politically isolationist policies during the 1930s could claim at least some Wilsonian inheritance, to the Republicans who had blocked accession to the League. Moreover, it explicitly made the case that world order rested on American involvement in international institutions and on effective collective security measures. Further, it had the added benefit of pandering to the American ego.

For the architects of postwar internationalism, then, it was certainly convenient and perhaps even necessary to contend that isolationism had been naive or immoral in the 1920s as well as being wrong in the 1940s. The effect of the Soviet-American rupture and the slide into Cold War, however, was to increase still further the need to delegitimate America's isolationist history. Given the Founding Fathers' admonitions against entangling alliances—which NATO even more clearly than the United Nations represented—the need to discredit "isolationism" became imperative. It was necessary to argue that what had been wise for a weak state in the eighteenth century was no longer wise for a strong power in the twentieth century. The 1920s "pathway of peace" had to be described not as the fulfillment of a covenant with America's Founding Fathers but as an anachronistic error and an act of immaturity. Moreover, if 1920s isolationists could be tarred with the brush of World War II guilt, this would strengthen the case for North Atlantic internationalism in the 1940s by providing a useful analogy: Failure of "liberal democratic" powers to join together in the League had meant accommodation to Hitler, and failure of liberal democratic powers to join together in NATO would mean accommodation to Soviet Russia. The supercooled world of Soviet-American rivalry after 1947 hardened positions. Criticism of

America's commitment to collective security, present or past, became nothing less than unpatriotic: it implied an abandonment of European allies, and this lay outside the pale of legitimate political discourse.

Thus, during the Cold War, study of the 1920s experience was inevitably premised on the conclusion, regarded as unarguable and self-evident, that America's decision to stay out of the League and to seek security through arms control and principled accommodation with other great powers, was wrong. Debate was limited to the question of why this wrong-headed choice was made.

Ironically, for the radical and revisionist critics of American Cold War internationalism, as for the Cold Warriors themselves, the 1920s were a useful shibboleth. From the radical or revisionist perspective, the 1920s were not a period of isolationism at all: What was striking about the period was the extraordinary global expansion of unfettered American capitalism. If, in the 1920s, American capitalists managed to manipulate and exploit the world to their benefit without the open use of force and without engaging in classical imperialism, this merely reflected the increasing sophistication of capitalist strategies. Hughes's achievements in stopping the naval arms race, stabilizing great-power relations, codifying the Open Door in China, and beginning what would later be called the "Good Neighbor" policy in Latin America were merely skilled strategic measures to increase the ability of American industry and capital to penetrate foreign markets. The so-called liberal isolationism of the 1920s was, in this view, simply an effort to construct "an empire without tears."[43] If the Depression, World War II, and the Cold War were, for radical and revisionist thinkers, the bitter harvest of global capitalism, then the 1920s were the summer days of this noxious crop. To see the 1920s in any other light would be to question the whole radical and revisionist intellectual edifice.

THE 1920s AS A TRIUMPH OF STATESMANSHIP

It is one thing to argue that the 1920s foreign policies have been perjured and another to argue that they were a triumph of statesmanship. I seek to do both.

In 1920, America faced at least six major external obstacles to its efforts to build a safe and stable liberal world order. First and most immediately pressing was the looming security dilemma that was sucking the great powers into a deepening whirlpool of arms construction, diplomatic hostility, and political conflict. Second, there was the problem of poor bilateral relations between America and not one but every one of the other great powers: American foreign policy makers were faced with increasingly bitter relations with Britain, long-standing U.S.-Japanese animosity, German-American relations disrupted by the war and its intense nationalist propaganda, general antipathy between American and French political establishments, and American nonrecognition of and military intervention against the new Soviet government. Third, there was the long-standing problem of China—how to end imperialist expansion there and create the conditions for stable national governance. Fourth, there was the new challenge of rebuilding and stabilizing Europe; the connected issues of continued Franco-German rivalry, German reparations, German economic recovery, and allied war debts left the continent a politico-military flash spot. Fifth, there was the perennial dilemma of Latin America, where the legacy of U.S. imperialism left a flawed foundation for building amity. And sixth, there was the need to establish, modernize, and expand international institutions to deal with the evolving twentieth-century agenda of (technical and justiciable) issues.

Impressively, American administrations of the 1920s scored important progress in all six of these areas. By the mid-1920s, the security dilemma that looked so unmanageable had been definitively resolved: Competitive Anglo-American-Japanese naval construction was halted, fleets were slashed, and the unwarranted suspicions that had driven the construction programs were dispelled. On the bilateral front, Anglo-American relations had been restored to utmost cordiality; Japanese-American relations were enormously improved, despite the disaster created by the Immigration Act of 1924 and by congressional misconstrual of the Hanihara letter; German-American relations reached a new plateau of amity; with the Kellogg-Briand Pact of 1928, Franco-American relations were placed on a mutually acceptable (if not, from either side's perspective, ideal) footing; and although America continued its policy of Soviet nonrecognition, with the end of American intervention, massive American aid during the famine of 1921, and American pressure on Japan to end its occupation of Siberia, on a practical level a minimally acceptable degree of Soviet-American amity was established.[44] Perhaps most astonishing, great power agreement on China, establishing an open door and committing the great powers to Chinese sovereignty, was achieved; equally amazing, practical implementation steps, including a Sino-Japanese arrangement on the controversial question of Shantung, were taken.

Admittedly, progress in rebuilding a stable European order was less satisfactory. While short-term stability was achieved and the dangerously unpromising French approach of 1922–1923 was reversed, the breathing space created by American diplomacy was not used to advantage: The underlying problems went unaddressed, as Congress short-sightedly tied the executive branch's hands on the issue of debt repayment and successive Republican administrations failed to recognize the impossibility of achieving liberal European and Atlantic political orders while pursuing illiberal trade policies. In Latin America, by contrast, the intellectual and political foundation for Franklin Roosevelt's "Good Neighbor" policy was laid, and America began disentangling itself, however slowly, from the imperialist interventions that both Theodore Roosevelt's corollary to the Monroe Doctrine and Wilsonian interest in supporting democratic forces had generated. And with some success, the United States pursued agreements and arrangements to facilitate cooperation on issues such as the drug trade, disease and public health, international crime, disaster relief, customs policies, and arms sales.[45]

Three specific foreign policy achievements of the early 1920s deserve special discussion not only because of their immediate significance in clearing the political storm clouds in the Pacific, Europe, and Latin America, but also because of the clarity with which they illustrate the logic of liberal isolationism in practice. The first was the Washington Naval Conference of 1921–1922 and the three major treaties resulting from it. The second was the Dawes Plan and Dawes Commission. The third was the public abandonment of the Roosevelt Corollary and the redirection of American efforts in Latin America.

The Washington Treaties, Security Dilemmas, and Asian Order

Often mischaracterized during the Cold War years as an idealistic folly, the Washington Naval Treaties represented a masterstroke of American diplomacy, simultaneously resolving the great power security dilemma, eliminating the principal irritants in Anglo-American and Japanese-American relations, and committing the great powers to a sovereign China.[46] Demonstrating the value of diplomatic surprise and the power of global public opinion, Hughes overcame deep national suspicions and outraged military bureaucracies by springing a fully developed proposal for dramatic, equitable naval reductions on the unsuspecting assembled delegates in the welcoming session on November 12, 1921. Hughes's extraordinary tactic generated an unstoppable groundswell of global public support, transforming a conference that most astute observers had assumed would be dead on arrival into a highly productive summit.[47]

The most important agreement reached in Washington was the Five-Power Treaty that created, in Harold and Margaret Sprout's aptly chosen phrase, a "new order of sea power."[48] The Five-Power Treaty established a 5:5:3:1.75:1.75 ratio for American, British, Japanese, French, and Italian capital ship tonnage, essentially halted the massive building programs then underway, scrapped a substantial number of older battleships, declared a ten-year capital-ship construction holiday, and limited the size of future capital ships.[49] In a stroke, the great power security dilemma was eliminated: Each of the great powers retained a capacity to protect itself and its vital interests, and each was reassured of the others' intentions. As Hughes bluntly put it: "Preparation for offensive naval war will stop now."[50]

To understand the full implications of the Five-Power Treaty, however, it is important to recognize that Hughes was seeking to transform domestic realities as well as international ones. With his November 12 theatrics, he intended not only to score a tactical victory but also to shatter how Americans, as well as other national publics, thought of their world and of security. On the one hand, by making American naval construction explicitly contingent on the naval construction of the other powers, Hughes took aim at the pacifist and realist isolationist elements in America that were pressing for unilateral disarmament or naval economies regardless of the consequences of such an action for the rest of the world. At the same time and more obviously, the Five-Power Treaty was aimed at, and generated consternation in, the circles where realist perspectives were most deeply ingrained, for example in the "Big Navy" community. The difficulty of Hughes's task—shattering deeply held worldviews rooted not only in culture but also sometimes in bureaucratic and parochial self-interest—should not be underestimated. Hughes's disarmament proposal could never have been developed had the U.S. Navy been consulted; and yet, as testimony to Hughes's success, note that three years after the conference the Navy's General Board would concede that "the great accomplishment . . . was not in the fixing of a definite ratio of ships, with its attendant economies, but in effecting an agreement making aggressive warfare across the ocean more difficult."[51] In other words, Hughes succeeded in changing how Navy planners thought of the world and their place in it, helping them to see security not in terms of a balance of power but in terms of security dilemmas.

But Hughes needed to transform foreign domestic realities as well as American ones: He needed to create a belief in the possibility of international amity in foreign hearts as well as in American ones. Here, too, he was surprisingly successful. Within two days of Hughes's speech demanding the destruction of twenty-three British battleships "built or building" and British abandonment of a policy of naval superiority, Winston Churchill was telling the American ambassador to the Court of Saint James's that "he could not find words to express his rejoicing as an Englishman and his pride in his American ancestry. His hat was not only off but as high as he could throw it."[52]

If the isolationist character of the treaty—basing security on the amelioration of security dilemmas and on the abandonment by the great powers of a capacity to intervene in each other's home waters, rather than on the creation of mutual politico-military obligations and the retention of fleets able to enforce the international community's will—is obvious, so too is its liberal character. From the realist perspective of the post-World War II years, the Five-Power Treaty was criticized—probably wrongly, even given realist assumptions about the nature of security in an anarchic world—on two grounds. First, the treaty precluded fortification of bases across a broad swathe of the Pacific. When World War II came, this made defense of the Philippines impossible, while secret Japanese violation of the treaty in the mandated islands made reconquest more difficult. What critics overlooked, however, was that defense of the Philippines would probably have been impossible even had the approaches to Manila been effectively fortified, given the overwhelming concentration of Japanese air, sea, and land power that was possible, and that Japanese fortification efforts in the 1930s were widely suspected but the American government refused to challenge Japanese violations. More to the point, even opponents of the nonfortification provision conceded that, given congressional sentiment and budget concerns, there was no serious possibility that America would undertake fortification, treaty or no treaty. Second, the treaty was criticized for lulling America into a false security, which in turn led the United States not to build its naval forces up to treaty limits. While no counterfactual is possible, this argument probably misreads American willingness to support naval construction under any circumstances short of an all-out great-power arms race: Substantial public and congressional pressure to slash naval expenditures predated rather than followed from the treaty. The alternatives to the Five-Power Treaty were probably either an uncontrolled spiral of great-power hostility or sullen American withdrawal to Fortress America, not the American naval predominance advocated by realist internationalists.

The Five-Power Treaty was accompanied by the Four-Power Treaty (involving the United States, Britain, Japan, and France) and the Nine-Power Treaty (involving Belgium, China, Italy, the Netherlands, and Portugal as well). Together these eliminated what America regarded as the four principal irritants in the great powers' Pacific and Asian relationships—the long-standing Anglo-Japanese alliance, Japanese imperialism in Asia, the Sino-Japanese dispute over Shantung, and Japanese-American disputes over mandated islands in the Pacific.

The Four-Power Treaty bound the signatories to respect each other's insular Pacific territories, to submit any disputes to an international conference, and to consult and cooperate in response to aggression by any other state. In essence, it replaced the Anglo-Japanese alliance (seen by those two powers as necessary for guaranteeing the security of each of their Pacific territories but viewed by the United States as potentially aimed against America and certainly as representing a threat to the Philippines) with a general commitment to recognize and uphold the status quo. The inclusion of France in the agreement was sought by the United States to avoid any perception of a trilateral Anglo-Japanese-American alliance and to soothe French amour-propre.[53]

The remarkable brevity and unremarkable generality of the Four-Power Treaty should not belie its significance:

> This Four-Power Pact was the cement of good faith that held together the settlements reached as to other issues. The consultation pledge afforded a means by which disputes in the Pacific could be settled if there was any will to settle

them. But of much greater importance than the obligations it created were the obligations it removed. By destroying the Anglo-Japanese alliance, Hughes detached the British from their tacit support of Japanese policy in the Far East and in effect aligned them with American policy. That is an achievement from which great historic consequences have flowed.[54]

Consistent with the logic of liberal isolationism, in the Four-Power Treaty Hughes did not attempt to create some sort of binding institution or agreement for imposing peace. (Indeed the treaty eliminated the one such institution in the Pacific—the Anglo-Japanese alliance.) Rather, the treaty enunciated mutually acceptable arrangements that would provide a foundation for amicable relations, eliminated unwarranted suspicions about intentions, and created a presumption in favor of adjudication of any disputes that would lend themselves to it. In other words, the Four-Power Treaty assumed a harmony, or at least compatibility, of interests in the Pacific and recognized that institutional efforts by any of the powers to enhance their security risked triggering a security dilemma for the others.

Where the Four-Power Treaty constructively addressed the problem of Pacific security and broke the old *Realpolitik* alliance system, the Nine-Power Treaty resolved the Chinese situation on liberal terms long sought by America. It pledged the great powers

(1) To respect the sovereignty, the independence, and the territorial and administrative integrity of China; (2) To provide the fullest and most unembarrassed opportunity to China to develop and maintain for herself an effective and stable government; (3) To use their influence for the purpose of effectually establishing and maintaining the principle of equal opportunity for the commerce and industry of all nations throughout the territory of China; (4) To refrain from taking advantage of conditions in China in order to seek special privileges which would abridge the rights of subjects or citizens of friendly States, and from countenancing action inimical to the security of such States. . . . The Contracting Powers agree not to enter into any treaty, agreement, arrangement, or understanding, either with one another, or, individually or collectively, with any Power or Powers, which would infringe or impair the principles stated.[55]

The Treaty went on not only explicitly to affirm the American "Open Door" principle by name but also to detail the expectations that followed from this, including a renunciation of political or economic spheres of influence. This was a stunning success for American diplomacy, among other things eliminating the apparent public concession made by Secretary of State Robert Lansing in 1917 that had acknowledged Japanese "special interests" in China. "The language could not have been more emphatic in avowing respect for the open door and the integrity of China."[56]

As with the Four-Power Treaty, the Nine-Power Treaty "was a mutual promise of self-discipline, not a guarantee to use force."[57] It was, however, accompanied by practical steps toward implementation. A nine-power agreement on Chinese tariffs signed in Washington provided the basis for Chinese government finances and moved toward eliminating internal barriers to trade. Even more important, Washington reversed the retrograde motion put underway at Versailles: Under diplomatic pressure from the United States and Britain, China and Japan negotiated a compromise on Shantung, control over which had been given to Japan in the peace negotiations.

Consistent with the logic of liberal isolationism, perhaps the most important impact of the Washington Conference was not to create international institutions or mechanisms for regulating the behavior of the great powers but to change the way the most powerful nations of the world viewed each other. What Hughes sought and to an astounding degree achieved was a change in how nations "constructed" themselves and the world in which they interacted. It was a change in "state of mind" that was critical. Hughes put it this way a few months after the conference:

> The most important results are those which are unwritten and imponderable; those that relate to sentiment and purpose, to good will and a better understanding. When there is friendship and confidence, treaties to maintain peace are of least importance, and where suspicion and hatred dominate the thought of peoples it may be wise to interpose the mechanism of conciliation but the best assurance of peace is lacking. If you would measure the work of the Conference, contrast the present opinion as to peace in the East with the view that was widely held and constantly expressed before the Conference was called. The mists, which many called war clouds, have been dispelled. Confidence has been restored, fears allayed, and a new feeling of respect and friendship engendered. Quite apart from specific engagements, it was worth all the efforts of the Conference to produce a new state of mind with respect to our relations with the Far East.[58]

What the conference accomplished was to shatter the realist paradigm in the minds of attentive publics and elites. "The conference," argued Britain's Lord Lee of Fareham, "produced a complete change in the attitude of mind of the nations there assembled and, if I may so describe it, made them think in terms of peace rather than in terms of war."[59] The argument that national security necessarily rested on national military capability, and that maximizing national power was the only or surest route to safety and well-being in an anarchic international environment, was set aside by national governments, much to the dismay of military establishments around the world. Hughes recognized that this achievement was not necessarily permanent— that the belief (or "autosuggestion" as he went so far as to describe it) in a liberal order between nations was not necessarily self-maintaining or self-replicating. Nowhere did Hughes suggest that the liberal accommodation of the 1920s would make the resurgence of realism and aggressive nationalism impossible. He only suggested the possibility, not the certainty, of continued liberal order; "it will be," Hughes argued, "the part of wisdom to maintain this attitude and to frown upon those who seek to change it."[60]

Liberal Isolationism, Europe, and Latin America

If the Washington Conference rendered manageable the great-power security dilemma, shattered realist visions of an international security order, and put Pacific relations on an amicable foundation, the American liberal isolationists of the 1920s were less successful when they turned their attention to Europe. Here, of course, the problem was the inability of successive Republican administrations to convince Congress to forego debt repayment and their unwillingness to rebuff the domestic interest groups favoring protectionism. Given the failure to create a basis for long-term economic stability, what is perhaps most impressive are the short-term accomplishments of American foreign policy. Most notable among these are the Dawes Plan and Dawes Commission, which largely depoliticized the German reparations problem, provided a basis for German reconstruction, defused Franco-German tensions, and by defusing Franco-German tensions resolved a growing Anglo-French split.

The approach pursued by Hughes—to establish an international committee of experts to determine Germany's ability to pay reparations and to use U.S. government pressure to ensure a flow of private capital into Germany that would permit reconstruction and reparations payment—was typical of Hughes's thinking: Where possible, he separated technical and justiciable issues from political ones and resolved the former as a means of reducing the irritations and misperceptions that clouded judgments regarding the latter. International institutions—courts, commissions, standing committees—could help resolve these technical and justiciable matters, but they would not be effective in resolving underlying political disputes or imposing peace when implacable political wills clashed: Only good will and amity could resolve underlying political questions, but when technical and justiciable issues no longer inflamed passions, good will and amity might indeed prevail.[61] In proposing what became the Dawes Commission, Hughes neatly the separated the question of how much Germany could pay from more inherently political issues and refused to put America in the position of appearing to make a political decision either on Germany's capacity to pay or on the justness of reparations.

> Some of our own people have suggested that the United States should assume the role of arbiter. . . . I do not think that we should endeavor to take such a burden of responsibility. We have quite enough to bear without drawing to ourselves all the ill feeling which would result from disappointed hopes and a set-

tlement which would be viewed as forced upon nations by this country which at the same time is demanding the payment of the debts owing to it.

But the situation does call for a settlement upon its merit. The first condition of a satisfactory settlement is that the question should be taken out of politics.

If . . . statesmen cannot agree . . . what is to be done? . . . The fundamental condition is that in the critical moment the merits of the question, as an economic one, must alone be regarded. Sentiment, however, natural, must be disregarded; mutual recriminations are of no avail; reviews of the past, whether accurate or inaccurate, promise nothing; assertions of blame on the one hand and excuses on the other come to naught.

If statesmen cannot agree, and exigencies of public opinion make their course difficult, then there should be called to their aid those who can point the way to a solution.

Why should they not invite men of the highest authority in finance in their respective countries, men of such prestige, experience, and honor that their agreement upon the amount to be paid . . . would be accepted throughout the world as the most authoritative expression obtainable. . . . If governments saw fit to reject the recommendation upon which such a body agreed, they would be free to do so, but they would have the advantage of impartial advice and of an enlightened public opinion.

I do not believe that any general conference would answer the purpose better, much less that any political conference would accomplish a result which premiers find it impossible to reach. . . . It would be time enough to consider forcible measures after such an opportunity had been exhausted.[62]

The approach proved successful. Though Hughes and his successors were careful not to become politically involved or politically responsible (beyond informing the French government that if it rejected the Dawes Plan, America would wash its hands of the situation) because they believed that the issues were essentially ones among the European powers that only indirectly affected the American people, Hughes used his good offices and his ability to pressure American banks into making massive German loans to assist in creating amity in Europe.

The third obvious illustration of liberal isolationism in practice came in Latin America. There the realist interventionism of Theodore Roosevelt and the liberal interventionism of Wilson had left U.S. foreign policy in a dangerous dead end and poisoned U.S. relations with states throughout the hemisphere. Hughes immediately, though with varying degrees of success, set about winding down American occupations in the Caribbean,[63] and he removed from the Monroe Doctrine the various twentieth-century accretions used to justify U.S. intervention in domestic affairs. (At the same time Hughes was candid in acknowledging that the United States had interests in Latin America in addition to the prevention of European colonialism—for example, American concern with the protection of the Panama Canal and with the protection of American lives and legitimately acquired property—and that these might bring the United States into conflict with its neighbors.[64])

In Latin America as in Europe, the policy of liberal isolationism certainly did not equate to U.S. inaction. In 1922–1923, for example, Hughes sponsored a general conference of Central American states that resulted in some thirteen treaties, resolved a number of outstanding regional quarrels, and established a basis for mutual noninterference.[65] Similarly, the 1923 Pan-American Conference in Santiago yielded not only a host of technical agreements designed to improve interaction among American states but also created a procedure for resolving justiciable matters. The theme that ran through Hughes's Latin American policy was the need to build amity, not to build institutions or to impose values or order.

> The real accomplishments of the Pan-American conferences, he said, "are not to be found in any formal acts or statements but in the generation of helpful and friendly influences which draw peoples together through a better mutual understanding." In short . . . the institutions of a community are mainly significant insofar as they build and intensify the sentiment upon which that community is based. Once these attitudes are understood, many of his activities vis-à-vis the Latin American republics become meaningful. On many occasions, he devoted himself to projects in which it is difficult to find any basic motive other than his conviction that the United States had an interest in promoting peace and friendship among American nations.[66]

Perhaps the clearest explanation of what liberal isolationism implied for U.S. relations with its southern neighbors and what it implied about military intervention in general was offered by Hughes in Havana in 1928, at the Sixth Pan-American Conference. In what may have been the most extraordinary speech of his career, made extemporaneously and without notes, Hughes offered a candid summary of his view on American intervention in Latin America, one that continued his long repudiation of both Wilsonian interventionism and the Roosevelt Corollary:

> We yield to none in the establishment of the ideal of sovereignty and independence for every one of the American republics from the greatest to the smallest. . . . We do not wish the territory of any American republic. We do not wish to govern any American republic. We do not wish to intervene in the affairs of any American republic. We simply wish peace and order and stability and recognition of honest rights properly acquired so that this hemisphere may not only be the hemisphere of peace but the hemisphere of justice. . . . Now what is the real difficulty? Let us face the facts. The difficulty, if there is any, in any one of the American republics is not of any external aggression. It is an internal difficulty. . . . What are we to do when government breaks down and American citizens are in danger of their lives? Are we to stand by and see them butchered in the jungle because a government in circumstances which it cannot control and for

which it may not be responsible can no longer afford reasonable protection?. . .
Now it is a principle of international law that in such a case a government is fully
justified in taking action—I would call it interposition of a temporary character—for the purpose of protecting the lives and property of its nations. . . . Of
course the United States cannot forgo the right to protect its citizens. . . . The
rights of nations remain, but nations have duties as well as rights . . . we cannot
codify international law and ignore the duties of States by setting up the impossible reign of self-will without any recognition upon the part of a State of its obligations to its neighbors. . . . I have made this statement merely to avoid any
possible misunderstanding. I am too proud of my country to stand before you
as in any way suggesting a defense of aggression or of assault upon the sovereignty or independence of any State. I stand before you to tell you that we unite
with you in the aspiration for complete sovereignty and the realization of complete independence.[67]

In more eloquent terms, this was the double-barreled critique he leveled
against Wilson's Mexican policy in 1916: Intervention to impose a government, even a democratic government was not justified, but intervention to
protect American lives and property was. Against all expectations, Hughes's
lawyerly analysis of the rights *and duties* of sovereignty in a liberal world
carried the day in Havana, turning an apparent American foreign policy debacle into a memorable success.

The 1920s and the 1930s

Critical readers, particularly those schooled within the realist tradition,
may well respond, "yes, but." If the liberal isolationist policies of the 1920s
bought their victories at the price of the future—if the remarkable accomplishment of calming the troubled waters of the 1920s came at the cost of disorder, political collapse, and war in the following decade—then they can
hardly be considered a success, or much of one anyway. In their efforts to
remove the fears and suspicions that risked inflaming political passions,
Hughes and his successors gravely weakened the *Realpolitik* system of alliances and balancing in Europe and completely dismantled key elements of
it in Asia. In the short term—during the 1920s—this defused tensions and
yielded an extraordinary degree of harmony. But did this create a vacuum
that made later conflict unpreventable or unmanageable? Were the efforts to
dismantle *Realpolitik*—efforts shared by both Wilson and Hughes—not only
naive but also a significant contributor to the disaster of the 1930s? Or was
the slide into the abyss during the 1930s a consequence of terrible economic
and social stresses that would have strained any system, incomplete and mis-
managed efforts to implement the liberal vision (particularly in the area of
trade), and a failure by leaders during the 1930s to acknowledge that states
might step off the pathway of peace? I argue the latter view. Since two of the

liberal isolationist agreements of the 1920s, the Washington Treaties and the Kellogg-Briand Pact, drew the brunt of realist ire during the Cold War, it is useful to focus on these.

However successful the Washington Treaties were in halting the arms spiral and calming the turbulent Pacific seas of the 1920s, they failed to prevent a resurgence of Japanese militarism and Japan's return to imperial expansion in the 1930s. It is certainly fair, therefore, to ask whether the collapse of a liberal order in the Pacific reflected inherent flaws in the liberal isolationist vision or simply faulty implementation of that vision. Realists note that the Washington Treaties effectively isolated Japan, severing the Anglo-Japanese tie that had both protected Japanese interests and served as a check on Japanese behavior. In place of the British alliance, the Washington Treaties provided a more nebulous sort of Anglo-Franco-Japanese-American partnership. Though Japan would have preferred a tacit American alliance, and many observers in Japan both then and later concluded that this was indeed what Japan was offered, such an alliance would have been both inconsistent with the logic of liberal isolationism and politically impossible given American domestic realities.[68] What Hughes envisioned was shared American and Japanese membership in a new liberal order. The question therefore arises: Did peace in the Asia-Pacific region break down because the liberal isolationist vision (and domestic politics) precluded the former but nonetheless dictated the destruction of the *Realpolitik* Anglo-Japanese pact, or did it break down because protectionists and the Depression blocked the latter? In the absence of a counterfactual, any answer is speculative. The timing of events, however, tends to support the latter interpretation—that it was not the politico-military isolation of Japan but the social dislocation of the Depression, the collapse of international markets, and the failure of America to support free trade that were the principal stimuli for Japan's abandonment of the liberal order, for its decision to pursue military solutions to its politico-economic problems, and for its eventual abrogation of the Naval Treaties. With the Great Depression, Japan found American and European imperial markets closed, and not surprisingly felt it had been cheated out of the bargain it had struck in Washington. Japan's embrace of liberalism and commitment to the liberal pathway of peace, fragile in any case, was broken by these passion-heightening developments. Would a Japanese-American alliance, or the preservation of the Anglo-Japanese alliance, have changed how the Japanese came to understand themselves and their world in the 1930s or resolved the economic and social issues that led Japan to embark on a course of aggressive expansion? Frankly, it is hard to see how. A more complete American commitment to a liberal economic order might have been valuable, but an American commitment to Japanese security, or a British commitment to Japanese security, seems beside the point.

In Asia, America actively destroyed *Realpolitik* institutions; in Europe, the failure was to create them. Perhaps the most consistently caricatured and reviled piece of liberal isolationist diplomacy has been the Kellogg-Briand Pact of 1928, renouncing war. Taken out of context, especially given the history of following two decades, the Pact does indeed appear a striking example of idealistic moralizing and liberal naivete. In context, however, it is a much more interesting demarche, still vulnerable to realist criticism but a far more sophisticated bit of diplomacy than it is usually presented as being. France sought a Franco-American nonaggression treaty. Particularly given the *Realpolitik* tenor of French foreign policy, the United States was unwilling to enter into any bilateral Franco-American agreement, even one as apparently consistent with liberal isolationism as a renunciation of aggressive war, that would appear to suggest a special Franco-American relationship. The Kellogg-Briand Pact neatly solved this problem. By making the Franco-American nonaggression treaty open to all signers, it expressed in universal language and as a universal commitment the reality of Franco-American amity.[69] While not the naive, moralistic document that realists have portrayed it as being (remarkably, given that Kellogg's cosignatory, and the principal instigator of the Pact, was Aristide Briand, hardly an exemplar of liberal naivete), the Pact is nonetheless interesting for what it is not: a Franco-American alliance. Would a Franco-American, or an Anglo-Franco-American, alliance have been a good thing? Perhaps. But in 1928, German and Italian fascism still lay in the future, and French intransigence as much as German revanchism appeared a threat to peace. Unless one concludes that by 1928 it was already certain that Germany and Italy would threaten the liberal order, a decision to forego a *Realpolitik* Franco-American alliance was indeed a sensible one.

A fair appraisal of the 1920s would thus seem to be that the successes of liberal isolationism were extraordinary; the failures were due to incomplete execution, not to a flaw in the basic vision. Sadly, the conditions necessary for the "peaceful order based on the shared political values of a freely cooperating community of equals"[70] that Hughes and his colleagues sought disappeared in the 1930s as societies around the world turned off the liberal pathway of peace. But this does not detract from the achievement of the 1920s or suggest that an alternative route would have led to a happier destination.

A LIBERAL ISOLATIONIST POLICY FOR TWENTY-FIRST CENTURY AMERICA?

Even if one accepts the proposition developed above, that liberal isolationism was a productive approach to dealing with the challenges facing America and the world in the 1920s, this in no way necessarily implies that liberal isolationism makes sense today. I would argue, however, not only that the fundamental premises underlying liberal isolationism are correct but also that today's realities are in important regards quite similar to those of the 1920s. For this reason, the kinds of policies that made sense in the 1920s make sense again today.

Liberal isolationism is rooted in a vision of the world that has not been widely accepted during the last half century. Three assumptions about international politics lie at the heart of this vision. The first, contrary to the tenets of realist internationalism that shaped American thinking during the Cold War years, is that a global international harmony is possible. Security need not rely on the possession of countervailing force or on the maintenance of a favorable balance of power. Properly understood, the search for security and well-being is not a competitive undertaking, but a common one. To be sure, in some circumstances when dealing with immature adversaries, the pursuit of power may be necessary (that is to say, there is no reason to believe that any liberal policy, however well-executed, would have turned Hitler or the Japanese militarists into responsible members of an international *res publica*); but the realist pursuit of power can never yield the optimum outcome.

Second, contrary to the views of liberal internationalist critics of realism, achievement of international harmony depends not on the creation of international institutions for cooperation but on the maturation of individuals and societies. While international institutions are indeed valuable for coordinating actions and eliminating friction, in the end it is necessary for political actors, whether individual or collective, to be able to understand and act on their mature self-interest. They must construct for themselves an identity and self-awareness that permits them to rise above childish myopia and passionate petulance, and to subordinate emotions to reason. Given the natural harmony of relations between nations, mutual reason yields amity and amity yields cooperation and peace. By eliminating irritations and suspicions, international institutions may make subordinating passions like anger and fear to reason easier, and may make it easier to turn amity into cooperation and peace. But if reason and amity are not present, institutions cannot ensure cooperation and peace.

Third, the ability to subordinate passion to reason depends on the healthy organic development of well-ordered societies, through education, culture, and domestic institution-building (including the construction of democratic norms and structures). Healthy societal growth can be fertilized through international cultural contacts and economic ties, but it is by its nature a process *organic* to a particular society: In general, liberal values and domestic institutions cannot be imposed from outside, either at the point of a gun or by international fiat. The Japanese and German post-World War II experiences, of course, provide exceptions, though arguably they are exceptions that illustrate the rule: In both countries it took devastating military defeat and unconditional surrender, prolonged occupation, and the ability to rewrite constitutions and imprison or execute hostile elites in order to remove the illiberal weeds that had choked the field, turn the clock back twenty years, and regrow the society around the liberal plants that had survived from earlier years.

This belief that societies develop organically and resist external pressures for radical transformation means that the liberal notion of self-determination is taken more seriously in this vision of world politics than in the Wilsonian one, both normatively and positively. Normatively, the vision suggests that nations have a right not only to possess their own state but also to develop the political institutions and political culture that meet their particular needs. Positively, it suggests that while nations may learn from one another about the benefits of political and economic liberalism, in general they will either resist or be unable to incorporate institutions and cultures that are imposed on them.

The rejection of the 1920s liberal isolationist vision—first in favor of Franklin Roosevelt's liberal internationalist vision with its emphasis on global institutions, then in favor of a realist internationalist vision of Cold War containment and deterrence, and finally in favor of a hybrid realist/liberal internationalist vision that yielded detente, Desert Storm, and Dayton—has had important consequences. Visions shape realities. Both in our hearts and minds and through our policies we construct the world within which we operate and which in turn shapes our lives. To be sure, we do not (and cannot) do so with disregard to objective facts. But these objective facts are underdetermining of behavior and open to multiple understandings. Within the constraints imposed by the laws of physics, chemistry, biology, and mathematics, human beings remake themselves and their political world according to the images they construct. Thus to accept the assumptions underlying liberal isolationism—that a natural harmony of interests between nations can exist, that human reason permits the discovery and pursuit of this natural harmony, and that the individual and cultural development necessary for this exercise of reason must occur organically within particular societies—is to construct a very different understanding of reality than that which guided the Roosevelt, Truman, Nixon, or Clinton administrations.

Back to the Future: The 2000s as the 1920s

One reason to look back to the 1920s, then, would be the suspicion that the liberal isolationists of that era were on to something: that their interpretation of human nature and of national development offered the potential for a better world. But if the 2000s were not in important regards like the 1920s, it would nonetheless be a mistake not to look back for lessons. After all, the pathway of peace, however attractive, cannot be walked alone—it takes two to be at peace. If there is no prospect for amity in today's world, we are driven by default to pursue realist policies and power. As in the 1920s, however, this is not the case.

Thus the first important similarity to the 1920s is the absence of great powers with fundamentally revisionist or revolutionary agendas. The world today is (more or less) a world of status quo powers. Whatever irritants may exist between the great powers and whatever modifications in the status quo particular great powers might prefer (for example, Chinese interest in reasserting control over Taiwan), none see great-power war as necessary or even as a serious option. This is hardly the kind of world of great-power balancing and war of all against all that realists presume.

A second similarity is the existence of worrisome clouds on the horizon of this sunny day. In this regard, today may offer a fairer prospect than did 1920. But even the most optimistic observer in the year 2000 would have to worry about China's future stability; the continued implosion of the Russian economy and disintegration of Russian political life; the economic stagnation, collapse of state institutions, and increasingly endemic violence across sub-Saharan Africa; the regional trouble-making of the inveterate illiberal "rogues"—North Korea, Iraq, Iran, Libya; the long-standing hostile passions marring relations between India and Pakistan; and an Arab world in which violence remains an accepted tool of politics. And while it would be wrong to invest the problem with a permanence or fundamentality that it does not deserve, it is also true that the liberal Western world faces a clash of civilizations—friction between nations with different worldviews, different expectations, and different styles and modes of communication. As in the 1920s, looking to the future one would have to conclude that conflict is neither inevitable nor unlikely, and the task of statesmanship will be to clear the skies before storms break. A key element in this statesmanship will be dealing with security dilemmas, both between regional powers, such as India and Pakistan, and between great powers, such as the United States and China.

Third, again as in the 1920s, nations are confronted by major social upheaval. Then, societies around the world were wrestling with the challenges of modernity—that is, with the challenges of developing social, cultural, political, and economic institutions sufficient to cope with the tensions of industrialization, urbanization, and mass-nationalization. Today, advanced industrial societies are wrestling with the challenges of postmodernity. In the transition now underway, modern societies face the social consequences of deindustrialization, exurbanization, political multiculturalization, and economic globalization. These are challenges that will severely tax, and may even threaten the legitimacy of, existing political institutions, and will alienate many ordinary citizens from existing sources of political and social authority. As during industrialization, the erosion of traditional authority, the

need to overcome economic and social alienation, and the task of constructing a collective political identity will make appeals to passion and to myopic
and simplistic definitions of interest politically attractive. All of Hughes's
worries about the capacity of democracies to behave unwisely, to succumb
to demagoguery and to the politics of parochial self-interest, must be faced
again today.

These are problems not only abroad, but also at home. To be capable of
meeting the challenges of foreign policy leadership and of building a harmonious world order, Americans will have to subject themselves and their
own society to critical scrutiny.

Five Principles of a Liberal Isolationist Foreign Policy

If we do turn to the 1920s for lessons, what principles can we identify? Let
me suggest five.

1. *Don't be preoccupied with international institutions.* Today's liberal institutionalists, like their Wilsonian predecessors, misunderstand the nature of institutions. Institutions are superstructure. They are valuable
   superstructure. But they are superstructure. Most obviously, institutions
   are valuable because they help actors achieve shared goals, overcoming dilemmas of collective action and market failures. Institutions may
   also be valuable as a vehicle for cross-national communication and idea
   sharing, and may thereby encourage the construction of national identities that facilitate international amity. The European Union nicely illustrates both points. In general, however, international institutions do
   not change how actors construct their identity, nor do they change how
   actors conceive of their interests. It is not that these are permanent or
   fixed. They are, to the contrary, malleable in important ways. It is just
   that the process by which these identities and interests are constructed
   is an organic one, overwhelmingly shaped by forces, histories, and realities within individual societies. A nation's understanding of itself and
   its appropriate behavior may be influenced by forces above or outside
   its borders—nations may certainly learn from each other—but except
   in unusual circumstances (for example, the social and political reconstruction of Germany and Japan following their complete defeat, unconditional surrender, and occupation) these understandings are likely
   to be relatively immune to deliberate outside pressure or manipulation.
   Thus, while the relationship between institutions and identity plainly
   runs both ways, the more important causal arrow runs not from institutions to identity but the reverse direction: Changes in constructed identity (and therefore in constructed understanding of interest) yield
   changes in institutions. Building liberal international institutions in the

absence of a mature, liberal understanding of one's self and self-interest is building an edifice on sand: however impressive and however well-designed, it is weak and impermanent.

This is not to suggest that the United States should cease to participate in the United Nations, NATO, the IMF, the World Bank, or the vast number of other global and regional institutions in which it plays an important role. But it is to argue against reifying these institutions. It is to suggest that these institutions be understood for what they are: useful fora for dialog and generating friendly contact, a means of overcoming problems of collective action and market failure, and a tool for resolving justiciable and technical disputes. They are not, however, instruments for creating political transformation. Political transformation must first occur within the minds of individuals and within the culture of national societies. Except perhaps in the most extraordinary circumstances, this can not be imposed by external institutions.

2. *Build amity.* Realists misunderstand both human nature and the nature of world politics. Human beings are social creatures, capable of amity. They are able to organize themselves in familial, local, national, or international *res publicas*. The fullest achievement of self-interest demands the creation of an amicable, harmonious order, not the subjugation of all to one. Ultimately, politics is not about power but about maximizing happiness or, as economists would have it, maximizing utility.

The construction of amity involves a reconstruction of identity, a maturing capacity to act on reason rather than passion, and a recognition of the potential for harmonious order. The key goals of statecraft, therefore, are the removal of irritants that inflame passions and an encouragement of the process of self-discovery and maturation that allows nations to reconstruct their identity in ways that highlight shared interests and strengthen ties of amity.

In specific terms, though, what does this mean for American foreign policy? At one extreme, the injunction to build amity degenerates into platitude—that the American state conduct its national policies so that when neighboring nations think of fairness, caring, and integrity, they think of America. Fortunately, however, it is possible to see more concrete prescriptions as well.

In the first place, this injunction suggests an active, forward-looking (i.e., nonreactive) diplomacy aimed at eliminating security dilemmas and international disputes. It therefore calls for a vigorous and creative search for arms control measures, and for a foreign policy that encourages and facilitates the pursuit of arms control by other states. Discussions need to be aimed at helping nations recognize the ways in which their actions distress or alarm their neighbors; in many cases, appar-

ently grand achievements like nuclear test bans may be of less consequence than apparently trivial agreements on transparency or confidence-
building. The need to focus on resolving international disputes also
highlights the importance of active efforts to establish institutions of
mediation and arbitration, able to resolve international disputes while
they are still technical or justiciable and before they acquire a harder
political shell or move into the realm of political passion. In an era of
globalization, in which the points of contact (and potential grievance)
among nations grow constantly, the need for new institutions of dispute resolution grows in tandem.

A point worth underscoring here is that U.S. foreign policy should
aim at depoliticizing issues—that is, on finding ways to resolve issues
on their technical or juridical merits rather than dealing with them as
political clashes to be resolved through an appeal to power. One of the
dangers of realism is its tendency to focus narrowly on power. To be
sure, power is the ultimate arbiter (and, in the end, military power is the
ultimate, ultimate arbiter). But resorts to power are costly and in the
long run counterproductive. It is true that spousal disputes may be resolved by one partner denying the other financial support or by one
partner beating the other; the long-term prognosis for such relationships, however, is not good.

In the second place, this injunction to build amity dictates a foreign
policy that gives high priority to increasing transnational contact. When
building amity is placed at the center of the foreign policy agenda, then
cultural, technical, and educational exchanges become essential pillars
of foreign policy rather than pleasant afterthoughts. Exposure to liberal
values does not guarantee their transmission. Indeed, it may provoke a
reaction against them. The growth and evolution of social and political
institutions are, after all, organic processes, and societies find their own
distinct paths to their future. Nonetheless, because liberal values are
widely attractive and because individuals and nations can, in some circumstances, learn lessons about the construction of stable, mature domestic political institutions from observing conditions in other societies, transnational contact becomes centrally important.

3. *Accept differences.* Difference need not imply conflict. The "clash of civilizations" thesis advanced by Sam Huntington should be regarded as
only half right: it is true that the whole world is not Western and liberal,
but this does not necessarily imply a violent interaction between the
West and the rest. While maturity, far-sightedness, and an acceptance of
the ultimate harmony of international society are necessary for a peaceful international order, these are qualities not necessarily limited to the
West. Creating amity across cultural and civilizational lines may be more
difficult than creating it within a particular culture or civilization, but it

is not necessarily impossible. (And since even if one wanted to impose a homogenous Western culture—a debatable goal—there is no practical way to do so, liberally inclined foreign policy makers have no option but to try to create transcivilizational amity.)

This suggests two corollary observations. First, the West does not need vainly to try to compel the world to remake itself in a Western image. Peace does not depend on the rest of the world becoming a pale copy of the West. Western-dominated international institutions do not need to be burdened with the impossible task of remaking national societies. Second, while there may from time to time be aggressive adversaries that must be contained, isolated, or counterbalanced, in general the realist presumption that the "other" is hostile, either because of its will to power or because of its fears of exploitation in an anarchic system, is mistaken.

4. *Accept that violence will occur.* We do not have universal liberalism. And even if we did, it would not necessarily imply an end to history or an end to the violent disputes that represent the stuff of history. Individuals and societies, even liberal ones, are capable of yielding to passions such as anger, fear, and myopic greed. Neither mature understanding of an overarching harmony of interest nor wise policies to resolve the clashes of interest that will still inevitably arise are guaranteed. To use Hughes's image, there may be a pathway of peace, but peace is a path to be walked, not a goal that can be achieved once and for all time. Even those individuals, societies, and nations that attempt to travel the path are likely sometimes to step off it. Millennial visions are deceptive. As much as we loathe and deplore violence, its occurrence does not mean we have failed, only that we need to continue to try harder.

At any given time there will be some societies that lack the institutions or cultural tools necessary if they are to forego violence as a routine means of political action. These institutions and cultures cannot be imposed. They must develop organically. And until they develop, our ability to create peace, either within or between such societies, is limited.

This does not mean the United States should wash its hands of places like Rwanda, the Congo, Somalia, the Sudan, Sierra Leone, Liberia, the former Yugoslavia, and Colombia, where violence now appears endemic. But it does argue that the approach must be long term and involve efforts to encourage organic cultural change, rather than assume an end to the fighting can be imposed and maintained by outside force. Appeals to superior American military power must be regarded with enormous suspicion. In some cases intervention may be politically necessary to protect American lives and property. In other cases it may be morally necessary given the magnitude and clarity of the crimes against humanity being conducted. But even in these cases American military intervention must be regarded as the lesser of two evils, not as a solution; and it must be undertaken with trepidation and regret rather than with enthusiasm and pride.

5. *Don't expect an end of history at home, either.* Perhaps the most important realization, though, is that the gravest threats to American well-being and happiness are at home. The point here is not simply that the most pressing problems to be resolved are domestic ones, though this is probably true. Rather the point is that America's ability to act in a wise, mature fashion in its foreign policy cannot be taken for granted. Building a harmonious international system for the long haul demands constant attention be given to domestic values and institutions. And this does not mean simply preserving the liberal values and institutions that exist. As organic creatures, societies are constantly in motion. Values and institutions cannot be fixed. Change is necessary, unstoppable, and desirable. The challenge is to prevent the emergence of values and institutions that interfere with the intelligent, mature pursuit of a global harmony.

NOTES

1. The phrase is Hughes's. He used it both as the title of one of his major foreign policy addresses, delivered in 1923, and as the title of his collected foreign policy addresses, published in 1925. See Charles Evans Hughes, *The Pathway of Peace* (New York: Harper and Brothers, 1925).

2. To be fair to Hughes, he did realize the ill-advisedness of insisting on repayment of war debts, but found his hands tied by congressional legislation. See, for example, Hughes, "Some Aspects of Our Foreign Policy," in Hughes, *Pathway of Peace*, p. 55.

3. On this subject see, for example, Selig Adler, *The Isolationist Impulse* (London: Abelard-Schuman, 1957), 27.

4. For an analysis of the interplay of domestic cognitive, cultural, economic, and institutional forces shaping foreign policy readjustment, see Peter Trubowitz, Emily O. Goldman, and Edward Rhodes, eds., *The Politics of Strategic Adjustment: Ideas, Interests, and Institutions* (New York: Columbia University Press, 1999).

5. The standard biographies of Hughes are Dexter Perkins, *Charles Evans Hughes and American Democratic Statesmanship* (Boston: Little, Brown, 1956) and Merlo J. Pusey, *Charles Evans Hughes*, 2 volumes (New York: Macmillan, 1951). Drawing on these earlier works, Betty Glad's study of Hughes offers a brilliant analysis of Hughes's cognitive framework and the intellectual forces that shaped his worldview: see Betty Glad, *Charles Evans Hughes and the Illusions of Innocence* (Urbana: University of Illinois Press, 1966). On Hughes as governor of New York, see Robert F. Wesser, *Charles Evans Hughes: Politics and Reform in New York, 1905–1910* (Ithaca, N.Y.: Cornell University Press, 1967). On Hughes's two tenures on the Supreme Court, see Samuel Hendel, *Charles Evans Hughes and the Supreme Court* (New York: Columbia Uni-

versity Press, 1951) and Kenneth Bernard Umbreit, *Our Eleven Chief Justices*, volume 2 (Port Washington, N.Y.: Kennikat Press, 1969 [1938]), 451–500. Regarding Hughes's service as secretary of state, see Charles Cheney Hyde, "Charles Evans Hughes," in Samuel Flagg Bemis, ed., *The American Secretaries of State and Their Diplomacy*, volume 10 (New York: Alfred A. Knopf, 1929), 221–401. Hughes's own thinking on foreign policy questions is detailed in his published memoirs, drafted in 1941–1945 but based on notes made for him earlier, and in numerous carefully reasoned public addresses, published contemporaneously or at the close of his tenure as secretary: David J. Danelski and Joseph S. Tulchin, eds., *The Autobiographical Notes of Charles Evans Hughes* (Cambridge, Mass.: Harvard University Press, 1973); and, *inter alia*, Charles Evans Hughes, *Conditions of Progress in Democratic Government* (New Haven, Conn.: Yale University Press, 1910); Hughes, *The Pathway of Peace*; Charles Evans Hughes, *Our Relations to the Nations of the Western Hemisphere* (Princeton, N.J.: Princeton University Press, 1928); and Charles Evans Hughes, *Pan American Peace Plans* (New Haven, Conn.: Yale University Press, 1929).

6. His defeat has generally been attributed to bungled efforts to heal the 1912 Republican-Progressive split in California and to California governor Hiram Johnson's antipathy. For a detailed analysis of the 1916 campaign, see S. D. Lovell, *The Presidential Election of 1916* (Carbondale: Southern Illinois University Press, 1980).

7. See, for example, Pusey, *Hughes*, volume 1, pp. 352–359.

8. Hendel, *Hughes and the Supreme Court*; Pusey, *Hughes*, volume 2, pp. 731–772.

9. See, for example, L. Ethan Ellis, *Republican Foreign Policy* (New Brunswick, N.J.: Rutgers University Press, 1968) and L. Ethan Ellis, *Frank B. Kellogg and American Foreign Relations, 1925–1929* (New Brunswick, N.J.: Rutgers University Press, 1961).

10. For a discussion of these competing visions of American foreign policy, see Edward Rhodes, "Constructing Peace and War: An Analysis of the Power of Ideas to Shape American Military Power," *Millennium Journal of International Relations*, Spring 1995.

11. See, for example, Danelski and Tulchin, *Autobiographical Notes*, pp. 188, 210.

12. Pusey, *Hughes*, volume 1, p. 395.

13. Hughes, as cited in Pusey, *Hughes*, volume 1, p. 396. See also Danelski and Tulchin, *Autobiographical Notes*, p. 210.

14. Hughes, as cited in Danelski and Tulchin, *Autobiographical Notes*, pp. 210–211. Hughes's biographer suggests that Hughes was particularly concerned that Article X would bind the United States to support Japan in the event that China attempted to recover Shantung, which had been yielded to Japan at Versailles, by force of arms. See Pusey, *Hughes*, volume 1, p. 398.

15. Hughes, as cited in Danelski and Tulchin, *Autobiographical Notes*, p. 211.

16. Hughes, as cited in Danelski and Tulchin, *Autobiographical Notes*, p. 211.

17. Hughes, as cited in Danelski and Tulchin, *Autobiographical Notes*, pp. 211–212.

18. Hughes to Senator Eugene Hale, July 24, 1919, as cited in Danelski and Tulchin, *Autobiographical Notes*, p. 212.

19. On the impact of the "Committee of 31" see, for example, Adler, *Isolationist Impulse*, pp. 112–114.

20. Hughes, "Pathway of Peace," pp. 11–12.

21. Hughes, "Pathway of Peace," pp. 12–13.

22. For an extraordinary account of the exegesis of Hughes's thought, see Glad, *Hughes.*

23. Hughes, Speech of February 22, 1908, as cited in Glad, *Hughes,* p. 89.

24. Hughes, "Pathway of Peace," pp. 3–4.

25. "The Pathway of Peace" was delivered to the Canadian Bar Association in Montreal on September 4, 1923. Hughes used it as the introductory essay in his collected secretarial addresses, also titled *Pathway of Peace.*

26. Hughes, *Conditions of Progress,* pp. 6–7, 8. See also pp. 8–9, 21–22 both on the dangers of popular passion, privileged special interests, and reckless partisan leadership, and on the capacity of a community to overcome them. Despite his constant refusal to support dramatic ("nonorganic") change in domestic institutions, Hughes's Progressive instincts were apparent during both of his tenures on the Supreme Court. He saw expanded government power as necessary to the protection and advancement of the community, but was concerned lest that power be perverted to protect powerful private interests or be abused by demagogues.

27. Hughes, as cited in Pusey, *Hughes,* volume 2, p. 764.

28. Hughes, "Pathway of Peace," p. 7.

29. See Pusey, *Hughes,* volume 2, pp. 794–795.

30. Hughes's letter to Frederic R. Coudert, as cited in Pusey, *Hughes,* volume 2, pp. 795–796.

31. Hughes, "Pathway of Peace," pp. 7–8, 17.

32. On the origin of the Dawes Plan see, for example, Hyde, "Hughes," pp. 374–393.

33. The literature on the Washington Naval Treaties is substantial. In addition to works on Hughes, however, see in particular Harold and Margaret Sprout, *Toward a New Order of Sea Power: American Naval Policy and the World Scene, 1918–1922* (Princeton, N.J.: Princeton University Press, 1940); Emily O. Goldman, *Sunken Treaties: Naval Arms Control Between the Wars* (University Park: Pennsylvania State University Press, 1994); and Robert Gordon Kaufman, *Arms Control During the Pre-Nuclear Era: The United States and Naval Limitation Between the Two World Wars* (New York: Columbia University Press, 1990).

34. Wilson's proposed 1916 Democratic Party platform plank, as cited in Lovell, *Election,* pp. 56–57.

35. See, for example, Ellis, *Republican Foreign Policy,* pp. 328–363, or Adler, *Isolationist Impulse,* p. 245. Adler underscores both the League's unwillingness to act on its collective security pledges and America's unwillingness to jeopardize great-power peace. "By any ordinary interpretation of Japan's actions, the League was obligated to come to the help of China. . . . The Hoover administration set an all-time record for close cooperation with the League in the Manchurian crisis, but the President refused to countenance any American action that might risk war." Though offering no condemnation of his friend Hoover's timidity, Hughes's own evaluation, for what it is worth, is similar: "Certainly as to the action of Japan in Manchuria in 1931, when we consider Secretary Stimson's efforts, his collaboration with the League, his 'seizing the initiative both in direct remonstrances with Tokyo and in the introduction of proposals at Geneva,' his acting 'more boldly than Great Britain or the League,' the attitude of the British Government, and the final result, there is no basis for saying that this

result would have been altered by our membership in the League." See Danelski and Tulchin, *Autobiographical Notes*, p. 219. Hughes is quoting A. Whitney Griswold, *The Far Eastern Policy of the United States* (New York: Harcourt, Brace, 1938), pp. 417–418, 431, 438.

36. Hughes, "The Pathway of Peace," p. 7.

37. Hughes, as cited in Danelski and Tulchin, *Autobiographical Notes*, pp. 220, 221.

38. Hughes, as cited in Danelski and Tulchin, *Autobiographical Notes*, p. 219.

39. Adler, *Isolationist Impulse*, p. 169.

40. See, for example, Hyde, "Hughes," pp. 236–252, and Pusey, *Hughes*, volume 2, pp. 445–452.

41. On the motivations of the Wilson administration's enormous 1919 naval construction program see, for example, Sprout and Sprout, *New Order*, pp. 47–69. "The administration's purpose . . . was primarily to fashion a club to hold over the European Allies in general, and over Great Britain in particular, pending their adherence to President Wilson's comprehensive plans for reduction of armaments and creation of a new world order" (p. 56). In the secret Anglo-American agreement of April 9, 1919, Wilson agreed to temporarily halt the building program in return for British acceptance of a league of nations, but the threat of resuming construction was retained as a means of forcing further British concessions, particularly on freedom of the seas, British naval construction, and British alliance policies. Drawing on memoranda prepared by the naval staff, the Sprouts make the point that logically the long-term implications of membership in a league (given the unresolved differences in American and British worldviews) were that America would have to continue to use American naval construction and expanded American naval power as a lever and threat.

> 'At a time when all the world is seeking to form a league of nations that will secure justice to great and small nations alike, the British prime minister announces that the British alliance with France will continue forever.' And the Anglo-Japanese Alliance still continued in the Far East. Such combinations seemed . . . 'to contain elements of grave danger and to demand . . . extraordinary measures.' Nothing less than full equality upon the sea would enable us to hold our own, whether in conference or in armed conflict, in the clearly impending Anglo-American struggle for position, power, profit, and prestige. Such equality . . . was also necessary to secure the ends of world peace and international justice. If the projected league of nations was to fulfill its mission, it must have available sufficient force to overpower 'any recalcitrant member. . . .' Such force was not to be found in a 'heterogeneous' collection of naval craft assembled by the League, unless 'that assemblage' included 'one group of a single nationality . . . equal in strength' to the naval power of the nation under coercion. Thus 'as long as Great Britain insists on retaining her overwhelming naval force, the only answer for the purposes of the League is the building of an equal force by some [other] nation.' (pp. 67–68)

42. Hughes, "Some Aspects of Our Foreign Policy," pp. 32–58.

43. The term is Warren Cohen's. See Warren I. Cohen, *Empire Without Tears: America's Foreign Relations, 1921–1933* (Philadelphia, Penn.: Temple University Press, 1987).

44. On the Immigration Act of 1924 and the Hanihara letter see, for example, Pusey, *Hughes*, volume 2, pp. 512–517. Pusey notes that under Hughes's guidance and as a consequence of the Washington Naval Treaties, "our relations with Japan

had reached a high state of cordiality. The American people had generously aided Japan after her 'bewildering devastation' by the earthquake of 1923. The gratitude of the Japanese strengthened the good relations that had taken firm root at the Washington Conference. Then suddenly this hopeful amity was poisoned by rancor because Congress intemperately wrote a Japanese exclusion clause into the Immigration Act of 1924" (p. 512). In an effort to forestall congressional action and at Hughes's suggestion, Japanese Ambassador Hanihara agreed to make public the terms of the previously confidential Japanese-American "Gentlemen's Agreement" of 1907 limiting Japanese emigration; Hanihara's letter of April 10, which represented an extraordinary attempt at accommodation (and powerful testimony to the effectiveness of Hughes's Japanese diplomacy), unfortunately included a passing reference to concerns shared by Hanihara and Hughes about "grave consequences" that the Act would have for "the otherwise happy and mutually advantageous relations between our two countries," and this phrase was interpreted in Congress and the yellow press as a threat. Hughes's effort to reaffirm the Gentlemen's Agreement was defeated in the Senate by a vote of 76–2 and Hanihara had no choice but to resign. Hughes, Japanese Foreign Minister Shidehara, and the new Japanese ambassador, Matsudaira, were faced with the task of calming public opinion on both sides of the Pacific and rebuilding the "friendship policy." That they were able to do so, and that Japanese-American relations continued on a positive tack until the collapse of Japanese liberalism in the late 1920s, is extraordinary.

On the reconstruction of German-American relations see, for example, Adler, *Isolationist Impulse*, pp. 175–179. On the genesis of the Kellogg-Briand negotiations in French interest in some sort of Franco-American nonaggression pact to round out France's network of treaty arrangements and the evolution of these negotiations to yield a multilateral arrangement acceptable to America but still serving French purposes, see, for example, Ellis, *Kellogg*, pp. 193–212. On American policy toward the Soviet Union see, for example, Perkins, *Hughes*, pp. 125–128; for Hughes's explanation and justification of this policy see Hughes, "Russia," in Hughes, *Pathway of Peace*, pp. 59–64.

45. See, for example, Pusey, *Hughes*, volume 2, p. 435.

46. For balanced but critical appraisals see, for example, Kaufman, *Arms Control*, and Goldman, *Sunken Treaties*. For the texts of the treaties and agreements resulting from the Washington Conference, see Goldman, *Sunken Treaties*, pp. 273–307.

47. Summaries from the world press and from elite comments amply support the conclusion that until the opening session "fear that the great undertaking in Washington would simmer down to pious mouthings signifying nothing was dominant." (Pusey, *Hughes*, volume 2, p. 466.) Hughes's opening speech, on November 12, 1921, was a surprise to all but about a half dozen in the American government who had been party to its preparation or had necessarily been informed, including the ever-amiable president. William Allen White, writing twenty some years later would claim that "of all human conclaves I have ever witnessed, the gathering of the Disarmament Conference in Washington furnished the most intensely dramatic moment I have ever witnessed." More contemporaneously, the head of the British delegation, Arthur Balfour, described Hughes's speech as "one of the most remarkable utterances which has ever been made by any statesman under any circumstances" and concluded that "it was the inspired moment of November 12th on which all the greatness of this great transaction

really depends." (As cited by Pusey, *Hughes*, volume 2, pp. 472, 473.) Four days after the conference's opening, the *New York Times* reported "What was an impossibility is now a fact." (See Pusey, *Hughes*, volume 2, p. 474. For the text of Hughes's
speech see Hughes, "Limitation of Naval Armament," in Hughes, *Pathway of Peace*,
pp. 20–31.) Journalists recorded with naughty glee the impact of Hughes's plan on
the assembled delegates. The British, whose fleet was sunk first and therefore without any warning whatsoever, had the hardest go of it:

> Admiral Beatty, First Sea Lord of the British Admiralty, was seen to come forward in his
> chair, a 'slightly staggered and deeply disturbed expression' on his countenance, remind-
> ing one of a 'bulldog, sleeping on a sunny doorstep, who has been poked in the stomach
> by the impudent foot of an itinerant soap-canvasser seriously lacking in any sense of the
> most ordinary proprieties. ' Admiral Chatfield, one of Beatty's colleagues, 'turned red and
> then white, and sat immovable.' Lord Lee of Fareham, civilian head of the Admiralty, be-
> trayed intense excitement. . . . Others noted the 'deep silence' that prevailed while Hughes
> sank more British battleships 'than all the admirals of the world had destroyed in a cycle
> of centuries.' . . . Giving his listeners no time to recover from this shock, Hughes passed
> on to Japan. . . . Although warned by what had gone before, 'there was no discounting the
> surprise of Prince Tokugawa, Baron Kato, and Ambassador Shidehara, the delegates from
> Japan.' (Sprout and Sprout, *New Order of Sea Power*, pp. 151, 152.)

48. See Sprout and Sprout, *New Order of Sea Power*.

49. Hughes's November 12 proposal was to scrap sixty-six battleships and battle-
cruisers "built and building," with a combined tonnage of 1,878,043 tons: the United
States would stop construction on fifteen capital ships and scrap fifteen more, while
Britain would halt work on four capital ships and scrap nineteen, and Japan would
scrap one battleship just launched and ten older vessels, stop work on six more capital ships, and abandon plans for a further eight. In the end, Japanese insistence on
keeping the newly launched *Mutsu* forced some marginal modification of this plan,
but it was approved in its essentials.

50. Hughes, "Limitation of Naval Armament," p. 31.

51. As cited in Pusey, *Hughes*, volume 2, p. 509.

52. Ambassador George Harvey, as cited in Pusey, *Hughes*, volume 2, p. 473.

53. See, for example, the history of the negotiations offered by Pusey, *Hughes*, volume 2, pp. 491–500.

54. Pusey, *Hughes*, volume 2, p. 500.

55. "A Treaty Between All Nine Powers Relating to Principles and Policies To Be
Followed in Matters Concerning China," as cited in Goldman, *Sunken Treaties*, pp.
299–300.

56. Pusey, *Hughes*, volume 2, p. 502.

57. Pusey, *Hughes*, volume 2, p. 502.

58. Hughes, "Some Aspects of Our Foreign Policy," pp. 39–40.

59. Lee of Fareham, speech to the Royal Colonial Institute, London, May 9, 1922,
as cited by Pusey, *Hughes*, volume 2, p. 507.

60. Hughes, "Some Aspects of Our Foreign Policy," p. 40.

61. For Hughes's views on the utility of joint investigative commissions see Hyde,
"Hughes," pp. 357–358, or Hughes, "Pathway of Peace," in Hughes, pp. 2, 16.

62. Hughes, "Some Aspects of Our Foreign Policy," pp. 55–58.

63. Hughes announced a withdrawal from the Dominican Republic in June 1921, though this was not completed until 1924. The withdrawal of the last American troops in Nicaragua was announced in 1923 and was completed in 1924, but civil war forced the return of American troops. Conditions in Haiti did not permit the removal of American Marines, but Hughes sought to create a long-term policy that would permit American disentanglement.

64. Hughes dealt with the issues explicitly in his 1928 Stafford Little lectures at Princeton. See Hughes, *Our Relations to the Nations of the Western Hemisphere*, pp. 11–20. For an excellent discussion of Hughes's thinking, see also Glad, *Hughes*, pp. 236–253.

65. Though perhaps a historical footnote, this conference is interesting in at least two regards. First, the success of this conference demonstrated the value of liberal isolationism and of U.S. refusal to be drawn into dictating the terms of agreement: as one chronicler dryly notes,

> the Central American delegates were not assembling at Washington with a view to accepting the dictation of a powerful northern neighbor. Sensitive as to their right freely to object to whatever might be deemed incompatible with their respective interests, they were likely to resist any proposals that the United States might press with vigor. On the faintest grounds for suspicion they might be expected to impute to the United States some selfish design as the reason for the wisest proposal. (Hyde, "Hughes," p. 267.)

In a world of jealously sovereign states, Wilsonian imposition was counterproductive to positive change.

Second, the content of the agreements reached at this conference is also a revealing indication of what liberal isolationism meant in practical application. The treaties between the five Central American republics dealt with a range of issues including disarmament, free trade, education, labor legislation, social welfare, finance, transportation, improvement of cultural ties, and treatment of each other's nationals. The most important of the treaties, however, pledged the Central American republics not to assist or recognize revolutions or coups d'etat unless or until this was approved by some sort of democratic process; not to recognize leaders who came to power violently; not to intervene in each other's civil wars; not to permit reelection of presidents and vice presidents; and "not to intervene, under any circumstances, directly or indirectly, in the internal political affairs of any other Central American republic." (See Danelski and Tulchin, *Autobiographical Notes*, pp. 268–69, and Hyde, "Hughes," pp. 266–270.) The treaties also established a tribunal and international commissions designed to mediate any judiciable issues that would arise between the republics.

66. Glad, *Hughes*, p. 257.

67. Hughes, as cited in Pusey, *Hughes*, volume 2, pp. 559–560.

68. I am grateful to Michael Adas, Osamu Ishii, Ryo Oshiba, and Jitsuo Tsuchiyama for their insights on this point. They do not share my conclusions.

69. For a useful account of the diplomacy leading to the Kellogg-Briand Pact, see Ellis, *Kellogg*, pp. 193–212.

70. Glad, *Hughes*, pp. 258–259.

10

The Limits of Alliance: Conflict, Cooperation, and Collective Identity

Ronald R. Krebs

On the hustings in 1996 President Bill Clinton trumpeted the Atlantic Alliance's virtues—not its capacity for deterrence proven during the Cold War, nor its growing ability to project military power out of area, but its internal conflict resolution mechanisms. In Detroit, a traditional stop on the election tour of ethnic America, Clinton, who had become an ardent supporter of NATO enlargement several years before,[1] declared, "through NATO, Western Europe became a source of stability instead of hostility. France and Germany moved from conflict to cooperation. . . . I came to office convinced that NATO can do for Europe's East what it did for Europe's West."[2] The conventional wisdom, widely shared in both the policy and scholarly worlds, is that alliances are useful means of promoting cooperation and even collective identity among their members. That claim, more often asserted than systematically argued, is not as much wrong as it is crude. Relations between allies—both in NATO and in the less deeply institutionalized alliances of the past—have historically been associated with both cooperation and conflict, for "allies often clash with each other more than they unite in common cause."[3] The facts of intra-alliance competitive dynamics and violent conflict suggest the need to examine critically the validity and scope of the belief that alliances are magically transformed over time into zones of peace in which war is unthinkable.

It is indeed tempting to consider alliances as unproblematically producing cooperation (the coordination of behavior) and collective identity (the convergence of interests). Decision makers understandably find it far more difficult to justify membership in an institution with cross-cutting consequences and trade-offs than in one whose effects flow in only one, fully salutary and desired direction. Scholars have an additional incentive to engage in a selective reading of the history of intra-alliance relations: simplifying assumptions about alliances are useful tools in social scientific model building. But such insensitivity to history and complexity leads to ill-considered policy and poor theory.

This chapter ranges widely across theory, history, and policy discourse in offering several arguments about the consequences of alliance membership. First, I take issue both with structural realists, who see alliances as epiphenomenal, and with neoliberal institutionalists, who view alliances, like other institutions, as promoting cooperation within their boundaries. Alliances have independent causal impact: they critically shape their members' patterns of interstate interaction. But, drawing on the insights of collective action theory, I argue that, under particular conditions, alliances can make possible and even exacerbate tensions and heighten the possibility of intra-alliance conflict. These hypotheses suggest the limits of neoliberal institutionalist logic and take tentative first steps toward a "realist institutionalism."[4]

In the second half of the chapter, I evaluate the general claim that alliance is conducive to the emergence of a security community and critically review six causal mechanisms proposed within recent constructivist literature. Some are deeply flawed at the level of theory, others are plausible but remain theoretically underdeveloped and hence unfalsifiable, and others fail on empirical grounds in the crucial most-likely case, NATO. At best, constructivist scholars have a great deal of work ahead of them in specifying scope conditions to their broad claim about the power of alliance to shape identity. At worst, they—and policy makers who have endorsed similar views—have overstated their case and have placed far too much explanatory weight on common alliance commitments.

This chapter proceeds in four sections. First, I provide a few examples of the tendency to exaggerate the harmony of alliance, drawing on the statements of political leaders as well as on academic writings. Sections two and three assess the causal logic and empirical evidence linking alliances with in-turn cooperation and collective identity. Finally, I conclude with a brief discussion of the implications both for international relations theory and for American foreign policy in the uncertainty and flux that continue to characterize international politics a decade after the end of the Cold War.

FRIENDS BUT ALSO FOES

When states band together, whether to promote aggressive or defensive goals, their joint commitment presumes some common interest, but that hardly precludes the possibility that other conflicting aims, perhaps no less important in the hierarchy of objectives, will undermine the alliance. This seems an obvious point, yet scholars and policy makers alike have tended either to assume that the shared interest overrides all other concerns or to overestimate the degree of common interest.[5] Bill Clinton was hardly alone in treating an alliance as the panacea for the ills of European great power competition. In a speech to the French Senate in 1911, the French Foreign Minister Alexandre Ribot proclaimed that the alliance between his nation and Russia reflected a wide range of shared interests beyond defense: "When two great nations enter into a permanent bond of friendship they join forces in foreign policy, not merely with the object of maintaining the peace of the world, but also of dealing jointly with all sorts of eventualities which cannot at the moment be foreseen. . . . They accordingly keep a watchful eye on events with a view of framing a suitable joint policy."[6]

Students of international relations, rooted in a variety of theoretical traditions, have equally fallen prey to such fallacies. In constructing his expected-utility theory of war, Bruce Bueno de Mesquita assumes that allies have absolute utility for their partners, that they lack any conflicting objectives. Seeking to account for the counterintuitive empirical finding that allies have engaged in war with each other a surprising fifteen times between 1816 and 1974—nearly 20 percent of all interstate conflicts in that period—he argues that any change that might affect the other's foreign policy signals a forthcoming deterioration in relations and generates incentives to war. However, Bueno de Mesquita provides no evidence that would substantiate his causal story, and the logic of his explanation is entirely dependent on the patently unrealistic assumption that allies possess identical goals across the board.[7] Jonathan Mercer's work on reputation formation, grounded in psychology, is explicitly counterposed to rationalist theories of deterrence, but he implicitly agrees with Bueno de Mesquita's formulation of intra-alliance relations. One key to Mercer's argument is that allies always find desirable each other's demonstrations of resolve (and that antagonists are necessarily displeased with such behavior), but this assumption cannot be justified unless one accepts an idealized view of allied and adversarial dynamics, in which cooperation (or conflict) on a limited set of security questions leads to agreement (or disagreement) on all issues.[8]

Realist statements on the nature of allied relations have also been ambiguous.[9] Focused on alliance formation and dissolution, realists have generally regarded alliances as epiphenomenal and paid little attention to the politics within them. Often alliances are in this view merely fleeting agglomerations of military capabilities, "only temporary marriages of convenience, where today's alliance partner might be tomorrow's enemy, and today's enemy might be tomorrow's alliance partner."[10] With relative gains concerns as powerful in alliance as they are for states unsheltered from the buffets of anarchy, states pass the buck, forcing their allies to bear the costs of confronting a common threat. However, at times realists have implied that once states enter alliance, their behavior exhibits a near-identity of interest and residual clashes do not arise. Although Kenneth Waltz famously noted that states "are compelled to ask not 'Will both of us gain?' but 'Who will gain more?'" he also explained European integration as a consequence of the Soviet menace. Bound together by their common fear, Germany, France, and the other former great powers of Europe overcame centuries of hostility and strife, and even welcomed their fellows' growth and development. Among these consumers of security, "not all impediments to cooperation were removed but one important one was—the fear that the greater advantage of one would be translated into military force to be used against the others."[11]

Alliances are tools for achieving common ends, but conflict can nonetheless creep into their members' relationships from two directions. First, insofar as states continue to seek aims beyond the *casus foederis* of the alliance, they often remain competitors in other dimensions, blurring the distinction between allies and adversaries. Even at the height of the Cold War, France was suspicious of American diplomacy in Indochina as a threat to the integrity of its overseas empire. Agreement on the broad outlines of containment obscured the allies' divergent regional priorities and "the subtle competition for spheres of influence that often underlined their diplomacy toward the Third World."[12] Moreover, states have often sought to control an adversary by enmeshing it in an alliance. Alliances, Paul Schroeder has observed, are "associative-antagonistic relationships": they are as often devices that unite rivals as they are means of linking friends.[13] Thus conflict may exist within alliance for the same reasons that it had before the allied states made common cause. Second, it is also possible, and I shall argue on behalf of this view, that under certain conditions alliance can itself exacerbate states' conflictual relations. Conflict may arise then not despite, but because of, alliance.

ALLIANCE, COOPERATION, AND CONFLICT

The Atlantic Alliance's greatest achievement in its first forty years lay in the realm of the invisible, in scenarios avoided, in communism averted. But, in the eyes of many, Franco-German reconciliation—the process by which these two long-standing continental rivals became the cornerstone of peace in Western Europe, "the alliance within the alliance"[14]—places a very close second. When policy makers and scholars ascribe such healing powers to NATO, they often conflate the distinct propositions that the alliance promoted "cooperation" between these two former great powers and that it fostered the emergence of a "collective security identity." The first describes mutual policy coordination between actors whose interests are, for theoretical purposes, treated as exogenous, while the second denotes that states' interests themselves have converged.[15] This section of the essay focuses on the relationship between alliances and cooperation, while the next examines the contribution of alliance membership to the formation of collective identity.

The most developed set of theoretical arguments on behalf of alliances' ability to nurture cooperation derives from institutionalist reasoning. Although Robert Keohane insisted a decade ago that "alliances *are* institutions,"[16] few of his disciples have turned their analytical lenses in that direction, preferring to focus on institutions of low politics such as international economic regulatory agencies or environmental regimes. The occasional exceptions to this rule, rather than employ the framework to explain patterns of cooperation among allies as a function of institutionalization, have generally focused on questions such as the persistence of alliance policies or the search for new missions as old ones become obsolete.[17] Nevertheless at first glance institutionalists should be capable of offering several coherent arguments as to how alliances, like other institutions, promote international cooperation among their members.[18]

First, institutions are characterized by rule-governed interaction, which encourages an increased number of transactions among participants, thereby discouraging cheating among states that are reasonably sensitive to the "shadow of the future." Second, by providing a framework for further agreement, institutions reduce the costs associated with the bilateral negotiation, monitoring, and verification of individual accords, making cooperation more profitable and attractive.

Third, institutions link issue areas, different zones of state interaction, creating greater opportunities for side payments and raising the price of defection. As Keohane explains, "Clustering of issues under a regime facilitates side payments among these issues: more potential *quids* are available for the *quo*. Without international regimes linking clusters of issues to one another, side payments and linkages would be difficult to arrange in world politics."[19] Such linkages also make cheating more costly, for they provide the victim with multiple issue areas in which to exact revenge. Fourth, institutions increase the level of transparency among members, raising the expected cost of cheating within an institutional context, as the likelihood of detection and retaliation increases. Moreover, the expected gain decreases, since transparency permits prospective victims to take protective measures.

If in a neorealist world states are reluctant to remain in alliances longer than they must because they do not trust others, institutionalists expect that formalized, well-integrated alliances help their members overcome incentives to internal mobilization, attenuate the fear of unequal gains, and foster numerous cooperative ventures.[20]

Upon closer inspection, however, such institutionalist hypotheses are, without emendation, indeterminate with regard to the consequences of alliance membership for cooperation.[21] First, repeated interaction under a long shadow of the future does not logically produce cooperation. As James Fearon points out, "though a long shadow of the future may make *enforcing* an international agreement easier, it can also give states an incentive to *bargain harder*, delaying agreement in hopes of getting a better deal."[22] Where the stakes are unusually high as when war, rather than the mere failure to achieve a mutually beneficial accord, is the possible outcome one would expect to observe especially intense bargaining: under such circumstances, the costs of not reaching an agreement would certainly be quite high, but the terms would consequently also be more important.[23] Among states with a potentially militarizable conflict of interest, the rule-governed interaction sponsored by alliance therefore seems likely to encourage tough bargaining rather than mutual concessions.

Second, the additional issue areas supplied by the institution can give states more to fight over, exploding the boundaries of an initially limited conflict. Rather than generate cooperation, institutions may, through issue-linkage, contribute to the deterioration of the relationship.[24] Keohane has himself acknowledged, though only in a footnote, that in highly conflictual situations "linkages . . . may well impede cooperation."[25] Practitioners and specialists have also argued that the presence of multiple issue areas has often served as a hindrance to cooperation, broadening and deepening conflict, and they have consequently suggested decoupling issues. A former American ambassador to Greece has observed that instead of enabling Greece and Turkey "to reconcile their differences by direct negotiation, their common alliance with the United States and Western Europe often appears to act as an impediment. Bilateral disputes acquire a multilateral dimension."[26]

Third, transparency may improve the quantity and quality of information available, but the question remains: information about what? In a modern alliance, high levels of coordination demand that allies keep each other informed of their respective military capabilities, but inferring intentions and projected use is hardly straightforward. The same resources that can be justified on the basis of alliance tasks can also be turned profitably against an allied adversary. In such cases, estimates regarding intent derive less from accurate information regarding forces than from worst-case analysis and the weight of the past. Moreover, such information may not improve a state's defensive capabilities against a surprise attack in a limited campaign; protective measures may simply be impossible in the face of surprise, and the expected gains from cheating will then be unaffected.

Perspicacious policy makers have at times grasped institutions' potential to thwart cooperation. After World War I, French statesmen, particularly Foreign Minister Aristide Briand, feared that alleviating German security concerns to the West through the Treaty of Locarno would give rise to German aggression in the East. From that perspective, the accord they eventually negotiated was particularly poorly designed. Although the pact permitted

France to assist its allies in East-Central Europe, the circumstances under which it could do so were highly constrained: except in the case of a direct attack on France itself or a League of Nations pronouncement branding Germany an aggressor, a French invasion on behalf of its allies would violate the treaty and possibly force Britain to intervene on the German side. In the words of one historian, thanks to Locarno, "Germany's western flank would receive a measure of protection in the event of a Polish attack on Germany or in case Germany in the distant future were to use force to revise its eastern frontiers—a contingency which neither the Reichwehr nor the Wilhelmstrasse ruled out if attempts at peaceful revision failed." At the end of the day, however, the security of France itself came first, and France did not make evacuation of the Rhineland contingent on an "eastern Locarno."[27]

British leaders had a different, if related, concern, worrying that a security pact with France would destabilize the continent by giving France further incentive to provoke Germany: as Prime Minister MacDonald warned the Committee of Imperial Defense in 1924, "There was the danger that if we made [the] French secure, thereby we would give her a free hand to work out her own political and economic policy in Europe and relieve her of all military implications which might result from her policy."[28] Similarly, in the early years of the Cold War, John Foster Dulles repeatedly cautioned that the short-term exigencies of American security policy, which demanded an alliance with ravaged Western Europe, might impede the long-run aim of American military withdrawal from the continent, which depended on European unity and recovery. As early as 1948 Dulles warned George Marshall and Robert Lovett that the agreement that would become the North Atlantic Treaty "might seem to guaranty the status quo and make it less likely, rather than more likely, that the western European democracies would unite as to create strength between themselves."[29]

Such nagging fears have not proved entirely unwarranted, as alliance membership has at times convincingly resulted in perverse consequences. Elsewhere I have argued that the Atlantic Alliance had a destructive impact on the Greco-Turkish relationship. Made enemies by a long history of mutual exploitation and cycles of revenge, the two countries brokered a rapprochement in 1930 when faced with aggressive threats from Bulgaria and Italy, and the bonds grew tighter after World War II despite Greek resentment at perceived Turkish betrayal during the war. In the early 1950s the Turkish premier paid a visit across the Aegean, and the Greek royal couple did the same; meanwhile leading policy makers floated the idea of confederation. But, shortly after the pair's accession to NATO, nearly a quarter-century of warm relations dissolved in bickering over the fate of Cyprus.[30]

Neither institutionalist nor structural realist logics can explain why and under what conditions alliances might undermine cooperation and even spur conflict. The theory of collective action, which has been applied in limited fashion to alliances, can prove helpful in this regard. Drawing from his home discipline of economics, Mancur Olson pointed to the difficulty of cooperation among rational egoists with regard to public goods, which are characterized by (1) nonexcludability (those who do not purchase or pay for the good cannot be kept from consuming it, from enjoying its benefits), and (2) jointness of supply (additional consumption of the good does not diminish the amount available to others).[31] Although the actors share an interest in provision of the public good, each also wishes to minimize his or her own contribution and shift the onus primarily onto others. As each shirks, collective action fails, and all suffer. That actors seek to gain benefit from a public good without bearing proportional costs, that they might ride free on the efforts of their partners, is a phenomenon familiar to anyone who has ever engaged in a collaborative enterprise. Grounded in economics, Olson spoke the language of costs and payments, and his work had obvious application to burden sharing within alliances; soon thereafter a vibrant research program sprung up examining the distribution of costs within NATO and averring that the Europeans were, as Olson had expected, exploiting the United States and contributing less than their fair share.[32] But the narrowness of this research has been unfortunate, for collective action theory has implications that extend beyond burden sharing to the broader question of alliance commitment.

Actors, in this case states, ride free because they believe that they will enjoy the same amount of the good, in this case security, regardless of their behavior. States spend less on defense because allies will pick up the slack. But the further implication is that they can devote less attention to the common objective, for others are guaranteeing their security (or, in the case of an offensive alliance, ensuring that their shared goals are attained). Free-riding applies not just to tangible monetary burdens, but even to interests, as allies shift the focus of their foreign policy to secondary goals. Consequently revisionist states espy an opportunity to further their ends, which may run counter to those of fellow allies, and, for status quo states, the traditional rival replaces the alliance's target as the primary threat, even if that rival is an ally. And since states are very often satisfied with respect to some issues and less content with respect to others, they can simultaneously exhibit both patterns of behavior.

However, this logic applies only to those allies, typically small powers, whose national efforts are relatively inconsequential for the coalition's effectiveness. Olson noted that perverse effects were somewhat mitigated in an intermediate case, when "the contribution or lack of contribution of any one individual in the group will have a perceptible effect on the burden or benefit of any other individual or individuals in the group."[33] The incentive to ride free is vastly reduced when that actor's *individual* behavior would cause insufficient provision of the good. If a single great power or even an important mid-sized state were to shift its foreign policy away from the primary goal, the credibility and capacity of the alliance would be markedly diminished. In contrast, a small state may aid the alliance by sitting along a vital strategic corridor or by serving political and symbolic purposes, but its actual military contribution remains largely insignificant to the project's success. With the deterrence of the primary security threat, or achievement of the offensive goal, no longer falling on their shoulders, small-state decision makers turn inward and focus more intently on secondary concerns, particularly their long-standing conflicts with regional adversaries. When that adversary also happens to be an ally, as in the Greco-Turkish case, accession renders possible intra-alliance conflicts that had previously been put aside.

Membership in a multilateral alliance, therefore, thrusts small allies back into a world in which unequal gains are feared, in which the security dilemma operates. Once accession to the alliance has prompted the rivals to turn their attention to secondary foreign policy objectives and thus to their conflicts of interest with each other, the very means that contemporary alliances adopt to bolster their collective strength—economic and military assistance, technology transfer, and so on—transform a bounded dispute into a sweeping threat. Such arms transfers are a mixed blessing, simultaneously reassuring and threatening. Although the larger patrons provide arms to the allied enemies to meet shared objectives, their plans for using them remain partly inscrutable. Weapons intended for use against opposing forces can be turned against an ally. Alliance military assistance compounds intra-alliance suspicion as it provides the capacity for offensive action and thus contributes to a broader sense of insecurity.

Finally, under these conditions, the features of institutions that supposedly promote cooperation serve to ratchet up the conflict. Rivals link issues not to offer side payments, but rather to seek greater gains across the board. Transparency yields just slight gains against the uncertainty of anarchy, and of course inhibits cooperation when improved information reveals that suspected wolves really are wolves. Last, institutions are themselves not apolitical venues through which states achieve agreement, but are sources and instruments of power; rather than cultivating cooperation, institutions become the site and object of contest as states have significant incentives to capture them for their own ends. The argument is not that alliances spur only competitive dynamics, for certain features do undeniably promote cooperation.[34] Rather alliance institutions can promote effects that cut in both directions, simultaneously making possible and exacerbating, yet also moderating the rivalries within.

A Brief Case Study: NATO, France, and Germany

This framework yields insight not only into important cases of intra-alliance conflict, as in Greece and Turkey, but even into the Atlantic Alliance's great triumph: Franco-German reconciliation. Unlike among the far smaller allies in the southeast Mediterranean, NATO as an institution was the keystone supporting future cooperation between France and the Federal Republic of Germany. The terms of West Germany's accession to NATO and the Brussels Treaty Organization (later, the Western European Union), enshrined in 1954 in a series of agreements, placed strict limits on the size of its armed forces and on the weaponry in its arsenal, particularly with regard to nonconventional arms, long-range missiles, strategic bombers, and large warships. With its troops operating exclusively under NATO authority and without a national general staff, West Germany could pose little military threat to its neighbors. Finally, and most important, the United States committed itself to stationing forces in the country, thereby guaranteeing the peace in Western Europe.[35] When, after several years of tenacious opposition, the French finally did put aside their fears and accept German rearmament, these particular institutional arrangements that enmeshed West Germany in a restrictive web made it palatable. That the alliance engaged in monitoring, sponsored information exchange, and otherwise nurtured transparency was critical to ensuring these agreements' long-term stability and survival.

The NATO regime laid the foundation for the Franco-German rapprochement, but it exerted a differential impact on these two European powers, as a perspective informed by the collective-action problem would expect. At the close of World War II, France played a classic zero-sum game, laboring hard to keep Germany small, weak, and demilitarized, but as the Soviet threat emerged, French fears of German revanchism took a back seat. Such concerns sprang up again only after the militarization of the Cold War and the deeper institutionalization of the Atlantic Alliance, after the American military commitment to the continent had been solidified in the wake of the Korean War; manifest in French opposition to German rearmament, these qualms led to the defeat of the European Defense Community, which France had initially proposed. While Germany stood, divided, astride the continent's central cleavage line, France was, thanks to NATO, relatively sheltered and could afford to maintain its independent Gaullist priorities. With Germany and allied forces a buffer between its borders and the Soviet bloc, France had the luxury of resisting integration into the alliance's joint military structures and eventually withdrawing its forces from NATO's military wing. French investment in its military was so skewed toward its (post-)imperial needs that, as time passed, the armed forces' ability to defend against a Warsaw Pact assault declined substantially.[36]

In contrast, especially under Konrad Adenauer, West Germany was the model ally, identifying its own fate with that of the alliance as whole. Confronted daily with the threat posed by the Soviet bloc, Germany was an integral member of the alliance and could not afford to realign its foreign policy priorities, as had France; with 30 percent of its population and 25 percent of its industrial capacity located within sixty miles of the border, only West Germany exceeded the American contribution to the forward defense of Western Europe.[37] When West Germany was dissatisfied with the alliance's policy-making processes, as in the case of the United States' refusal to share nuclear targeting and strategy information in the 1950s, it sought solutions within the organization, through nuclear control-sharing arrangements and later the Nuclear Planning Group; similarly discontent, France chose a different path, striking out on its own and developing an independent nuclear force. France's foreign policy reflected its peculiar insulated position that permitted it to decrease its devotion to alliance aims without undermining provision of the public good—that is, security from the Soviet menace. Meanwhile, Germany had less leeway for riding free, for a reduced German commitment would have undermined alliance effectiveness and contributed to marked underprovision of security.[38]

Moreover, the larger pattern of Franco-German cooperation during the Cold War is explained less by the abstract mechanisms highlighted by institutionalist theory (issue linkage, side payments, heightened iteration, reduced transaction costs) than by a combination of domestic politics (the ideology of state leaders, the limits imposed by coalition politics) and fears of American abandonment. Whereas a structural realist would have expected improving superpower relations to have undermined European integration and bilateral cooperation, the effect was in fact the opposite. European statesmen recognized that whether the elephants were fighting or making love, the grass was sure to be crushed; their fears of abandonment and entrapment were simply two sides of the same coin.[39] When Soviet-American relations seemed to portend that the collective good that NATO and the United States had supplied would no longer be plentiful, France and Germany found security cooperation far easier to attain.

As the superpower détente approached its zenith, a pervasive sense of isolation drove the French desire for cooperation with Germany, particularly in military affairs. Even though it had achieved warmer relations with the eastern bloc through *Ostpolitik,* Germany also found the U.S.-USSR rapprochement worrisome and sought to bind itself more closely to its neighbor to the west. The ascendance to power of Valèry Giscard d'Estaing in France and Helmut Schmidt in Germany paved the way for renewed progress in their countries' integration, in defense no less than in economics. The election of Jimmy Carter in 1976 fueled European skepticism about American reliability, and Germany's Schmidt was particularly worried as Carter suddenly decided in 1978 to cancel the deployment of enhanced radiation weapons after Schmidt had, at great personal political risk, promised to deploy them. Close cooperation between France and Germany emerged not as part of a broader American-led effort to counter the Soviet threat or as a happy consequence of NATO's institutional design, but out of a growing fear that the United

States was not committed to Western Europe's defense and might seek a separate solution with the Soviets.

The aspirations of Giscard and Schmidt went unfulfilled as they could not overcome domestic political weakness, and thus the next great wave of Franco-German security cooperation got under way roughly as Soviet-American relations began to undergo a sea change in the mid-1980s. That Francois Mitterand and Helmut Kohl, despite different general ideological predilections, shared similar views on NATO and the Soviet Union was certainly important, and they began to move their countries closer even before the transformation of the Cold War environment, but these leaders also recognized that changing geopolitical conditions might lead the United States to retrench its global commitments and withdraw its forces from the continent. To Europeans nervous about American abandonment, the signing of the 1987 Intermediate-Range Nuclear Forces (INF) Treaty was but the culmination of a longer process whose roots lay in the early years of the Cold War and that Ronald Reagan had reinvigorated. The Franco-German bilateral advances came fast and furious in the middle years of the decade as Reagan's obsession with the Strategic Defense Initiative raised the specter of a new isolationism, as growing American budget deficits seemed to bode ill for future levels of defense spending, as American attention seemed to shift from the European theater to Latin America and the Pacific Basin, as Reagan appeared willing at the 1986 Reykjavik Summit to trade the nuclear umbrella over Europe, and as the ink dried on the INF Treaty. As a French parliamentarian rhetorically posed the question in 1987, "Do you think 320 million Europeans can continue forever to ask 240 million Americans to defend us against 280 million Soviets?"[40]

The steadily deepening cooperation of the 1980s—from the institutionalization of meetings at all levels to improved French capabilities for participation in the forward defense of West Germany to unprecedented joint exercises to the French decision to consult Germany on the employment of tactical nuclear weapons—was remarkable. Differences still persisted between French and German security policy, particularly over whether bilateral cooperation would serve as the central pillar of a European security community that would replace NATO and largely exclude the United States (France) or would be at most a European complement to the older transatlantic partnership (Germany). But by the late 1980s these two major European powers had indeed become close collaborators in security affairs. However, the common wisdom on NATO's role in effecting the transformation seems wrong. NATO did lay the foundation for Franco-German reconciliation, but the institution cannot account for the ebb and flow of their security relationship. The brief account here is only suggestive, and far greater research would be required for firmer conclusions. But at first glance it would seem that the supposed feather in the neoliberal institutionalists' cap has been blown away by the empirical winds.

ALLIANCES AND COLLECTIVE IDENTITY

Narrowly crafted institutionalist arguments regarding cooperation are less popular, however, than the far grander claim that NATO has contributed in substantial fashion to the formation of a transatlantic security community: a group of states that share a social identity, a sense of "we-ness," and whose interactions are marked not by short-term self-interest and self-help, but by diffuse reciprocity, trust, and even altruism.[41] Within this community, "dependable expectations of peaceful change" reign; war has become inconceivable. Rooted in the seminal work of Karl Deutsch and his collaborators, this argument has more recently been articulated by theorists of a constructivist bent, who have begun to place the initial insight on firmer footing and who have sought to craft more generalizable causal chains.[42] Evaluating this newer literature, I maintain that careful examination of the mechanisms purportedly linking alliance to collective identity reveals that the transformative capacity of alliances has been exaggerated. Moreover, NATO, a critical test of the general hypothesis, cannot bear the bulk, if much at all, of the explanatory burden, suggesting the emphasis on alliance has been misplaced.

The constructivist claim is that, through common membership in a deeply institutionalized alliance, states forge a collective identity, reflected in what Deutsch termed a security community. Such states would not escape anarchy and self-help—the international system would continue to lack a dependable means of enforcing commitments—but they would expand the boundaries of the self to include their allies. The allies would no longer define their interests by themselves alone, but would positively identify with "the welfare of another, such that the other is seen as a cognitive expression of the self." The result would be "empathetic rather than instrumental or situational interdependence between self and other."[43] Proceeding from an ontology that stresses the social construction of reality, the importance of intersubjective in addition to material structures, contemporary students of security communities have distanced themselves from Deutsch's behavioralist underpinnings and emphasis on quantitative measures of transactions and have instead devoted attention to the emergence of an imagined, cognitive region.[44] The existence of a collective security identity does not imply that interstate relations are completely harmonious, but rather that when disputes arise, they are resolved peacefully, even when strategically rational actors might opt for war.

Two strategies assist in assessment of this argument. First, I cull from the literature six proposed causal mechanisms linking alliances and collective identity and critically evaluate their *theoretical* plausibility as either useful generalizations or contingent explanations. Second, I offer preliminary *empirical* evidence drawn from the history of NATO regarding those hypotheses that are sufficiently well-developed to permit falsification and that seem minimally reasonable. The depth of NATO's institutionalization and the intensity of the interstate interactions it sponsored renders it a most-likely case for the alliance-collective identity connection, and not surprisingly NATO has been widely cited as having just such effects. If NATO should prove less influential than most have thought, it would raise serious questions about the hypothesis.[45]

1. *Powerful States and Ideational Influence.* At the level of structure, it has been asserted that great powers, and especially hegemonic powers, nudge others toward and compel them to adopt and maintain a collective stance. Stated in more ideational terms, "because of the positive images of security or material progress that are associated with powerful and successful states, security communities develop around them."[46] Whatever the plausibility of this hypothesis or the extent to which it captures the imagining that surrounds the emergence of a security community, it has little to do with the institutionalized features of an alliance and much to do with the relations between the powerful and the weak; both the alliance and the security community would then independently be products of the gap in relative power, and the causal relationship between them would be spurious. The alliance might provide the hegemon with an additional means of coercion, with a lever over its allies, but the institution would hardly account for the bulk of the action, except possibly in moments "after hegemony."

2. *The Interstate Contact Hypothesis.* Constructivist scholars have argued that collective experiences and social identities follow from an impressive level of interstate transactions, from high "dynamic density." The greater the quantity, velocity, intensity, and diversity of exchanges of various kinds, the more likely they are to give rise to collective interstate identities,[47] and deeply institutionalized alliances are important sponsors of such influential interactions. This proposition bears close kinship to the venerable "contact hypothesis," which has roots stretching back to Montesquieu, and extends its domestic logic to the international level. However, the simple contact hypothesis—which suggests that intense and extensive interaction among individuals and groups would, as a function of increasing knowledge about the other, eventually eliminate prejudicial attitudes and behavior and reduce consciousness of difference—has been conclusively rejected. In his studies of prejudice, the social psychologist Gordon Allport formulated a more sophisticated version to distinguish "casual contact" from "true acquaintance," proposing three additional criteria that would break down the barriers to meaningful communication.[48] But, despite a highly active research program that has flourished for decades, the causal claims of the contact hypothesis remain unverified, and even the sophisticated variant has received little empirical support.[49]

Constructivists therefore stray awfully close to the liberal fallacy, and they know it: in tortured language, they have sought desperately to distinguish themselves from the liberals of yesteryear. While Emanuel Adler and Michael Barnett caution that "not all transactions will produce a collective identity; after all, interactions are also responsible for creating an 'other' and defining threats," they also state, without caveat, that "increased interactions . . . encourage the development of new social institutions and organizational forms that reflect diffuse reciprocity, shared interests, and perhaps even a collective identity."[50] Constructivists are well aware of, but have not found a satisfactory reply to, the truism that although contact with others may foster friendship, harmony, and a sense of common destiny, familiarity may also breed contempt. As distances narrow and contact increases, cooperation may become profitable, but conflicts of interest that sharpen the lines of demarcation are equally likely to arise. True understanding of the other's aims, demands, fears, and methods of operation may just as easily contribute to deadlock, to the recognition that goals are entirely incompatible, as it will to the feeling of commonality. As Andrew Sullivan has observed, "It is one of the most foolish clichés of our time that prejudice is always rooted in ignorance, and can usually be overcome by familiarity with the objects of our loathing."[51]

Realist writers on international relations have convincingly rebutted such liberal claims. John Lewis Gaddis concludes that "the conquest of distance" over the course of the latter half of the nineteenth century "did not strengthen Russian-American friendship; instead it worsened matters by injecting disputes over geopolitics and human rights into a relationship in which remoteness had heretofore encouraged the appearance of complementary interests."[52] An ironic, if somewhat tendentious, example also dates from the end of the nineteenth century, when two languages that aspired to universality, Esperanto and Volapük, rapidly descended into a bitter feud. A common language could not even bind together the disciples of Volapük, who split after a quarrel over grammar.[53] Even Alexander Wendt has observed that "the vulnerabilities that accompany interdependence may generate perceived threats to self-control, and rising similarity may generate fears that the state has no raison d'être if it is not different from others. States may respond to these systemic processes, in other words, by redoubling their efforts to defend egoistic identities."[54]

Although even manifold and diverse transactions would appear not to be related in any straightforward fashion to the emergence of collective identity, they may make the participants aware of underlying similarities they had not previously recognized or serve as a multiplier.[55] Colin Kahl, for example, adds that only under conditions such as "the *positive* nature of interdependence" and "a *proper* foundation" will intense contact yield a shared sense of identity and purpose; these caveats are clearly reminiscent of Allport's version of the contact hypothesis, but Kahl does not go even as far as Allport in identifying the factors that render high levels of interaction conducive to the varied outcomes.[56] Other proponents have retreated from the strong form of the proposition, admitting that "increasing interaction, whether of groups or individuals, intensifies and magnifies processes already underway."[57] These more plausible, and more humble, forms of the contact hypothesis are, however, unverifiable and hence unassailable in the absence of further theoretical development. Without a priori specification of the "proper foundation," such arguments tend toward committing the *post hoc ergo propter hoc* fallacy, asserting the existence of this basis and the operation of the causal mechanism whenever a collective identity appears to have taken shape. Nor can one measure interaction's causal effect as a multiplier without specifying precisely what impact such ongoing processes would have had if such interaction had not taken place.

3. *Monitoring and Trust.* Alliances, like other international organizations and institutions, establish behavioral norms, monitoring mechanisms, and sanctions that are the basis for the trust that lies at the heart of the security community. However, the process linking such features of institutional design to the emergence of deep-seated trust is highly undertheorized. Not only do such structural inducements not always successfully engender cooperation, but few such cooperative enterprises blossom into the full-fledged, almost unthinking trust one would associate with a security community. What are the intervening factors that encourage or impede the transformation of cooperation into trust? Is trust simply an extreme form of cooperation such that differences in degree become differences in kind, as this mechanism implies? Or is it perhaps an entirely different phenomenon produced by entirely different processes? Since interstate relations, even among allies, are rarely composed solely of cooperative episodes but usually entail both cooperative and competitive interactions, states must somehow pick and choose from among the mounds of contradictory data when composing their portrait of the other. Why are some events accented and others ignored? Institutions may be sites of learning, but whence the content of the lessons?[58]

The answers to these questions have been at best suggestive. Adler and Barnett, for example, characterize trust as the product of "a lifetime of common experiences and [emerging] through sustained interactions and reciprocal exchanges, leaps of faith that are braced by the verification offered by organizations, trial-and-error, and a historical legacy of actions and encounters that deposit an environment of certitude notwithstanding the uncertainty that accompanies social life."[59] This is roughly equivalent to saying: trust emerges when it emerges; we are not quite sure how; but we are sure monitoring must be a major piece of the puzzle. Until such insights are recast and formulated as testable hypotheses, it is impossible to know whether monitors and sanctions are themselves sufficient for trust and identity. It is not even clear that international institutional monitoring mechanisms are necessary for trust: for instance, today a liberal democracy cannot conceive of being attacked militarily by a fellow liberal democracy, regardless of the pair's current or past institutional memberships.

4. *Socialization (I)—Domestic Structures.* Collective identity may also emerge as states become increasingly similar in their domestic political structures, ideologies, or cultures. Insofar as international institutions, and more particularly alliances, help engineer a transnational convergence of values and regime types, they figure centrally in the formation of collective identity. The chief mechanism is socialization—that is, the internalization of a given social community's constitutive beliefs and practices by embedding them in domestic decision-making processes. Part of NATO's purpose has been to spread and support democratic institutions, and the recent NATO enlargement was widely justified as assisting in the transition to and consolidation of democracy in East-Central Europe.[60]

How effective alliances, and particularly NATO, prove at this task is an empirical question, but there are reasons for skepticism. Alliances are, first and foremost, politico-military tools of statecraft that aggregate military capability to counter external threats, constrain the at times hostile power of allies, or pursue revisionist ends. In principle and in practice, other functions may be and often are grafted onto alliance, notably reshaping their members' domestic political and cultural systems. But precisely in those moments when alliances are most necessary and most important and therefore most influential, when the stakes are high and momentous questions of security are at issue, states are unlikely to allow the core role to suffer. Policies aimed at inducing homogeneity will be more successful if pursued bilaterally or through other institutional webs.

NATO's record in this regard is mixed. The Atlantic Alliance seems to have played relatively little role in establishing and consolidating democracy in the largest such project on the European continent—the transformation of postwar Germany; accounts that stress NATO's socialization function in the German case typically conflate alliance and American factors and policies.[61] Students of democratic transitions have routinely credited NATO with preventing particularly Spain, and some-

Chapter 10

times even Greece and Portugal, from slipping back into military rule
by giving support to military missions and identities based on enhanced
professionalism.[62] This claim is suspect, however, as the Spanish armed
forces had little formal interaction with NATO, as, soon after the country's accession to the alliance in 1982, the new Socialist Prime Minister
Felipe González, who had been swept into office in large part on the
strength of his anti-NATO stance, immediately froze integration into
NATO's military command structures. To the extent that the Spanish
armed forces learned the meaning of professionalism from their foreign
counterparts, it seems probable that the bilateral relationship with the
United States, which dated from 1953, was more consequential than the
alliance. And Greece had been active in the alliance for some fifteen
years before the 1967 coup; although the military's integration into the
alliance since the resumption of civilian rule in 1974 has been relatively
limited as a consequence of the conflicts with Turkey, the country has
remained coup-free. Finally, Turkey, a member of the alliance since
1952, is home to a shaky democracy in which coups have been frequent and in which the military still operates relatively autonomously.
Relatedly, if anything the alliance, by way of expansion, has slowed the
transition to liberal democracy in post-Cold War Russia by strengthening the political hand of antidemocratic forces.

   NATO does seem able to claim one recent and important success,
however. For the former Soviet bloc states of East-Central Europe,
membership in NATO is highly attractive: it provides a guarantee
against attack by their hulking neighbor to the East, signals to investors
a certain stability, and, beyond such strategic rationales, indicates that
one's country falls within the boundaries of the West. Over the last
decade, NATO has held out the prospect of membership to induce
these states to undertake democratic and economic reforms and to settle their outstanding territorial and ethnic conflicts.[63] How critical NATO
was to this process is contested,[64] and how permanent and deep-seated
are these agreements and institutions remains to be seen. Not participation in NATO forums (which is what is usually implied by socialization), but simply the possibility of Western acceptance (for which
NATO was a proxy) was the operative mechanism assisting in the
process of democratization.

5. *Socialization (II)—Security Experts and Epistemic Communities.* A
   number of observers have argued that alliance institutions more effectively foster a convergence of member interests by socializing security-
   policy elites toward a common set of norms. Under the auspices of the
   alliance, particular groups in member states—such as military officers
   and civilian security analysts—engage in intensive, structured interaction and collaborate to achieve shared corporate goals. Alliance forums

provide numerous opportunities to persuade other actors and change their beliefs, and over time the institution comes to serve as the home for an epistemic security community: a cohesive transnational group of civilian and military experts on international security who agree broadly on the definition of central concepts, cause-and-effect relationships, methods of truth-testing, and the objective of maximizing intra-alliance coordination.[65] Such expert communities have great influence because they are key suppliers of information to central state decision makers and work to reshape their states' interests in ways that promote trust and collective identity. In support of this socialization process, there is some evidence that American and European military officers serving in NATO forces have developed a unique alliance perspective and some degree of loyalty to the collective body.[66]

Underlying this argument, however, are two questionable premises. First, by envisioning that an expert consensus gradually evolves within alliance circles, this socialization hypothesis ignores the high political stakes that accompany alliance decisions. A more deeply political perspective recognizes that even as members' civilian and military representatives seek to further their common purpose, they also compete to control the alliance agenda, to devote greater collective attention to their own pet projects, to reduce their share of the burden, to conduct military operations in a fashion that accords with their own capabilities and strategic culture, and so on. Persuasion may certainly take place even within such a political environment, but it is more a rare and contingent outcome than a regular and predictable one.

Second, the epistemic community hypothesis presumes that the experts in question have unique and virtually unchallenged access to central state decision makers and consequently have great influence over the latter's policy preferences (and, presumably, in the long run over the state's conceptions of the self). When the epistemic community resides within the government as it largely does in the case of alliance, rather than within academia or the world of political activism, this argument certainly carries greater weight. Nonetheless, at least in democracies, a wide range of views from a variety of sources both within and outside government clamor for attention, and usually no one group will be able to monopolize decision makers' ears. While epistemic communities might dominate governmental decision making with regard to seemingly technical questions about, for example, the consequences of pollution or the details of military force employment, the mechanism seems less accurately to describe how state leaders acquire their information about basic issues in international relations. Unless equipped with a more powerful theory of domestic politics than any in the political scientist's tool kit, the hypothesis cannot explain who will triumph

in the contest that inevitably surrounds such important policy decisions. Thus while the hypothesis may still have explanatory power in
cases in which the community of experts does possess unparalleled access and influence, it cannot serve as the basis for a broader general-
ization about alliance and collective identity.

6. *Social Identity Theory.* Finally, numerous social-psychology experiments, associated most closely with Henri Tajfel, have established that
group identity is often rooted in nothing more than framing the group
as such, in the classification itself. Psychologists have found that the
simple act of placing an individual in a minimal group leads to in-group
preference and out-group prejudice: a person will believe his or her
group better, friendlier, more competent, and stronger than others.
Tajfel has argued that viewing the group in positive terms enhances
one's self-esteem (social identity theory, or SIT), while John Turner
has suggested that such framing yields perceptions of similarity (self-
categorization theory).[67] Applying this finding to the question at hand,
it seems plausible that alliance members would, especially over time,
consequently develop a special affinity for their fellow allies.

The problem is that individuals (and states for that matter) are enmeshed in overlapping and cross-cutting webs of loyalties. Not only
members of group A, they may also be children or parents, workers or
industrialists, Democrats or Republicans, pro-choice or pro-life; when
such identity commitments come into conflict with each other, social
identity theory ceases to yield a distinctive set of predictions. Countries
that have joined an alliance to achieve particular aims may find themselves at odds over other issues and thus subject to a different, conflicting set of in-group-out-group biases, and their formal adversaries
may on occasion be informal allies. Social psychologists have not explored the consequences of cross-cutting cleavages for SIT and have
not offered a coherent explanation for which identity triumphs in this
competition or whether both are abandoned in favor of a third.[68]

Collective Identity in Conclusion

Much discussion of the consequences of alliance membership has implied
a powerful, generalizable link with the formation of collective identity. By
carefully evaluating the proposed causal mechanisms, I have argued that this
claim is not sustainable. At best, alliance may prove a critical piece of the
causal story in particular cases. When the "proper" foundation is present, intense alliance-sponsored interaction may help generate expansive definitions of the self, perhaps more quickly and more deeply than in its absence.
When the alliance itself homogenizes states' domestic political structures,
perceptions of similarity and collective identity may follow. When epistemic
communities have achieved consensus within alliance forums and have un-

rivaled access to decision makers at home, they influence leaders' policy preferences and state identity. These paths remain open, but they are highly contingent. Perhaps further theoretical development will provide clearer scope conditions as to when a common alliance gives rise to collective identity and when it does not, but the difficulty of further specifying the hypotheses may also simply reflect the uncertain nature of social reality. Such indeterminacy is deeply problematic for those who seek nomothetic explanation, but those who are sensitive to powerful interaction effects, to the reflexivity of social subjects and the possibility of learning from experience, to the impossibility of holding everything else constant, will find less troubling accounts that stress "can" rather than "will." The capacity of alliance to reshape state identities is not universal, but it is also not, at least in principle, nonexistent.

Neither the constructivist project nor the concept of a security community has been the target here. War does seem to have become unthinkable among major advanced industrialized countries in a way that transcends calculations of costs and benefits, and approaches that bring states' definitions of interests to the heart of the analysis are most likely to provide satisfying answers. That the boundaries of the "European" security community are not coterminous with NATO may point the way: On the one hand, Greece and Turkey share little trust and certainly lack dependable expectations of peaceful change, while several states that are not members of the alliance, such as Australia and New Zealand, would seem to belong.

At least two candidates deserve further consideration. First, it may be no accident that the security community is most firm among those states whose regimes are consolidated liberal democracies and that the non-NATO members of the security community also fall into that category. The attributes that define relations within a security community—shared identity, diffuse reciprocity, trust—overlap in large measure with the nature of foreign relations among democracies.[69] The roots of the security community may lie not in alliance, but in the interactions among states of a particular regime type. Second, it is possible that the security community is far broader still. John Mueller has argued that a norm has developed against major war, at least among those states most likely to engage in it—that is, advanced industrialized states.[70] As an increasing number of states falls into this rank, the security community may go global. These hypotheses may be right or wrong, but they are noted here merely as two constructivist alternatives that place far less weight on alliance.

ALLIANCES: THEORY AND POLICY

Students of international relations have not been particularly sensitive to the complexity of alliances and their politics. Like many debates, that surrounding international institutions has developed into a sterile dichotomy: For some, institutions matter and are associated with cooperation, whereas others counter that they are epiphenomenal, only products of the distribution of power. Drawing on collective action theory, I have sought to articulate a third position that (1) argues institutions have independent causal impact; (2) suggests that alliance membership may, under particular conditions, make possible and even exacerbate conflictual dynamics; and (3) specifies the scope of neoliberal institutionalist hypotheses. Thus put, the question is no longer whether, but how, institutions matter, and the structural realist response to the neoliberals gives way to a realist institutionalism that is more consistent with realism's philosophical core.[71] But such system effects cannot account fully for the flux of relations among allies, from near-war to moments of rapprochement. Further research would, I hope, marry the hypotheses suggested above to other systemic factors as well as to domestic politics to arrive at more complete explanations of intra-alliance conflict and cooperation.

The constructivist turn in international relations in the last decade has drawn attention to previously ignored phenomena, distinguishing even regular cooperative behavior from the patterns associated with collective identity. Constructivist writers on security communities have identified a prior alliance as a key sufficient causal factor in effecting the emergence of a collective social identity among a given group of states. In particular, they have credited NATO with giving birth to the transatlantic security community. Carefully examining the theoretical logic and empirical plausibility of the proposed causal mechanisms, six in all, and drawing on preliminary evidence from the NATO case, I argue that constructivist scholars have vastly overstated the alliance-security community connection and have failed to supply sufficiently well-specified hypotheses that identify when alliance is conducive to collective identity and when it has little causal impact. At the end of the analysis, several pathways remain open, but much theoretical and empirical work remains to be done before any firm conclusions can be reached.

Unrealistic assumptions and contentions about the consequences of alliance have equally been a part of American policy discourse. Unlike Europeans schooled in *Realpolitik*, American statesmen have typically not been attracted by the mere *management* of conflict, but rather have sought to *resolve* disputes. Perhaps as a consequence of their professional training, perhaps for reasons deeply rooted in American history and culture, they have, in their efforts to bring to an end international competition and conflict, often placed undue faith in legalism and in formal institutions.[72] The confluence of these two tendencies has made American leaders particularly susceptible to espousing the fallacy that alliances, by their very nature, breed cooperation and reshape fundamental interests. This unwarranted belief has certainly not been confined to Americans, nor to our own age, but it has shaped American political debate to an unusual extent. It informed the discussions surrounding the establishment of the Atlantic Alliance, and it played a prominent role in the discourse of NATO enlargement. Alliances are often useful tools of statecraft and valuable means of expressing common interests, but very rarely do all good things go together. They generate pressures in multiple directions and have cross-cutting consequences for their members. They are marked by moments of cooperation for which they can take credit, but also by competition and conflict for which they must accept blame. They may coincide with the emergence of a zone of peace, a security community, but their causal role is likely to be small.

This chapter does not, therefore, contain a simple lesson for American policy makers as they continue to confront the problem of order in the post–Cold War world. Alliances, as well as other international institutions, have their place and can make important contributions to achieving our foreign policy ends, but they should be neither overestimated nor oversold. Coming to terms with complexity is never comfortable, for individuals dealing with everyday life or for policy makers facing challenges on the international scene. But recognizing the full range of costs and benefits associated with alliance membership is essential for wise policy. Foreknowledge of the consequences that joining NATO would have for Greco-Turkish relations would probably not have changed Dean Acheson's calculations, but it might have led the United States and its partners to design more carefully the modalities of accession, and it most certainly would have prevented American statesmen from reacting with as little understanding as they did. The most recent expansion of NATO may very well not have such perverse consequences for East-Central Europe, perhaps because most states there seek membership not to protect themselves from a revival of Russian imperial ambitions but to send a message to potential investors, perhaps because larger allies will refuse to foot the bill to modernize their militaries and they cannot on their own afford new sophisticated armaments, perhaps because the Western commitment to their security is so obviously tenuous. These issues remained absent from the rancorous debate on enlargement and will probably not be addressed as future waves are considered. But these questions deserve a hearing if the costs of enlargement are not to prove far greater than anyone had anticipated.

NOTES

1. James M. Goldgeier, "NATO: Expansion: The Anatomy of a Decision," *Washington Quarterly* 21:1 (Winter 1998): 85–102; Goldgeier, *Not Whether but When: The U.S. Decision to Enlarge NATO* (Washington, D.C.: Brookings Institution Press, 1999).
2. *New York Times*, 23 October 1996, A20. As early as 1994, Secretary of State Warren Christopher declared that "now our challenge is to extend the zone of security

and stability that the Alliance has provided to extend it across the continent to the east." See "NATO: Extending Stability in Europe," *U.S. Department of State Dispatch* 5:48 (28 November 1994): 790.

3. Paul W. Schroeder, "Alliances, 1815–1945: Weapons of Power and Tools of Management," in Klaus Knorr, ed., *Historical Dimensions of National Security Problems* (Lawrence: University Press of Kansas, 1976), 256–257.

4. Portions of this chapter, particularly in the section on alliances and cooperation, draw on Ronald R. Krebs, "Perverse Institutionalism: NATO and the Greco-Turkish Conflict," *International Organization* 53:2 (Spring 1999): 343–377.

5. On these tendencies, see Robert Jervis, "Hypotheses on Misperception," *World Politics* 20 (1968): 463.

6. Quoted in Glenn Snyder, *Alliance Politics* (Ithaca, N.Y.: Cornell University Press, 1997), 356–357.

7. Bruce Bueno de Mesquita, *The War Trap* (New Haven, Conn.: Yale University Press, 1981). For a similar critique, see Jack S. Levy, "The Causes of War: A Review of Theories and Evidence," in Philip E. Tetlock et al., *Behavior, Society, and Nuclear War*, Vol. I (New York: Oxford University Press, 1989), 249, 306. James Lee Ray refines the coding and empirical analysis, but fails to move theoretically beyond Bueno de Mesquita's explanation. See Ray, "Friends as Foes: International Conflict and Wars between Formal Allies," in *Prisoners of War?* Charles Gochman and Alan Ned Sabrosky, eds. (Lexington, Mass.: D.C. Heath, 1990), 73–92

8. Jonathan Mercer, *Reputation and International Politics* (Ithaca, N.Y.: Cornell University Press, 1996).

9. By realism in this context, I mean structural realism. Classical realists would find my perspective quite familiar.

10. John J. Mearsheimer, "The False Promise of International Institutions," *International Security* 19:3 (Winter 1994/95): 11.

11. Kenneth N. Waltz, *Theory of International Politics* (New York: McGraw-Hill, 1979), 105, 70–71.

12. Steven Hugh Lee, *Outposts of Empire: Korea, Vietnam, and the Origins of the Cold War in Asia, 1949–1954* (Montreal: McGill-Queen's University Press, 1995), 7.

13. Schroeder, "Alliances." See also Patricia Weitsman, "Intimate Enemies: The Politics of Peacetime Alliance," *Security Studies* 7 (Autumn 1997): 156–192.

14. David G. Haglund, *Alliance within the Alliance? Franco-German Military Cooperation and the European Pillar of Defense* (Boulder, Colo.: Westview, 1991).

15. For this widely accepted view of cooperation, see Robert O. Keohane, *After Hegemony* (Princeton, N.J.: Princeton University Press, 1984); Helen Milner, "International Theories of Cooperation among Nations: Strengths and Weaknesses," *World Politics* 44 (April 1992). On collective identity, see Alexander Wendt, "Collective Identity Formation and the International State," *American Political Science Review* 88:2 (June 1994): 384–396.

16. Keohane, "Alliances, Threats, and the Uses of Neorealism," *International Security* 13:1 (Summer 1988): 174.

17. Such exceptions include John S. Duffield, "Explaining the Long Peace in Europe: The Contributions of Regional Security Regimes," *Review of International Studies* 20 (1994): 369–388; Duffield, "NATO's Functions after the Cold War," *Political Science Quarterly* 109:5 (Winter 1994–95): 763–787; Duffield, *Power Rules: The*

Evolution of NATO's Conventional Force Posture (Stanford, Calif.: Stanford University Press, 1995); Robert B. McCalla, "NATO's Persistence After the Cold War," *International Organization* 50:3 (Summer 1996): 445–475; Celeste A. Wallander and Robert O. Keohane, "Risk, Threat, and Security Institutions," in Helga Haftendorn, Keohane, and Wallander, eds., *Imperfect Unions: Security Institutions over Time and Space* (New York: Oxford University Press, 1999), 21–47; Steve Weber, "Shaping the Postwar Balance of Power: Multilateralism in NATO," *International Organization* 46 (1992): 633–680. Focusing directly on alliances and cooperation is Fred Chernoff, *After Bipolarity: The Vanishing Threat, Theories of Cooperation, and the Future of the Atlantic Alliance* (Ann Arbor: University of Michigan Press, 1995).

18. The following discussion draws on Keohane, *After Hegemony*; Keohane, *International Institutions and State Power: Essays in International Relations Theory* (Boulder, Colo.: Westview, 1989); Keohane with Lisa L. Martin, "The Promise of Institutionalist Theory," *International Security* 20:1 (Summer 1995): 39–51. See also Mearsheimer, "False Promise," 342–353; Milner, "International Theories of Cooperation"; Kenneth Oye, ed., *Cooperation Under Anarchy* (Princeton, N.J.: Princeton University Press, 1985).

19. Keohane, *After Hegemony*, 91.

20. See Christian Tuschhoff, "Alliance Cohesion and Peaceful Change in NATO," in Haftendorn, Keohane, and Wallander, eds., *Imperfect Unions*, chapter 5.

21. Of the four mentioned above, I will not discuss one popular institutionalist mechanism—the implications of reduced transaction costs. Transaction costs are very difficult to specify ex ante, and the importance of reducing them has typically figured in institutionalist accounts as a post hoc explanation lacking empirical referents; they offer, in other words, a just-so story of cooperation.

22. Fearon, "Bargaining, Enforcement, and International Cooperation," *International Organization* 52:2 (Spring 1998): 269–305, at 270.

23. On the differences between security and nonsecurity areas, see Robert Jervis, "Security Regimes," in Stephen D. Krasner, ed., *Regimes* (Ithaca, N.Y.: Cornell University Press, 1982), 174–176; Charles Lipson, "International Cooperation in Economic and Security Affairs," *World Politics* 37 (1984): 1–23.

24. On the weakness of the logic connecting issue-linkage and cooperation, see James Sebenius, "Negotiation Arithmetic: Adding and Subtracting Issues and Parties," *International Organization* 37 (Spring 1983): 281–316; and Joanne Gowa, "Rational Hegemons, Excludable Goods, and Small Groups" *World Politics* 42:3 (1989): 307–324.

25. Keohane, *International Institutions*, 18, n. 20.

26. Monteagle Stearns, *Entangled Allies: U.S. Policy Toward Greece, Turkey, and Cyprus* (New York: Council on Foreign Relations Press, 1992), 5. See also Van Coufoudakis, "Greek-Turkish Relations, 1973–1983: The View from Athens," *International Security* 9:4 (Spring 1985): 215.

27. Jon Jacobson, *Locarno Diplomacy: Germany and the West, 1925–1929* (Princeton, N.J.: Princeton University Press, 1972), 41, 29–30, 40–41, 155–156, and passim. While this seems hardly to have concerned the British, Polish and Czechoslovakian elites were understandably worried that security guarantees in the West would produce insecurity in the East. See Piotr S. Wandycz, *France and Her Eastern Allies, 1919–1925* (Minneapolis: University of Minnesota Press, 1962), 328, 335,

341–368, and passim. In Wandycz's estimation, "It stood to reason that an abandonment by France of her offensive powers on the Rhine would facilitate German expansion to the east, a fact emphasized by the French during the Paris Peace Conference and recalled over and over again by [Polish Foreign Minister Count Aleksander] Skrzynski" (360).

28. Cab 2/4/188(2), Committee of Imperial Defense (CID), Minutes of Meeting 188, 2 October 1924, Public Records Office (PRO). Winston Churchill, as Chancellor of the Exchequer, raised similar arguments a few months later; see Cab 2/4/195, CID, Minutes of Meeting 195, February 13, 1925, PRO. I am indebted to Timothy Crawford for suggesting these examples and providing the PRO materials. See also Arnold Wolfers, *Britain and France Between Two Wars: Conflicting Strategies of Peace Since Versailles* (New York: Harcourt Brace, 1940), especially 237–239; and Jacobson, *Locarno Diplomacy*, 18.

29. Dulles expressed the same concern to the Senate Foreign Relations Committee a year later. See James McAllister, "The Reluctant Pacifier: America, the German Question, and the Future of Europe," Ph.D. Dissertation, Columbia University, 1999, 234, 238. On American policy makers' wish to withdraw from the continent, see Marc Trachtenberg, *A Constructed Peace: The Making of the European Settlement, 1945–1963* (Princeton, N.J.: Princeton University Press, 1999).

30. Krebs, "Perverse Institutionalism." Accounts of the Greco-Turkish relationship are not surprisingly often biased depending on the author's personal predilections and ethnic origins. With this caveat in mind, for useful discussions of Greco-Turkish relations from the late nineteenth century through the postwar period, see Tozun Bahcheli, *Greek-Turkish Relations Since 1955* (Boulder, Colo.: Westview, 1990); James Brown, *Delicately Poised Allies: Greece and Turkey* (London: Brassey's, 1991); and Coufoudakis, "Greek-Turkish Relations."

31. Mancur Olson Jr., *The Logic of Collective Action* (Cambridge, Mass.: Harvard University Press, 1965). In contrast to many economists, Olson, however, argues that "jointness of supply" is not a necessary attribute of public goods.

32. For the theory's initial application to burden sharing in alliances, see Mancur Olson Jr., and Richard Zeckhauser, "An Economic Theory of Alliances," *Review of Economics and Statistics* 48 (August 1966): 266–279. For a recent, representative empirical test of the hypothesis, see John R. Oneal, "Testing the Theory of Collective Action: NATO Defense Burdens, 1950–1984," *Journal of Conflict Resolution* 34 (September 1990): 426–448. For a challenge to the collective-action alliance literature, see Charles A. Kupchan, "NATO and the Persian Gulf: Examining Intra-Alliance Behavior," *International Organization* 42 (Spring 1988): 317–346.

33. Olson, *Logic*, 45.

34. For an empirical analysis, albeit largely from a realist noninstitutionalist perspective, see Christopher Gelpi, "Alliances as Instruments of Intra-Allied Control," in Haftendorn, Keohane, and Wallander, eds., *Imperfect Unions*, chapter 4.

35. See Stephen A. Kocs, *Autonomy or Power? The Franco-German Relationship and Europe's Strategic Choices, 1955–1995* (Westport, Conn.: Praeger, 1995), 17–18; Duffield, "Explaining the Long Peace," 384.

36. Kocs, *Autonomy or Power?*, 253.

37. David Garnham, *The Politics of European Defense Cooperation: Germany, France, Britain, and America* (Cambridge: Ballinger, 1988), 2, 12.

38. The differing French and German attitudes toward the alliance persisted throughout the Cold War period. For good discussions of the two countries' strategic concepts, see Kocs, *Autonomy or Power?*; and Philip H. Gordon, *France, Germany, and the Western Alliance* (Boulder, Colo.: Westview, 1995).

39. See Haglund, *Alliance within the Alliance*, 5. For general discussions of abandonment and entrapment, see Snyder, *Alliance Politics*; and Michael Mandelbaum, *The Fate of Nations* (New York: Cambridge University Press, 1988), 101–112.

40. On these points, see Gordon, *France, Germany, and the Western Alliance*; David S. Yost, "Franco-German Defense Cooperation," *Washington Quarterly* 11:2 (Spring 1988): 173–195; Garnham, *Politics of European Defense Cooperation*, 16–22, quote at 33; Robbin F. Laird, ed., *Strangers and Friends: The Franco-German Security Relationship* (London: Pinter, 1989).

41. Even Glenn Snyder, whose work has been unusually sensitive to the political bargains at the core of alliance, asserts that allies "acquire each other's interests to some extent as a result of allying." Conflicts between allies "will be weaker when the parties begin to think of themselves as friends rather than enemies." See his *Alliance Politics*, 25.

42. See Karl W. Deutsch et al., *Political Community and the North Atlantic Area: International Organization in the Light of Historical Experience* (Westport, Conn.: Greenwood, 1969 [1957]); Emanuel Adler and Michael Barnett, eds., *Security Communities* (Cambridge: Cambridge University Press, 1998).

43. Wendt, "Collective Identity Formation," 386. Wendt's language here is a bit confusing, as there may still be many "others" who remain outside the construction of the self, but his intention is to argue that state interaction can collapse such boundaries. I cannot review here the foundations of constructivist ontology and epistemology, nor can I contest constructivists' definitions of terms such as identity and security community. For an important perspective on identity, rooted not in phenomenology but in social networks, see Charles Tilly, "International Communities, Secure or Otherwise," in Adler and Barnett, eds., *Security Communities*, chapter 12.

44. See Emanuel Adler, "Imagined (Security) Communities: Cognitive Regions in International Relations," *Millennium* 26:2 (1997): 249–277; Adler, "Europe's New Security Order: A Pluralistic Security Community," in Beverly Crawford, ed., *The Future of European Security* (Berkeley: University of California Press, 1992), 287–326.

45. Except where noted, the following discussion draws on Adler and Barnett, "A Framework for the Study of Security Communities," in Adler and Barnett, eds., *Security Communities*, chapter 2; Deutsch, *Political Community*; Wendt, "Collective Identity Formation." Further notes refer only to particular passages in these texts.

46. Adler and Barnett, "Framework," 39–40. See also G. John Ikenberry and Charles A. Kupchan, "Socialization and Hegemonic Power," *International Organization* 44:3 (Summer 1990): 283–315.

47. On Durkheim's concept of dynamic density, see John Gerard Ruggie, "Continuity and Transformation in the World Polity: Toward a Neorealist Synthesis," in Robert O. Keohane, ed., *Neorealism and its Critics* (New York: Columbia University Press, 1986), 131–157. Communication lay at the heart of Deutsch's intellectual project; see *Political Community*, and also his *Nationalism and Social Communication: An Inquiry into the Foundations of Nationality* (New York: Wiley, 1953). For a summary of this argument, see Colin H. Kahl, "Constructing a Separate Peace: Constructivism,

Collective Liberal Identity, and Democratic Peace," *Security Studies* 8:2/3 (Winter 1998/99–Spring 1999): 120–122.

48. See Gordon W. Allport and B. M. Kramer, "Some Roots of Prejudice," *Journal of Psychology* 22 (1946): 9–39; Allport, *The Nature of Prejudice* (Reading, Penn.: Addison-Wesley, 1954). The contextual conditions held to be conducive to eliminating prejudice through increased communication have changed little during the half-century of research that has followed. See D. M. Taylor and F. M. Moghaddam, *Theories of Intergroup Relations: International Social Psychological Perspectives*, 2nd ed. (Westport, Conn.: Praeger, 1994), at 180.

49. See Walter G. Stephan, "The Contact Hypothesis in Intergroup Relations," in Clyde Hendrick, ed., *Group Processes and Intergroup Relations* (Newbury Park, Calif.: Sage, 1987), 13–40; J. W. Jackson, "Contact Theory of Intergroup Hostility: A Review and Evaluation of the Theoretical and Empirical Literature," *International Journal of Group Tensions* 23 (1993): 43–65; and Hugh D. Forbes, *Ethnic Conflict: Commerce, Culture, and the Contact Hypothesis* (New Haven, Conn.: Yale University Press, 1997).

50. Adler and Barnett, "Framework," 47, 53.

51. Sullivan, "What's So Bad About Hate," *New York Times Magazine*, 26 September 1999.

52. John Lewis Gaddis, *We Now Know: Rethinking Cold War History* (New York: Oxford University Press, 1997), 4.

53. Geoffrey Blainey, *The Causes of War*, 3rd ed. (New York: Free Press, 1988 [1973]), 21–22; see also all of his classic chapter, "Paradise is a Bazaar."

54. Wendt, "Collective Identity Formation," 390.

55. I am grateful to Aaron Lobel for helpful discussion on this point.

56. Kahl, "Constructing a Separate Peace," 120, emphasis added.

57. Thomas F. Pettigrew, *Racially Separate or Together?* (New York: McGraw-Hill, 1971), 275, cited in Forbes, *Ethnic Conflict*, 22–23.

58. Students of security communities might, for example, draw on social psychology for answers to some of these questions. Mercer, *Reputation*, addresses similar issues of data aggregation.

59. Adler and Barnett, "Studying Security Communities in Theory, Comparison, and History," in Adler and Barnett, eds., *Security Communities*, 414.

60. See Mary N. Hampton, "NATO at the Creation," *Security Studies* 4:3 (Spring 1995): 610–656; Hampton, "NATO, Germany, and the United States: Creating Positive Identity in Trans-Atlantia," *Security Studies* 8:2/3 (Winter 1998/99–Spring 1999): 235–269; and Frank Schimmelfennig, "NATO Enlargement: A Constructivist Explanation," *Security Studies* 8:2/3 (Winter 1998/99–Spring 1999): 198–234.

61. For good examples of this problem, see Hampton, "NATO at the Creation," and Hampton, "NATO, Germany, and the United States."

62. See Samuel P. Huntington, *The Third Wave: Democratization in the Late Twentieth Century* (Norman: University of Oklahoma Press, 1991), 245–247; Juan J. Linz and Alfred Stepan, *Problems of Democratic Transition and Consolidation* (Baltimore: The Johns Hopkins University Press, 1996), 219–220. This claim is, with little evidence, also commonly made by regional experts. See, among others, Angel Viñas, "Spain and NATO: Internal Debate and External Challenges," in John Chipman, ed., *NATO's Southern Allies* (London: Routledge, 1988), 140–194; and various essays in Federico G. Gil and Joseph S. Tulchin, eds., *Spain's Entry into*

NATO: Conflicting Political and Strategic Perspectives (Boulder, Colo.: Lynne Rienner, 1988); and Kenneth Maxwell, ed., *Spanish Foreign and Defense Policy* (Boulder, Colo.: Westview, 1991). Noting the absence of hard data demonstrating this link is Gregory F. Treverton, "Spain: Domestic Politics and Foreign Policy," *Adelphi Papers* 204 (Spring 1986).

63. See Schimmelfennig, "NATO Enlargement," 217–225.

64. According to some accounts, the CSCE/OSCE has been more successful along these lines. See Gregory Flynn and Henry Farrell, "Piecing Together the Democratic Peace: The CSCE, Norms, and the Construction of Security in Post-Cold War Europe," *International Organization* 53:3 (Summer 1999): 505–535; and Emanuel Adler, "Seeds of Peaceful Change: The OSCE's Security Community-Building Model," in Adler and Barnett, eds., *Security Communities*, chapter 4.

65. On the concept of the epistemic community, see Peter Haas, *Saving the Mediterranean* (New York: Columbia University Press, 1990); and Haas, ed., *Knowledge, Power, and International Policy-Coordination, International Organization* 46 (Winter 1992).

66. On German military elites, see Hampton, "NATO, Germany, and the United States," 249; more broadly, see Tuschhoff, "Alliance Cohesion and Peaceful Change in NATO," 148–150. On the socialization of Chinese bureaucrats within ASEAN, see Alastair Iain Johnston, "The Myth of the ASEAN Way? Explaining the Evolution of the ASEAN Regional Forum," in Haftendorn, Keohane, and Wallander, eds., *Imperfect Unions*, 287–324.

67. See Henri Tajfel and John C. Turner, "The Social Identity Theory of Intergroup Behavior," in S. Worchel and W.G. Austin, eds., *Psychology of Intergroup Relations* (Chicago: Nelson-Hall, 1986), 7–24; and John C. Turner, *Rediscovering the Social Group* (Oxford: Basil Blackwell, 1987). For discussions with application to international relations, see Jonathan Mercer, "Anarchy and Identity," *International Organization* 49 (1995): 229–252; and Daniel Druckman, "Nationalism, Patriotism, and Group Loyalty: A Social Psychological Perspective," *Mershon International Studies Review* 38 (1994): 48–50.

68. I am grateful to Rose McDermott for helpful discussion on this subject.

69. See Bruce Russett, *Grasping the Democratic Peace: Principles for a Post-Cold War World* (Princeton, N.J.: Princeton University Press, 1993); Michael E. Brown, Sean M. Lynn-Jones, and Steven E. Miller, eds., *Debating the Democratic Peace* (Cambridge, Mass.: MIT Press, 1996); John Owen IV, *Liberal Peace, Liberal War: American Politics and International Security* (Ithaca, N.Y.: Cornell University Press, 1997). For explicitly constructivist explanations, see Thomas Risse-Kappen, "Democratic Peace—Warlike Democracies? A Social Constructivist Interpretation of the Liberal Argument," *European Journal of International Relations* 1:4 (1995): 491–517; and Kahl, "Constructing a Separate Peace."

70. John Mueller, *Retreat From Doomsday: The Obsolescence of Major War* (New York: Basic Books, 1989).

71. See Lisa L. Martin and Beth A. Simmons, "Theories and Empirical Studies of International Institutions," *International Organization* 52:4 (Fall 1998): 729–757; and Randall L. Schweller and David Priess, "A Tale of Two Realisms: Expanding the Institutions Debate," *Mershon International Studies Review* 41, supplement 1 (Spring 1997): 1–32.

72. For an insightful analysis, see Stanley Hoffmann, *Gulliver's Troubles, or The Setting of American Foreign Policy* (New York: McGraw-Hill, 1968).

11

Transatlantic Relations after the Cold War: Theory, Evidence, and the Future

John S. Duffield

One of the more frequent subjects of Richard Ullman's extensive scholarship has been U.S.-European relations. And whether his primary purpose has been to analyze the current state of affairs or to prescribe policy to transatlantic leaders, he has always proved a perceptive observer and timely commentator. In the early 1980s, he endeavored to plot a route "out of the Euromissile mire" in which NATO had become stuck. Later that decade, he illuminated the underlying imperatives for security cooperation that endured even among estranged allies through his exposé of the "covert French connection." As the Cold War began to wind down, he was one of the first to grasp the potential opportunities for "enlarging the zone of peace" on the continent and "securing Europe" as a whole. And where the rapid consolidation of democratic institutions and liberal values proved elusive, he did not flinch from offering a sober assessment of the difficulties faced by the West in addressing regional conflagrations, as in his analysis of "the world and Yugoslavia's wars."

Even this very brief and incomplete survey suggests the considerable impact that Richard Ullman has had on our thinking about the close but often conflicted ties shared by the United States and Europe in the postwar era. Consequently, it is only fitting on this occasion to take stock of transatlantic relations, especially as they have evolved since the end of the Cold War. An underlying theme of this chapter is that, although many of the issues have changed, especially in the realm of security affairs, the analytical perspectives emphasized by Richard Ullman in his teaching continue to be helpful tools for furthering our understanding of the subject.

For some four decades after World War II, transatlantic relations were shaped largely by two shared imperatives. Internationally, the imperative of containing Soviet power and influence did much to force convergence among the foreign policies of the United States and its West European allies. Domestically, the imperative of creating jobs and providing rising living standards generated considerable impetus for the reduction of trade barriers, the liberalization of capital flows, and macroeconomic coordination across the Atlantic.

During the past decade, however, transatlantic relations have unfolded within a rather different context. The first of these imperatives was largely removed by the end of the Cold War and the disintegration of the Soviet Union. No longer must the United States and Europe coordinate their political-military affairs with a constant eye on Moscow. Although the second imperative remains important, its implications for transatlantic relations have become increasingly ambiguous as the West approaches the limits of the benefits of economic openness and principled multilateralism.

Consequently, the period since 1990 has been a time of soul-searching in U.S.-European relations.[1] Fundamental questions have been raised about all aspects of transatlantic ties. Will the North Atlantic Treaty Organization (NATO) be preserved and continue to play an important role in European security affairs? Specifically, will the United States remain engaged militarily on the continent? Will the transatlantic partners continue to enjoy high levels of trade, or will they erect ever more barriers to one another's products amid a flurry of mutual recriminations? More generally, will the United States and Europe work together to promote common interests, or will they increasingly find themselves at cross purposes?

Needless to say, observers have offered a wide range of answers to these questions. Some have adopted a pessimistic stance, arguing that the foundations of postwar transatlantic cooperation have been irrevocably shattered by the end of the Cold War (Mearsheimer, 1990; Walt, 1998). Others have been much more sanguine, maintaining that those same foundations remain largely intact (Kahler, 1996). And a third school of thought contends that while serious fissures have opened up, they can nevertheless be closed through concerted effort on both sides of the Atlantic, should the will to do so exist (Gompert and Larrabee, 1997).

This lack of consensus, while frustrating to those looking for clear-cut answers, should come as no surprise. At bottom, it reflects divergent views about the underpinnings of transatlantic cooperation during the Cold War and the nature of the post–Cold War world. In order to assess the merits of the various positions, therefore, it is necessary to clarify the assumptions on which they are based and to spell out logically the implications of those assumptions in ways that enable us to weigh them against the accumulating evidence.

A potentially valuable tool for this purpose is the scholarly literature on international relations. Much of this work is often zealously scrupulous about specifying its assumptions, deriving hypotheses, and, space and resources permitting, subjecting the latter to careful empirical tests. Moreover, this literature contains a range of theories that either have been previously applied to questions of transatlantic relations or hold out the promise of helping us to understand them.

In fact, the application of international relations theory to post-Cold War transatlantic relations promises to be of benefit to scholars and policy makers alike. For members of the academy, the recent history of U.S.-European interactions offers a useful laboratory for evaluating and, if necessary, refining theories that purport to explain patterns of interstate cooperation and conflict. Indeed, a handful of scholarly works have tried to do just that (e.g., Haftendorn and Tuschhoff, 1993; Peterson, 1993 and 1996; Featherstone and Ginsberg, 1996; Guay, 1999).

For their part, members of the policy community can profit from such an exercise in at least two related ways. First, theory can suggest the types of developments that are more or less likely to occur. As a result, policy makers can focus their attention on more plausible scenarios. The following analysis shows, for example, that the more pessimistic assessments of transatlantic relations are exaggerated. A significant decline in U.S.-European cooperation is not inevitable. Rather, solid theoretical grounds exist for concluding that a high degree of cooperation will remain possible well into the future. Nevertheless, the glue that bound the United States and Europe together during the Cold War is not as strong as it once was. Consequently, leaders who value a strong Atlantic partnership cannot afford to become complacent but must be pro-active in seeking to manage the relationship.

This conclusion raises the question of what types of steps should be taken, and once again, theory can help to provide some of the answers. By prioritizing the underlying causes of events, theory suggests where policy makers should concentrate their efforts. The following analysis underscores the important roles that international institutions play in transatlantic relations and thus the need to be attentive to their possibilities and limitations. Another finding concerns the stabilizing impact that flows of goods, investments, people, and ideas across the Atlantic can have where these promote the development of better understanding, common values and interests, and even mutual identification.

Accordingly, the chapter is divided into three parts. It first introduces three leading theoretical perspectives on international relations—the realist, the liberal, and what I term the transformational—and asks how each approach would expect U.S.-European relations to evolve after the Cold War. It then evaluates the usefulness of each perspective for accounting for the actual pattern of transatlantic relations since 1990. To what degree do the events of the past decade lend support to each of the three perspectives? In the third part of the chapter, I draw on the preceding analysis to reflect on the likely future course of transatlantic relations and, where possible, to offer theoretically grounded prescriptions for their successful management in the next decade and beyond.

Before proceeding, it may be useful to make explicit some of the limitations of the following analysis. In the first place, the portrait I intend to present will perforce take the form of broad brush strokes rather than a highly detailed rendering of transatlantic relations. To accomplish much more in a single chapter would be impossible. Consequently, some of the specific events of the past decade may seem to fit poorly with the interpretation provided. By the same token, the predictions and policy prescriptions offered below must necessarily be pitched at a high level of generality. Second, it is probably still too early to draw definitive conclusions about the subject. Some important consequences of the end of the Cold War may not yet be fully manifest. This possibility should serve only as a reason for caution, however, not as a justification for deferring consideration of the topic. Rather, it is incumbent on scholars to use the analytical tools at their disposal to make informed judgments about such matters in a timely manner, even as they acknowledge the provisional nature of their findings.

ALTERNATIVE THEORETICAL
PERSPECTIVES AND THEIR EXPECTATIONS

Theories are useful tools for making sense of the world. They help us to gain our bearings in the face of an often dizzying array of "facts" by providing conceptual frameworks for ordering and selecting among those facts. At a minimum, a theory should provide a map of the most important features of the structure underlying the phenomena we wish to understand as well as an indication of the relationships between those features and the processes that connect them. In this way, it enables us to focus our attention on a relatively small number of factors that may be particularly important in determining the trajectories and outcomes in which we are interested.

International relations scholars have articulated a number of distinct theories for explaining patterns of interstate cooperation and conflict. Indeed, to the uninitiated, the diversity of specific theoretical approaches present in the literature may seem bewildering. Nevertheless, most can be grouped into a relatively small number of theoretical perspectives that reflect common assumptions about the nature of the most important actors and causal factors in world politics.

Three theoretical perspectives—the realist, the liberal, and what I term the transformational—hold particular promise as tools for understanding transatlantic relations after the Cold War. As I will argue below, no single perspective—and certainly no single theory—is able to account for all important aspects of the subject, especially one so complex and multifaceted. Each perspective offers valuable insights. But some are clearly more useful than others.

The Realist Perspective: Power and Threats

Perhaps the most commonly invoked theoretical perspective on international relations is realism. The term "realism" has been used to describe a number of specific theories, not all of which are compatible with one another. Despite such differences, however, most realist theories share a common set of basic assumptions (Mearsheimer, 1994/95; Waltz, 1979): that the main actors in international relations are sovereign states whose most fundamental motive is to ensure their own survival; that most states have the ability to inflict physical harm on and, in some instances, to destroy one another; that the basic organizing principle of the international system is anarchy;[2] and that states can never be certain about the intentions or capabilities of others.

The most important consequence following from these assumptions is that states are fundamentally insecure. The use of force is always possible in relations among them, and every state is a potential—if not an actual—threat to every other state, although some are more threatening than others. Consequently, "governments worry a lot about security and pay close attention to potential threats" (Walt, 1998:8).

Two variants of realism are particularly relevant to the question of transatlantic relations after the Cold War: balance of power theory and hegemonic stability theory. Both offer pessimistic predictions, in the form of declining cooperation and increasing conflict between the United States and Europe.

Balance of Power Theory

Balance of power theory argues that states will seek to balance the power of threatening states.[3] In order to do so, states will sometimes undertake unilateral balancing efforts. Where two or more states perceive a common threat, however, they may engage in various forms of military cooperation, including but not limited to forming a military alliance. The existence of a common threat may also promote economic cooperation, since the economic benefits that accrue to either ally will enhance their combined power. Conversely, the decline and, especially, the disappearance of the common threat will undermine the basis for both types of cooperation. Military cooperation will no longer be perceived as necessary, while economic cooperation may be viewed as dangerous, depending on the distribution of benefits, since an erstwhile partner might be able to convert its economic gains into greater relative military power (Grieco, 1988).

Balance of power theory explains postwar transatlantic relations, especially its cooperative aspects, as a response to the commonly perceived Soviet threat. The military power and expansionist ideology of the Soviet Union prompted the United States and Western Europe to form what was arguably the most highly developed peacetime military alliance in history—NATO—and to engage in high levels of economic cooperation. Whatever conflicts might have existed between them were overshadowed by the need to maintain a united front.

From this perspective, however, the collapse of the Soviet Union, by eliminating the overriding common interest, should have deleterious consequences for transatlantic cooperation. First, the United States and its European partners should perceive little to be gained from continued participation in NATO while feeling ever more acutely the restrictions on state autonomy imposed by alliance membership. Thus we should not expect NATO to outlive the Cold War by long (Mearsheimer, 1990; Williams et al., 1993; Harries, 1994). Moreover, the United States and Europe should become increasingly concerned about the relative gains of economic cooperation to the degree that each now represents the other's greatest potential strategic rival. As a result, we should also expect growing transatlantic conflict in economic affairs (Asmus, 1997; Walt, 1998/99; Bergsten, 1999).

To be sure, some realists have appended caveats to this scenario. The former Soviet threat, while greatly reduced, might nevertheless provide sufficient glue to hold the alliance together, at least in the medium term, given Russia's nuclear capabilities and unpredictable politics (Duffield, 1994/95). Alternatively, other commonly perceived threats, such as terrorism or nuclear proliferation, might suffice to fill, at least in part, the void created by the collapse of the Soviet Union and serve as a basis for continued transatlantic security cooperation. Nevertheless, the general thrust of balance of power theory is pessimistic for U.S.-European relations.

Hegemonic Stability Theory

A second variant of realism, hegemonic stability theory, is hardly more optimistic about the prospects for enduring transatlantic cooperation, albeit for a different set of reasons. In contrast to balance of power theory, hegemonic stability theory seeks primarily to explain patterns of economic relations. It nevertheless shares with balance of power theory a healthy skepticism about the prospects for cooperation. Also like balance of power theory, it identifies a set of circumstances in which the usual hurdles can be overcome.

For hegemonic stability theory, however, these circumstances involve not the presence of a common threat but that of a singularly dominant, or hegemonic, power. Through a combination of threats and promises, a hegemon, can induce—or coerce—smaller states to open their markets and, more generally, to adhere to common rules of commercial intercourse. By the same token, a declining hegemon will find it increasingly difficult to elicit such behavior, and previously established cooperative economic arrangements will tend to break down (Keohane, 1980).

Hegemonic stability theory has been invoked to account for the ups and downs of the postwar Western economic order, especially its transatlantic component. Following World War II, the United States, which had emerged as the dominant power in the world, spearheaded the creation of a new set of arrangements for the governance of international trade and financial relations. Although these arrangements corresponded closely with American preferences at the time, they nevertheless served the interests of most of the other noncommunist developed countries. As the relative power of the United States began to decline in the 1960s and, especially, the 1970s, however, the postwar economic order was subjected to a series of shocks that threatened to bring the whole edifice crashing down (Keohane, 1980).

In terms of hegemonic stability theory, the end of the Cold War per se has no clear consequences for transatlantic relations. It may nevertheless coincide with a continuation, if not an acceleration, of America's relative decline. Not only have the countries of the European Union taken important steps toward economic integration and the creation of an economic power on par with the United States, but other dynamic market economies, notably those of East Asia, have emerged to pose serious challenges to U.S. ascendancy. In such circumstances, the United States should be even less willing to shoulder burdens of international leadership and less able to elicit behavior on the part of others in accordance with established rules, with predictably negative consequences for the stability of the postwar economic order (Sandholtz et al., 1992; Thurow, 1992; Bergsten, 1999).

The Liberal Perspective: Institutions and Values

Not all of international relations theory offers such pessimistic views of transatlantic relations after the Cold War. A second leading theoretical perspective, what is often called "liberalism," is much more positive about the prospects for continued cooperation between the United States and Europe. Liberal theories are not inattentive to the role of power and threats in shaping state behavior and international outcomes. They insist, nevertheless, that international relations are far more than a rough-and-tumble scramble among states for physical security. Two principal liberal approaches in particular promise to speak to the question of transatlantic relations after the Cold War: institutional theory and liberal democratic peace theory.

Institutional Theory

Institutional theory, as developed perhaps most fully in the work of Robert Keohane and his associates, shares a number of important features

with realism. Like realism, it views states as the most important actors in
world affairs, treating them as largely unitary and rational. Similarly, it regards domestic politics as relatively inconsequential.

In contrast to most variants of realism, however, this liberal approach assigns considerable importance to international institutions. Institutional theory starts from the premise that international relations are characterized by
numerous situations in which states could in principle achieve considerable
joint gains through concerted action but are often in practice prevented from
doing so because of transaction costs, uncertainty, fears of cheating, and
other obstacles to cooperation. Where such obstacles exist, however, states
can overcome them in order to realize the potential gains through the creation of international institutions designed to lower transaction costs, reduce
uncertainty, deter cheating, and so on (Keohane, 1984; Keohane and Martin,
1995).

Once such institutions are established, participating states have strong incentives to maintain them and to comply with the rules they contain. The
preservation of international institutions ensures the continuation of the benefits that they were originally intended to produce. Even when conditions
change and an established institution becomes less than ideal, participants
may find that it is difficult to construct superior institutional alternatives or
that the short-term costs of doing so outweigh the discounted present value
of anticipated gains. Moreover, it may be easier to adapt existing institutions
to meet new needs than to build new ones from the ground up. Only where
an institution becomes clearly dysfunctional will it be rational for member
states to cease to participate.

From the perspective of institutional theory, the end of the Cold War need
not spell the demise of transatlantic cooperation. In the security arena, postwar U.S.-European relations were conducted largely within the context of
NATO. The disintegration of the Warsaw Pact and the collapse of the Soviet
Union itself clearly deprived the alliance of one of its most compelling rationales. But deterrence and defense against external aggression did not constitute NATO's only purpose, and others, such as stabilizing relations among
the states of Europe, have attained new prominence with the decline of the
former Soviet threat (Duffield, 1994/95). It could be expected, moreover, that
NATO members would attempt to use such a highly developed and capable
organizational structure to address any new challenges that might arise in the
region, if not further afield (McCalla, 1996).

The implications of institutional theory for transatlantic economic relations
are less clear, given that the United States and Europe established few primarily transatlantic institutions to govern their interactions in this area during the Cold War. Nevertheless, the transatlantic partners were the principal
architects of and the major players in the broader Western institutional structures created after World War II to promote economic cooperation, such as

the General Agreement on Tariffs and Trade (GATT), the International Monetary Fund (IMF), and, later, the Group of Seven (G-7). Thus insofar as these institutions continue to represent valuable tools for pursuing U.S. and European economic interests and coping with global economic difficulties, one should expect continued compliance with their dictates even as individual states seek to modify their functions, structures, and rules in order to better suit the states' current needs.

Liberal Democratic Peace Theory

Liberal democratic peace theory represents an even greater departure from the tenets of realism. In particular, it rejects the assumption that states can be treated as unitary actors, contending instead that due attention must be given to the individuals and private associations that constitute society, the values they hold, and the domestic institutions that serve to aggregate their value-based preferences into state policy (Moravcsik, 1997).

Liberal democratic peace theory has been developed over the past decade and a half to explain a striking empirical anomaly: the fact that no two liberal democracies have ever gone to war with each other. To account for this phenomenon, international relations scholars have advanced two complementary theoretical arguments concerning the roles of democratic political institutions and liberal values, respectively (Doyle, 1986; Owen, 1994). Democratic political institutions can make it difficult for a state to move toward war until it is sorely provoked. The existence of a free press and open public debate can make it harder for leaders to act in secrecy. Regular, competitive elections ensure that those same leaders can be held accountable for their actions and thus punished if they resort to war without good reason or public support. And the distribution of foreign policy decision-making authority among multiple bodies or individuals means that steps toward war will be slower and more cumbersome.

The presence of such domestic institutions is no guarantee of pacific behavior, however. Not only have democracies participated in wars with no less frequency overall than their authoritarian counterparts, but they have sometimes even initiated military conflicts. Thus it is also important to consider how these institutional effects can be reinforced by liberal values. Liberal societies place a high intrinsic value on each individual and his or her well-being. Typically, this value is accompanied by a depreciation of war as a means of progress, given its potentially high cost in human terms, except where the use of force may be required to ensure the community's security or, in extreme cases, to preserve liberty and justice. Instead, liberal societies exhibit a strong preference for peaceful methods of resolving disputes and regulating competition. A further consequence is that societies marked by liberal values will have a special affinity for one another. They tend to regard each other as fundamentally just and peaceful and thus deserving of accommodation, whereas illiberal states will be viewed as hostile and potential threats (Doyle, 1986).

Arguably, the contribution of liberal democratic peace theory to understanding transatlantic relations during the Cold War is relatively small. The United States and Western Europe had good reason to cooperate with one another when confronted with the power and expansionist ideology of the Soviet Union. Nevertheless, liberal democratic peace theory may help to explain why the transatlantic partners came together so readily and why they cooperated so extensively, creating institutions (like NATO) without precedent (Risse-Kappen, 1996). It also helps to account for the limits they placed on security and, especially, economic cooperation with illiberal states such as Greece, Spain, and Portugal until the 1970s and 1980s.

The expectations of liberal democratic peace theory for transatlantic relations after the Cold War are similarly indefinite. While this approach may predict the absence of military conflict between the United States and Europe, it cannot forecast with any precision the forms of active cooperation in which they are likely to engage. Perhaps the most that can be said at this point is that they should possess a shared interest in preserving democratic institutions and liberal values at home and promoting their spread abroad where possible.

The Transformational Perspective:
Changes in Beliefs, Interests, and Identities

The third theoretical perspective that I will consider, what I term the "transformational," is derived from the broader set of theories that seek to explain international relations and state behavior in terms of ideational factors, such as belief systems, images, cognitive maps, collective identity, and culture. The term transformational is intended to distinguish those theories that emphasize the protean nature of the beliefs, values, interests, and even the identities of the actors in international relations and call for more attention to how and why such ideational phenomena may change over time. As such, transformational approaches share liberalism's critique of realism and build on the insights of the former, especially its emphasis on the role of values.[4] At the same time, however, they implicitly criticize liberalism—and other existing idea-based theories—for offering too static a picture of world politics.

Learning Theory and Social Constructivism

The two most prominent transformational approaches are learning theory and social constructivism. Learning theory, which was the first to be developed, is just what it claims to be: a theory of what and how actors—typically individual policy makers—learn from experience, observation, and study. In its most basic form, it concerns any changes in the beliefs and values held by these individuals rather than connoting some form of human progress; learning can be maladaptive and dysfunctional as well as productive and beneficial (Levy, 1994).

Scholars have typically differentiated between two types of learning. Simple learning involves changes in factual knowledge and cause-effect beliefs. This type of learning is manifested when actors alter the strategies they employ to achieve a fixed set of goals. Complex learning, in contrast, involves changes in values, interests, and the basic goals of policy themselves. Thus this second type of learning may result in even more profound behavioral modifications (Nye, 1987).

Social constructivism, which borrows heavily from modern social theory, requires a bit more explication. The starting point of constructivist analyses is the assumption that the agents in any social system are not autonomous but, rather, are embedded in social structures of shared norms that do much to define their interests and identities. Such arrangements of agents and structures are not static but evolve over time through a process of mutual constitution: the actions (physical and communicative) of agents shape and reshape the normative structures, which simultaneously constitute and reconstitute the agents (Wendt, 1995 and 1999).

The intensity of such transformational processes can vary considerably, although most social constructivists would maintain that they are always present to some degree. What is important for our purposes, however, is the idea that repeated interactions among states and the people who compose them can result in changes in their interests and even their identities over time. Moreover, this process can easily go beyond the development of complementary interests and similar identities (e.g., as liberal democratic states) and lead instead to the emergence of common interests and a common identity (e.g., as an Atlantic community), an identity that could perhaps even serve as the basis for the construction of a new polity and that might exclude otherwise similar states located elsewhere.

In addition, there are good reasons to expect that the types of transformational phenomena posited by learning theory and constructivism will occur with particular frequency in the context of formal international institutions. Membership in such institutions is likely to alter the nature of interstate and transnational interactions in ways that facilitate the processes of interest and identity formation. Other things being equal, interactions among the individuals that represent participating states and various unofficial actors are likely to be of greater frequency, intensity, density, and duration than those among nonmembers. This effect should be characteristic of a wide variety of types of interactions, including direct human contacts, the establishment of transnational and transgovernmental links, information flows, and resource transfers (Risse-Kappen, ed., 1995). Thus although institutionalist theory and social constructivism start from very different premises, international institutions should play a prominent role in many constructivist accounts of international relations.

Hypotheses about Transatlantic Relations

The transformational perspective is perhaps the least useful for explaining transatlantic relations during the Cold War (Risse-Kappen, 1995). What it would emphasize during that period is not the impact of accumulating changes in beliefs, interests, and identities but the very occurrence of such changes in the context of frequent and highly institutionalized transatlantic interactions. Since ideational changes of this type are likely to be gradual in nature, their behavioral consequences should require some time to emerge.

The post-Cold War era, however, is probably not too early a period in which to expect such consequences to become manifest. Thus transformational approaches would suggest that, independently of the continued existence of common threats, interlinking international institutions, and shared liberal democratic traditions, transatlantic relations after the Cold War should be different from what they might otherwise have become because of fundamental changes in the nature of the United States and the European countries, or at least in the beliefs and values held by their elites, mass publics, or both (Wendt, 1992:417–418).

The exact nature of the likely impact of such changes on U.S.-European relations is harder to specify; it depends crucially on the precise ways in which—and the degree to which—beliefs, values, interests, and identities have evolved under the impact of transatlantic interactions over the previous four decades. As a working hypothesis, however, one might posit, for example, the existence of altered beliefs (especially in the United States) about the interdependence of U.S. and European security and thus the value of continued American engagement in European security affairs. Closely related might be convergent transatlantic interests in European peace and stability, and not only because of the corresponding economic benefits. And some scholars have gone so far as to claim the emergence of a transatlantic security community based on a common identity (Risse-Kappen, 1995). Such developments would militate strongly in favor of a high level of continued cooperation, perhaps especially in the area of security.

WEIGHING THE AVAILABLE EVIDENCE

Three leading theoretical perspectives offer often contrasting expectations about the likely course of transatlantic relations after the Cold War. How do these expectations hold up against the empirical record since 1990? Although even a decade of experience is perhaps too short a period on which to base firm conclusions about so broad a subject, it should provide us at least with some indication of likely trends.

Before attempting to draw any conclusions, however, it is important to make note of the most obvious difficulties that will attend such an effort. Three related problems stand out. First, a good deal of uncertainty exists regarding the expectations of each theory. In order to make more accurate predictions, it is necessary to have more detailed descriptions of the causal antecedents that each approach emphasizes. Concrete realist hypotheses are likely to be the easiest to generate, since the configurations of power and threat that they emphasize are relatively easy to specify, although, in fact, subjective perceptions of them may vary considerably. In contrast, the task of ascertaining the beliefs, interests, and identities stressed by transformational theories may be quite demanding and fraught with pitfalls.

Second, even if the achievement of greater specificity were possible, the various theories considered above would not necessarily offer rival hypotheses. Thus the same phenomena may provide support for more than one approach. The task of differentiating between the outcomes predicted by the liberal and transformational perspectives, respectively, will be especially challenging. Nevertheless, it should be relatively easy to distinguish between the generally pessimistic expectations about transatlantic cooperation of realist theories and the more optimistic ones of their liberal and transformational counterparts.

Third, even where hypotheses can be clearly differentiated and where evidence seems to be consistent with the expectations of one theory or another, it may be difficult to establish with any certainty that the causal factors emphasized by that theory were indeed responsible for the observed outcome. In any case, to do so with a high degree of confidence would require a much more detailed examination of the evidence than is possible within the confines of a single chapter, since one may need to inquire into the motives and calculations of multiple decision makers. Here, it will be possible only to examine the broad contours of transatlantic relations since 1990 and not to delve into primary sources.

With these caveats in mind, I now evaluate the usefulness of the three perspectives for understanding the recent evolution of U.S.-European relations. How should one go about doing so? Each of the theories considered above purports to explain the presence or absence of cooperation among states. Consequently, one should begin by looking for evidence of transatlantic cooperation. International cooperation has been usefully defined as "the voluntary adjustment by states of their policies so that they manage their differences and reach some mutually beneficial outcome" (Grieco, 1990:22; see also Keohane, 1984:51–52). With this broad definition as a starting point, one might further distinguish among three more specific forms of cooperation in situations where policy preferences diverge:

- Making an effort to address common challenges or problems jointly, rather than acting independently. In some cases, this will involve using appropriate preexisting institutional fora.
- Exhibiting a willingness to compromise one's preferred course of action in order to achieve common policies. In some cases, this will entail the creation of new institutional structures or the modification of existing ones.
- Faithfully implementing common policies, even where this involves some cost or inconvenience in comparison with unilateral action. In some cases, this will involve complying with agreed institutional rules.

In conducting this analysis, consider first the security and then the economic aspects of the subject. Although this organizational structure is somewhat arbitrary and, more importantly, may obscure important links between the two components and tend to marginalize other significant aspects of transatlantic relations, it is nevertheless common in the literature and thus should facilitate comparison with other works.

Transatlantic Security Relations

The post-Cold War record in the area of security affairs provides considerable support for the liberal and transformational perspectives. Despite a number of episodes involving strained transatlantic ties, many of which seemed to confirm realist expectations, the United States and Europe have continued to engage in high levels of security cooperation. Along the way, they have transformed NATO into an institution that is better able to address their likely future security concerns in the region and thus can serve as a sturdy platform for joint action. Harder to establish is the role of transformational processes in accounting for these and related developments.

Evidence of Cooperation and Conflict

To be sure, many developments in the early to mid-1990s suggested that the realist dynamic of alliance disintegration would prevail in transatlantic security relations. As the Soviet threat declined, NATO countries engaged in rapid, largely unilateral force reductions and troop withdrawals, raising questions about the viability of the alliance's integrated military structure. Simultaneously, a number of European states, including many NATO members, expressed an interest in developing strong pan-European and/or West European security structures, suggesting that the old alliance with the United

States was no longer deemed necessary or at least that the U.S. role in Europe could be significantly reduced.

In addition, NATO was almost immediately buffeted by challenges of a different nature, which placed in stark relief the question of the alliance's continued relevance to the problems of European security after the Cold War. These challenges stemmed from the allies' differing responses to the conflicts that wracked the former Yugoslavia, beginning in mid-1991. Initially, of course, the desire of the Europeans to take the lead in dealing with the conflicts and U.S. willingness to defer to them resulted in a brief period of transatlantic harmony. The failure of these European efforts as well as those of the United Nations to put an end to the fighting and the concomitant recognition of the need for NATO involvement, however, soon brought U.S.-European differences to a head. One result was the early impasse triggered by the American proposal for a policy of "lift and strike" in Bosnia, which found little support on the continent. Such episodes of paralysis generated in turn a chorus of cries, especially in the United States, that NATO either had to go "out of area" or it would go out of business. And even where the allies could agree in principle to act, as on the policy of enforcing the U.N.-declared no-fly-zone over Bosnia, they frequently clashed publicly over the precise measures to be taken in response to violations. Clearly, the nature of the threat posed by ethnic conflict in the Balkans was not sufficient to compel a unified front (Ullman, 1996).

At approximately the same time, the NATO allies began to disagree openly over the desirability of admitting new members from Central and Eastern Europe. Although perhaps never as heated as the intra-alliance debates over what to do about Bosnia, the enlargement issue nevertheless further manifested the fissiparous tendencies existing within the alliance after the Cold War. Indeed, one realist has described it as the clearest sign of an eroding strategic consensus (Walt, 1998:19).

When all is said and done, however, it is clear that no fundamental breakdown has occurred in transatlantic security cooperation. To the contrary, the United States and Europe have continued to try to work together on regional security issues and have usually been able to overcome their differences in order to arrive at and carry out common policies. NATO has been not only preserved but substantially modified, both doctrinally and structurally, in order to be better able to address the likely challenges of the future. As a result, it remains a central—and, in many cases, *the* central—focus of the security policies of its members. Indeed, even France, which severed its military ties to the alliance in the 1960s, has seen fit to involve itself once again in NATO's defense bodies.

Likewise, the early concerns raised by the prospect of alternative European security structures turned out to be misplaced. Less progress has occurred than many had initially hoped or feared, in no small part because of the transatlantic alliance's continuing utility. And insofar as new structures have been established, they have been increasingly viewed as complementary to rather than competing with NATO, which has itself taken steps, such as the development of the Combined Joint Task Forces (CJTF) concept, to ensure their mutual compatibility.

Finally, the United States and the Europeans were able to work through their most important initial differences on the question of enlargement in the span of a few years, paving the way for the admission of three new members from Central and Eastern Europe in 1999. Likewise, they were ultimately able to achieve a high level of cooperation in Bosnia, beginning with the enforcement of U.N. sanctions in the mid-1990s and continuing through a half decade-long deployment of peacekeeping forces there. The Bosnia experience was followed by a much less contentious process of decision making and joint military action in response to the subsequent crisis in Kosovo, notwithstanding the lack of a clear U.N. mandate.

Accounting for Cooperation

More difficult than describing this generally cooperative pattern of outcomes is the task of accounting for it in terms of the three theoretical perspectives outlined above. Even realists—never ones to concede a point readily—might argue that, notwithstanding the collapse of the Soviet Union, the United States and Western Europe faced common threats of sufficient magnitude to ensure continued security cooperation. In the face of a nuclear armed Russia, actual and potential ethnic conflicts on their borders, and the new risks posed by proliferation and terrorism, the allies may not yet have been ready to go their separate ways. In terms of the material factors emphasized by realism, however, it is hard to see why the United States possesses a stronger interest in institutionalized security cooperation with Europe than it did, say, during the interwar years or immediately after World War II, both occasions on which it sought to disengage. And even if U.S. engagement were not problematic, the particular form that transatlantic cooperation has taken—the preservation of NATO—and the ways in which the organization has been used are not readily accounted for by balance of power theory.

Instead, the trajectory of post-Cold War transatlantic security relations seems less puzzling when viewed through the lenses provided by the liberal and transformational perspectives. Institutional theorists can explain NATO's persistence in terms of the utility and adaptability of existing international institutions. Even if the nature of the security challenges facing the United States and Europe changed, as they did to a significant extent, it was always more efficient to rely on NATO and to make organizational adjustments as necessary than to react to events on an ad hoc basis. Thus an alliance that had once emphasized the deterrence of threats and acts of aggression against its members has been employed to stabilize and promote reform in the states of Central and Eastern Europe and, where actual hostilities occurred, to coordinate international military interventions for the purposes of peacekeeping and peace enforcement. Indeed, all of these operations would have been much more difficult, if not impossible, to mount in the absence of NATO's organizational machinery. With the acquisition of experience and the development of new capabilities, moreover, such new cooperative ventures could be undertaken with ever greater speed, confidence, and efficiency—compare NATO's responses to the Bosnian and Kosovo crises, respectively.

The other strand of liberalism considered in this chapter, liberal democratic peace theory, would emphasize the specific types of strategies jointly employed by the United States and Western Europe to enhance their security after the Cold War. The allies were not content simply to wall themselves off from potential dangers, to engage in military cooperation with nonmembers insofar as possible, or to extinguish regional military conflicts. To the contrary, they have placed at least as much emphasis on transforming former adversaries into fully fledged members of the community of liberal, democratic states. Thus the North Atlantic Cooperation Council (now the Euro-Atlantic Partnership Council), the Partnership for Peace (PFP), and the NATO enlargement process concerned not only the creation of new security ties but also the export of Western models of civil-military relations, transparent defense policy making, treatment of national minorities, and the like. Likewise, the interventions in Bosnia and Kosovo have been closely linked to the goal of constructing political communities based on the principles of tolerance and representative government in those devastated regions.

Harder to establish is the impact of the types of factors emphasized by transformational perspectives, although this difficulty should not discourage us from looking for their influences. It would be an exaggeration to state that the United States and Europe have developed a common identity that could serve as a solid foundation for cooperation—indeed, such a claim would be premature even in the case of the members of the much more integrated European Union—although the first elements of such a transatlantic identity may be present. Even where American and European security interests seem to have coincided, moreover, it would be reckless without much more careful analysis to attribute such coincidences wholly to earlier interactive processes rather than to the common strategic circumstances of the moment.

Nevertheless, we can adduce at least some evidence for the existence of transformational phenomena in the rationales offered by political leaders for the policies that their respective states have pursued. These include, for example, frequent references to the United States as a European power, one with a permanent role to play in the security affairs of the continent (Holbrooke, 1995). Today, such views, which would have found few adherents following either of the world wars, seem much more than just wishful thinking. By the same token, very few American elites today regard renewed isolationism as a responsible option.

Perhaps even more striking have been the justifications provided by political leaders in Germany, which is arguably the European linchpin of transatlantic security cooperation. The Federal Republic, more than any other European state, has been transformed by its participation in NATO and its close relations with the United States during the postwar era. Consequently, successive German governments of varying political stripes have been ardent supporters of the alliance and continued strong security ties with the United States, including an American military presence on German soil, to an extent that seems to exceed even what can be rationalized in terms of the expected practical benefits of such a policy (Duffield, 1998).

Finally, one might point to evidence of ongoing learning since the end of the Cold War with regard to how to respond to ethnic conflict in the Balkans and perhaps elsewhere on the continent. Having started at different positions, the transatlantic partners now appear to have arrived at a consensus about the importance of timely intervention, the need for American leadership, and the utility of NATO. These altered beliefs no less than the institutional changes that have occurred in the alliance are necessary for explaining the differing Western responses to fighting in Croatia, Bosnia, and Kosovo. In a similar manner, U.S. and European views about the meaning and value of European efforts to develop an autonomous capability for military action have exhibited considerable convergence.

Transatlantic Economic Relations

A similar pattern of outcomes and influences would seem to obtain in the area of transatlantic economic relations since the end of the Cold War. Here, too, one finds some empirical support for the increasingly conflictual dynamics predicted by realism. The preponderance of evidence, however, points in the direction of a liberal interpretation. Whether transformational processes have played much of a role is more difficult to say.

Evidence of Cooperation and Conflict

As realists might have anticipated, U.S.-European economic relations have been characterized by a number of high-profile disputes, especially in the area of trade. Whether the issue was bananas, hormone-treated beef, and Hollywood movies or more arcane subject like export subsidies and the extraterritorial application of American sanctions, such disputes have made headlines and raised concerns that transatlantic commercial ties might soon be strained to the breaking point. And at the beginning of the 1990s, the

Uruguay Round of global trade negotiations came close to collapse, largely due to transatlantic differences.

Yet the overall record of transatlantic economic relations is one of continued cooperation, notwithstanding attention-getting disagreements. The United States and Europe have continued to try to work together on economic issues, seeking amicable solutions to their conflicts. These efforts have included the creation and elaboration of formal arrangements between the United States and the European Union (EU) for the bilateral discussion of nonsecurity issues, including biannual summits at the presidential level, as called for in the 1990 Transatlantic Declaration (Kahler, 1995: 61; Reinicke, 1996: 42–43; Eichengreen, 1998: 1).

With regard to the area of trade, one should also remember that high-profile disputes are not a purely post-Cold War phenomenon. To the contrary, they have long been a staple irritant of transatlantic relations, even if the specific bones of contention have changed over the years. Moreover, important past objects of conflict, such as strategic trade with the Soviet bloc, access to resources in the developing world, and the protection of agriculture, have been diminished with the end of the Cold War, a steady decline in the price of most commodities, and significant reforms in the EU's Common Agricultural Policy (CAP) (Kahler, 1995: 2–3).

What really matters, in any case, is the broader impact of such disputes, and this impact appears to have been modest, if not negligible. Disputes in one area have not readily spilled over into others but have remained largely contained.[5] In absolute terms, moreover, the level of transatlantic trade remains substantial, at around 20 percent of the U.S. total.[6]

It is also noteworthy that the United States and the EU were ultimately able to overcome the deep differences that had obstructed global trade negotiations and to achieve agreements that served as the basis for the successful 1993 conclusion of the Uruguay Round, which resulted in the establishment of the World Trade Organization (WTO). Not only were the principles governing trade in manufactured goods extended into new areas, such as services and intellectual property rights, but they were supplemented with new decision-making bodies and dispute settlement procedures. Since then, the two sides have regularly taken their grievances to the WTO and have sought to comply with its rulings rather than resorting to unilateral measures in order to obtain redress.

The evidence in the area of monetary relations is more ambiguous. The post-Cold War era has seen no major conflicts in this area thus far. Nevertheless, the degree of transatlantic coordination in response to the financial crises—first in Mexico, later in Asia—that threatened to bring down the global financial system has been less than ideal. Moreover, it is too soon to assess the consequences of the establishment of a monetary union among eleven European states in 1999 (Eichengreen and Ghironi, 1998).

Accounting for Cooperation

To an important extent, it seems possible to account for this general pattern of continued cooperation in terms of the multiple international institutions of relevance to transatlantic economic relations. In contrast to the security realm, however, many of these institutions are global rather than purely regional in nature or, if not global, include one or more extraregional states. One important general mechanism for policy coordination has been the G-7, to which Japan and Canada belong. Although the G-7 is only loosely institutionalized, its annual summit meetings provide a unique forum for the discussion of issues and the achievement of consensus among the world's largest industrialized countries. During the first half of the 1990s, the G-7 served as a principal venue for the coordination of Western assistance to the former Soviet Union. With a larger, though still far from universal, membership and a lower profile is the Organization for Economic Cooperation and Development (OECD), which provided a forum for the negotiation by the United States and Europe of an agreement on measures to limit corruption by their corporations (Schott, 1998: 59).

The most developed set of international institutions governing transatlantic economic relations have been those concerned with trade, especially the GATT and its successor organization, the WTO. The existence of these complex frameworks of rules and procedures, and the benefits that they generate in terms of market access and the regulation of competition, has given the United States and Europe additional strong incentives for seeking to contain and resolve their differences. Indeed, these global institutions have reduced barriers to transatlantic trade to such an extent that relatively little would likely be gained from any purely bilateral liberalization measures, such as a U.S.-EU free trade area in services and industrial goods (Schott, 1998: 41).

As for monetary relations, transatlantic cooperation is pursued in a variety of international institutions, including the G-7, the OECD, the IMF, and the Bank of International Settlements (BIS). In contrast to trade, however, this realm is characterized by few specific rules and relatively weak mechanisms for policy coordination (Eichengreen and Ghironi, 1998). Consequently, should serious U.S.-European conflicts ever arise in this area, it may be possible to attribute them in at least part to the absence of adequate institutional arrangements.

The liberal democratic nature of the societies involved may have also played a role in promoting transatlantic economic cooperation, albeit a more indirect one. On balance, cooperation seems to have been favored by the level and nature of economic interdependence that has existed between the United States and Europe. While a high volume of trade increases the potential for conflict across the Atlantic (Eichengreen, 1998:1), it also raises the stakes, providing both sides with an incentive to make sure that disputes are resolved or at least contained. In addition, transatlantic trade is highly balanced, thereby removing a source of rancor that repeatedly roils U.S. relations with Asia. Finally, cooperation has been undergirded by continuing high levels of direct investment, which has a strong positive impact on trade.[7] Economic interdependence is in turn, however, strongly associated with liberal democracy. In particular, recent studies have found that democratic states trade significantly more with each other than they do with states that have other types of political systems (Morrow, Siverson, and Tabares, 1998).

Considerable evidence also suggests that transformational dynamics have been present. U.S. and European concepts about the proper ordering of the world economy have undergone considerable convergence during the postwar era. Whereas the United States and its principal European allies were frequently at odds over such issues as imperial preference half a century ago, they have developed highly similar, if not always identical, preferences for economic openness and market competition (Kahler, 1996; Guay, 1999). Whether this convergence can be attributed primarily to the types of processes posited by the transformational perspective is harder to establish. Nevertheless, at least one perceptive observer has argued that "five decades of close collaboration have produced societies on either side of the Atlantic that share broadly common views on international economic governance" (Kahler, 1996:24).

CONCLUSION: FINDINGS, FUTURE PROSPECTS, AND POLICY IMPLICATIONS

This chapter has inquired into the usefulness of three leading theoretical perspectives for understanding transatlantic relations after the Cold War. It has found that realist approaches, while providing a useful starting point for analysis, are unable to account for the general pattern of considerable cooperation that has continued to characterize relations between the United States and Europe in both the security and economic arenas. Balance of power theory and hegemonic stability theory both predict a decline in cooperation as a result of the end of the Soviet threat and American hegemony vis-à-vis Europe, respectively.

Instead, the record of the past decade is much more consistent with the expectations of liberal theories of international relations. As institutional theory would predict, the strong security and economic institutions created by the transatlantic partners in the wake of World War II and in response to the Cold War have continued to serve as valuable instruments for addressing their concerns and pursuing their national interests. As a result, the very existence of these institutions has both facilitated and generated strong incentives for continued cooperation, even as they have been modified and supplemented to conform better to the exigencies of the post-Cold War era. While the predictions of liberal democratic peace theory are not as specific, it too is nevertheless compatible with the high degree of cooperation witnessed between the United States and Europe.

Hardest of all to assess is the contribution of the transformational perspective to an explanation of transatlantic relations. Certainly, the pattern of continued cooperation is not inconsistent with this approach's emphasis on the effects of convergent beliefs, interests, and even identities. Rather, the problem lies in establishing with any degree of confidence that such transformational dynamics have indeed occurred and that they can be primarily attributed to the interactive processes that transformational approaches presuppose, as opposed to some other (perhaps random) mechanism. This problem, however, is not an absolute one but an artifact of the relative novelty of these theoretical approaches, the relatively greater difficulty of measuring the ideational variables that they emphasize (in comparison with power distributions or international institutions), and the relatively limited resources that scholars have thus far devoted to exploring their validity.

In fact, further research on the subject of transatlantic relations is likely to result in new theoretical syntheses in which the transformational perspective is treated as an essential complement to realism and liberalism as scholars find it increasingly difficult to disentangle the causal processes posited by these various approaches. This is because the impact of seemingly objective factors such as power and institutions on international relations is necessarily mediated by the perceptions, meanings, and understandings that are attached to them. Thus how one responds, for example, to Germany's economic power and military potential is largely a function of what one might expect Germany to do with the resources at its disposal. Likewise, the utility of a particular international institution such as NATO is as much a learned or imagined quality as it is something that can be straightforwardly divined from the organization's formal structures and processes. Consequently, it may ultimately be impossible to understand realist and liberal dynamics except through a transformationalist lens that helps to explain how the world came to be perceived and understood in a particular way.

A final observation concerns the sufficiency of the theoretical perspectives employed in this analysis. While one or more of them may be necessary to understand post-Cold War transatlantic relations, they are not necessarily able to account, singly or jointly, for all of the events and trends of the past decade that one might deem important. Although each of the three perspectives is pitched in broad terms in order to embrace multiple theories, they do not by any means encompass all of the theoretical approaches that might be of use in this enterprise. Indeed, the very nature of these approaches may obscure important features that are essential to a more fully satisfying understanding of the subject.

As a first step, it may be useful to question the tendency of the preceding analysis to treat Europe (or at least Western Europe) as a single entity. Although this assumption is perhaps more reasonable than at any time in the past in view of the impressive strides made recently by the EU, the truth remains that the region is populated by a number of distinct nation-states that often hold conflicting interests on particular issues. Indeed, these intra-European differences may at times be as substantial as those that characterize transatlantic relations as a whole. Thus it may be advisable to disaggregate Europe and to explore the additional obstacles and opportunities for cooperation that such a model suggests.

Going a step further in this direction, it may sometimes be useful to disaggregate the states themselves into their constituent parts, such as governments, which may in turn be separated into their executive, legislative, and judicial components; societies, which may in turn be divided along lines of economic interest, class, ethnicity, and so on; and the various institutions of interest representation that link the state and society. Such an analytical move may help to highlight additional important constraints on or pressures for cooperation as well as aid in the process of identifying strategies for overcoming the former and harnessing the latter.

Both of these departures from the simpler model employed in this chapter suggest the potential relevance of the family of theories that concern the primarily domestic sources of foreign and security policy. Indeed, it may be impossible to comprehend particular trade disputes or the zig-zagging course of allied discussions on the question of NATO enlargement without reference to such factors. Nevertheless, it is useful to begin an analysis of this type by examining how far theories that consider the transatlantic system as a whole, rather than the often idiosyncratic characteristics of its component parts, are able to take us.

Future Prospects

What does the preceding analysis suggest about the future course of transatlantic relations? Clearly, attempts at political forecasting are fraught with potential pitfalls. Often, it is impossible to anticipate developments that prove to be primary determinants of future events. Could but Western leaders have foreseen the rise of a national-socialist dictatorship in Germany, the world might have been spared a second global conflagration. Likewise, those in positions of political power at the end of World War II could hardly have imagined the degree to which relations with the Soviet Union would deteriorate during the following five years.

Nevertheless, if one is to prognosticate, one cannot dwell on the unpredictable. And perhaps the best we can do is to project recent trends into the future, even as we recognize the possibility of departures from a linear path. In that case, the prospects for transatlantic relations are generally bright. We can anticipate a continuation of the generally high levels of cooperation between the United States and Europe that have prevailed during the past decade. Such an optimistic forecast also follows from a consideration of the factors emphasized by the theoretical perspectives that we have found particularly useful for illuminating post-Cold War U.S.-European relations thus far. The liberal and transformational perspectives provide good grounds, especially when taken together, for expecting continued cooperation, notwithstanding the greater potential for conflict, or at least a drifting apart, that the realist perspective identifies.

In the first place, the United States and its European partners remain well-established liberal democracies that will be naturally inclined to cooperate in the many areas in which their interests coincide. And where their interests diverge on specific issues, they will tend to evince understanding of each other's positions and to exercise restraint in their dealings with one another, placing sharp bounds on the potential for conflict.

In the second place, the United States and Europe remain jointly enmeshed in a number of well-developed international institutions that simultaneously provide opportunities and good reasons for continued collaboration. Most of those that were created during the Cold War have been successfully adapted, like NATO, so as to maintain their relevance in the face of new international realities and in some cases, such as the WTO, given additional powers. Moreover, some new ones, including the first purely transatlantic arrangements for the discussion of political and economic issues, have been established. Although these institutions and their operation have themselves at times been at the center of disagreements, they remain, on balance, valuable instruments for the pursuit of national interests. Thus their participants are likely to continue to work through them and to respect the limits that they place on national action even in cases where doing so seems disadvantageous.

One further word on the liberal perspective may be in order at this point. Thus far, I have treated institutional theory and liberal democratic peace theory as distinct approaches to understanding international relations. In fact, however, they are complementary insofar as international institutions and liberal democracy are mutually reinforcing. On the one hand, liberal democratic states are more likely to create and maintain international institutions than are other types of states. One reason for this is the intrinsic value that liberal democracies place on cooperation. Another is the importance assigned to the rule of law in such societies. The development of international law and organizations is merely the extension of familiar law-governed domestic processes to the international sphere. On the other hand, international institutions will be not only more abundant among liberal democracies but also more consequential. Liberal democracies are more likely to regard the rules institutions contain as authoritative and binding and thus to treat those rules with deference. This further line of argument suggests the existence of even stronger grounds for expecting a continued high level of transatlantic cooperation after the Cold War (Kupchan, 1999).

Finally, as the transformational perspective would emphasize, the United States and Europe may have grown through a half century of frequent and wide-ranging interactions into convergent ways of thinking about themselves, their interests, and one another that reinforce the institutions and liberal values that already dispose them toward cooperation. Externally, they have been increasingly bound by the shared goal of enlarging the areas of the world that possess functioning market economies and are governed by the rule of law. Vis-à-vis one another, in the words of a leading German observer of transatlantic relations, "the distinction between foreign and domestic policy has blurred as [their] societies have interwoven," a process that seems only likely to accelerate with the growth of the internet (*New York Times*, 28 May 2000; see also Guay, 1999).

Of course, the possibility remains that, in the long run, corrosive realist pressures may ultimately prevail over these cooperative tendencies. Nor can one guarantee that all the circumstances that currently promote cooperation will not change. For example, the relative, if not absolute, degree of transatlantic economic interdependence—and thus the consequences of a fundamental rupture—could decline as more and more U.S. trade shifts from Europe to Asia. As a result, the United States could become increasingly willing to take a hard line vis-à-vis Europe in defense of its perceived economic interests.

In addition, there is uncertainty about the implications of the further evolution of the EU. The 1990s witnessed first the completion of a single European market largely free of barriers to the movement of goods, services, capital, and labor, and then the successful introduction of a true European economic and monetary union (EMU) involving a common currency and a single central bank, the feasibility of which had long been doubted. Now the EU is poised to streamline its internal decision-making processes in preparation for the accession of new members from Central and Eastern Europe and to add a true capacity for military action.

As a result of these developments, relations with the United States could be strained in two somewhat contradictory ways. On the one hand, such significant integrative steps would seem not only to evidence the existence of a Europe that was more willing and able than ever to assert its independence but also to set the stage for drawn-out future conflicts over both economic and security policies between more evenly matched rivals. On the other hand, problems with the EMU and enlargement could cause the EU to turn inward, hampering efforts at transatlantic economic cooperation (Eichen-green and Ghironi, 1998).

Policy Implications

In short, the road ahead is unlikely to be an entirely smooth one. Just as during the last decade, the transatlantic relationship will encounter frequent bumps and the occasional pothole. Thus the generally optimistic picture painted above should not be allowed to foster complacency. To the contrary, the forward progress of U.S.-European relations will always stand to benefit from active management and enlightened leadership. This observation seems especially true in view of the fact that some important sources of post-war U.S.-European cooperation, particularly those emphasized by the realist perspective, are no longer present or much reduced. Consequently, the possibility that misdirected policies—or the absence of policy—could eventually lead to a fundamental breach in the relationship, although perhaps small, is not negligible. The good news is that the situation is not entirely beyond human control. Today's and tomorrow's leaders have it in their means to take steps that can help to preclude an extensive breakdown of cooperation.

What prescriptions follow from the theoretical perspectives considered in this paper? Once again, it is necessary to begin by qualifying what can be achieved here. It is no more possible to derive highly specific policy guidance from such broadly framed theoretical perspectives than it is to offer detailed predictions about transatlantic relations. A tradeoff usually exists between the range of instances to which a theory might apply and the degree to which it can illuminate a specific case. Consequently, perhaps the most that can be hoped for are very general guidelines, including an indication of the types of conditions and policy instruments to which policy makers should devote their attention.

When it comes to offering advice, realism is in one respect the least useful of the three perspectives, since the factors that it emphasizes are the least subject to conscious manipulation. There is not much one can do about the loss of the unifying Soviet threat or about the relative decline of American power vis-à-vis Europe. Nor would it be worth attempting to resurrect the Soviet threat or to construct a substitute merely for the sake of preserving allied unity even if one could do so.

Nevertheless, realism can help to suggest the forms of cooperation that are more or less possible and sustainable in the altered geopolitical circumstances of the post-Cold War era. In the area of security affairs, it makes clear that a high level of U.S. involvement in Europe will be more difficult to justify and thus to sustain than in the past, absent the reemergence of a compelling threat. Consequently, it behooves the Europeans to take the steps necessary to become collectively a more equal military partner of the United

States, one that can bear a greater share of the burdens of regional defense—and now peacekeeping—efforts than they have been able to do thus far, and it behooves the United States to encourage this process. To be sure, the United States may sometimes chafe at having to relinquish the disproportionate influence over NATO policy that has come with being the dominant member of the alliance. But this equalization of U.S. and European roles will be compensated for by a commensurate readjustment of their respective responsibilities and the elimination of lingering European resentments.

Similarly, in the area of economic affairs, realism underscores the importance of establishing and maintaining a balanced relationship. In the absence of a hegemonic power, asymmetrical flows of goods and capital risk prompting the erection of trade barriers and controls on investment. Indeed, this goal would already seem to have been largely achieved, at least in comparison with other bilateral relationships, thereby creating a relatively sound foundation for future U.S.-European economic ties.

The liberal perspective offers a different but complementary set of prescriptions. Institutional theory instructs policy makers to be attentive to the role that international institutions can play in promoting cooperation. Thus it would caution against moving too hastily to abandon or dismantle existing international institutions, even if they seem outdated, and would instead underscore the importance of identifying the ways in which they may continue to be of use, even if some modifications are necessary. Likewise, while recognizing that the creation new institutions is not the solution for every thing that ails transatlantic relations, it reminds us that they can sometimes help to resolve specific sources of conflict. Thus, as noted above, a transatlantic free trade agreement would probably not represent any improvement upon the WTO. But with traditional trade barriers having been largely eliminated, there may be a place for new U.S.-European institutions that could address so-called behind-the-border issues, such as differences in government regulation and corporate taxation (Kahler, 1995; Reinicke, 1996).

For its part, liberal democratic peace theory emphasizes the value of promoting the inculcation of liberal values and the establishment democratic institutions in countries that lack them and preserving them where they already exist. Liberal democracy seems well-entrenched in the countries covered in this analysis. Thus the most immediate prescription that follows from this theory is the need to seek to enlarge the "zone of peace" (Ullman, 1990) within Europe, if only as a means of reducing the likelihood and magnitude of crises and conflicts in neighboring areas that might strain transatlantic relations. In fact, Western leaders would seem to have already understood this lesson, judging by the efforts that they have made to promote political and economic reforms in Central and Eastern Europe.

In this regard, the two strands of liberal theory considered in this paper come together. Although regional institutions serve a number of purposes, they have proven themselves to be among the most useful instruments for fostering liberal democracy where it is not already present. This goal has informed some of the most noteworthy NATO initiatives of the past decade, such as the PFP, as well as the EU's more gradual but nevertheless significant progress toward strengthening ties with Central and Eastern Europe. Although the potential drawbacks of admitting additional countries into NATO and the EU, especially if done so too hastily, should not be minimized, neither should they be allowed to justify interminable delays in the enlargement process.

Perhaps less obvious is the fact that international institutions will also have a role to play in preserving the impressive liberal democratic gains that were achieved within the existing transatlantic community during the postwar era. Here the case of Germany is especially instructive. Although German democracy may be no less inherently stable than democracy in other West European countries, it may be potentially more subject to corrosive external pressures because of Germany's central geographical location on the continent and its heavy dependence on exports. Thus policy makers should bear in mind how NATO and other European security structures can help to buffer Germany against potentially disruptive security threats, while the EU and the WTO can help to ensure access for German products in foreign markets.

Because of the relatively undeveloped nature of the transformation perspective, it is perhaps the least capable of generating concrete guidance for policy. At a minimum, it is useful for reminding policy makers that national beliefs, interests, and even identities are not immutable. Rather, these important determinants of state policy and international relations are themselves malleable and, indeed, somewhat subject to conscious manipulation. Thus policy makers eager to sustain transatlantic cooperation should be ever on the lookout for ways of fostering common understandings and interests.

Typically, such transformational dynamics are associated with international contacts and the flow of people, information, and material resources across national boundaries. Such exchanges, moreover, are likely to take place in the context of or be promoted by international institutions. Consequently, policy makers should be attentive to—and prepared to exploit—the transformational potential of NATO and other transatlantic institutions, even if these were established for different reasons and continue to be justified on other grounds.

Unfortunately, it is difficult to be much more specific at this point, given that transformational processes are still poorly understood. Much more research is required in order to clarify the mechanisms through which and the conditions under which national perspective, interests, and even identities may grow together. Scholarly efforts directed toward this end are likely to be well worthwhile, however, because of their substantial potential policy relevance, and not just for the management of transatlantic relations.

NOTES

1. One need only examine the titles of many of the books that have recently appeared on the subject. See, for example, Coker, 1998; Geipel and Manning, 1996; Kaase and Kohut, 1996; Serfaty, 1997; and Weidenfeld, 1996.

2. By anarchy, in this context, we do not mean a state of chaos; international relations can be quite orderly, even from a realist perspective. Rather, anarchy means a lack of hierarchy and, in particular, the absence of any central authority capable of enforcing agreements between states or of protecting them if they are threatened or actually attacked by one another.

3. The most rigorous presentation of balance of power theory remains Waltz (1979). A valuable refinement focuses on the role of threats, rather than power alone, in stimulating balancing behavior (Walt, 1987).

4. Indeed, insofar as liberal democratic peace theory emphasizes values as opposed to formal domestic institutions, it too falls within this expansive camp.

5. For example, the tariffs (approximately $300 million) that the United States has threatened to impose on European products over the banana and beef-hormone disputes would amount to only about one-tenth of 1 percent of the total volume of transatlantic trade.

6. In 1996, the EU ranked just behind Canada as the leading U.S. partner in merchandise trade ($270 billion in total exports and imports versus $290 billion) (Schott, 1998: 38–39).

7. In 1998, 44 percent of all U.S. foreign direct investment (FDI) was in Europe, while 58 percent of all FDI in the United States originated in the EU (Guay, 1999: 82; see also Schott 1996: 41 and 44). According to one estimate, trade between parent firms and their affiliates on the other side of the Atlantic amounts to one-third of all transatlantic trade (Schott, 1996: 44).

BIBLIOGRAPHY

Asmus, R. (1997) "Double Enlargement: Redefining the Atlantic Partnership after the Cold War." In D. Gompert and F. Larrabee, eds. *America and Europe: A Partnership for a New Era.* New York: Cambridge University Press.

Bergsten, C. (1999) "America and Europe: Clash of the Titans?" *Foreign Affairs* 78 (2): 20–34.

Cohen, Robert (2000) "Tiffs over Bananas and Child Custody." *New York Times*, May 28, Sect. 4, p. 1.

Coker, C. (1998) *Twilight of the West.* Boulder, Colo.: Westview.

Doyle, M. (1986) "Liberalism and World Politics." *American Political Science Review* 80: 1151–1169.

Duffield, J. (1994/95) "NATO's Functions after the Cold War." *Political Science Quarterly* 109 (5): 763–788.

Duffield, J. (1998) *World Power Forsaken: Political Culture, International Institutions, and German Security Policy After Unification.* Stanford, Calif.: Stanford University Press.

Eichengreen, B., ed. (1998) *Transatlantic Economic Relations in the Post-Cold War Era*. New York: Council on Foreign Relations.

Eichengreen, B., and F. Ghironi. (1998) "European Monetary Unification and International Monetary Cooperation." In B. Eichengreen, ed., *Transatlantic Economic Relations in the Post Cold War Era*, 69–98.

Featherstone, K., and R. Ginsberg. (1996) *The United States and the European Union in the 1990s*. New York: St. Martin's.

Geipel, G., and R. Manning. (1996) *Rethinking the Transatlantic Partnership: Security and Economics in a New Era*. Indianapolis, Ind.: Hudson Institute.

Gompert, D., and F. Larrabee, eds. (1997) *America and Europe: A Partnership for a New Era*. New York: Cambridge University Press.

Grieco, J. (1988) "Anarchy and the Limits of Cooperation: A Realist Critique of the Newest Liberal Institutionalism." *International Organization* 42, no. 3 (Summer): 485–507.

Grieco, J. (1990) *Cooperation among Nations: Europe, America, and Non-tariff Barriers to Trade*. Ithaca, N.Y.: Cornell University Press.

Guay, T. (1999) *The United States and the European Union: The Political Economy of a Relationship*. Sheffield, England: Sheffield Academic Press.

Haftendorn, H., and C. Tuschhoff, eds. (1993) *American and Europe in an Era of Change*. Boulder, Colo.: Westview.

Harries, O. (1994) "The Collapse of the West." *Foreign Affairs* 72 (4): 41–53.

Holbrooke, R. (1995) "America, a European Power." *Foreign Affairs* 74 (2): 38–51.

Kaase, M., and A. Kohut. (1996) *Estranged Friends? The Transatlantic Consequences of Societal Change*. New York: Council on Foreign Relations.

Kahler, M. (1995) *Regional Futures and Transatlantic Economic Relations*. New York: Council on Foreign Relations Press.

Kahler, M. (1996) In M. Kahler and W. Link, eds., *Europe and America: A Return to History*, 1–28. "Revision and Prevision: Historical Interpretation and the Future of the Transatlantic Relationship."

Keohane, R. (1980) "The Theory of Hegemonic Stability and Changes in International Economic Regimes, 1967–1977." In O. Holsti, R. Siverson, and A. George, eds., *Change in the International System*, 131–162. Boulder, Colo.: Westview.

Keohane, R. (1984) *After Hegemony: Cooperation and Discord in the World Political Economy*. Princeton, N.J.: Princeton University Press.

Keohane, R., and L. Martin. (1995) "The Promise of Institutionalist Theory." *International Security* 20 (1): 39–51.

Kupchan, C. (1999) "Rethinking Europe." *National Interest* 56: 73–79.

Levy, J. (1994) "Learning and Foreign Policy: Sweeping a Conceptual Minefield." *International Organization* 48: 279–312.

McCalla, R. (1996) "NATO's Persistence after the Cold War." *International Organization* 50: 445–475.

Mearsheimer, J. (1990) "Back to the Future: Instability in Europe After the Cold War." *International Security* 14 (4): 5–56.

Mearsheimer, J. (1994/95) "The False Promise of International Institutions." *International Security* 19 (3): 5–58.

Moravcsik, A. (1997) "Taking Preferences Seriously: A Liberal Theory of International Politics." *International Organization* 51 (4): 513–553.

Morrow, J., R. Siverson, and T. Tabares (1998) "The Political Determinants of International Trade: The Major Powers, 1907–90." *American Political Science Review* 92 (3): 649–661.

Nye, J. (1987) "Nuclear Learning and U.S.-Soviet Security Regimes." *International Organization* 41: 371–402.

Owen, J. (1994) "How Liberalism Produces Democratic Peace." *International Security* 19 (2): 87–125.

Peterson, J. (1993) *Europe and America in the 1990s: The Prospects for Partnership.* Brookfield, Vt.: Edward Elgar.

Peterson, J. (1996) *Europe and America: The Prospects for Partnership.* New York: Routledge.

Reinicke, W. (1996) *Deepening the Atlantic: Toward a New Transatlantic Marketplace?* Gütersloh: Bertelsmann Foundation Publishers.

Risse-Kappen, T. (1995) *Cooperation among Democracies: The European Influence on American Foreign Policy.* Princeton, N.J.: Princeton University Press.

Risse-Kappen, T., ed. (1995) *Bringing Transnational Relations Back In: Non-State Actors, Domestic Structures, and International Institutions.* New York: Cambridge University Press.

Risse-Kappen, T. (1996) "Collective Identity in a Democratic Community: The Case of NATO." In P. Katzenstein, ed., *The Culture of National Security: Norms and Identity in World Politics,* 357–399. New York: Columbia University Press.

Sandholz, W. et al. (1992) *The Highest Stakes: The Economic Foundations of the Next Security System.* New York: Oxford University Press.

Schott, J. (1998) "Whither U.S.-EU Trade Relations?" In B. Eichengreen, ed., *Transatlantic Economic Relations in the Post Cold War Era,* 36–68.

Serfaty, S. (1997) *Stay the Course: European Unity and Atlantic Solidarity.* Westport, Conn.: Praeger.

Thurow, L. (1992) *Head to Head: The Coming Economic Battle Among Japan, Europe, and America.* New York: Morrow.

Ullman, R. H. (1990) Enlarging the Zone of Peace. *Foreign Policy,* no. 80 (Fall): 102–120.

Ullman, R., ed. (1996) *The World and Yugoslavia's Wars.* New York: Council on Foreign Relations.

Walt, S. (1987). *The Origins of Alliances.* Ithaca, N.Y.: Cornell University Press.

Walt, S. (1998). "The Precarious Partnership: America and Europe in a New Era." In C. Kupchan, ed., *Atlantic Security: Contending Visions,* 5–44. New York: Council on Foreign Relations.

Walt, S. (1998/99) "The Ties That Fray: Why Europe and America are Drifting Apart." *The National Interest.* 54:1–11.

Waltz, K. (1979) *Theory of International Politics.* Reading, Mass.: Addison-Wesley.

Weidenfeld, W. (1996) *America and Europe: Is the Break Inevitable?* Gütersloh: Bertelsmann Foundation Publishers.

Wendt, A. (1992) "Anarchy Is What States Make of It: The Social Construction of Power Politics." *International Organization* 46:391–425.

Wendt, A. (1995) "Constructing International Politics." *International Security* 20 (1):71–81.
Wendt, A. (1999) *Social Theory of International Politics.* New York: Cambridge University Press.
Williams, P., P. Hammond, and M. Brenner. (1993) "Atlantis Lost, Paradise Regained? The U.S. and Western Europe after the Cold War." *International Affairs* 69: 1–18.

12

Realism, Liberalism, and German Foreign Policy

Thomas Banchoff

The foreign policy traditions of realism and liberalism are bound up with German experience in two related ways. On the one hand, the history of German foreign policy offers crucial examples of both traditions in practice. Otto von Bismarck's balance of power politics and Konrad Adenauer's embrace of a multilateral, supranational orientation are exemplars of realism's focus on interests and liberalism's attention to the effects of institutions. On the other hand, thinkers in the German tradition from Immanuel Kant through Max Weber and Hans Morgenthau have contributed to the evolution of realism and liberalism as theoretical paradigms. From Kant's *Perpetual Peace* to Morgenthau's *Politics among Nations*, the themes of cooperation and conflict in interstate relations have been a running German concern. The confluence of these analytical and policy streams is no coincidence. Germany's precarious position at Europe's center and disastrous legacy of armed conflict have, in different eras in different ways, confronted both leaders and thinkers with fundamental problems of power and purpose in foreign policy. In no other country, perhaps, have the theory and practice of international relations been so closely intertwined.

These relationships—between realism and liberalism, and between theory and practice—are central to the work of Richard Ullman. As a scholar and a teacher he approaches theory as a tool, not a dogma; as a means to illuminate puzzles, not as an end in itself. Dick combines critical analysis of foreign policy with rich appreciation of its complexity, of the contrasting demands that leaders must address and reconcile, often under time pressure. His work on the Russian civil war, American foreign policy, and post-Cold War Europe portrays leaders confronted with choice amid shifting constellations of material interests and political institutions, realist concerns, and liberal ideals.

This insistence on the complexity, contingency, and moral choice inherent in statecraft has challenged Dick's students to approach international relations theory with an eye to its limits. In the case of postreunification Germany, I argue, it can advance a fuller understanding of international relations in contemporary Europe.

Germany is a crucial case for the versions of realism and liberalism that now dominate international relations theory. The collapse of bipolarity and the emergence of a powerful Germany at Europe's center provoked some realist scholars to predict a foreign policy shift in a more assertive, national direction. Freed from the constraints of the Cold War, they argued, the Federal Republic would formulate and pursue its national interests more assertively (Mearsheimer 1990; Waltz 1993). Other scholars, drawing on the liberal tradition, pointed to the persistence of institutions like NATO and the European Union as a context for German foreign policy, and predicted its continued multilateral, supranational orientation (Anderson and Goodman, 1993; Katzenstein, 1997). As it happened, the complex interplay of interests and institutions during the decade after 1990 confronted German leaders with difficult choices, as they sought to adapt an established foreign policy orientation to new circumstances. Helmut Kohl, Gerhard Schröder, and their governments pursued German interests in military security and economic prosperity, but also remained committed to multilateral cooperation within European institutions. Their postreunification choices, I argue, challenge any stark opposition between realism and liberalism and underscore the importance of historical legacies and particular foreign policy ideas in shaping state action.

The argument proceeds in three parts. The first part describes the most striking aspect of postreunification foreign policy—the strong continuity in its direction across the 1990 divide. The new Germany, though more powerful and more sovereign, embraced a foreign policy orientation strikingly similar to that of its predecessor. Changes in the instruments of foreign policy, particularly the use of armed forces outside the NATO defensive perimeter and a more open recognition of German interests, remained embedded in a continuous pattern of multilateral, supranational orientation. The second section addresses the incapacity of neorealism and neoliberalism, the dominant contemporary versions of both traditions, to make sense of this continuity. Neither structural shifts in the balance of power nor broad institutional continuities, I argue, can adequately explain the post-1990 trajectory of German foreign policy. The third section then brings in the foreign policy ideas articulated and pursued by German leaders themselves. It shows how their embrace of both German material interests and multilateral cooperation, informed by a particular understanding of German history and its implications, cannot be fully understood within either the realist or liberal traditions.

EMBEDDED CONTINUITY:
THE PURSUIT OF INTERESTS WITHIN INSTITUTIONS

That postreunification foreign policy was marked by a high degree of continuity is not self-evident. The years after 1990 saw significant changes. The first and most obvious concerned the use of armed forces. The gradual German embrace of a military role outside NATO's defensive perimeter marked a break with a four-decade precedent. In 1995, Kohl's government lent its support to the alliance's air campaign over Bosnia, and participated in the subsequent NATO peacekeeping force. In the context of the 1999 Kosovo crisis, Schröder's government participated more actively—in the air campaign against Serbia and the multinational forces brought in to enforce the subsequent peace accord. This activity represented an important shift at the level of foreign policy instruments. At the same time, however, it can be situated within a broader pattern of continuity: the more active military role served to preserve alliance unity under new circumstances. Its genesis can be traced back to Western criticism of German nonparticipation in the Gulf War. Before the collapse of the Soviet threat, when German forces contributed decisively to overall Western security in Central Europe, external pressure for an out-of-area role had been all but nonexistent. In the absence that threat, the German contribution to Western security evolved in new directions after 1990. Adaptation served to preserve the strong Western orientation of previous decades in a changing context.

During the immediate postreunification period, this continued emphasis on solidarity with the West was not a foregone conclusion. The ardent German-Soviet bilateralism during and immediately after reunification raised some concern in Western capitals. Cooperation between Bonn and Moscow, which culminated in a far-reaching friendship treaty in November 1990, appeared to many to augur a more independent *Ostpolitik*. The treaty marked the end of a year of intense negotiations on reunification that reached its peak during the July 1990 Kohl-Gorbachev summit in the Caucasus. At that meeting, Gorbachev agreed to the core component of a broader East-West settlement: reunification within NATO in return for Kohl's pledge to limit German armed forces and provide financial support for the Soviet opening to the West. As it happened, German-Soviet bilateralism in 1990 did not lead to any loosening of German ties with the West. Gorbachev's fall and the collapse of the Soviet Union made ties with Moscow less of a foreign policy priority. In subsequent years, Kohl was careful to place his policy toward Russia squarely within a solid multilateral Western framework. And Schröder, in his dealings with Boris Yeltsin and Vladimir Putin, followed the same pattern.

A second, more significant apparent exception to the strong German emphasis on Western unity was the German decision to recognize Croatia and Slovenia in December 1991 (Crawford, 1996). During the second half of that year, Kohl and Foreign Minister Hans-Dietrich Genscher lobbied hard within the EU for the extension of diplomatic recognition to both former Yugoslav republics. But when Britain and France, fearful of an escalation of the Balkan civil war, demurred, the German government announced its intention to go ahead unilaterally. Under pressure, Paris and London agreed to follow Bonn's lead. The form of multilateralism was maintained, but a more assertive German *Ostpolitik* within the EU framework strained ties with key allies in the process. In the end, the controversy did not signal a shift toward a more independent German policy. Over the years that followed, Kohl followed the French, British, and U.S. lead in the Balkan crisis, abjuring further initiatives. Solidarity with the West remained the leitmotif of German foreign policy. Schröder's decision to participate actively in NATO's Kosovo policy marked a continuation of this pattern. Both leaders were also careful, in the years after 1993, to follow the U.S. lead on the issue of NATO expansion. They underscored its importance for German security, but were careful not to get ahead of their allies on the issue.

In the years after 1991, the German emphasis on solidarity with the West was not only apparent in security policy, relations with Moscow, and the war in former Yugoslavia. It also informed the German approach to two increasingly important, intertwined components of European policy: the deepening and widening of the EU (Deubner, 1995; Gardner Feldman, 1994). The centerpiece of the deepening program, agreed upon at the December 1991 Maastricht summit, was the proposed introduction of a single European currency by the end of the century. Kohl's ongoing support for economic and monetary union (EMU), a project with roots in the prereunification period, evidenced his strong pro-Western orientation amid changed circumstances. Despite the periodic objections of the Bundesbank, the opposition of much of German public opinion, and the painful fiscal austerity imposed by the Maastricht convergence criteria, Kohl remained an ardent supporter of the deepening project (Bulmer and Paterson, 1996). Both he and Schröder, wrestling with economic problems in the wake of reunification, sought to limit German contributions to EU coffers. But Kohl was careful not to let more attention to material interests disrupt good political ties with Germany's European allies, and France in particular. And Schröder, who had expressed periodic skepticism of EMU in the mid-1990s, threw his unequivocal support behind the project during his successful run for the chancellorship. And, once elected, he softened his stance on EU budget contributions.

Kohl's commitment to Western solidarity was not only clear in his continued support for deeper integration; it was also evident in his cautious approach to the question of widening the EU eastward. In the wake of the collapse of the Soviet bloc, Kohl continually reiterated the importance of integrating former communist states into Western institutions. His early support for widening peaked in 1993, when the German government appeared to make the creation of a "zone of stability" in Central and Europe—particularly Poland, Hungary, and the Czech Republic—a top foreign policy priority. In 1994–1995, however, partly in response to French concerns about the possible negative effects of widening on deepening—and about an eastward shift in the EU's center of gravity—Kohl tempered his enthusiasm for a rapid expansion eastward. During the German presidency of the European Council in late 1994, for example, he did not press for a timetable for expansion. And he subsequently agreed that detailed discussions of widening should only take place after the Intergovernmental Conference of 1996–1997. Both before and after taking office, Schröder was similarly cautious about pressing for EU expansion, although his motivations were apparently more economic and political than strategic—concern about the costs and a possible backlash among German voters.

The overall pattern of German foreign policy in Europe through the mid-1990s, then, was one of continuity amid change. Despite the political earthquake of 1989–1991—the collapse of the Warsaw Pact, reunification, and the dissolution of the Soviet Union—German foreign policy remained very focused on the West. Strong transatlantic bonds and Franco-German solidarity persisted as core themes; new policy challenges in the East, while important, commanded relatively less attention. Germany had more than its allies to gain through economic, political, and security stability in Central and Eastern Europe—and more to lose through instability. And German leaders frankly acknowledged the country's interests in the region. Still, both Kohl and Schröder continued to make *Ostpolitik* clearly subordinate to *Westpolitik*. Kohl's engagement in the East went only as far as unity with the West would allow—a pattern that can be traced back to the earliest years of his chancellorship. And once in office, Schröder continued the same manner. He and his cabinet were more forthright in articulating and pursuing German interests within Atlantic and European institutions. But like Kohl before them, they refused to adopt a more assertive, national orientation.

NEOREALISM, NEOLIBERALISM, AND
POSTREUNIFICATION GERMAN FOREIGN POLICY

What explains this striking overall continuity in German policy across the 1990 divide? Contemporary versions of the realist and liberal traditions, taken in isolation, provide inadequate accounts (Baldwin, 1993). Each points to salient constraints on Germany after reunification—the balance of power and the institutional constellation. But both fail to capture the complexity of the post-1990 constellation and the new trade-offs and opportunities facing German leaders.

Neorealist approaches to foreign policy begin with the distribution of material resources at the international level (Waltz, 1979; Keohane, 1986). They envisage state conduct as a rational response to international structure, to the constraints posed by the constellation of economic and military capabilities at any particular juncture. Neorealist analyses can diverge along several important dimensions: the relative importance of military and economic security concerns, of maximizing and satisfying calculations, and of absolute and relative gains. But whatever their differences, neorealists of different persuasions concur that shifts in the distribution of material power engender shifts in patterns of international politics. The constellation of economic and military capabilities creates a baseline constraint for foreign policy decisions.

The case of post-1990 Germany presents a challenge for neorealism. Shifts in the balance of power might have been expected to drive a shift in German foreign policy. The end of the Cold War and reunification produced a clear increase in absolute and relative German power. The addition of East German resources widened the economic distance between the Federal Republic and its two main EU partners, France and Britain. The Federal Republic moved to fill the power vacuum left by the Soviet retreat from Eastern Europe. And the decline in U.S. power on the continent increased Germany's relative influence within the Atlantic Alliance. An emphasis on shifts in the distribution of material power led John Mearsheimer, for example, to entertain the possibility that the new Germany might break with its strong Western orientation and pursue economic, political, and even military hegemony in Europe (Mearsheimer, 1990). Clearly, such a perspective cannot account for the fact that the new Germany continued to make Western solidarity its top priority after 1990, forswearing national ambitions outside a multilateral framework—not to mention a drive for European hegemony.

A neorealist perspective more attuned to the ongoing limits on German military and economic power can better account for the pattern of foreign policy continuity. While reunification saw German power increase in absolute terms, the Federal Republic's economic and military resources remained dwarfed by those of France and Britain combined. Moreover, even after the collapse of bipolarity, the FRG remained dependent on the U.S. nuclear and conventional deterrent against a possible revival of the Russian threat. This more nuanced neorealist stance, articulated by Kenneth Waltz, would predict the embrace of a more independent, assertive foreign policy—and perhaps even German access to nuclear weapons—in the medium term or long term. It, too, has problems accounting for developments in the 1990s. On the whole, German power certainly increased over the decade. German leaders may not have been in a position to strike out on their own and assert hegemony in Europe. But they could have pressed their interests in the East more actively within a Western multilateral framework. They could have placed less overall emphasis on association with the West and more emphasis on engagement in the East, for example in making the expansion of the EU eastward a priority over its deepening. A focus on changes in the balance of power cannot explain why they did not.

Neoliberal approaches to foreign policy place international institutions at the center of their analysis (Keohane and Martin, 1995). They tend to view foreign policy through the lens of norms and rules embedded in institutions such as alliances and trade regimes. Neoliberals do not ignore the importance of the material context; they acknowledge the centrality of economic and military capabilities as a baseline constraint for foreign policy calculations. But they perceive competition for wealth and power to be mediated by international institutions designed to limit conflict and promote cooperation. Neoliberals, like their realist cousins, disagree with one another along a number of important dimensions: the relative autonomy of institutions from the states that constitute them, the relationship between international norms and national interests, and the sources of institutional change. But they tend to concur that institutions are not just an effect but also a cause of broad trends in international politics.

Viewed from one angle, the case of post-1990 German foreign policy challenges the neoliberal perspective. Changes in international institutions might have been expected to drive a change in German foreign policy orientation. The collapse of Eastern institutions—the Warsaw Pact and Comecon—transformed the context of German foreign policy. Flux in Western institutions had a similar effect. NATO, long designed primarily to defend Western Europe against the Soviet threat, stumbled to redefine its role. And the European Union, faced with the twin challenges of economic and monetary union, on the one hand, and eastward expansion, on the other, faced an uncertain future. Viewed in this light, an unstable institutional constellation constrained the new Germany less effectively than it had its predecessor. The FRG was in a position to pursue its national interests more forcefully within a more fluid institutional framework. The fact that it did not—that German foreign policy was marked by broad continuity—cannot be fully explained from this institutional perspective.

The neoliberal perspective fares better if one emphasizes similarities between the pre-and post-1990 institutional constellations in Europe. The Atlantic Alliance and the European Union, their dynamics altered by the collapse of bipolarity, nevertheless continued to form the context for German policy (Anderson and Goodman, 1993). Reunification took place in NATO, a sine qua non for the assent of the United States, France, and Britain. And the drive for EMU had its roots in the late 1980s. Institutional continuity produced foreign policy continuity. But this more nuanced neoliberal argument, too, is not fully persuasive. While attention to the resilience of Western institutions can explain the absence of a German break with multilateralism, it cannot account for the reluctance to press particular interests in the East within those institutions more assertively. Nor can it explain the German willingness to participate in military operations, a new posture not prescribed by institutions themselves. Given this institutional ambiguity, German leaders confronted a significant degree of choice. A neoliberal approach cannot explain the choice made: a continued focus on the priority of deepening existing institutions in the West.

Both structural perspectives, the neorealist and the neoliberal, offer explanations of post-1990 continuity that are plausible in many respects. But neither is adequate. Structure can always be invoked as an ex post facto explanation for action: By definition, actions are compatible with the structure within which they take place. However, a focus on structure alone can obscure the existence of alternative courses of action in a given situation. There is often more than one way to pursue material interests in security and prosperity. And institutional norms will often permit more than one policy alternative. In the postreunification case, German leaders could have made interests in the East a higher priority and pressed more actively within Western institutions for their realization. An adequate explanation of postreunification German foreign policy must also address the contingent choices of German leaders in their historical and political context.

INTERESTS, IDEALS, AND THE WEIGHT OF HISTORY

Structural approaches to the problem of German foreign policy continuity are less flawed than they are incomplete. They neglect an important part of the explanatory puzzle: the historically informed priorities articulated and pursued by German leaders, and the domestic political constellations that underpinned them. Through the mid-1990s, Kohl faced an international constellation that allowed for choice. At the same time, he enjoyed a secure position atop the Christian Democratic Union (CDU) and in the office of the chancellor, that reinforced his freedom of action. The foreign ministry, first under Genscher and then, after 1992, under Klaus Kinkel, was in the hands of the Free Democratic Party (FDP). But Kohl's constitutional right to set policy guidelines and his considerable prestige as the "chancellor of German unity" gave him leverage to shape the direction of postreunification foreign policy. After 1998, Schröder had similar advantages: the authority to set the course of policy, and the support of a loyal coalition partner, Foreign Minister Joschka Fischer of the Greens. But the domestic political foundations of his foreign policy were much less secure. The left wing of the SPD and the fundamentalist wing of the Greens had opposed Kohl's gradual embrace of a more active security policy. And neither party had a pro-European tradition as strong as that of the CDU.

The major policy statements by Kohl, Schröder, and other government officials reveal a pragmatic stance that combined attention to interests and ideals against a historical backdrop. There was a broad recognition that German power had grown, and that the Federal Republic should pursue interests in economic prosperity and military security amid new circumstances.

But there was also a conviction that multilateral and supranational institutions should continue to bound the pursuit of those interests. Ultimately, for Kohl, Schröder, and their governments, German interests and those of its allies were inseparable; an independent German *national* interest did not exist within an emergent European Union. For Timothy Garton Ash and other critical observers, the invocation of "Europe" and international institutions represented a sort of veil for the pursuit of specifically German interests, a disturbing legacy of the German idealist tradition (Garton Ash, 1994). An analysis of German foreign policy statements against the backdrop of German foreign policy practice supports a more benign interpretation—that the lack of any analytical distinction between interests and ideals was a rational response both to the lessons of German history and to the post-1990 European constellation (Banchoff, 1999).

Kohl justified his strong commitment to multilateralism within NATO as consonant with German interests and as an expression of alliance solidarity. During the mid-1990s, he acknowledged that the new Germany, given its geography, had particular interest in the expansion of NATO eastward. But he insisted on the importance of following the U.S. lead. There were, of course, balance of power reasons for doing so. The Federal Republic remained ultimately dependent on the American nuclear deterrent. But Kohl couched his priorities in political terms. He construed the alliance not simply as a military organization, but as a grouping of democratic nations bound by mutual trust. In the January 1994 Bundestag Debate on the Partnership for Peace initiative, he noted German support for eventual eastward expansion, but added that "international trust in the reliability and dependability of German foreign policy" constituted "important capital" for present and future German foreign policy. Placing alliance unity first, and the preservation of trust, made sense for historical reasons. From Kohl's perspective, the "historical success of the alliance" in ending the Cold War and bringing about reunification "rested on strong security ties between North America and Europe." Therefore, for Kohl, NATO remained in Germany's "existential interest"(13 January 1994).

The same fusion of interests and ideals in Kohl's thinking was evident in his gradual embrace of a more active military security policy. Around the time of reunification, Kohl repeatedly asserted that German foreign policy was and remained "a policy of peace" (November 15, 1990). Subsequent FRG participation in out-of-area operations was not, from his perspective, an example of an economic and political power now becoming a military one. In his November 1994 government declaration, Kohl insisted a more active role had nothing to do with any militarization of German foreign policy (24 November 1994). Clear military security interests were indeed in play in the Balkans. Germany had a strong interest in the peaceful resolution of conflict in former Yugoslavia, and Kohl admitted as much. But participation in joint operations was, in his view, first and foremost a means of maintaining the unity of the Western alliance, and avoiding German isolation within it. NATO should be preserved as a multilateral framework for the pursuit of German security interests, and Germany should therefore leave the policy lead to others. From Kohl's perspective, this reticence represented neither free-riding nor a psychological aversion to the use of force, but rather an imperative response to the lessons of German history. As he put it in the context of the escalating conflict in Bosnia in January 1994, "We Germans in particular" should "be careful about giving advice to others" (13 January 1994).

On balance, the security rhetoric of Schröder and Fischer during their first year in office marked a slight shift in the direction of a more national, less multilateral orientation. Ironically, the Green foreign minister was more inclined to view the international constellation through a balance of power lens. On the occasion of NATO's fiftieth anniversary, he spoke of a "contradiction" (*Widerspruch*) between Germany's Atlantic and European interests that needed to be addressed in the future, a formulation unthinkable for Kohl or Genscher (22 April 1999). But in the same address, he argued that the United States should stay in Europe, and that there were "shared interests" in doing so. At a security policy conference in Munich two months earlier, he had portrayed Europe on the verge of becoming a "political subject" in its own right. But he had also stressed the importance of U.S. presence, and of its "congruent" interests with Europe. As with Kohl, the focus on common interests rested not just on straightforward calculations, but on shared democratic norms and a shared history. He echoed Kohl's argument about the importance of strong U.S.-European ties in view of the disastrous course of twentieth-century history (6 February 1999).

Schröder's approach to the Kosovo crisis also marked a slight shift of focus from Kohl's—away from an Atlantic toward a more European orientation. At the same Munich security conference, he noted that Europe would be willing to assume greater "political and military responsibility" where "European interests" are at stake (6 February 1999). And he subsequently surprised observers by coming forward with a European proposal for a ceasefire in Kosovo. At the same time, however, like Kohl, Schröder conceived of German interests within the context of the Atlantic alliance and of broader historical experience. In a Bundestag address of April 1999, he argued that "against the backdrop of German history, there must not be any doubt about our reliability, determination, and steadfastness." He continued: "Germany's integration into the community of Western states is part of German reason of state. We do not want a German *Sonderweg*" (15 April 1999). Fischer, who struggled successfully to maintain his party's support for German military deployments, continued to articulate a more European perspective. Kosovo, he argued, was about how Europeans could bring their "political interests to bear." And a failure to stop aggression in Europe, he contended, threatened the future of the integration process, the "greatest achievement of modern European history" (21 July 1999).

This tendency of postreunification governments to justify a continued strong Western orientation in terms of European or Western, as opposed to exclusively German interests, was also evident in the context of the European integration. More than in the security sphere, Kohl and Schröder were likely to acknowledge the existence of specifically German interests. In May 1994, for example, Kohl reminded the Bundestag that "Germans secure great economic advantages from the European Union. With respect to the existing Twelve, one can say, the greatest" (31 May 1994). Earlier that year, he also acknowledged that the Federal Republic had "its own vital German interests" in the expansion of the EU eastward, and that it was "unimaginable that the German-Polish border should remain the eastern border of the European Political Union" (13 January 1994). But in pressing for monetary and political union, and making them a priority over EU expansion eastward, Kohl more often invoked arguments about institutions and ideals: the importance of political union for cooperation within established European institutions, and of EMU for making military conflict unimaginable. His rhetoric made no clear distinction between German and European interests. German support for Maastricht, he told the Bundestag in December 1991, was "proof" that a united Germany "remains committed to what we have always said, namely that German unity and European Unity are two sides of the same coin" (13 December 1991).

Schröder and Fischer were also more comfortable with the language of interests in the context of European integration. In the wake of difficult budget negotiations in April 1999, for example, the chancellor insisted on the imperative to "subordinate national interests to a reasonable overall solution." In the same Bundestag address, he contrasted "individual interests" with "shared responsibility," but also referred to "national and European interests," as if the two were inseparable—a formulation similar to Kohl's (14 April 1999). In another address the previous month, Fischer made a similar distinction between two kinds of national interest, the "shortsighted" version, and one compatible with "European unity" (26 March 1999). As this use of key terms makes clear, the greater use of the word "national" did not represent a reorientation of German foreign policy in a realist direction. Not only did Schröder and Fischer consider national interests inseparable from European ones. They also echoed Kohl's claims that German support for European integration was also sharp break with a destructive historical legacy. As Fischer put it before the European Parliament in July 1999, European integration was ultimately about "building a European Peace Order on the continent" (21 July 1999).

In a September 1999 address to the German Foreign Policy Association (DGAP), Schröder squarely addressed the question of a reorientation of FRG foreign policy. He said he "could not really understand" why his government was sometimes accused of placing too much emphasis on 'German interests,'" and continued:

Foreign policy is interest politics (*Interessenpolitik*). Any foreign policy that claimed not to be pursuing interests would be the purest hypocrisy. Like all our neighbors, the Germans also have national interests. The critical point is how one defines interests, and how one pursues them. The latter point is particularly important, because in an age of globalization, no one can be successful with a strictly national policy.

German foreign policy should therefore be a policy of "enlightened self-interest," Schröder continued. It should be openly articulated and clearly formulated. But "national interests should be coordinated with those of our friends, in order to be able to represent common positions." Germany's interests existed, but could not be conceptualized in isolation from the interests of its partners. Atlantic and European institutions represented the starting point for their pursuit. As with Kohl, this insistence reflected not only a recognition of the institutional web within which Germany was enmeshed. It was also consonant with a particular view of German history and its implications:

> I understand German foreign policy today as policy in and with Europe. That is the responsibility (*Auftrag*) from history, but also obligation for the present and the future. The time of the German *Sonderweg* and its disastrous consequences is thankfully and finally over with. (2 September 1999)

This analysis of official justifications for German foreign policy suggests the inseparability of interests and institutions in the conceptualization and conduct of German foreign policy. Clearly foreign policy does not simply spring from the heads of leaders. It represents responses to international problems mediated by countless political pressures at the level of bureaucracies, parties, interest groups, and public opinion. But ideas about foreign policy—when articulated by different rivals for national leadership—can frame the terms of the political struggle and shape the broad outlines of policy. Such ideas are, of course, closely related to the constraints posed by the international system—to what is possible. But constraints often leave room for choice, as they did in Germany after 1990. Greater attention to German interests, embedded within a continued emphasis on Western solidarity, represented an adaptation of an established multilateral, supranational orientation to new circumstances. The insistence of Kohl and Schröder on the inseparability of interests and institutions was not hypocrisy; it constituted a successful foreign policy formula in practice. A focus only on institutions would have undermined German prosperity and security, while a much greater emphasis on interests would have generated historically charged mistrust. A sometimes untidy mix of self-interest and ideals, difficult to capture within overarching theoretical frameworks, served the Federal Republic well.

CONCLUSION

Dick Ullman was among the first scholars to acknowledge the enduring postwar transformation of German foreign policy. His 1991 book, *Securing Europe*, emphasizes the Federal Republic's ongoing commitment to the territorial status quo, and to a multilateral, supranational foreign policy. While realists at the time were predicting that the new, more powerful Germany might again pose a threat to its neighbors, he envisioned the new Federal Republic instead as a foundation for a more secure Europe in the years ahead. His optimism has proved justified. Germany has been an active partner in efforts to reform NATO and extend it eastward. And it has sought to bring Central and Eastern Europe closer to the political and economic institutions of the European Union. While the German role in Europe continues to develop, and the precise mixture of national interests and international institutions in its foreign policy will change from one context to the next, the overall pattern is one of continuity with the multilateral, supranational foreign policy of the postwar decades. German leaders have proven able to exercise their greater national power within established European institutions.

The record of postreunification German foreign policy, I have argued, underscores the limitations of the two leading theories of international relations, neorealism and neoliberalism. But it also suggests the continued relevance of the traditions within which they are embedded. Neither contemporary approach can provide an adequate explanation of postreunification foreign policy on its own. This has to do with their focus on structural constraints and neglect of the element of choice. But it may also be a function of their analytical insistence on the clear separation of interests, on the one hand, and institutions on the other. In foreign policy practice, leaders have always had to combine the pursuit of power and wealth with attention to norms and rules—in different ways. In today's Europe, with its thick set of overlapping multilateral and supranational institutions, both sets of calculations are more inseparable than ever. Realism and liberalism are closely intertwined in practice, and not just for Germany. In analytical terms, this suggests the continued relevance of realist theorizing more attentive to the contingency and choice facing national leaders. But it also suggests that, at least in the case of Germany, the institutions highlighted by liberalism now form a starting point for calculations of interest in Europe.

BIBLIOGRAPHY

Anderson, Jeffrey, and John B. Goodman. (1993) "Mars or Minerva: A United Germany in a Post-Cold War Europe." In Robert O. Keohane and Stanley Hoffmann, eds. *After the Cold War: International Institutions and State Strategies in Europe, 1989–1991.*Cambridge, Mass.: Harvard University Press.

282 *Chapter 12*

Banchoff, Thomas. (1999) *The German Problem Transformed: Institutions, Politics, and Foreign Policy, 1945–1995.* Ann Arbor: University of Michigan Press.

Baldwin, David A., ed. (1993) *Neorealism and Neoliberalism. The Contemporary Debate.* New York: Columbia University Press.

Bulmer, Simon, and William E. Paterson. (1996) "Germany in the European Union: Gentle Giant or Emergent Leader?" *International Affairs* 72, no. 1: 9–32.

Crawford, Beverly. (1996) "Germany's Unilateral Recognition of Croatia and Slovenia: A Case of Defection from Multilateral Cooperation." *World Politics* 48, no. 4: 482–521.

Deubner, Christian. (1995) *Von Maastricht zu Kerneuropa.* Baden-Baden: Nomos Verlag.

Fischer, Joschka [All Web sites were accessed April 30, 2001.]

———. 6 February 1999, Address at Munich Security Conference, http://www.auswaertiges amt.de/

———. 26 March 1999, *Verhandlungen des deutschen Bundestages,* series 14, and

———. 22 April 1999, *Verhandlungen des deutschen Bundestages,* series 14, [both http://dip.bundestag.de/]

———. 21 July 1999, Address before the European Parliament, http://www.auswaertiges amt.de/

Gardner Feldman, Lily. (1994) "Germany and the EC: Realism and Responsibility." *Annals of the American Association of Political Science,* No. 531: 25–43.

Garton Ash, Timothy. (1994) *In Europe's Name: Germany and the Divided Continent.* New York: Random House.

Katzenstein, Peter, ed. (1997) *Tamed Power. Germany in Europe.* Ithaca: Cornell University Press.

Keohane, Robert O., and Lisa L. Martin. (1995) "The Promise of Institutionalist Theory." *International Security* 20, No. 1: 39–51.

Keohane, Robert O., ed. (1986) *Neorealism and its Critics.* New York: Columbia University Press.

Keohane, Robert O. (1984) *After Hegemony. Cooperation and Discord in the World Political Economy.* Princeton, N.J.: Princeton University Press.

Kohl, Helmut [Web site: http://dip.bundestag.de/, accessed April 30, 2001]

———. 15 November 1990, *Verhandlungen des deutschen Bundestages,* series 12

———. 13 December 1991, *Verhandlungen des deutschen Bundestages,* series 12

———. 13 January 1994, *Verhandlungen des deutschen Bundestages,* series 12

———. 31 May 1994, *Verhandlungen des deutschen Bundestages,* series 12

———. 24 November 1994, *Verhandlungen des deutschen Bundestages,* series 13

Mearsheimer, John J. (1990) "Back to the Future: Instability in Europe after the Cold War." *International Security* 15, No. 1: 5–56.

Schröder, Gerhard [All Web sites accessed on April 30, 2001]

———. 15 April 1999, *Verhandlungen des deutschen Bundestages,* series 14, http://www.bundesregierung.de/frameset/index.jsp

———. 2 September 1999, Address at German Foreign Policy Association, http://dgap.org/

Waltz, Kenneth N. (1993) "The Emerging Structure of International Politics." *International Security* 18, No. 2: 44–79.

Waltz, Kenneth. (1979) *Theory of International Politics.* New York: Addison-Wesley.

13

Strategic Competition among China, Japan, and Taiwan

David B. H. Denoon

The rise of China and the problems it poses have been the central issue for most strategists and Asia specialists in the past five years.[1] The focus on China's capabilities and intentions is understandable given the rapid growth of its economy, the number of border disputes Beijing has with its neighbors, and China's long history of grievances toward the West. Also, given the preeminent position of the United States in global military and economic affairs, it is not surprising that assessing U.S.-China relations has become a central issue for American foreign policy specialists as well.[2]

Nevertheless, this focus on China has led many observers to pay insufficient attention to a related but distinct development in East Asia: the emergence of a three-way competition between China, Japan, and Taiwan. The intent of this chapter is to demonstrate that the emerging triangular interaction between China, Japan, and Taiwan is more dynamic and prone to change than the U.S.-China relationship. Hence, though observers need to keep a close eye on the Washington-Beijing barometer, they may be better able to understand future strategic developments in East Asia if they can identify trends in Beijing-Tokyo-Taipei relations.

CHANGING SECURITY PERSPECTIVES IN EAST ASIA

In the 1972–1989 period there was a remarkably stable strategic equilibrium in East Asia. The U.S. opening to China and the Shanghai Communique had forced policy makers in Moscow to recognize that preemptory action in the region could lead to the United States and China cooperating militarily. China was still going through the final pangs of the Cultural Revolution and the political transition after Mao Zedong's death, so it had little incentive to precipitate change. The Japanese were concentrating on economic performance and were happy with the status quo. Until 1986, Taiwan had authoritarian leaders who perpetuated the myth that they might eventually reconquer the Chinese mainland; thus, they suppressed any sentiment for Taiwan's independence and supported a one-China policy. The United States was still trying to recoup from the embarrassment of the debacle in Vietnam and was more concerned with maintaining good working relationships in South Korea and Japan than in taking on any new Asian ventures.

A key turning point was the period 1989–1990, however, because the decline of Soviet power and the disintegration of the Soviet Union took away the rationale for the U.S.-China entente. China was no longer threatened on its northern border, and the United States no longer worried about the expansion of Soviet power in Asia. The Tiananmen Square incident in June 1990 further strained U.S.-China relations because it revealed, very publicly, the harsh behavior of China's rulers.

By the mid-1990s, the strategic picture in East Asia had been significantly transformed. Democratization in Taiwan had led to a growing interest in greater autonomy, if not independence, from China. Beijing had responded with increasing shows of force, notably testing missiles off the Taiwan coast during 1995 and 1996 in the months before the Taiwan presidential elections. The Japanese public became alarmed by these new signs of assertiveness on China's part, and that made it far easier for Japanese politicians to support closer defense cooperation with the United States.[3] China's behavior, in combination with the North Korean test of a medium-range Taepodong II missile through Japanese airspace, led the Obuchi government to proceed with research and development expenditures for Theater Missile Defense (TMD).[4]

Taiwan, which was initially intimidated by the Chinese missile firings in 1995 and 1996, regained its confidence and most of the residents concluded that China was not ready to invade. This emboldened President Lee Teng-hui to raise Taiwan's international profile; and, in July 1999, he took the carefully calculated step of asserting that relations between China and Taiwan should be "state to state" relations. This infuriated the leadership in Beijing, which has long maintained that Taiwan is merely a province of China. However, other than massing mobile missiles in Fujian Province (opposite the Taiwan coast) and cutting off planned diplomatic discussions with Taiwan, China made a relatively muted response.

The only non-Asian power capable of changing the balance in the region is the United States; but, for the foreseeable future, the United States is a status quo power, in most regards content with the current economic and security arrangements. Some Americans are deeply concerned with the soaring trade imbalances that continue with every major country in East Asia, while others are more focused on human rights abuses. Yet, there is only limited

American sentiment for a major reduction of commitments in the region and most of the debates in Washington on Asia policy center on modest adjustments in goals and tactics. Overall, the United States is seen as satisfied with its role in East Asia, not willing to be displaced, but not seeking new or expanded obligations either. Hence, mainstream administrations, whether Democrat or Republican, are likely to keep the primary links with Japan and South Korea, maintain ties in the Association of Southeast Asian Nations (ASEAN), and attempt to channel China's behavior in cooperative directions.

The question then becomes: How much room for maneuver do the principal players inside the region have? This is the main issue we explore in this chapter. The Chinese are clearly dissatisfied with their current role in the region—being subordinate to the United States—and have gone to considerable effort to expand both their military and diplomatic options.[5] In turn, Chinese restiveness has led Japan to expand its diplomatic initiatives, first courting the Russians and then patching up old rifts with the South Koreans.[6] With the leadership on Taiwan also dissatisfied, one can then anticipate different alignments and various efforts at testing how stable the current strategic balance actually is.

Thus we assess if a new pattern of strategic competition is developing; and, if so, how it is affecting the character of interaction in the region. For our purposes, strategic competition is defined as conscious moves by states to use political, military, economic, and cultural ties to promote their long-term interests over those of their neighbors in a manner that stresses relative gains in power and influence, rather than joint gains and cooperative activity.

The central argument of this chapter is:

1) Relations *within* Asia are now more likely to determine the future dynamics of politics in the region than the behavior of external actors.
2) The linchpin of future East Asian relations will be the pattern of interaction among China, Japan, and Taiwan.
3) In the period 1972–1989 there was a stable equilibrium in the triangular relationship among China, Japan, and Taiwan. None of the three needed an alliance with any of the others and all had internal reasons for preferring the status quo.
4) In the 1990s both China and Taiwan would like changes; and, though Japan still prefers the status quo, there are situations under which two of the three parties may form linkages. This situation creates uncertainty and potential instability in the triangular interaction.

To evaluate this argument, we look first at the strategic and sociopolitical environment East Asia faces and then turn to a detailed evaluation of how the three-way competition and interaction among China, Japan, and Taiwan may develop.

THEORETICAL APPROACHES TO
EXPLAINING EAST ASIAN COMPETITION

There have been three principal schools of thought dominant in the literature on East Asian security: the realist, liberal internationalist, and what will
be called here the historical uniqueness school. Each of these approaches
has been highly developed, has important contributions to make in explaining behavior, and yields clusters of propositions that provide a guide to future trends in East Asia.[7] Our purpose here is to summarize the salient features of these schools, point out their differences, and then comment on the
extent to which they can provide insight into the likely competition among
China, Japan, and Taiwan.

The realist literature on East Asia is extensive. It starts from familiar assumptions: that states place the highest premium on ensuring security, they
expect their neighbors to coerce or co-opt them if there is no outside pro-
tector, and international relations are, ultimately, about competition and
dominance. With this approach, realists then look at the current situation in
East Asia and generally conclude that China is the central player inside the
region. By weighting traditional measures of power potential (size and
growth rate of the economy, population, geographic size, and extent of military forces), China is, unquestionably, a looming presence.[8] In addition, Beijing's willingness to use force against Vietnam in 1979 and in the Spratly Islands in the 1980s and 1990s makes China feared by all its neighbors.

This has led most realists to conclude that there are two plausible directions in which strategic alignments in Asia could move: either (1) toward alliances that seek to *balance* against Chinese power or (2) toward various
types of cooperation with Beijing, *bandwagoning*, where neighboring states
preserve their formal autonomy but agree to cooperate with and take their
lead from China.[9] If Washington was fully committed to balancing against
Beijing, the United States has the economic resources and military prowess
to do so. However, many of the East Asian states realize that they would pay
a future price if they joined an effort to contain China and subsequently
found the United States exiting the region or unwilling to bear the burden of
continuously balancing China.

Thus, many realists think that bandwagoning is the likely outcome. Here
there is an interesting split among realists: most think that an Asia conciliat-
ing Beijing is deeply inimical to U.S. interests,[10] but a small minority see
China as inherently a land power with little likelihood of projecting military
force beyond its direct borders.[11] This split among realists leads some to conclude that China's strategic clout is being overstated,[12] while others are
deeply concerned that the United States and its allies are selling technology
that will come back to haunt American forces.[13] Hence, on balance, we see
realists deeply concerned about the rise of Chinese power and the likelihood

that neighboring Asian states will accommodate to Beijing, leading to a reduction or expulsion of U.S. influence in the region.

Liberal internationalists have looked at recent developments in East Asia in a very different perspective.[14] In general, they are optimistic that increased economic and cultural interaction will reduce tensions between states and think that links between businesses and nongovernmental organizations will form a set of bonds that further mitigate the chances of conflict.[15] Clearly there are important differences among liberal internationalists: some stress the power of economic ties, while others emphasize the importance of culture and ideas as a means to reduce tension.[16]

Yet, despite their differences in emphasis, liberal internationalists broadly support policies and programs that encourage states to conform with international norms (like trade and human rights conventions) and policies that will encourage greater trade and economic interaction (like lowering tariff barriers). Thus, liberal internationalists have urged that the United States and China's neighbors make various offers that would induce Beijing to behave in a cooperative manner. Since 1994, when the Clinton administration dropped its intense focus on human rights, Washington has sent a dual message to Beijing by openly encouraging "engagement" and a "strategic partnership" yet, at the same time, building up military links with Japan, Taiwan, and South Korea. So, both realists and liberal internationalists could see elements of their preferred approaches in Clinton policies. In its early months, the Bush administration has been preoccupied with recovering the aircraft and the crew after a U.S. reconnaissance plane collided with a Chinese jet fighter off Hainan Island. This has heightened tensions between the United States and China and delayed the enunciation of more detailed aspects of the Bush administration's China policy.

Many Asia specialists are unhappy with both realism and liberal internationalism; so for lack of a better term, we will cluster their views under the banner of historical uniqueness. A long-standing tradition in China studies is to emphasize the intense humiliation that Chinese felt during the period of Western domination. Believing that their civilization was the center of the universe and, in fact, being far ahead of Western Europe technologically until the 1600s, it is not surprising that most Chinese resented their treatment at the hands of Western businessmen and governmental representatives.[17] Some in this school emphasize that much of the difficulty in dealing with the West was self-imposed because many Chinese didn't master the functioning of the Western state system: in essence, "China is a civilization pretending to be a state."[18]

Regardless of the precise explanation, there is little doubt that deep resentments still exist among the Chinese elite toward the West and that this tends to amplify the difficulties of handling complex interactions.[19] Most Americans are familiar with the history of China's interaction with the West but, in addition, Asia specialists stress that emotional scars due to colonial and cultural dominance within the region affect much of East Asia's international relations. This is evident in difficulties in all of the following interactions: Koreans toward Japanese, Taiwanese toward Mainlanders, Vietnamese toward Chinese, Malaysians toward Singaporeans, and Indonesians toward Chinese.[20]

The historical uniqueness approach is not a focused paradigm but it leads to some policy warnings. For example, (a) don't assume that countries that have rational common interests will necessarily be able to cooperate effectively, (b) don't assume that economic interaction will enhance political ties, economic closeness may exacerbate relations, and (c) despite many protestations about resentment of Westerners, they are not seen as likely invaders so may be perfectly acceptable strategic partners.

With these three orienting concepts for background, let us now turn to the specific questions we hope to deal with regarding the changing character of international relations in East Asia.

WHY WILL RELATIONS INSIDE ASIA BE THE CRITICAL ONES?

The *first* and most critical reason is that no outside state has both the desire and ability to alter the strategic balance in East Asia.

As discussed above, there is a broad political consensus within the United States that the security commitments to Japan and South Korea are desirable and that American power provides a stabilizing influence throughout East Asia.[21] Many analysts see the United States continuing to provide nuclear guarantees and substantial conventional defense for at least the next decade.[22] Equally important, it would not be in the U.S. interest for there to be a major conflict in East Asia or for any new power to come to dominate the region militarily. Therefore, one can anticipate that the United States would resist either China or Japan establishing a dominant role in the region. Moreover, an alliance between China and Japan that would, necessarily, diminish U.S. influence, would probably also be resisted by Washington.

The Europeans have neither the military capability nor the intention to intervene significantly in Asia. There are two other possibilities that need to be watched closely: Russia and India, yet neither appears capable now of fundamentally altering the course of events in East Asia. The Russians still have an active diplomatic role in Asia, and clearly aspire to reestablish themselves as an important player, but the chances of that occurring depend on the revitalization of Russia's economy.[23] India's aspirations are more plausible; and, now that India has been invited to join the ASEAN Regional Forum, it would not be surprising to see India play some security role on the perimeters of East Asia. Yet, India was bloodied badly in its 1962 war with China, and there is little enthusiasm in New Delhi for a direct strategic competition with East Asian states.[24]

The *second* explanation of why relations within Asia will be the dominant ones comes from looking at the economic and social trends in the region. Trade within Asia is now greater than trans-Pacific trade and investment between Asian states is now greater than trans-Pacific investment.[25] Also, the rise of a burgeoning middle class in the region makes it likely that governments will reflect more nationalistic sentiments and be less prone to accept the lead of states from outside the region.[26]

This more assertive stance by East Asian states has been in evidence during debates over human rights issues and, very prominently, during the bargaining over conditionality for external loans during the 1997–1998 economic crisis.[27] As the region recovers from the economic downturn, we could expect a return to more discussion about "Asian solutions to Asian problems." Although there is a very clear desire of the smaller states in the region to keep American and European involvement as a counterweight to Japanese and Chinese strengths, there are cultural and ethnic sensitivities as well that pull toward resolving issues within the region.

A *third* reason for expecting relations within Asia to be critical is the speed of China's rise to prominence. Since there is no other state of China's scale and Beijing has been unable to project power for the past 150 years, it is not surprising that China's neighbors are uncertain about the forthcoming regional power alignments. Few analysts expect China to be able to maintain annual economic growth rates of over 10 percent in the next decade.[28] Yet, even if her growth rate slips to one-half that pace, China will have enormous resources to devote to military modernization if she so chooses. Although the Chinese leadership routinely stresses its desire for peaceful relations with its neighbors, many of Beijing's policy pronouncements also include direct references to a desire for greater influence in the region.[29] It is these mixed messages that create uncertainty about China's intentions.

In addition to all the usual uncertainties about predicting foreign policy behavior, there are two elements of China's recent rise to prominence that make forecasts even more problematic: (a) the spurt in economic growth since 1979 has created significant regional disparities in per capita income and tens of millions of migrants, which would challenge the authority and capacity of any government,[30] and (b) there are millions of descendants of Chinese immigrants living throughout Southeast Asia, many of whom have become successful in business.[31]

Therefore, when countries in East Asia try to assess the directions that China may pursue, they have worries not only about its scale but how stable its course will be and how some of their most prominent citizens will react if China pursues more assertive policies. Nevertheless, this strengthens the basic themes noted above as attention is being focused inside Asia, not on comments on policies from outside the region.

WHY ARE CHINA, JAPAN, AND
TAIWAN GOING TO BE THE LINCHPIN?

There is no debate that China and Japan are the two most critical East Asian states for determining the future military balance within the region. In terms of population, size of economy, and size of military forces, China and Japan dwarf their neighbors.[32] Even if one thinks about information technology and precision-guided munitions, that leaves Japan dominant in the region, with China lagging somewhat behind but still ahead of all of its neighbors except South Korea and Taiwan.

If we then begin a process of exclusion, which other countries could seriously affect the regional balance of power?

South Korea is a plausible candidate. Although it went through an enormous shock in December 1997 when its foreign exchange was depleted and the won plummeted, under President Kim Dae Jung, Korea has stuck to a stringent recovery strategy and GDP has grown at over 5 percent in 1999. It is not clear if Korea will be able complete the industrial restructuring that many observers feel is necessary to return the country to a high growth path in the future.[33] Yet, South Korea has impressive technical competence in computation, electronics, software, and armaments manufacture, so there is no doubt that it could definitely be a factor in the regional balance of power.

The great uncertainty in Seoul's future is whether there can be peaceful reunification on the Korean Peninsula and, if so, at what cost. If North Korea remains a separate and hostile state, Pyongyang's maneuvering will inevitably occupy most of South Korea's attention. However, even if there is agreement on reunification, it would certainly be a decade or two before a united Korea could exert influence outside its borders. An even bigger issue is whether reunification would trigger a withdrawal of American forces from Korea and how that would affect regional balances.[34] Thus, for our purposes, we can assume that Korea will remain a key country for security calculations, but that, in the near-term future, it is unlikely to be projecting power or influence in other parts of East Asia.

The growing political links between the countries of Southeast Asia makes ASEAN another potential actor. However, the economic turmoil in the past two years illustrated how little the Southeast Asian states were willing to do for each other in the face of economic disaster.[35] If one combines that passivity on economic cooperation with deep splits over how to respond to China's aggressiveness over the Spratly Islands question, there is ample grounds for skepticism that ASEAN and its Regional Forum will be able to shape events outside their own area.[36]

Thus, we are left with the possibility that Taiwan is the only actor that could conceivably join China and Japan in shaping the East Asian regional power balance.[37] Is Taiwan up to the task? Almost certainly, yes. Although it has only 21 million people, Taiwan has foreign exchange reserves of over $100 billion, a dynamic and modern industrial sector that only paused briefly during the 1997–1998 Asian economic crisis, and most important, the will to resist pressure from Beijing.

Most Taiwanese strategists are convinced that top military planners in China see the dominance of Taiwan and the South China Sea as the first steps in their broader ability to shape outcomes in East Asia.[38] Recent PLA budget increases and procurement decisions (especially coproduction and manufacturing agreements with Russia) have favored the PLA Air Force and Navy, and are often interpreted as laying the basis for a true power projection capability.[39] Naturally, the Taiwanese see these developments as quite threatening, and, in some ways, a stimulus to resist.

The scale of the recent Taiwanese military buildup is impressive. Mirroring the PLA moves, efforts in Taiwan have been concentrated on the Air Force, in air defense, and in antisubmarine warfare. The purchase of 150 F-16s, 54 Mirage 2000s, early warning aircraft, and Patriot and Improved Hawk batteries all give Taiwan a potent defense force.[40] When this is combined with Taiwan's expertise in information technologies, Taiwan has a military presence and political flexibility that few entities her size possess. The sale of new U.S. destroyers and submarines will additionally strengthen Taiwan's navy. Though Taiwan cannot compete directly with either China or Japan, it cannot be overwhelmed easily and has to be considered as the swing factor in the emerging strategic competition in Asia.

WHY ARE STRATEGIC ALIGNMENTS LESS CERTAIN TODAY?

As noted above, the 1972–1989 period in East Asia was one of strategic equilibrium. It appeared, briefly, in the 1975–1979 period that the Soviet Union was expanding its influence in the region as Hanoi consolidated power throughout Vietnam and invaded Cambodia. Yet, once it became clear that Vietnam's foray into Cambodia was creating its own quagmire, other states in the region became more confident. From that point on until the end of the Cold War, none of the other major players in East Asia had an incentive to try to disturb the balance of forces.

What is different now? The two most critical changes affecting the China-Japan-Taiwan triangle are (a) the fading of Soviet/Russian power, and (b) the dramatic transformation of China's economy.

China had options after 1989 that were simply not feasible while the Soviet Union was a military threat. Few in Beijing in the 1980s would have thought that, a decade hence, Russia would be selling high-performance ground attack aircraft to China.[41] So, the Soviet/Russian demise produced a twofold benefit for China: Beijing was free to concentrate on its economic performance and could proceed with its military modernization at its own pace. Moreover, as the threat from the north receded, China could pay more attention to the long-simmering dispute with Taiwan and its territorial claims in the South China Sea.

These changes mean that today China has a far more complex calculus in its foreign policy decision making than prior to 1989.[42] Several examples will illustrate the new choices to be made. In the energy sector, there is little doubt that China will become a major net oil importer. The scale of the imports and where they will come from is uncertain.[43] If the Chinese private sector is allowed to operate freely, oil imports will increase rapidly and oil could substitute for coal, particularly in the fast-growing southern provinces.[44] Rising oil imports would raise the significance of sea lanes, the Spratly Islands, and the PLA Navy. If China focuses more on internal sources of energy, then there will be a concerted effort to limit imports and more government controls. Also, if this latter course is taken, there could be less Chinese courting of Persian Gulf oil-supplying countries.

In military policy, a key short-run objective is to dominate the waters and airspace around Taiwan. Yet, in the process of purchasing and manufacturing the weapons to do this, Japan and Taiwan will be increasingly threatened. Beijing faces the same dilemma on nuclear policy. Though China has signed the nuclear Comprehensive Test Ban Treaty and the Non-Proliferation Treaty and appears to want world approval for cooperative behavior, its military still sees that possessing nuclear weapons distinguishes it from all its East Asian neighbors (other than Russia).[45] Overall, China sees its relative power in the region growing and wants to use the levers at its command to gain substantially greater influence in East Asia and prevent Taiwan from achieving greater autonomy or independence.[46]

Japan is a status quo power dealing with a rapidly changing set of circumstances around it.[47] Polling of Japanese citizens shows that the public overwhelmingly opposes the development of nuclear weapons and is almost as skeptical of efforts to establish a more robust defense capability. Since the end of the Cold War, Japan's immediate need for U.S. protection has actually declined. Yet, two generations have accepted the American security umbrella and the alliance with the United States because the costs of the arrangement have already been adjusted to and there is no consensus on an alternative.

Various Japanese security specialists have attempted to suggest alternative routes to a higher profile, more independent strategy for Japan. Some have urged closed links with ASEAN,[48] others think greater autonomy overall is an advantage,[49] while still others urge more willingness to deal with problems outside East Asia.[50]

On the key issue of how to deal with the rise of Chinese power, there is deep ambivalence in Japan. When the Japanese public saw China using force in the Spratly Islands and threatening Taiwan with risky missile tests in

1995–1996, it created considerable trepidation. Those circumstances allowed Prime Minister Hashimoto to go ahead with revisions of the U.S.-Japan Defense Guidelines (which provide the details for how the Security Treaty will be implemented) without having the Socialist and Sakigake members of his coalition in revolt.

To date, however, there has only been one prominent Japanese strategist who has openly called for efforts at balancing or containing Chinese ambitions.[51] Although there is no consensus on what kind of "security architecture" is ideal for Japan, there is a growing recognition among the Japanese elite that Taiwan represents a real prize. If China were to completely dominate Taiwan, that would vastly increase the foreign exchange reserves, GDP, and technological capability under Beijing's control.

Hence, many Japanese have quietly adopted the view that it would be to their advantage if Taiwan kept its autonomy—at least "until China becomes a democratic state." The Japanese elite is quite content for the United States to bear the brunt of Beijing's wrath regarding Taiwan's autonomy, but they recognize that it is in their interest to see an indefinite postponement of Taiwan's reunification with China.

Taiwan is the most vulnerable of the three players in the triangular competition. Yet, Taiwan has survived by its wits and the political leadership has no intention of getting coerced into an unfavorable reunification agreement.

In the past decade and a half, two fundamental changes have transformed Taiwanese politics: (a) the steady moves toward democratization, and (b) the KMT decision to give up the 1950s–1970s position that it is the legitimate government of all of China. Democratization has proceeded smoothly, starting in 1986 with the ending of martial law and then moving on to local elections, parliamentary elections, and finally direct elections for the presidency in March 1996. This has meant that Taiwanese, not Mainlanders who emigrated, now control political life; and this, almost inevitably, led to the rise of a desire for greater autonomy from China.

The democratization of Taiwan has had important international consequences, as sympathy for the island has increased. Popular support combined with skillful lobbying has enhanced Taiwan's international stature and maneuverability since the shock of losing recognition in the 1970s.[52]

Taiwan's basic strategic dilemma is that it has 21 million people and, in the long run, will not alone be able to balance a determined China. Thus, despite Taiwan's remarkable buoyancy, its relative position vis-à-vis China is declining. Taiwan's current strategy has several elements: attempting to attract a broad range of foreign investment,[53] using its military upgrading to make China realize it would pay an enormous price to subdue Taiwan,[54] and trying to use its foreign aid and technology as inducements for support.

An interesting dilemma for Taipei is whether to encourage or inhibit business investment in China. Since much of the Taiwanese investment in China is routed through Hong Kong, it is hard to know the exact extent of this capital transfer, but it is estimated at tens of billions of dollars per year—making Taiwan the second or third largest investor in China. In one sense this should give Taipei influence in Beijing, as the PRC clearly wants to keep the capital inflow coming and thus to avoid overly harsh behavior toward Taiwan that would stop it. On the other hand, leaders in Taipei are now worried that Taiwanese businessmen protecting their interests will, ultimately, become defenders of the regime in Beijing. This raises the issue: Does interdependence between actors of different sizes create mutual accommodation or asymmetric vulnerability?

Therefore, though Taiwan would clearly prefer a strengthened link with the United States and some type of entente with Japan, its fall-back position is at least to maintain current links with Washington and to urge Japan not to join with China in any agreement that forecloses Taiwan's autonomy.

ALTERNATIVE WAYS TO PORTRAY UNCERTAINTY IN EAST ASIA

In this section we explore alternative ways to analyze the evolving strategic alignments in East Asia. We concentrate on a game-theoretic approach to the issues but start with a brief summary of the pros and cons of using expert polling and scenarios as methods of exposition.

Expert polling has been useful as a means for helping policy makers decide which issues warrant the greatest attention. During the past five years, expert polling has been remarkably consistent in identifying the Korean Peninsula, China-Taiwan tensions, and territorial disputes in the South China Sea as the three issues most likely to turn into full-scale crises and conflict.[55] If such polling is well-designed and implemented, and it reaches specialists who do not have access to policy makers, then it can provide a useful source of outside opinion. However, polling does not yield an analytic structure or a long-run guide to action.

Scenarios that highlight the implications of different policy choices can often provide important insights into likely patterns of government decision making.[56] One variant of scenario building concentrates on making choices that hedge alternatives for governments and, therefore, focus attention on preserving options if desired policies are thwarted or fail.[57] Since there is broad agreement among a wide variety of analysts that neither the United States nor Japan should take actions that threaten China or encourage her military buildup, the question then becomes: How can policies be designed to encourage cooperative behavior by Beijing while, at the same time, imposing costs on China if it continues its aggressive actions toward Taiwan and its Southeast Asian neighbors? Scenario building that attempts to highlight these constraints is definitely needed.

The discussion below presents a game-theoretic approach to the central themes raised above. Obviously, reducing the myriad of choices for the key actors in East Asia to five options is a substantial oversimplification, but this should show the essence of the strategies China, Japan, and Taiwan have now and may pursue in the near future. The term "alliance" is used in its broadest sense, meaning agreed linkages, not necessarily formal treaties.

Table 13.1 below, Equilibrium: 1972–1989, presents an ordinal ranking of the preferences of the three actors. Without covering all the entries in the table, the principal points are:

Taiwan would have preferred an alliance with Japan but feared being taken over by China, so it settled for no alliance, given the U.S. defense guarantees in the Taiwan Relations Act of 1979. Japan could not have joined with revolutionary China and saw little to gain from linking with Taiwan so it stayed with the U.S.-Japan Security Treaty. China would have resented an alliance between Taiwan and Japan but, given the Soviet threat and its focus on internal developments, settled for no alliance.

Table 13.1   Equilibrium: 1972–1989

T = Taiwan	1 = lowest preference
J = Japan	4 = highest preference
C = China	

| | Country Rankings | | |
	T	J	C
TJ	4	2	1
TC	1	2	4
JC	2	1	2
No Alliance	3	4	3
Grand Alliance	1	1	1

Table 13.2 below, Potential for Disequilibrium: The Present, presents the current rankings and illustrates how significantly the strategic picture has changed since 1989.

Table 13.2   Potential for Disequilibrium: The Present

T = Taiwan	1 = lowest preference
J = Japan	4 = highest preference
C = China	

| | Country Rankings | | |
Potential Alliances	T	J	C
TJ	4	2	1
TC	1	1	4
JC	1	2	3
No Alliance	3	4	2
Grand Allinace (TJC)	1	2	3

Taiwan still prefers an alliance with Japan, but now recognizes that there is a possibility that China and Japan may form some kind of understanding. This would isolate Taiwan, so the Taipei leadership seeks to press harder for its own links to Japan. Taiwan also does what it can to keep a rapprochement from developing between China and Japan.

Japan changes its ratings only modestly. Recognizing that the U.S.-Japan Security Treaty may not last indefinitely and that some form of agreement with China may be desirable, the Japanese then slightly raise their rating of an alliance with China. Yet, their preference is still for No Alliance among the three Asian states.

China changes its ratings significantly. It still see a Taiwan/Japan Alliance as undesirable and still works to reunify with Taiwan but, now it sees that it may be able to play the lead role in the entire region if it forms a direct link with Japan. Hence, China works to undercut Japan's links with the United States and tries to avoid any moves that directly threaten Japan. This explains the change in China's position in 1998 regarding the desirability of the U.S. military presence in Asia. During the Cold War, China saw the United States as a potential ally against the Soviet Union; now the U.S.-Japan Security Treaty and the U.S. links with Taiwan are an inhibition to its potential leading role in the region.[58]

Thus, today we have a situation where two of the three actors in the fulcrum of Asia are seriously exploring a changed set of relationships. Both China and Taiwan will be courting Japan. However, Japan is not willing to join either as long as the U.S.-Japan Security Treaty is in place and functioning satisfactorily. This clearly creates a potential for disequilibrium because two of the three states will actively try to change the choices of the other parties.

In the Outcome Matrix below (table 13.3), we present the results of how bargaining might proceed. From table 13.2 we see that neither Taiwan nor Japan is willing to join with China; thus Beijing cannot succeed diplomatically now. The real crux of decision making is in the hands of Japan and Taiwan. Taiwan *actively seeks* an alliance with Japan. If, however, Japan wants an alliance with China, Taiwan is not able to stop it. Finally, if Japan prefers to remain uncommitted with the region, then No Alliance is an acceptable fall-back position for Taiwan.

In the Payoff Matrix below (table 13.4), we present a sequential or extensive form, cooperative game. Taiwan is trying to entice Japan into an alliance, while Tokyo is trying to sort out what its interests are. In row 1, Taiwan strongly prefers an alliance. In row 2, Japan sees some merit in joining with China but knows that it will have to take a subordinate position in such an alliance—so finds that type of compromise unappealing as long as the U.S.-Japan Security Treaty is still available. On balance, however, neither an alliance with Taiwan nor China is attractive, so Japan sticks with No Alliance in row 3. There are two equilibria and one of them (no alliance, with Taiwan

Table 13.3   Outcome Matrix

T = Taiwan	TJ = Taiwan/Japan Alliance
J = Japan	JC = Japan/China Alliance
C = China	Ø = No Alliance

Taiwan Seeks

		Alliance	No Alliance
	Alliance with Taiwan	TJ	Ø
Japan Considers	Alliance with China	JC	JC
	No Alliance	Ø	Ø

Table 13.4   Payoff Matrix

1 = lowest payoff
4 = highest payoff

Taiwan Seeks

		Alliance	No Alliance
	Alliance with Taiwan	2,4	4,3
Japan Considers	Alliance with China	2,1	2,1
	No Alliance	4,3	4,3

still courting Japan) is associated with the weakly dominant strategies of the both states.

Several critical exogenous factors are not represented in these matrixes. For example, the United States might be amenable to a grand alliance (CJT) in East Asia if China becomes democratic and there was a generally peaceful situation. Yet, if China keeps its present regime and major power ambitions, then an alliance between China and Japan would be inimical to American interests.

Also, we have left out Korea, which could be important. As long as Korea remains divided between North and South, Seoul will want its security guarantee from the United States. If reunification proceeds, then there is a possibility U.S. forces would be asked to leave and some chance that Korea would go neutral or even lean toward China. In that situation, Japan would probably still want to maintain its links with the United States but might consider allying in some fashion with Taiwan.

CONCLUSION

1) There are good reasons to assume that the principal factors for future change in strategic relations within East Asia will come from within the region.
2) The China-Japan-Taiwan triangle is the central locus for determining the future military balance in East Asia and this relationship can be put in formal terms.
3) The relationship among China, Japan, and Taiwan was quite stable in the 1972–1989 period as none of the three had an incentive to change their triangular interaction. China was consumed with the Soviet threat and internal problems; Japan was content with its links to the United States; and Taiwan was, until 1986, undemocratic and claiming that it represented all of China.
4) Although the situation today still favors no alliance, Taiwan would very much like to link with Japan (while still keeping its guarantee from the United States) and the strategically oriented elite in Tokyo is beginning to see that an autonomous Taiwan is advantageous to Japan.
5) Since neither Japan nor Taiwan currently wants an alliance with China, present maneuverability rests with Japan and Taiwan. However, if China is able to entice or coerce a change in this triangular relationship, then the future regional balance and structure of East Asian relations would change abruptly.

NOTES

1. For an overview of the economic issues that China's growth poses, see W. Overholt, *The Rise of China* (New York: Norton, 1993); for a survey of the security issues, see T. Christensen, "China, the U.S.-Japan Alliance, and the Security Dilemma in East Asia," *International Security,* Vol. 23, No. 4, (Spring 1999):49–80.

2. For a review of positions on U.S-China relations, see M. Oksenberg and E. Economy, *Shaping U.S.-China Relations* (New York: Council on Foreign Relations, 1997).

3. Although many outsiders viewed the changes in the U.S.-Japan Defense Guidelines agreed on between President Clinton and Prime Minister Hashimoto in 1996 as modest adjustments in responsibilities, they did obligate Japan to support the United States in certain contingencies outside Japanese territorial waters. This type of enhanced role has long been controversial inside Japan. See M. Mochizuki and M. O'Hanlon, "Rethinking Alliances—A Liberal Vision for the U.S.-Japan Alliance," *Survival,* Vol. 40, No. 2 (Summer 1998): 127–134.

4. N. Yamaguchi, "New Challenges in U.S.-Japan Defense Relations," *JEI Report,* No. 34a (September, 3, 1999): 1–5.

5. W. Broad, "Spies vs. Sweat: The Debate Over China's Nuclear Advance," *New York Times*, September 6, 1999, pp. A1–4, and M. Swaine, "Chinese Military Modernization and Asia-Pacific Security," RAND Working Paper, May 1999, pp. 35–40.

6. H. French, "Seoul and Tokyo, United by Common Interests, Are Drawing Closer as Anger Fades," *New York Times*, September 30, 1999, p. A-7.

7. For an overview of competing schools in international relations, see R. Tanter and R. Ullman, eds., *Theory and Policy in International Relations* (Princeton, N.J.: Princeton University Press, 1972).

8. For an survey of traditional means of estimating national power potential, see O. Morgenstern, K. Knorr, and K. Heiss, *Long-Term Projections of Power* (Lexington, Mass.: Ballinger, 1974).

9. A good summary of these arguments appears in R. Betts, "Wealth, Power, and Instability: East Asia and the United States after the Cold War," *International Security*, Vol. 18, No. 3 (Winter 1993–94): 34–77.

10. J. Lilley, and C. Ford, "China's Military: A Second Opinion," *The National Interest*, No. 57 (Fall 1999): 71–77.

11. R. Ross, "The Geography of the Peace: East Asia in the Twenty-first Century," *International Security*, Vol. 23, No. 4 (Spring 1999): 81–118.

12. G. Segal, "Does China Matter?" *Foreign Affairs*, Vol. 78, No. 5 (September/October 1999): 24–36.

13. A. Friedberg, "Arming China Against Ourselves," *Commentary*, July–August 1999, pp. 27–33, and W. Hawkins, "For All the Tea in China: The 'Commercial Temptation' in U.S. Foreign Policy," *Strategic Review*, Vol. XXV, No. 4 (Fall 1997): 7–18.

14. Since the mid-1990s, some members of the liberal internationalist academic community have focused increasingly on institutions, rather than trade or capital flows as the means of achieving cooperative outcomes. Thus, some are now calling themselves liberal institutionalists. See R. Keohane and L. Martin, "The Promise of Institutionalist Theory," *International Security*, Vol. 20, No. 1 (Summer 1995): 34–46.

15. For an overview of these arguments, see R. Keohane, *Cooperation and Discord in the World Political Economy* (Princeton, N.J.: Princeton University Press, 1984), and J. Frieden and D. Lake, eds., *International Political Economy—Perspectives on Global Power and Wealth* (New York: St. Martin's Press, 1995).

16. J. Nye, *Bound to Lead* (New York: Basic Books, 1990), 173–201.

17. J. Fairbank, ed., *The Chinese World Order—Traditional China's Foreign Relations* (Cambridge, Mass.: Harvard University Press, 1968).

18. L. Pye, "China: Erratic State, Frustrated Society," *Foreign Affairs*, Vol. 69, No. 4 (Fall 1990): 58.

19. H. Harding, *A Fragile Relationship—The United States and China since 1972* (Washington, D.C.: Brookings, 1992).

20. G. Gong, ed., *Remembering and Forgetting—The Legacy of War and Peace in East Asia* (Washington, D.C.: Center for Strategic and International Studies, 1996).

21. For the details of the military commitment made by the Clinton administration to keep 100,000 troops in the Pacific Theater, see J. Nye, "The Case for Deep Engagement," *Foreign Affairs*, Vol. 74, No. 4 (July/August 1995): 90–115.

22. R. Montaperto, ed., *Cooperative Engagement and Economic Security in the Asia-Pacific Region* (Washington, D.C.: National Defense University Press, 1993).

23. H. Chikahito, *Russia and North-east Asia*, Adelphi Paper No. 310 (London: International Institute of Strategic Studies, 1997).

24. For an overview of Indian foreign policy objectives, see S. Ganguly and T. Greenwood, eds., *Mending Fences—Confidence and Security Building Measures in South Asia* (Boulder, Colo.: Westview Press, 1996).

25. Pacific Economic Cooperation Council, *Pacific Economic Outlook—1996 to 1997* (San Francisco: P.E.E.C., 1996), Appendix Table 1, p. 62.

26. This trend appears in both democratic and authoritarian regimes as the middle class becomes more knowledgeable about foreign influence, pressure, and inducements.

27. *The Economist*, "Asian Economies—On their feet again?" August 21, 1999, pp. 16–18.

28. N. Lardy, *China's Unfinished Economic Revolution* (Washington, D.C.: Brookings Press, 1998) and S. Lawrence, "Reality Check: At least Premier Zhu isn't hiding China's problems," *Far Eastern Economic Review* (March 18, 1999): 26.

29. See, for example, Liu Huaqui, "China Will Always Pursue a Peaceful Foreign Policy of Independence and Self-Determination," *Beijing Qiushi*, No. 23, December 1, 1997, in FBIS-CHI-98-07, March 19, 1998.

30. D. Shambaugh, "Losing Control: The Erosion of State Authority in China," *Current History* (September 1993): 253–259.

31. M. Yahuda, "The Foreign Relations of Greater China," *The China Quarterly* (December 1993): 687–710.

32. International Institute for Strategic Studies, *The Military Balance—1998/99* (Oxford: Oxford University Press, 1998).

33. S. Len, "Korean Conglomerates Remain Entrenched," *New York Times*, September 21, 1999, p. C–8.

34. M. Armacost, and K. Pyle, *Japan and the Unification of Korea—Challenges for U.S. Policy Coordination, NBR Analysis*, Vol. 10, No. 1 (Seattle: The National Bureau of Asian Research, 1999).

35. D. Denoon, and E. Colbert, "Challenges for the Association of Southeast Asian Nations," *Pacific Affairs*, Vol. 71, No. 4 (Winter 1998–98): 505–523.

36. M. Leifer, *The ASEAN Regional Forum*, Adelphi Paper No. 302 (Oxford: Oxford University Press for the I.I.S.S, 1996).

37. As discussed above, both Russia and India could have an impact in the long-term future, but neither is currently able or willing to do so.

38. A. Huang, "The Chinese Navy's Offshore Active Defense Strategy—Conceptualization and Implications," *Naval War College Review*, Vol. XLVII, No. 3 (Summer 1994): 7–31.

39. N. Halloway, and C. Bickers, "Brothers in arms—the U.S. worries about Sino-Russian military cooperation," *Far Eastern Economic Review* (March 13, 1997): 20–21.

40. A. Leung, "The Reinforced Fortress," *Military Technology* (March 1996): 65–74.

41. *Reuters*, "China seals deal to buy 30 advanced Russian jets," Beijing, October 8, 1999. The arrangement apparently involves the sale of SU-30s as well as manufacturing technology for air-to-ground and air-to-air missiles.

42. For a summary of the new factors in Chinese foreign policy decisions, see Xiaoxiong Yi, "China's U.S. Policy Conundrum in the 1990s," *Asian Survey*, Vol. XXIV, No. 8 (August 1994): 675–691.

43. Ji Guoxing, "Energy Security Cooperation: An Agenda Facing the Asian Pacific Countries," *PacNet*, No. 13 (Honolulu: Pacific Forum, March 28, 1997).

44. Kang Wu, and F. Feshariaki, "China Energy: Short Memos, Number VI" (Honolulu: East-West Center, December 23, 1994).

45. A. I. Johnston, "China's New 'Old Thinking'—The Concept of Limited Deterrence," *International Security*, Vol. 20, No. 3 (Winter 1995–96): 5–42.

46. It is also worth noting that China's 1998 White Paper on Defense was the first to directly state that Beijing sought the reduction of U.S. influence in East Asia.

47. G. Curtis, ed., *The United States, Japan, and Asia* (New York: W.W. Norton, 1994), chapter 8.

48. S. Sudo, "Towards the Pacific Century," *Far Eastern Economic Review* (January 31, 1991): 30–31.

49. T. Inoguchi, *Japan's Foreign Policy in an Era of Global Change* (London: Pinter, 1993).

50. A. Tanaka, "A Model for Japanese Security in the 21st Century," *Japan Review of International Affairs*, Vol. 10, No. 4 (Fall 1996): 276–290.

51. H. Okazaki, "For Balance of Power Capable of Achieving Peace," *Yomiuri Shimbun*, May 20, 1996, Foreign Broadcast Information Service, EAS-96-103, May 28, 1996.

52. R. Manning, "Now It's Taiwan's Turn," *PacNet*, No. 28 (Honolulu: Pacific Forum, July 11, 1997).

53. W. Donaldson, and C. Wharton et al., *Taiwan's Role in the East Asian Economy* (New York: Asia Society, 1997).

54. J. Davis, and C. Perry, *Asia-Pacific Issues and Development* (Washington, D.C.: National Security Planning Associates, 1996), 16–29.

55. See R. Ebinger, "The Top Five Threats to Asian Security: The Korean Peninsula Tops the List; China Issues Loom Large," *PacNet* No. 32 (Honolulu: Pacific Forum, August 20, 1999).

56. See C. Doran, "Why Forecasts Fail: The Limits and Potential of Forecasting in International Relations and Economics," *International Studies Review*, Vol. 1, No. 2 (Summer 1999): 11–42.

57. For two different variants of this approach see R. Manning and J. Przystup, "Asia's Transition Diplomacy: Hedging Against Futureshock," *Survival*, Vol. 41, No. 3 (Autumn 1999): 43–67, and N. Sirivudh, "ASEAN 10 Meeting the Challenges," *PacNet* No. 24 (Honolulu: Pacific Forum, June 18, 1999).

58. State Council of China, *Defense White Paper* (Beijing: State Council of China, July 1998).

Publications by Richard Ullman

BOOKS

Anglo-Soviet Relations, 1917–1921
Vol. I: Intervention and the War, Princeton, N.J.: Princeton University Press, 1961.
Vol. II: Britain and the Russian Civil Wa, Princeton, N.J.: Princeton University Press, 1968.
Vol. III: The Anglo-Soviet Accord, Princeton, N.J.: Princeton University Press, 1973.
Theory and Policy in International Relations (co-editor, with Raymond Tanter), Princeton: Princeton University Press, 1972.
Western Europe and the Crisis in U.S.-Soviet Relations (co-editor, with Mario Zucconi), Greenwood, Conn.: Praeger, 1987.
Securing Europe, Princeton, N.J.: Princeton University Press, 1991.
The World and Yugoslavia's Wars (editor), New York: Council on Foreign Relations Press, 1996.

ARTICLES AND CHAPTERS IN BOOKS (IN ORDER OF PUBLICATION)

"The Davies Mission and the United States-Soviet Relations, 1937–1941," *World Politics*, Vol. IX, No. 2 (January 1957): 220–239.
"Stamp Collecting and Grade-A Beef: Some Thoughts on Graduate Professional Education for International Affairs," *Foreign Service Journal*, September 1968.
"Education and Training for the New Diplomacy," *Annals of the American Academy of Political and Social Science*, November 1968.
"The Pentagon's History as History," Foreign Policy, No. 4 (Fall 1971): 150–157.
"No First Use of Nuclear Weapons," *Foreign Affairs*, Vol. 50, No. 3 (July 1972): 669–683.

"After Rabat: Middle East Risks and American Roles," *Foreign Affairs*, Vol. 53, No. 2 (January 1975): 284–296.

"Alliance With Israel? " *Foreign Policy*, No. 19 (Summer 1975): 18–33.

"The 'Foreign World' and Ourselves: Washington, Wilson, and the Democrat's Dilemma," *Foreign Policy*, No. 21 (Winter 1975–1976): 97–124.

"200 Americans," *The New York Times Magazine*, October 12, 1975.

"Trilateralism: 'Partnership' for What?" *Foreign Affairs*, Vol. 55, No. 1 (October 1976): 1–19.

"The Realities of George F. Kennan," *Foreign Policy*, No. 28 (Fall 1977): 139–155.

"Human Rights and Economic Power: The United States versus Idi Amin," *Foreign Affairs*, Vol. 56, No. 3 (April 1978): 529–542.

"Human Rights–Toward International Action," in Jorge I. Dominguez et al., *Enhancing Global Human Rights*, 1980s Project/Council on Foreign Relations, New York: McGraw-Hill, 1979, pp. 1–17.

"Salvaging America's Rhodesian Policy," *Foreign Affairs*, Vol. 57, No. 5 (Summer 1979): 1, 111–122.

"Keeping Cool at the Khyber Pass" (with Leslie H. Gelb), *Foreign Policy*, No. 38 (Spring 1980): 3–18.

"Seguridad Internacional en los anos ochenta," *Estudios Internactionales*, Vol. XIII, No. 50 (April–June 1980): 208–235.

"Ten Years of *Foreign Policy*" (with C. William Maynes), *Foreign Policy*, No. 40 (Fall 1980): 3–17.

"Out of the Euromissle Mire," *Foreign Policy*, No. 50 (Spring 1983): 39–52.

"Redefining Security," *International Security*, Vol. 8, No. 1 (Summer 1983): 129–153.

"At War with Nicaragua," *Foreign Affairs*, Vol. 62, No. 1 (Fall 1983): 39–58.

"Some Reflections on Intervention," *Revista Juridica de la Universidad de Puerto Rico*, Vol. 52, No. 1 (1983): 127–139.

"Human Rights and American Foreign Policy" *The Center Magazine*, Vol. XVII, No. 1 (March–April 1984): 21–29.

"Denuclearizing International Politics," *Ethics*, Vol. 95, No. 3 (April 1985):567–588.

"Reducing U.S. and Soviet Nuclear Arsenals" (with Harold A. Feiveson and Frank von Hippel), *Bulletin of the Atomic Sciences*, Vol. 41, No. 7 (August 1985): 145–150.

"Arresting the Militarization of the Third World," in Jagat S. Mehta, ed., *Third World Militarization: A Challenge to Third World Diplomacy*, Austin: Lyndon B. Johnson School, University of Texas, 1985, 201–216.

"Paths to Reconciliation: The United States in the International System of the Late 1980s," in Sanford J. Ungar, ed., *Estrangement: America and the World*, New York: Oxford University Press, 1985, 277–306.

"Avoiding Nuclear War," *The American Oxonian*, Vol. 73, No. 1 (Winter 1986): 8–13.

"America, Britain, and the Soviet Threat in Historical and Present Perspective," in Hedley Bull and W. Roger Louis, eds., *The "Special Relationship": Anglo-American Relations Since 1945*, Oxford: Clarendon Press of Oxford University Press, 1986, 103–114.

"Back from the Brink: The Case for a New U.S. Nuclear Strategy," (with McGeorge Bundy, Morton H. Halperin et al.), *The Atlantic*, Vol. 258, No. 2 (August 1986): 35–41.

"Nuclear Arms: How Big a Cut?" *The New York Times Magazine*, November 16, 1986, 70–78.
"Containment and the Shape of World Politics," in Terry L. Deibel and John Lewis Gaddis, eds., *Containing the Soviet Union*, New York: Pergammon, 1987, 120–138.
"Western Europe and the Options for America's Soviet Policy," in Richard Ullman and Zucconi, eds., *Western Europe and the Crisis in U.S.-Soviet Relations*, Greenwood, Conn.: Praeger, 1987, 1–16.
"Ending the Cold War," *Foreign Policy*, No. 72 (Fall 1988): 130–151.
"The Covert French Connection," *Foreign Policy*, No. 75 (Summer 1989): 3–33.
"A Superpower Code of Conduct in the Third World," in Thomas G. Weiss, ed., *The United Nations in Conflict Management: American, Soviet, and Third World Views*, New York: International Peace Academy, 1990, 68–76.
"Enlarging the Zone of Peace," *Foreign Policy*, No. 80 (Fall 1990): 102–120.
"Minimum Deterrence and International Security," in David Carlton and Carlo Schaerf, eds., *The Arms Race in an Era of Negotiations*, London: Macmillan, 1991, 73–99.
"Europe's Security after the Cold War," *New European*, Vol. 4, No. 6 (1991): 25–29.
"The United States, Latin America, and the World After the Cold War," in Abraham F. Lowenthal and Gregory F. Treverton, eds., *Latin America in a New World*, Boulder, Colo.: Westview, 1994, 13–27.
"Promoting Democracy: America's Mission?" in *Great Decisions 1995*, New York: Foreign Policy Association, 1995, 81–91.
"Introduction: The World and Yugoslavia's Wars," in Richard H. Ullman, ed., *The World and Yugoslavia's Wars*, New York: Council on Foreign Relations Press, 1996, 1–8.
"The Wars in Yugoslavia and the International System After the Cold War," in Richard H. Ullman, ed., *The World and Yugoslavia's Wars*, New York: Council on Foreign Relations Press, 1996, 9–41.
"Strong States, Strong Hopes: Guidelines for Post-Cold War United States Foreign Policy and Foreign Assistance Policy," Occasional Paper, Washington D.C., Aspen Institute. December 1997, 39 pp.
"Implementing NATO Enlargement: Difficult Choices Ahead" (with Scott D. Vesel & Damon M. Wilson) in *Great Decisions 1999*, New York: Foreign Policy Association, 1999, 67–76.
"Russia, the West, and the Redefinition of Security," in Alexei Arbatov, Karl Kaiser, and Robert Legvold, eds., *Russia and the West: The 21st Century Security Environment*, Armonk, N.Y.: M.E. Sharpe, 1999.
Reviews in *American Historical Review, American Oxonian, The Economist, The Guardian, Journal of Modern History, Los Angeles Times Book Review, New York Times Book Review, Oxford Magazine, Political Science Quarterly, Slavic Review, Survival,* and *University of Pennsylvania Law Review.*

Index

Obuchi government, 284
Ochmanek, David, 1–23
O'Hanlon, Michael, 111–30
Olson, Mancur, 214
Open Door principle, 184
openness, and legitimacy, 29–30
Organization for Security and
  Cooperation in Europe (OSCE), 95
Ostpolitik, 271–73
Ottawa process, 98
Outcome Matrix, in East Asia, 296–97
overridingness, in ethics, 50
Oxman, Stephen, 144

Pakistan, 136
Panama, 96, 114
Pan-American Conference, 188
Panic, Zivota, 143
Partnership for Peace (PFP), 253, 277
party politics, polarization of, 79–81
patriarch, definition of, 67
patriarchal privilege, 58–62
patriarchy, 57–73; definition of, 67
Payoff Matrix, in East Asia, 296–97
peace: Hughes on, 163, 166–67; liberal
  isolationism on, 154
peace operations. *See* intervention
peace theory, liberal democratic,
  245–46; and foreign policy, 263–64;
  on security cooperation, 253
perestroika, 25
peripheral regions, US foreign policy
  and, 136–37
Perry, William, 145
Persian Gulf War, 96
Peru, 68
PFP. *See* Partnership for Peace
Philippines, 182–83
Pinochet, Augusto, 57
Poland, 273
polarization: of Congress, 75–76, 80;
  and foreign policy, 82–86; of party
  politics, 79–81
political discourse, Ullman on, 12–14
political process, alienation from, 80–81
politics: among nonhuman animals, 59;
  Hobbes and, 62–63; US interests and,
  91–110

Pope, Alexander, 1
popular appeal, versus legitimacy, 28
Portugal, 183
Powell, Colin, 118, 147
power, and moral authority, 58
prescription, in ethics, 50
public, alienation from government,
  80–81
Public Citizen, 84, 86
public opinion: versus Congress, 75–90;
  interpretations of, 76–79
public responsibilities, ethics of, 47
Putin, Vladimir, 271

Ramsey, Paul, 51
Raznjatovic, Zeljko (Arkan), 143
Reagan administration, 12, 15–16
Reagan, Ronald, 218
realism: on alliance, 209–10; definition
  of, 241; on East Asian competition,
  286–87; on economic cooperation,
  256; and foreign policy, 257, 262–63;
  and German foreign policy, 269–82;
  on human nature, 164; and
  patriarchy, 57–73; post–Cold War,
  18–19; premises of, 161; on security
  cooperation, 252; structural, 102; on
  US–Europe relations, 241–43
realist illusion, 59, 62–65; after World
  War II, 65–67
realist institutionalism, 228
realist isolationism, and League of
  Nations, 159
realist neoisolationism, 153
reason, 192–93; Hughes on, 166
reconnaissance satellites, 123
regime theory, 102
relief agencies, and interventions, 97–98
religious freedom, and legitimacy, 28
repression, Ullman on, 12, 26
Republican Party, 80, 84; and CTBT,
  82–83; and UN dues, 85–86
Reservationists, 159–61
reserve forces, 127
Reyerson, William, 144
Rhodes, Edward, 153–205
Rhodesia, 100
Ribot, Alexandre, 209

About the Contributors

Thomas Banchoff is assistant professor of government at Georgetown University and a member of the Executive Committee of Georgetown's Center for German and European studies. He received his master's degree in history and political science from the University of Bonn in 1988 and his Ph.D. in politics from Princeton in 1993. His publications include *The German Problem Transformed: Institutions, Politics, and Foreign Policy, 1945–1995* (University of Michigan Press, 1999) and *Legitimacy and the European Union*, coedited with Mitchell Smith (Routledge, 1999). His current research interests include globalization and social policy, and the politics of higher education in Europe and the United States.

David Callahan is author of three books on U.S. foreign policy, including a 1990 biography of Paul Nitze and, most recently, *Unwinnable Wars: American Power and Ethnic Conflict*. He is currently director of research for a new public policy organization in New York City, the Network for American Renewal. He holds a Ph.D. in politics from Princeton University.

David B. H. Denoon is professor of politics and economics at New York University. He has a B.A. from Harvard University, an M.P.A from Princeton University, and a Ph.D. from MIT. He has served in the federal government in three positions: as program economist, USAID-Jakarta (1968–1971); vice president of the U.S. Export-Import Bank (1978–1979), and as deputy assistant secretary of defense (1981–1982). Two of his recent books are *Real Reciprocity: Balancing U.S. Economic and Security Policy in the Pacific Basin* (1993) and *Ballistic Missile Defense in the Post Cold War Era* (1995).

I. M. (Mac) Destler is professor at the School of Public Affairs, University of Maryland, and visiting fellow at the Institute for International Economics. He is a specialist in U.S. foreign policy making. His books include *Presidents, Bureaucrats, and Foreign Policy* (1972), *Our Own Worst Enemy: The Unmaking of American Foreign Policy* (1984, with Leslie Gelb and Anthony Lake), *American Trade Politics* (third edition, 1995), and *Misreading the Public: The Myth of the New Isolationism* (1999, with Steven Kull). He is currently collaborating with Ivo H. Daalder on an organizational history of the National Security Council, returning to the subject about which Dick Ullman advised him thirty years ago.

Michael W. Doyle is the Edward S. Sanford Professor of Politics and International Affairs and director of the Center of International Studies at Princeton University. He is the author of *Empires, U.N. Peacekeeping in Cambodia* and *Ways of War and Peace*; a coauthor of *Alternatives to Monetary Disorder*; and a coeditor of *Escalation and Intervention, Keeping the Peace*, and *Peacemaking and Peacekeeping for the New Century*. His current research focuses on U.N. peacekeeping and post-Civil War peacebuilding and he is a member of the research advisory committee of the U.N. High Commissioner for Refugees and the advisory committee of the Lessons Learned Unit of the U.N. Department of Peacekeeping Operations.

John S. Duffield was raised in Tucson and attended Williams College (B.A. 1980), Cambridge University (M.A. 1982), and the Woodrow Wilson School at Princeton University (M.P.A. 1985, Ph.D. 1989), where Richard Ullman served as his dissertation adviser. He has held faculty positions at the University of Virginia and the University of Georgia as well as research fellowships at the University of Southern California and Harvard University. His teaching and research interests lie in the areas of international security, international institutions, and international relations theory. His scholarly publications include *Power Rules: The Evolution of NATO's Conventional Force Posture* (Stanford University Press, 1995) and *World Power Forsaken: Political Culture, International Institutions, and German Security Policy After Unification* (Stanford University Press, 1998).

David C. Gompert is president of RAND Europe. From 1993 until 1999 he was vice president of RAND and director of its National Security Research Division. From 1990 to 1993, he served as special assistant to President George Bush and senior director for Europe and Eurasia on the National Security Council staff. He has held numerous positions at the State Department, including deputy to the under secretary for Political Affairs, deputy assistant secretary for European Affairs (1981–1982), and deputy director of the Bureau of Politico-Military Affairs (1977–1981). He worked in the private sector from 1983 to 1990. At Unisys (1989–1990), he was president of the Systems

Management Group and vice president for Strategic Planing and Corporate Development. At AT&T (1983–1989), he was vice president, Civil Sales and Programs, and director of International Market Planning. He holds a Bachelor of Science degree from the United States Naval Academy and a Master of Public Affairs from Princeton's Woodrow Wilson School.

Ronald R. Krebs is a doctoral candidate in the Department of Political Science, Columbia University. He has published articles on a variety of subjects in international security—intra-alliance dynamics, American Cold War strategy, NATO enlargement, demographic change, and international conflict—in such journals as *International Organization, The Journal of Strategic Studies*, and *The Harriman Review* as well as in edited volumes. He is also the author of *Dueling Visions: Reexamining Eisenhower Administration Objectives in Eastern Europe*, forthcoming from Texas A & M University Press and a revised version of his Princeton senior thesis supervised by Dick Ullman. He has received fellowships from the John M. Olin Institute for Strategic Studies at Harvard University, the Institute for the Study of World Politics, Columbia University, and the Kosciuszko Foundation.

Anthony Lake is distinguished professor in the Practice of Diplomacy at the Edmund A. Walsh School of Foreign Service at Georgetown University. He served during 1993–1997 as assistant to the president for National Security Affairs. From 1981–1992 he was Five College Professor of International Relations at Amherst and Mount Holyoke colleges. From 1977 to 1981 he served as director of Policy Planning in the U.S. Department of State. He received his A.B. from Harvard College in 1961 and read international economics at Trinity College, Cambridge, thereafter. He received his Ph.D. from the Woodrow Wilson School of Public and International Affairs in 1974. He is the author of several books, including *Somoza Falling* (1989) and *Our Own Worst Enemy: The Unmaking of American Foreign Policy* (coauthored with I. M. Destler, 1984).

Michael O'Hanlon is a senior fellow in the foreign policy studies program of the Brookings Institution and adjunct professor of public policy at Columbia University. At Brookings he specializes in U.S. defense policy and budgets, while also writing on security issues in Northeast Asia, the Balkans, and the Middle East. His latest Brookings book is *Defense Policy Choices for the Bush Administration, 2001–2005*. He has also recently published *Defending America: The Case for Limited National Missile Defense* (coauthored with James M. Lindsay). O'Hanlon previously worked at the Congressional Budget Office and served as a Peace Corps volunteer in the former Zaire. His undergraduate training at Princeton was in physics; he received a Ph.D. in Public Affairs from the Woodrow Wilson School.

David Ochmanek is a senior defense analyst at RAND. He has been associated with RAND from 1985 until 1993, and again since 1995. From 1993 until June 1995, he served as deputy assistant secretary of Defense for Strategy. Prior to joining RAND, Ochmanek was a member of the Foreign Service of the United States. From 1973 to 1978, he was an officer in the United States Air Force. He received his Bachelor of Science degree from the United States Air Force Academy in 1973 and a Master of Public Affairs degree from Princeton University's Woodrow Wilson School of Public and International Affairs in 1980. His most recent book is *To Find, and Not To Yield: How Information and Firepower Can Transform Theater Warfare.*

Edward Rhodes is director of the Center for Global Security and Democracy and associate professor of international relations in the Department of Political Science at Rutgers University. Rhodes received his A.B. from Harvard University and his M.P.A and Ph.D. from Princeton. The author of *Power and MADness: the Logic of Nuclear Coercion* and coeditor of *The Politics of Strategic Adjustment,* he has written widely on U.S. defense policy issues. In 1996–1997, as an International Affairs Fellow of the Council on Foreign Relations, Rhodes served on the U.S. Navy staff in its Strategy and Concepts (N513) branch. Rhodes has held research appointments at Harvard, Cornell, and Stanford universities. In 1995, he was named Rutgers' outstanding teacher of the year.

Robert Hunt Sprinkle, a physician, studied history at Dartmouth College and was a Social Science Research Council MacArthur Foundation Fellow in International Peace and Security at the Woodrow Wilson School of Public and International Affairs, Princeton University, where he earned his second doctorate in 1990. His history of political thought in the life sciences, *Profession of Conscience: The Making and Meaning of Life-Sciences Liberalism,* was published in 1994 by Princeton University Press. He joined the School of Public Affairs, University of Maryland, in 1995.

Scott Vesel is the manager of the president's office at the EastWest Institute in New York. Previous professional positions include serving on the staff of a member of the German Bundestag and as a teacher of English at Dresden Technical University. He received his B.A. from Yale in 1995 and his M.P.A from Princeton's Woodrow Wilson School in 1999. He has also studied at the University of Paris Sorbonne and at Moscow State University. His publications include "Implementing NATO Enlargement: Difficult Choices Ahead," in *Great Decisions 1999* (coauthored with Damon M. Wilson and Richard H. Ullman).

Thomas G. Weiss is presidential professor at The Graduate Center of The City University of New York, where he is director of the U.N. Intellectual History Project and the next editor of *Global Governance*. From 1990 to 1998 as a research professor at Brown University's Watson Institute for International Studies, he also held a number of administrative assignments (director of the Global Security Program, associate dean of the faculty, associate director), served as the executive director of the Academic Council on the U.N. System, and directed the Humanitarianism and War Project. Prior to that, he was executive director of the International Peace Academy and held several U.N. positions. His latest book is *Military-Civilian Interactions: Intervening in Humanitarian Crises* (1999). He studied with Richard H. Ullman as a graduate student at the Woodrow Wilson School (1969–1971) and worked with him on his dissertation (1974).